Harlem Speaks

A LIVING HISTORY OF
THE HARLEM RENAISSANCE

EDITED BY
CARY D. WINTZ

sourcebooks
mediaFusion

An Imprint of Sourcebooks Inc.®
Naperville, Illinois

810.9896
Har

Published by Sourcebooks, Inc.
P.O. Box 4410, Naperville, Illinois 60567–4410
(630) 961–3900
FAX: (630) 961–2168
ISBN-13: 978–1-4022–0436-4
ISBN-10: 1–4022–0436-1
www.sourcebooks.com

Library of Congress Cataloging-in-Publication Data

Harlem speaks : a living history of the Harlem Renaissance / [compiled by] Cary D.
Wintz.
    p. cm.
    Includes bibliographical references and index.
    ISBN-13: 978-1-4022-0436-4
    ISBN-10: 1-4022-0436-1
    1.   American literature--African American authors--History and criticism. 2.
Harlem (New York, N.Y.)--Intellectual life--20th century. 3.   African Americans--
Intellectual life--20th century. 4.   African American authors--Biography. 5.   African
American musicians--Biography. 6.   African American artists--Biography. 7.   African
American intellectuals--Biography. 8.   Harlem Renaissance. I. Wintz, Cary D., 1943-

    PS153.N5H267 2006
    810.9'896073--dc22

                                                    2006033609

Printed and bound in the United States of America
BVG   10 9 8 7 6 5 4 3 2 1

FOR

Alexander De Cordova Wintz,
who is just beginning his exploration of books

Contents

Part IV. Art and Image in the Harlem Renaissance:
The Visual and Performing Arts

Part V. Art and Politics:
The Renaissance Men of the Harlem Renaissance

Part VI. The New Negro:
Politics and Criticism in the Harlem Renaissance

ACKNOWLEDGMENTS

All books are collaborative projects. Authors depend on their editors, the production staff of their publisher, and, in the case of non-fiction, the librarians or archivists of the research institutions they consult. *Harlem Speaks* involved a level of collaboration that was both more complex and more rewarding than usual. It was complex because the Harlem Renaissance itself was a multifaceted movement that involved not only literature, but music, dance, theater, musical theater, and the visual arts, including painting, sculpture, and even film. It also involved race and politics. This book focuses specifically on five of these areas, and touches on the rest.

For this broad approach spanning multiple disciplines, we assembled a team of authors—twenty in all—to bring their expertise and insight on a wide range of topics. Working with this group of talented people made this an especially rewarding experience. First, I had the pleasure of working closely with scholars with whom I was already acquainted, and whose work I knew well. Also, as I explored the art, music, and theater of the Harlem Renaissance, I came to know scholars in these areas and their work, often for the first time. Each of these persons contributed greatly to this project. Without their efforts this book would not be.

The other complicating aspect of this project was the integration of recorded sound and photographs. Photographs I have worked with previously. For this book I sought images that evoked the time, the place, and the people involved in the Harlem Renaissance. I also sought at least some images that were original or different from those that are used again and again in publications on the Harlem Renaissance.

The Schomburg Center for Research in Black Culture of the New York Public Library provided access to their extensive photographic collection. Mr. Anderson and the rest of the staff in the Photographs and Prints Division of the center were extremely helpful in locating photographs. Additional images were found in the New York Public Library's digital collections. At the Library of

Congress, Vincent Virga provided valuable guidance in locating materials in that institution's on-line digital collections. Additional photographs were located in the extensive digital collection of the Beinecke Library at Yale University and in the Eubie Blake Collection of the Maryland Historical Society. James T. Hershorn at the Institute of Jazz Studies at Rutgers University provided a set of excellent photographs on the musical figures of the Harlem Renaissance.

The most challenging aspect of this research was locating recorded sound. Except in the field of music, the 1920s and 1930s did not leave a wealth of recorded sound. The Schomburg Center provided the most valuable resource. James B. Murray and Alison Quammie provided access to the David Levering Lewis "Voices of the Harlem Renaissance" oral history collection, which provided a great deal of information as well as some of the most interesting material included on the CD that augments the text. James Murray also arranged for me to see filmed interviews with Harlem Renaissance figures and to review other items of recorded sound that are in their extensive collections, and was extremely helpful in making materials available to the project.

The other major source for recorded sound was the Smithsonian Institute and its Folkways collection. Jeff Place provided access to these collections, which included a biographical interview with W. E. B. Du Bois and recordings of Langston Hughes, Claude McKay, Countee Cullen, and other Harlem Renaissance poets. While the Schomburg Center and the Smithsonian provided the basis of the audio material, additional sources included the Library of Congress, where Bryan Cornell, Jan McKee, and Karen Fishman provided valuable assistance; the Spingarn Library at Howard University, where Joellen El Bashir and Ida E. Jones were especially helpful; as was Robert Hill, director of the Marcus Garvey and Universal Negro Improvement Association Papers Project at UCLA.

Ultimately, much of the success of a book project lies outside the control of its author. My editor, Hillel Black, and the rest of the support staff from Sourcebooks deserve a great deal of credit for this book. Hillel Black first brought this project to me in the summer of

2004. He laid out its conception and its basic structure, and asked me to work with the project. His enthusiasm for the project and the challenge of working outside my comfort zone, both in terms of expanding the usual coverage of the Renaissance to include music and art, and especially the prospect of producing a book with recorded sound, sold me on the idea. Working closely with Hillel has been a pleasure. I greatly appreciate his wisdom, and I have learned much from his experience. He is both one of the most demanding and one of the best editors with whom I have worked. Likewise, it has been a pleasure to work with Todd Stocke who oversaw the project, Michael Ryder and Todd Green, who worked hands-on in the copyediting and with the photographs and sound recordings, and with Heather Moore, the publicity director for this project.

I would also like to express appreciation to my colleagues at Texas Southern University for their encouragement and support. I am especially appreciative of Merline Pitre, a friend, a colleague, and my Dean, who tolerated my absences and always encouraged and supported my efforts. Also I am indebted to Cliff Edwards of the University's School of Communications, who volunteered his time to digitize the cassette tapes that I collected so that I could edit the recorded sound. The university itself has my thanks for supporting me in this project and other projects I have been involved in, and for its support of scholarship and research among the faculty.

Several individuals deserve special mention. David Levering Lewis, whose books I have lived with for most of my career, I met for the first time. We had several discussions as the project was being conceptualized, and he kindly provided me access to the oral history interviews he had deposited with the Schomburg Center. These tapes contributed to the sound that is included with this book. Terry Waldo, who wrote the essay on Eubie Blake, also provided a personal tape featuring a conversation with Blake and a medley of Blake songs. Both Arnold Rampersad and George Hutchinson generously offered photographs for the project, while Amy Krischke provided access to material on Aaron Douglas. She put me in touch with George Adams, who provided images of the Aaron Douglas murals at Fisk during and after their restoration. Laurie Klein and Kathryn James of the Beinecke Library at Yale University were most helpful in coordinating the acquisition of many photographs from the Library's splendid and extensive collection of digital images. For their help with images of Langston Hughes, I'd like to thank Mimi Muray, Manager, Nickolas Muray Photo Archives, LLC, and Craig Tenney of Harold Ober Associates. James T. Hershorn of the Institute of Jazz Studies was most helpful in providing images of Louis Armstrong, Duke Ellington, and Ethel Waters, and he has my sincere thanks. Alicia Fessenden of the Artists Rights Society graciously granted permission for reproducing the Jacob Lawrence mural panel. Thanks also to Sarah Anderson of The Philips Collection in Washington, DC, for her help in securing rights to use this image.

Alvia Wardlaw submitted to an oral history interview that covered her meetings with Jacob Lawrence. Gene and Ann Jones extended their hospitality, and we shared two wonderful dinners during my research trips to New York. I enjoyed several long conversations with Martha Jane Nadell about the Harlem Renaissance and the career and activities of Alain Locke. Robert Hill, editor of the Marcus Garvey Papers at UCLA, helped me identify a fine young scholar to write the Garvey chapter, and provided access to two recorded Garvey speeches. My good friend Paul Finkelman provided his usual wisdom and guidance, especially in terms of arranging access to research materials. My son, Jason, gave me a quick and insightful lesson in how to edit sound with the complex sound editing software I had acquired for the project.

Finally, and most importantly, I must acknowledge the support of my wife and my best friend, Celia. She endured my repeated absences on research trips with grace and good humor, and also tolerated my more extensive "absences" when I was ensconced in my study, writing, researching, and otherwise managing the intricacies of this project, instead of attending to my duties as her husband and partner.

ON THE CD

Track	Description
1	Introduction: A montage of Harlem renaissance voices, including WEB DuBois and Langston Hughes, over music from the era from James Reese Europe and Charlie Johnson.
2	In 1972 Eubie Blake gave a private performance in a friend's home, playing a medley of songs including "Love Will find a Way" and ending with "I'm Just Wild About Harry," from *Shuffle Along*. In this previously unpublished recording, if you listen carefully you can hear the guests' quiet chatter as Blake begins playing.
3	Controversial *FIRE!!* author Bruce Nugent discusses his unexpected reaction to Carl Van Vechten and *Nigger Heaven*.
4	The works of many Harlem Renaissance artists played off and paid tribute to other black artists. Poet Sterling Brown reads his tribute to Ma Rainey that describes the singer and her impact on southern black audiences.
5	Ma Rainey, the "Mother of the Blues," recorded the song "Misery Blues" in August, 1927.
6	Langston Hughes pioneered the adaptation of the blues to poetry. Here he reads his best known blues poem, "The Weary Blues."
7	Langston Hughes reads his poem "Mother to Son," which he first published in *The Crisis* in 1922 when he was 20 years old. It became one of his most popular poems.

the time. Still, Wright conveys Bigger's fear and anger in the audio of this scene from the film.

17   Eubie Blake wrote "Troublesome Ivories" in 1911 but did not record the song until much later. This 1974 recording includes Blake's spoken introduction to the song.

18   "You Ought To Know" was from the 1924 Sissle and Blake musical *The Chocolate Dandies*. This 1926 recording features Eubie Blake on piano and Noble Sissle on vocals.

19   Hear Bessie Smith sing "Mean Old Bed Bug Blues," as recorded in September 1927.

20   Louis Armstrong leads His Hot Five and sings on this 1927 recording of "I'm Not Rough."

21   Under Irving Mills' management, Duke Ellington and the Kentucky Club Orchestra grew famous and recorded dozens of songs including this November 1926 recording of "The Creeper," with Bubber Miley on trumpet and Sonny Greer on drums.

22   This 1928 recording of "Do What You Did Last Night" is one of the few times Ethel Waters recorded with James P. Johnson, widely regarded at the time as the best piano player on the East coast.

23   In 1926 Josephine Baker, already a star in Paris for her nightclub act, began her singing career. One of her first recording successes was "Bye Bye Blackbird."

30   Marcus Garvey outlines the international perspective of
            the United Negro Improvement Association, and its
            objectives and beliefs in this excerpt from a recorded
            1921 UNIA membership appeal.

31   Throughout his career Alain Locke had sought the roots
            of African American culture in the race's African and
            Southern heritage. In 1940, he stressed the importance
            of "Negro Spirituals" in these introductory remarks for
            the Library of Congress concert commemorating the
            75th anniversary of the end of slavery.

32   In the 1930s and 1940s A. Philip Randolph had evolved
            from a labor leader to the most significant spokesperson
            for civil rights. His message, as presented in this speech,
            was racial equality and the need to secure for all Amer-
            icans their legal and Constitutional rights.

CONTRIBUTORS

Anne E. Carroll is an associate professor of English at Wichita State University. She is the author of *Word, Image, and the New Negro: Representation and Identity in the Harlem Renaissance* (2005), and of essays in *New Voices on the Harlem Renaissance* (2006), *Public Culture, American Literature, College Literature, Soundings, The Centennial Review*, and *In Process*. She also was a contributor to and an associate editor of *The Encyclopedia of the Harlem Renaissance* (2005).

Chip Deffaa is an ASCAP/Deems Taylor Award-winner as well as the author of eight books dealing with music and popular culture, including *Voices of the Jazz Age* and *Blue Rhythms* (both published by the University of Illinois Press). For eighteen years, he served as jazz critic for *The New York Post*, and he has contributed to most major jazz magazines. He is a member of NARAS and the Dramatists Guild, and recently wrote and directed the Off-Broadway show *George M. Cohan Tonight!*

Paul Finkelman is the President William McKinley Distinguished Professor of Law and Public Policy and Senior Fellow in the Government Law Center at Albany Law School. He is Editor-in-Chief of *The Encyclopedia of African American History*, published by Oxford University Press (2006); author of *Slavery and the Founders: Race and Liberty in the Age of Jefferson* (2001); and author or editor of more than twenty other books on slavery, race, legal history, and baseball. He received his Ph.D. in history from the University of Chicago and has held fellowships from numerous institutions and foundations including Harvard Law School and Yale University. He was the chief expert witness in the lawsuit over a 5,000-pound Ten Commandments monument placed in the rotunda of the Alabama Supreme Court building and also an expert witness in the suit over the ownership of Barry Bonds's seventy-third home run ball.

Kevin Gaines is Director of the Center for Afroamerican and African Studies and professor of history at the University of Michigan. He is author of *Uplifting the Race: Black Leadership, Politics and Culture During the Twentieth Century*, and most recently, *American Africans in Ghana: Black Expatriates and the Civil Rights Era*.

Abdul Goler is a freelance writer and budding Bearden scholar whose primary interests include museums and African American history and culture. A native of Detroit, he attended the University of Michigan and Seton Hall university. Mr. Goler has made several contributions to the field of American art history and museum education, including the Romare Bearden retrospective at the National Gallery of Art and the *Encyclopedia of African American Art and Architecture* (Oxford). He currently resides in Indianapolis.

Claudrena N. Harold is currently an Assistant Professor in the History Department and Carter G. Woodson Institute for African American and African States at the University of Virginia. She teaches African American history, black nationalism, and American labor history. She is finishing a book on the Marcus Garvey Movement in the urban South between 1918 and 1942.

William H. Harris is a former professor of history at Indiana University and former president of Payne College, Texas Southern University, and Alabama State University. He is the author of *The Harder We Run: Black Workers since the Civil War* and *Keeping the Faith: A. Philip Randolph, Milton P. Webster, and the Brotherhood of Sleeping Car Porters, 1925-37*. Harris is currently working on a biography of A. Phillip Randolph.

George Hutchinson is the Booth Tarkington Professor of Literary Studies and Chairman of the Department of English at Indiana University, Bloomington. He is the author of *The Ecstatic Whitman; The Harlem Renaissance in Black and White*; and, most recently, *In Search of Nella Larsen: A Biography of the Color Line*.

Gene Jones, writing with David A. Jasen, is co-author of three books on American popular music: *Spreadin' Rhythm Around: Black Popular Songwriters 1880-1930*; *That American Rag*; and *Black Bottom Stomp*. As an actor, he has worked on and off- Broadway, on *Chappelle's Show*, in Ken Burns's documentaries, and on film for the Coen Brothers.

Amy Helene Kirschke is an Associate Professor of Art History at University of North Carolina, Wilmington. She is the author of the major biography of Aaron Douglas, *Aaron Douglas: Art, Race and the Harlem Renaissance*, as well as a new book, *Art in* Crisis: *W. E. B. Du Bois and the Struggle for African American Identity*.

Dan Morgenstern has been Director of the Institute of Jazz Studies at Rutgers University since 1976, prior to which he served as editor of several periodicals, including *Down Beat*. He is the author of *Living with Jazz* (Pantheon Books, 2004) and has won six Grammy Awards for Best Album Notes, among them one for *Louis Armstrong—Portrait of the Artist as a Young Man 1923-1934*.

Martha Jane Nadell is a professor in the English Department at Brooklyn College, The City University of New York. She is the author of *Enter the New Negroes: Images of Race in American Culture* (2004), and is currently working on a cultural history of Brooklyn.

Arnold Rampersad, the Sara Hart Kimball Professor in the Humanities at Stanford University, is the author of several books, including the two-volume biography *The Life of Langston Hughes*. He has also edited the *Collected Poems of Langston Hughes*. His biography of Ralph Ellison is scheduled to appear in 2007.

Amritjit Singh is the Langston Hughes Professor of English and African American Studies, Ohio University. An editor for the MELA (Multi-Ethnic Literatures of the Americas) Series from Rutgers University Press, he has authored or co-edited well over a dozen books, including *Postcolonial Theory and the United States* (2000),

Collected Writings of Wallace Thurman (2003), and *Interviews with Edward Said* (2004). He is currently working on a documentary history of South Asians in North America.

Asli Tekinay is a professor of English and American Studies at Bogazici University, Istanbul. She received her MA in English from Southern Illinois University in 1987 and her Ph.D. from Bogazici University in 1992. Her main areas of research are African American Studies and contemporary British and American drama.

Lorenzo Thomas was a poet, literary scholar, and professor in the Department of English at the University of Houston-Downtown. Thomas is most widely known as a poet. His collections of poetry include *Chances Are Few* (1979), *The Bathers* (1981), and, most recently, *Dancing on Main Street* (2004). His academic publications include *Extraordinary Measures: Afrocentric Modernism and 20th-Century American Poetry* (2000) as well as a forthcoming book from the University of Michigan Press. Thomas died in the summer of 2005, shortly after he wrote the essay on Countee Cullen.

Tyrone Tillery, Associate Professor of History at the University of Houston, specializes in African American and civil rights history. He received his Ph.D. from Kent State University. His biography, *Claude McKay: A Black Poet's Struggle for Identity*, received a "Book of Note" citation from the *New York Times* and was the winner of the 1993 Gustavus Myers Center Outstanding Book Award on the subject of intolerance in the United States. He is a past executive director of the NAACP, Detroit Branch, and he is currently finishing work on a book on the history of race and inter-group relations in Detroit from 1943 to 1968.

Terry Waldo, the protégé of the late Eubie Blake, is a virtuoso ragtime-stride pianist, bandleader, composer, and singer who has produced over forty albums under his own name. He is also a scholar and historian who has written for the *Chicago Tribune*, *Village Voice*, and *American Heritage Magazine*. His *This Is Ragtime* is the definitive book on the subject, and his twenty-six-part National Public Radio series with the same title fueled the 1970's ragtime revival. Terry's recent appearances have included a tour of his one-man show, *Eubie & Me,* and a performance of the world premiere of a Eubie Blake concerto with the New York Pops at Carnegie Hall.

Alvia Wardlaw is Director of the University Museum at Texas Southern University and Curator of Modern and Contemporary Art at the Museum of Fine Arts, Houston. Over the past four years she has curated five significant exhibitions—"The Quilts of Gee's Bend;" "Something All Our Own: The Grant Hill Collection of African American Art;" "African Art Now: Masterpieces from the Jean Pigozzi Collection;" "Notes from a Childhood Odyssey: The Art of Kermit Oliver;" and "Thornton Dial in the Twenty-first Century and Gee's Bend: The Architecture of the Quilt." She is currently completing a book on African American artist Charles Alston and is continuing her research on African American artists of the southwest, the history of collecting African American art in the United States, and contemporary art in East Africa.

M. Genevieve West is an Associate Professor of English at Ferris State University, where she teaches African American, Native American, and women's literatures. Her essays and bibliographic work on Zora Neale Hurston have appeared in *Women's Studies* and *Analytical and Enumerative Bibliography.* Her study of Hurston's changed reputation, *Zora Neale Hurston and American Literary Culture,* appeared in 2005.

Cary D. Wintz is a professor in the History Department of Texas Southern University in Houston. He is the author or editor of numerous books on the Harlem Renaissance and African American history, including *Black Culture and the Harlem Renaissance* and, with Paul Finkelman, *Encyclopedia of the Harlem Renaissance.* He is currently working on two projects, the *Encyclopedia of African American History, 1896 to the Present,* and a historical dictionary of the Harlem Renaissance.

PART ONE

Harlem
and the
Harlem Renaissance

INTRODUCTION

To understand and appreciate the Harlem Renaissance it is necessary to recognize its situation in terms of time and place.

It began in the second half of the second decade of the twentieth
century, when African Americans, the United States, and the world
were being buffeted by forces of change that few people understood.
Within the African American community and the United States,
race and its connection to the past and the future of the nation was
so fundamental that few recognized it or paid it close attention. One
who did was W.E.B. Du Bois. He saw clearly, a decade earlier, that
"the problem of the twentieth century is the problem of the color-
line." In the first decades of the twentieth century, other forces

distracted Americans from this central issue. World War I and the economic and political forces it unleashed, especially the Bolshevik Revolution, seemed to be the defining events of the day. Yet they eventually faded away—the issue of the color line, on a national and international level, persisted.

The Harlem Renaissance occurred in this chronological context—emerging in the 1920s, following the First World War and spanning the two decades from the war through the Great Depression, and fading during the build up to the Second World War. It was the first concentrated involvement of African American artists, writers, musicians, singers, and intellectuals in an artistic and cultural movement that addressed the realities of the color line in all of its complexity.

In literary, cultural, or intellectual movements, beginnings and endings are rarely clear-cut. This is even more true of complex, multifaceted movements like the Harlem Renaissance, which involve numerous disciplines and fields—from literature to art to music—each with its individual (but sometimes interconnected) chronologies.

Place, fortunately, is an easier concept to define than time. For the Harlem Renaissance, place is Harlem, the focal point of the intellectual, cultural and artistic life in the African American community. In the nineteenth century, Harlem was predominately a white community on the northern edge of New York City. New York itself was not a particularly important place in the African American world. Washington, D.C., Philadelphia, Atlanta, even Boston were more important to black political, social, and cultural life, and to the arts, than was New York. By 1925, however, New York (and its Harlem) had surpassed these other cities and emerged as *the* black metropolis, the capital of African America.

This is not to say that the Harlem Renaissance did not have a connection to the entire United States and even to the Caribbean, Europe, and Africa. Harlem drew its population and its talent from all of these places; the Harlem Renaissance drew much of its literary and artistic influences, its writers, artists, and musicians, and especially its music, from outside of Harlem. But ultimately, it seemed all came to Harlem.

The two essays that follow explore these issues of time and place much more fully. The first, "The Harlem Renaissance," examines the full range of arts, events, and issues that occurred during the time of the Renaissance. The second essay, "Harlem," examines the place.

These dual essays provide the context for the twenty-one essays that follow.

Playbill for *Harlem*, by William Rapp and Wallace Thurman.
Beinecke Rare Book and Manuscript Library, Yale University.

TRACK 1

Introduction: A montage of Harlem renaissance voices, including WEB DuBois and Langston Hughes, over music from the era from James Reese Europe and Charlie Johnson.

The Harlem Renaissance

Cary D. Wintz

On the evening of March 21, 1924, at the Civic Club on Twelfth Street off Fifth Avenue in Manhattan, a gathering occurred that would dramatically alter African American literature and its relationship to American culture. Charles S. Johnson, the young editor of *Opportunity*, the monthly magazine of the National Urban League, conceived the event to honor Jesse Fauset upon the publication of her novel, *There Is Confusion*. Johnson planned for a simple dinner with about twenty guests—a mix of white publishers, editors, and literary critics, black intellectuals, and young black writers.

Professor Alain Locke of the Philosophy Department at Howard University agreed to preside if the dinner honored African American writers in general rather than one novelist. Consequently, the event mushroomed; over one hundred guests gathered for the celebration. Attendees included W.E.B. Du Bois, James Weldon Johnson, and other members of the black intelligentsia, along with Fauset and a representative group of poets and authors. White guests predominately were publishers and critics. Carl Van Doren, editor of *Century* magazine, spoke for this group, calling upon the young writers in the audience to make their contribution to the "new literary age" emerging in America. African American writers, he predicted, "will bring a fresh and fierce sense of reality to their vision of human life on this continent."

The Civic Club dinner significantly accelerated the development of the literary phase of the Harlem Renaissance. On that evening, Frederick Allen, editor of *Harper's*, sought Countee Cullen's poems for his magazine as soon as the poet finished reading them. As the dinner ended, Paul Kellogg, editor of *Survey Graphic*, lingered, talking to Cullen, Fauset, and several other young writers, then offered Charles S. Johnson a unique opportunity: an entire issue of *Survey Graphic* devoted to the Harlem literary movement. Under the editorship of Alain Locke, the "Harlem: Mecca of the New Negro" number of *Survey Graphic* hit the newsstands March 1, 1925. It was an overnight sensation. Later that year Locke published a book-length version of the "Harlem" edition, expanded and re-titled *The New Negro: An Interpretation*. In the anthology Locke laid down his vision of the aesthetic and the parameters for the emerging Harlem Renaissance; he also included a collection of poetry, fiction, graphic arts, and critical essays on art, literature, and music.

TRACK 2

In 1972 Eubie Blake gave a private performance in a friend's home, playing a medley of songs including "Love Will Find a Way" and ending with "I'm Just Wild About Harry," from *Shuffle Along*. In this previously unpublished recording, if you listen carefully you can hear the guests' quiet chatter as Blake begins playing.

The excitement in the literary world that followed the Civic Club dinner matched the enthusiasm three years earlier when *Shuffle Along* opened at the 63rd Street Musical Hall. *Shuffle Along* was a musical play written by a pair of veteran vaudeville acts— comedians Flournoy Miller and Aubrey Lyles, and composers/singers Eubie Blake and Noble Sissle. Most of its cast featured unknowns, but some, like Josephine Baker and Paul Robeson (who had only minor roles in the production), were on their way to international fame. Eubie Blake, recalling the significance of the production, pointed out that he and Sissle and Miller and Lyles accomplished something that other great

African American performers—Cole and Johnson, Williams and Walker—had tried, but failed to achieve. "We did it, that's the story," he exclaimed, "*We* put *Negroes* back on Broadway!"

Shuffle Along did more than break the color line on Broadway. In poet Langston Hughes's mind, it was responsible for the white fascination with Harlem and African American arts that was central to the Harlem Renaissance. It was "a honey of a show" he wrote in his autobiography, "Swift, bright, funny, rollicking, and gay, with a dozen danceable, singable tunes. Besides, look who were in it. The now famous choir director, Hall Johnson, and the composer, William Grant Still, were part of the orchestra. Eubie Blake and Noble Sissle wrote the music and played and acted in the show. Miller and Lyles were the comics. Florence Mills skyrocketed to fame in the second act. Trixie Smith sang 'He May Be Your Man, But He Comes to See Me Sometimes.' And Caterina Jarbors, now a European prima donna, and the internationally celebrated Josephine Baker were merely in the chorus. Everybody was in the audience—including me. People came to see it innumerable times. It was always packed."

Shuffle Along also brought jazz to Broadway. It combined jazz music with very creatively choreographed jazz dance to transform musical theater into something new, exciting, and daring. And it was a critical and financial success, running 474 performances before going on tour. It was a hit show written, performed, and produced by blacks, and it generated a demand for more. Within three years, nine other African American shows appeared on Broadway, and white writers and composers rushed to produce their versions of black musical comedies.

These two events mark the origin of the Harlem Renaissance, the most important event in twentieth-century African American intellectual and cultural life. While best known for its literature, it touched every aspect of African American literary and artistic creativity from the end of World War I through the Great Depression of the 1930s. Literature, critical writing, music, theater, musical theater, and the visual arts were transformed by this movement; it also affected poli-

A student in a metal craft class at the Harlem Community Art Center, 125th Street and Lenox Avenue, in the late 1930s. The Center was established by the WPA Federal Arts Program through the work of artist Augusta Savage and writer Gwendolyn Bennett. It hosted art exhibits and provided adult and youth art classes.
Photography Collection, Miriam and Ira D. Wallach Division of Art, Prints and Photographs, The New York Public Library, Astor, Lenox and Tilden Foundations.

tics, social development, and almost every aspect of the African American experience from the mid-1920s through the mid-1930s.

The Harlem Renaissance, then, was an African American literary and artistic movement centered in Harlem but drawing from and influencing African American communities across the country. It flourished in the late 1920s and early 1930s, but its antecedents and legacy spread many years before 1920 and after 1930. It had no commonly accepted name, but was known variously as the New Negro movement, the New Negro Renaissance, and the Negro Renaissance, as well as the Harlem Renaissance. It had no clearly defined beginning or end, but emerged out of the social and intellectual upheaval in the African American community that followed World War I, blossomed in the mid to late 1920s, and then faded away in the mid 1930s.

Contrary to popular belief, the Harlem Renaissance did not emerge out of a literary and cultural wasteland. By the end of the nineteenth century, there were stirrings of artistic creativity among African Americans in literature, music, and musical theater. In literature two writers, Paul Lawrence Dunbar and Charles Waddell Chesnutt, achieved some success and attracted the attention of white critics and publishers. Chesnutt achieved recognition initially for his short stories set in the plantation south written in the manner of Uncle Remus. When he turned to more serious subjects, especially those concerning race and racial prejudice, his popularity waned. Frustrated by his lack of critical or commercial success, Chesnutt stopped writing following the publication of his third novel in 1905.

Dunbar's career was equally frustrating as well as tragic. He first achieved fame for his dialect poetry of southern black life and then struggled to achieve recognition for his more serious literary efforts. The dialect poetry brought commercial success, but Dunbar's short stories and four novels failed to attract readers or please the critics. Nevertheless, before his untimely death in 1906 at age 38, he was supporting himself through his writing, had produced the first novel of black life in New York, and had collaborated with songwriter Will Marion Cook on a successful black musical.

African Americans made an even greater impact in music in the early twentieth century. The two great American music forms, the blues and jazz, emerged out of the African American experience around the turn of the century. From their origins in southern towns and cities like New Orleans, Memphis, and St. Louis, these musical forms spread across the country. The blues and black blues performers penetrated the vaudeville circuit with musicians like W.C. Handy and singers like Ma Rainey. The publication of W.C. Handy's "Memphis Blues" in 1912 and the first recordings a few years later brought this genre into mainstream American popular culture.

The origins of jazz are found in the creative musicians who played in the bars and brothels of the infamous Storyville district of New Orleans. Jelly Roll Morton claimed to have invented jazz there in 1902, but it is doubtful that any one person holds that honor. Jazz reached New York in 1905 at Proctor's Twenty-third Street Theater.

James Weldon Johnson described the band as "a playing-singing-dancing orchestra, making dominant use of banjos, mandolins, guitars, saxophones, and drums in combination, and [it] was called the Memphis Students—a very good name, overlooking the fact that the performers were not students and were not from Memphis. There was also a violin, a couple of brass instruments, and a double-bass." Seven years later composer and band leader James Reese Europe, one of the Memphis Students, took his Clef Club Orchestra to Carnegie Hall; during World War I, while serving as an officer for a machine-gun company in the famed 369th U.S. Infantry Division, James Europe, fellow officer Noble Sissle, and the regiment band introduced the sounds of ragtime, jazz, and the blues to European audiences.

In the postwar period these developments in music and literature accelerated. Europe continued his career as a successful bandleader until his untimely death in 1919. Ma Rainey and other jazz artists and blues singers began to sign recording contracts, initially with African American record companies like Black Swan Records, but very quickly with Paramount, Columbia, and other mainstream recording outlets. In Harlem one club opened after another, each featuring jazz orchestras or blues singers, while downtown *Chocolate Dandies* and a series of other black musical comedies cashed in on the success of *Shuffle Along*.

In literature, new writers expanded on the foundations Dunbar and Chesnutt had laid at the beginning of the century. James Weldon Johnson was the first of these. Johnson was actually a year older than Dunbar, but he did his most significant writing following Dunbar's death. He initially achieved recognition as a songwriter, teaming up with his brother, Rosamond Johnson, and Bob Cole. The three were a great success, composing about 200 songs for musical productions. Rosamond and Cole also were successful performers. While his partners were on the road, James Weldon Johnson turned to more serious literature. His most significant accomplishment at this time was the 1912 novel, *The Autobiography of an Ex-Colored Man*, and a book of poetry published in 1917, *Fifty Years and Other*

Poems. By World War I Johnson had become an officer of the NAACP and a promoter of African American writers and authors. He was also a literary scholar and anthologist. His 1922 collection, *The Book of American Negro Poetry*, chronicled the state of black poetry on the eve of the Harlem Renaissance.

Social and political upheaval added to the creative ferment of the period. World War I brought in its wake a series of devastating race riots culminating in the 1919 outbreaks in Washington and Chicago. Black politics shifted as Marcus Garvey mobilized tens of thousands of supporters and confronted the NAACP and the African American establishment with a mass political movement championing black nationalism and Pan-Africanism. A. Philip Randolph and the *Messenger* challenged traditional black leadership

Members of the Harlem-based 369th Regiment arriving in New York, 1919. World War I offered blacks both industrial jobs in northern cities, and the opportunity to serve, although in segregated military units. As one soldier noted, "When we have proved ourselves men, worthy to work and fight and die for our country, a grateful nation may gladly give us the recognition of real men, and the rights and privileges of true and loyal citizens of these United States." Photographs and Prints Division, Schomburg Center for Research in Black Culture, The New York Public Library, Astor, Lenox and Tilden Foundations.

from the socialist left. Meanwhile the black migration continued after the war, bringing north the hundred thousand or more who would transform Harlem into the Negro Metropolis. Along with the thousands of mostly poor, working-class blacks coming north into Harlem were the musicians, writers, poets, artists, dancers, actors, editors, publishers, critics, businessmen, professionals, and intellectuals who created and nurtured the Harlem Renaissance.

As the new decade began, the literary stirrings of the pre-War years and the social and political ferment that accompanied the troops returning from the war stimulated literary activity among a younger generation of black writers. In the early 1920s, Claude McKay's volume of poetry, *Harlem Shadows* (1922), Jean Toomer's experimental novel *Cane* (1923), and the initial published works of other young black writers contributed to Harlem's burgeoning cultural life.

Jamaican-born Claude McKay had already published two volumes of dialect island poetry before he came to the United States in 1912 to study agriculture. By 1915 he was living in Harlem pursuing a career as a writer. McKay used Harlem and the African American experience as the source and content of his best writing during this period, as evidenced in *Harlem Shadows*, his first and his finest American book of poetry. Washington resident Jean Toomer's primary literary connections were among whites—Waldo Frank, who helped guide the publication of his book, poet Hart Crane, artist Georgia O'Keeffe and photographer Alfred Stieglitz. His writing, though, was purely black in content and theme. His first and only book, *Cane*, was an experimental novel that excited African American critics with its daring and poetic style and for its probing of the black experience.

Other young writers surfaced in the early 1920s. Langston Hughes published his first poem, "A Negro Speaks of Rivers," in *The Crisis* in 1921, when he was a nineteen-year-old freshman at Columbia; by the spring of 1924, when he returned to New York after spending the better part of two years abroad, he was already something of a literary celebrity. Walter White, an officer of the NAACP, published his first novel, *The Fire in the Flint*, in 1924, as did Jessie Fauset, Du Bois's editorial assistant at *The Crisis*.

By the time of the Civic Club dinner a literary community was forming in Harlem. Charles S. Johnson mentioned an informal group of young writers and literati including poets Langston Hughes and Countee Cullen, writers Eric Walrond and Jessie Fauset, along with Regina Andrews, Harold Jackman, and others. This group likely met at the 135th branch of the New York Public Library or the apart-

The cover of *FIRE!!*, a quarterly "Devoted to Younger Negro Artists."
Beinecke Rare Book and Manuscript Library, Yale University.

ment at 580 St. Nicholas Boulevard that Regina Andrews shared with her roommates. Yet, up to this point there was no identifiable artistic movement; only a growing amount of creative activity.

Against this background of increasing literary activity, three events occurred between 1924 and 1926 that launched the literary phase of the Harlem Renaissance. The first was Charles S. Johnson's Civic Club dinner, which forged the link among the three major players in the literary Renaissance—the black literary-political intelligentsia, the white publishers and critics, and the young black writers. The second event signaled the unprecedented white fascination with Harlem, African Americans, and their music, art, and culture. This was the publication in early 1926 of white novelist Carl Van Vechten's *Nigger Heaven*, a spectacularly popular exposé of Harlem life. Despite controversy over its title—derived from a slang term for the balcony of a segregated theater—Van Vechten's novel and the immense popularity of black musical theater helped create the "Negro vogue" that drew thousands of sophisticated New Yorkers to Harlem's exotic nightlife and stimulated the national market for African American literature and music.

The third event symbolized the coalescence of a core group of young writers and artists into a movement. In the fall of 1926, a group of young black writers spearheaded by writer Wallace Thurman produced their own literary magazine, *FIRE!!* With *FIRE!!* poet Langston Hughes, writers Bruce Nugent and Zora Neale Hurston, and artist Aaron Douglas, along with other young writers and artists, joined Wallace Thurman in declaring their intent to assume ownership of the literary renaissance. In the process, they turned their backs on Alain Locke and W.E.B. Du Bois and others who sought to channel black creativity into what they considered to be the proper aesthetic and political directions. Pointedly, they rejected demands that they focus on uplifting content and themes that would present positive images of African Americans and in the process undermine prejudice and discrimination.

TRACK 3

Controversial *FIRE!!* author Bruce Nugent discusses his unexpected reaction to Carl Van Vechten and *Nigger Heaven*.

Instead, the creators of *FIRE!!* took delight in their ability to shock. Bruce Nugent recalled that he and Wallace Thurman decided "we should have something that gets the magazine banned in Boston" and there were two things that would do it: a story about prostitution and a story about homosexual relationship. They flipped a coin. Thurman wrote the prostitution piece and Nugent wrote the other. They achieved the result they intended. *FIRE!!* outraged Du Bois and offended most of the Harlem intelligentsia.

Despite the efforts of Thurman and his young colleagues, *FIRE!!* fizzled out after only one issue and the movement remained ill defined. In fact, this was its most distinguishing characteristic. There would be no common literary style or political ideology associated with the Harlem Renaissance. It was far more an identity than an ideology or a literary or artistic school. What united participants was their sense of taking part in a common endeavor and their commitment to giving artistic expression to the African American experience. If there was a statement that defined the philosophy of the new literary movement it was Langston Hughes's essay, "The Negro Artist and the Racial Mountain," published in *The Nation*, June 16, 1926.

> We younger Negro artists who create now intend
> to express our individual dark-skinned selves with-
> out fear or shame. If white people are pleased we are
> glad. If they are not, it doesn't matter. We know we
> are beautiful. And ugly, too. The tom-tom cries and
> the tom-tom laughs. If colored people are pleased we
> are glad. If they are not their displeasure doesn't mat-
> ter either. We will build our temples for tomorrow,
> strong as we know how, and we will stand on top of
> the mountain, free within ourselves.

This essay was the movement's declaration of independence—independence from the stereotypes that whites held about African Americans and the expectations that they had for their literary works; independence also from the expectations that black leaders and black critics had placed on the work of black writers.

The determination of black writers to follow their own artistic vision and the diversity that this created was the principal characteristic of the Harlem Renaissance. This diversity is clearly evident in the poetry of the period where subject matter, style, and tone ranged from traditional to more inventive. For example, in "The Weary Blues," Langston Hughes captured the life and language of the working class, and the rhythm and style of the blues:

> Droning a drowsy syncopated tune,
> Rocking back and forth to a mellow croon,
> I heard a Negro play.
> Down on Lenox Avenue the other night
> By the pale dull pallor of an old gas light
> He did a lazy sway . . .
> He did a lazy sway . . .
> To the tune o' those Weary Blues.

In contrast, Claude McKay applied the classical form of the son-

net to "If We Must Die," his well-know poem of protest and
resistance, written in 1919 in response to the vicious race riots:

> If we must die, let it not be like hogs
> Hunted and penned in an inglorious spot,
> While round us bark the mad and hungry dogs,
> Making their mock of our accursed lot.

In "Heritage," Countee Cullen combined a very traditional
poetic style and language with classical literary allusions as he questioned the African roots of his African American heritage:

> What is Africa to me:
> Copper Sun or scarlet sea,
> Jungle star or jungle track
> Strong bronze men or regal black
> Women from whose loins I sprang
> When the birds of Eden sang?
> *One three centuries removed*
> *From the scenes his fathers loved,*
> *Spicy grove, cinnamon tree,*
> *What is Africa to me?*

This diversity and experimentation characterized the blues of
Bessie Smith, as well as the range of jazz from the early rhythms of
Jelly Roll Morton to the instrumentation of Louis Armstrong and
the sophisticated orchestration of Duke Ellington. Aaron Douglas
used soft colors and pastels to create a veiled view for the African-
inspired images in his paintings and murals. Jacob Lawrence's paintings stood in stark contrast with their bright colors and sharply
defined images.

And yet, within this diversity, several themes emerged that set
the character of the Harlem Renaissance. No black artist expressed
all of these themes, but each did address one or more in his or her
work. The first of these themes was the effort to recapture the

African American past—its rural southern roots, urban experience, and African heritage. Interest in the African past corresponded with the rise of Pan-Africanism in African American politics, which was at the center of Marcus Garvey's ideology and also a concern of W.E.B. Du Bois in the 1920s. Poets Countee Cullen and Langston Hughes addressed their African heritage in their works, while artist Aaron Douglas used African motifs in his art. A number of musicians, from the classical composer William Grant Still to jazz great Louis Armstrong, introduced African-inspired rhythms and themes in their compositions. The exploration of black southern heritage was reflected in novels by Jean Toomer and Zora Neale Hurston, as well as in Jacob Lawrence's art. Hurston used her experience as a folklorist as the basis for her extensive study of rural southern black life in her 1937 novel, _Their Eyes Were Watching God_. Lawrence turned to African American history for much of his work, including two of his multi-canvas series of paintings, the Harriett Tubman series and the series on the Black Migration.

Harlem Renaissance writers and artists also explored life in Harlem and other urban centers. Both Hughes and McKay drew on Harlem images for their poetry, and McKay used the ghetto as the setting for his first novel, _Home to Harlem_. Some black writers, including McKay and Hughes as well as Rudolph Fisher and Wallace Thurman, were accused of overemphasizing crime, sexuality, and other less savory aspects of ghetto life in order to feed the voyeuristic desires of white readers and publishers, in imitation of white novelist Carl Van Vechten's exploitation of Harlem in _Nigger Heaven_.

A third major theme addressed by the literature of the Harlem Renaissance was race. Virtually every novel, play, and most of the poetry explored race in America, especially the impact of race and racism on African Americans. In their simplest form these works protested racial injustice. Claude McKay's "If We Must Die" was among the best of this genre. Langston Hughes also wrote protest pieces. Countee Cullen, not noted as a political activist, nevertheless addressed the theme of racism effectively in his deceptively pointed poem, "Incident":

Once riding in old Baltimore,
> Heart-filled, head-filled with glee,
I saw a Baltimorean
> Keep looking straight at me.

Now I was eight and very small,
> And he was no whit bigger,
And so I smiled, but he poked out
> His tongue and called me, "Nigger."

I saw the whole of Baltimore
> From May until December,
Of all the things that happened there,
> That's all that I remember.

Among the visual artists, Lawrence's historical series emphasized the racial struggle that dominated African American history, while Romare Bearden's early illustrative work often focused on racial politics. The struggle against lynching in the mid-1920s stimulated anti-lynching poetry as well as Walter White's carefully researched study of the subject, *Rope and Faggot*; in the early 1930s the Scottsboro incident stimulated considerable protest writing, as well as a 1934 anthology, *Negro*, which addressed race in an international context. Most literary efforts of the Harlem Renaissance avoided overt protest or propaganda, focusing instead on the psychological and social impact of race. Among the best of these studies were Nella Larsen's two novels, *Quicksand* (1928) and, a year later, *Passing*, both of which explored characters of mixed racial heritage who struggled to define their racial identity in a world of prejudice and racism. Langston Hughes addressed similar themes in his poem "Cross" and his 1931 play, *Mulatto*, as did Jessie Fauset in her 1929 novel *Plum Bun*. That same year Wallace Thurman made color discrimination within the urban black community the focus of his novel *The Blacker the Berry*.

Finally, the Harlem Renaissance incorporated all aspects of African American culture in its literature. This ranged from the use of black music as an inspiration for poetry or black folklore as an inspiration for novels and short stories. Best known for this was Langston Hughes, who used the rhythms and styles of jazz and the blues in much of his early poetry. James Weldon Johnson, who published two collections of black spirituals in 1927 and 1928, and Sterling Brown, who used the blues and southern work songs in many of the poems in his 1932 book of poetry *Southern Road*, continued the practice that Hughes had initiated. Other writers exploited black religion as a literary source. Johnson made the black preacher and his sermons the basis for the poems in *God's Trombones*, while Hurston and Larsen used black religion and black preachers in their novels.

Hurston's first novel, *Jonah's Gourd Vine* (1934), described the exploits of a southern black preacher, while in the last portion of *Quicksand* Larsen's heroine was ensnared by religion and a southern black preacher.

TRACK 4 & 5

Track 4: The works of many Harlem Renaissance artists played off and paid tribute to other black artists. Poet Sterling Brown reads his tribute to Ma Rainey that describes the singer and her impact on southern black audiences. Track 5: Ma Rainey, the "Mother of the Blues," recorded the song "Misery Blues" in August, 1927.

Through all of these themes Harlem Renaissance writers were determined to express the African American experience in all of its variety and complexity as realistically as possible. This commitment to realism ranged from the ghetto realism that created such controversy by exposing negative aspects of African American life, to beautifully crafted and detailed portraits of black life in small towns, such as in Hughes's novel, *Not Without Laughter*, to the witty and biting depiction of Harlem's black literati in Wallace Thurman's *Infants of the Spring*.

The Harlem Renaissance appealed to a mixed audience—the African American middle class and white consumers of the arts. African American magazines such as *The Crisis* (the NAACP monthly journal) and *Opportunity* (the monthly publication of the Urban League) employed Harlem Renaissance writers on their editorial staff, published their poetry and short stories and promoted

African American literature through articles, reviews, and annual literary prizes. They also printed illustrations by black artists. Also, blacks attempted to produce their own literary and artistic venues. In addition to the short-lived *FIRE!!*, Wallace Thurman spearheaded another single-issue literary magazine, *Harlem*, in 1927, while poet Countee Cullen edited a "Negro Poets" issue of the avant-garde poetry magazine *Palms* in 1926, and published an anthology of African American poetry, *Caroling Dusk*, in 1927.

As important as these literary outlets were, the Harlem Renaissance relied heavily on white-owned enterprises for its creative works. Publishing houses, magazines, recording companies, theaters, and art galleries were primarily white-owned, and financial support through grants, prizes, and awards generally involved white money. In fact, one of the major accomplishments of the Renaissance was to push open the door to mainstream periodicals, publishing houses, and funding sources. African American music also played to mixed audiences. Harlem's cabarets attracted both Harlem residents and white New Yorkers seeking out Harlem nightlife. The famous Cotton Club carried this trend to a bizarre extreme by providing black entertainment for exclusively white audiences. Ultimately, the more successful black musicians and entertainers moved their performances downtown.

The relationship of the Harlem Renaissance to white venues and white audiences created controversy. While most African American critics strongly supported the movement, others like Benjamin Brawley and even W.E.B. Du Bois were sharply critical and accused Renaissance writers of reinforcing negative African American stereotypes. Langston Hughes's assertion that black artists intended to express themselves freely, no matter what the black public or white public thought, accurately reflected the attitude of most writers and artists.

The Harlem Renaissance declined in the mid-1930s. A number of factors contributed to this. The Great Depression increased the economic pressure on both creative artists and the arts industry. As a result, organizations like the NAACP and the Urban League,

Three of the most gifted writers of the Harlem Renaissance, Zora Neale Hurston, Langston Hughes, and Jessie Fauset, in 1927, on the Tuskegee campus during a research trip to the South.
Beinecke Rare Book and Manuscript Library, Yale University.

which had actively promoted the Renaissance in the 1920s, shifted their interests to economic and social issues. Reflecting this change, both *The Crisis* and *Opportunity* suspended their literary prizes in the early 1930s. Actually, the role of *The Crisis* in promoting the Harlem Renaissance had diminished in the latter years of the 1920s following Jessie Fauset's departure as literary editor in 1926 and Du Bois's growing disillusionment with the direction black literature had taken and his inability to influence that direction. Charles S. Johnson's 1927 departure from the Urban League and *Opportunity* also redirected that organization's publication back toward social and economic issues in subsequent years. Book publishers and recording companies also became more careful in their selections. On the other hand, New Deal programs, especially those operating within the Works Progress Administration, offered employment to many writers, artists, musicians, and actors.

A second factor contributing to the decline of the Renaissance was the departure of many key figures in the late 1920s and early 1930s. In addition to Charles S. Johnson, James Weldon Johnson moved from Harlem back to the South in 1931, and W.E.B. Du Bois followed in 1934; Langston Hughes left Harlem in 1931 and did not return permanently until World War II. Josephine Baker based her career in Paris after 1925. Paul Robeson, beginning in 1927, worked mostly in London and did not return permanently to the United States until near the outbreak of World War II. Death also cut short many careers. Both Rudolph Fisher and Wallace Thurman died in 1934, and James Weldon Johnson died four years later. Ma Rainey died four years after she retired from the concert circuit in 1935. Bessie Smith's record sales plummeted in the 1930s, but she continued to perform for black audiences, especially in the South; she was killed in a car crash in 1937.

Josephine Baker in Paris as "La Venus Noire." Baker enthralled Parisian audiences and became an international superstar and the century's first sex symbol.
Beinecke Rare Book and Manuscript Library, Yale University.

Many of those that did not die or leave New York ceased or greatly curtailed their creative activity. Countee Cullen, faced with a significant decline in his literary income, took a full-time job teaching school in 1934; most of his writing after that time consisted of children's stories. Nella Larsen suffered an emotional breakdown and never completed her projected third novel. Claude McKay, returning to Harlem in 1934 after an absence of about twelve years, wrote that the few writers from the old days that were still around seemed to be at loose ends. His writing after his return consisted of an autobiography and a history of Harlem. In contrast, Zora Neale Hurston actually enjoyed her greatest period of literary output in the 1930s, but fell silent and largely dropped out of sight after the 1940s.

Sterling Brown and Arna Bontemps shifted their base of operations to black universities and their writing to literary criticism and literary history. Aaron Douglas accepted a job on the faculty at Fisk in 1940 and did very little painting after that time. Langston Hughes continued to support himself through writing after the 1930s, but he no longer considered himself part of a literary movement.

For a younger group of artists the 1930s marked the beginning of their careers. Richard Wright actually started serious writing in the mid-1930s; his most significant novel, *Native Son*, was published in 1940. Wright consciously separated himself from the Harlem Renaissance, criticizing the movement in his 1937 essay, "Blueprint for Negro Writing." Wright's criticism of the Harlem Renaissance and African American culture in general was intense, especially in terms of the relationship between black culture and white culture. "It either crept in through the kitchen in the form of jokes," he wrote, "or it was the fruits of that foul soil which was the result of a liaison between inferiority-complexed Negro 'geniuses' and burnt-out white bohemians with money." In spite of these protests Wright was deeply connected to the movement, especially in terms of his age (he was only slightly younger than Cullen and Hughes) and his commitment to expressing the African American experience.

Others also found life beyond the Harlem Renaissance. Visual artists like Jacob Lawrence and Romare Bearden both had productive careers that extended well beyond World War II, and their later work certainly evolved beyond what they had done in the Harlem Renaissance in terms of both content and style. Together with Wright they may be viewed as transitional figures that bridged the Harlem Renaissance and the world of African American artistic creativity in the post-war period. Likewise, musicians Duke Ellington and Louis Armstrong continued their careers into the post-war period without interruption.

Symbolically, any doubt that the era of the Harlem Renaissance had ended was put to rest by the Harlem Riot of 1935. This event shattered the illusion of Harlem as the "Mecca" of the New Negro that had figured so prominently in Renaissance folklore. Harlem was

Their Eyes Were Watching God, dust jacket, 1937. Zora Neal Hurston's novel was poorly received by black critics, but is now acclaimed as the best novel of the Harlem Renaissance and one of the finest literary works of the 20th century.
Beinecke Rare Book and Manuscript Library, Yale University. Reproduced with the permission of Harper Collins Publishers.

a ghetto, with all of the problems associated with American urban ghettos—high rates of poverty and crime, poor and overcrowded housing, inadequate city services, job discrimination, and control of government, the police force, and employment by the dominant white power structure.

Yet, in spite of all these problems, the Renaissance did not disappear overnight. Almost one-third of the books published during the Renaissance appeared after 1929, and Hurston's *Their Eyes Were Watching God*, arguably the best novel of the Renaissance, came out in 1937. In the final analysis, the Harlem Renaissance ended when most of those associated with it left Harlem or stopped writing, and the new young artists who emerged in the 1930s and 1940s no longer defined themselves by the movement.

What does the Harlem Renaissance mean to us today and to the African American experience of the last one hundred years? Some would acknowledge that it was an event of some interest in the early part of the last century, but dismiss it as having little to do with current events. Some, more critical, would dismiss it for its dependence on white money, audiences, and publishers. Others would celebrate it, if only for the quantity of the books written and the quality and originality of the music. But few read Countee Cullen today, or have the songs of Ethel Waters on their iPods. Furthermore, these approaches ignore the spirit and the uniqueness of the movement.

The spirit of the Harlem Renaissance was centered in its community of writers and artists, each expressing his or her own vision yet bound together in a shared undertaking, and with the community of intellectuals, critics, patrons, and publishers allied to create a revolution in African American culture—all of this was unique and sadly, would not appear again. The excitement generated by the Harlem Renaissance has not resurfaced in black arts and literature. The only similar experience occurred during the civil rights movement—beginning with Rosa Parks in Montgomery and culminating in Martin Luther King's "I Have A Dream" speech during the March on Washington D.C. Once again African Americans and their white friends united for a magic moment in history. But this time the focus was on politics, not on literature, art, and music. Thirty-five years earlier the Harlem Renaissance was another magic moment, filled with confidence, hope, and the dream that African American creative artists would free humankind and make real the dream of America.

where. There was assuredly no doubt of his where-
abouts. This was Negro Harlem.

Gillis then noticed the commotion in the street as trucks and
autos crowded into the intersection at the command of the traffic
cop—an African American traffic cop.

> The Southern Negro's eyes opened wide; his
> mouth opened wider. . . . For there stood a hand-
> some, brass-buttoned giant directing the heaviest
> traffic Gillis had ever seen; halting unnumbered tons
> of automobiles and trucks and wagons and pushcarts
> and street-cars; holding them at bay with one hand
> while he swept similar tons peremptorily on with the
> other; ruling the wide crossing with supreme self-
> assurance; and he, too, was a Negro!
>
> Yet most of the vehicles that leaped or crouched
> at his bidding carried white passengers. One of these
> overdrove bounds a few feet and Gillis heard the
> officer's shrill whistle and gruff reproof, saw the dri-
> ver's face turn red and his car draw back like a
> threatened pup. It was beyond belief-impossible.
> Black might be white, but it couldn't be that white!
>
> "Done died an' woke up in Heaven," thought
> King Solomon, watching, fascinated; and after a
> while, as if the wonder of it were too great to believe
> simply by seeing, "Cullud policemans!" he said, half
> aloud; then repeated over and over, with greater and
> greater conviction, "Even got cullud policemans."

Gillis was one of those who sought refuge in Harlem. He fled
North Carolina after shooting a white man. Now in Harlem the
policeman was black. Not that this changed his fate. At the end of the
story, Gillis was dragged away in handcuffs by another one of these
black policemen. The reality of Harlem could contradict the myth.

Harlem

CARY D. WINTZ

Harlem! To African Americans during the first half of the twentieth century the word evoked strong images—the Negro Metropolis, black Manhattan, the political, cultural, and spiritual center of African America, a land of plenty, a city of refuge. For some, the image of Harlem was more personal. King Solomon Gillis, the main character in Rudolph Fisher's "The City of Refuge," was one of these. Emerging out of the subway at 135th and Lennox Avenue, Gillis was transfixed:

> Clean air, blue sky, bright sunlight. Gillis set down his tan-cardboard extension-case and wiped his black, shining brow. Then slowly, spreadingly, he grinned at what he saw: Negroes at every turn; up and down Lenox Avenue, up and down One Hundred and Thirty-fifth Street; big, lanky Negroes, short, squat Negroes; black ones, brown ones, yellow ones; men standing idle on the curb, women, bundle-laden, trudging reluctantly home-ward, children rattle-trapping about the sidewalks; here and there a white face drifting along, but Negroes predominantly, overwhelmingly every-

Negro policemen, Harlem. One development during the Great Migration was the employment of blacks in law enforcement. Samuel Battle, the first African American assigned to the police department in Harlem, was appointed in 1910. To many southern black migrants, these officers symbolized the freedom of the North. Photographs and Prints Division, Schomburg Center for Research in Black Culture, The New York Public Library. *Black America*, 1929, pg. 232.

For poet Langston Hughes, Harlem was also something of a refuge. Following a mostly unhappy childhood living at one time or another with his mother or father, grandmother, or neighbors, Hughes convinced his stern and foreboding father to finance his education at Columbia University. He recalled his 1921 arrival: "I went up the steps and out into the bright September sunlight. Harlem! I stood there, dropped my bags, took a deep breath and felt happy again. I registered at the Y. When college opened, I did not want to move into the dormitory at Columbia. I really did not want to go to college at all. I didn't want to do anything but live in Harlem, get a job and work there." After a less than happy year at Columbia, Hughes did exactly that. He dropped out of school and moved into Harlem. Hughes, though, never lost sight of the fact that poverty, overcrowded, dilapidated housing and racial prejudice were part of the daily experience of most Harlem residents.

James Weldon Johnson saw a different Harlem. In his 1930 book *Black Manhattan*, he described the black metropolis as the race's

The Harlem Plains, 1812. In the early 19th century Harlem was rural and the site of large estates.
The Picture Collection of The New York Public Library.

Harlem-lane from Central Park to Manhattanville, 1865. By the middle of the century Harlem housed poor farmers and immigrants. It also had become a playground for the wealthy who raced their carriages along the rural roadways.
Picture Collection, The Branch Libraries, The New York Public Library, Astor, Lenox and Tilden Foundations.

Industrial night reception, about 1917. Over 400,000 people left the South between 1916 and 1918, at an aver-age rate of sixteen thousand per month, five hundred per day. Most, like these assembled at this employment cen-ter, came looking for higher-paying jobs.
Photographs and Prints Division, Schomburg Center for Research in Black Culture, The New York Public Library Astor, Lenox and Tilden Foundations.

Harlem's transition, once it began, followed fairly traditional pat-terns. As soon as blacks started moving onto a block, property val-ues dropped further as whites began to leave. This process was especially evident in the early 1920s. Both black and white realtors took advantage of the decline and the panic-selling that resulted when blacks moved in, and the pressure to provide housing for the city's rapidly growing black population. They acquired, subdivided, and leased Harlem property to African American tenants.

Year by year the boundaries of black Harlem expanded, as blacks, desperate for decent housing, streamed into Harlem as quickly as housing was made available to them. By 1910 they had established themselves as the majority group on the west side of Harlem north of 130th Street; by 1914 the population of black Harlem was esti-mated to be 50,000.

During the next two decades, black Harlem continued to grow as tens of thousands of migrants from the South were joined by thousands of immigrants from the West Indies, all finding their way to Harlem's streets and tenements. In 1920 black Harlem extended from 130th Street to 145th Street and from Fifth to Eighth Avenue, and contained approximately 73,000 blacks; by 1930 black Harlem had expanded north ten blocks to 155th and south to 115th; it spread from the Harlem River to Amsterdam Avenue, and housed approximately 164,000 blacks. The core of this community, bounded roughly by 126th Street on the south, 159th Street on the north, the Harlem River and Park Avenue on the east, and Eighth Avenue on the west, was more than 95 percent black.

A crowd in Harlem at Lenox Avenue and 134th Street. During the war thousands of migrants from the South transformed Harlem into the Black Metropolis.
Photographs and Prints Division, Schomburg Center for Research in Black Culture, The New York Public Library Astor, Lenox and Tilden Foundations.

By 1920, Harlem, by virtue of the sheer size of its black population, had emerged as the capital of black America. Its name evoked a magic that lured all classes of African Americans from all sections of the country to its streets. Impoverished southern farmers and sharecroppers poured northward, where they were joined in Harlem by black intellectuals such as W.E.B. Du Bois and James Weldon Johnson. Although the old black social elites of Washington, D.C., and Philadelphia were disdainful of Harlem's vulgar splendor, and while it housed no significant black university as did Washington D.C., Philadelphia, Atlanta, and Nashville, Harlem still became

The caption on this 1919 photograph reads: "Welcome home; All hail to the conquering heroes; When New York's Negro soldiers marched amid the cheering crowd, Harlem was mad with joy over the return of its own."
General Research & Reference Division, Schomburg Center for Research in Black Culture, The New York Public Library.

the race's cultural center and a mecca for its aspiring young. It housed the Urban League, A. Philip Randolph's Brotherhood of Sleeping Car Porters and the black leadership of the NAACP. Marcus Garvey launched his ill-fated black nationalist movement among its masses. Harlem became the geographical focal point of African American literature, art, and music. Harlem, in short, was where the action was in black America during the decade following World War I.

By the 1920s Harlem was a city within a city, with its own landmarks and neighborhoods. In large part the neighborhoods are defined by four major streets, which define a square—125th Street on the south, 135th Street running through the heart of Harlem, and two north-south avenues, Lennox and Seventh Avenue. Lennox was everyman's Harlem, characterized by street life, entertainment venues, and restaurants. At Lennox and 140th Street the Savoy Ballroom hosted most of Harlem's major social events and parties, where blacks and whites mingled on the dance floor and where the Lindy Hop was invented. It was also home to the Cotton Club, Harlem's most famous nightspot, which catered to white-only audiences and featured acts like Cab Calloway, Duke Ellington, and Ethel Waters.

Jungle Alley, a cluster of clubs and speakeasies along 133rd Street between Lennox Avenue and Seventh Avenue, provided a variety of entertainment options and a more eclectic and risqué environment. It catered to a racially mixed and sexually uninhibited clientele. In Jungle Alley everyone rubbed shoulders—gay and straight whites from across the city, working-class blacks as well as intellectuals, writers, musicians, artists, businessmen, criminals, and prostitutes. They drank bootleg liquor, had access to marijuana and harder drugs, and danced or just listened to jazz and blues artists, often until daybreak.

If Lennox Avenue and Jungle Alley were primarily devoted to entertainment, Seventh Avenue was the grand avenue where people went to see and be seen. It was a broad, tree-lined boulevard, with a median planted with trees and flowers, which stretched uninterrupted twenty blocks north from 125th Street. It was ideal for parades, and many passed down the street, including those in the

Harlem Street: 422–424 Lenox Avenue near 135th Street. This 1938 photo shows the mix of shops and institutions along Lenox Avenue, including, doctor's office, a meat and produce market, an auto school, a beauty salon, a barber shop, and women sitting on the steps of a church.
Photography Collection, Miriam and Ira D. Wallach Division of Art, Prints and Photographs, The New York Public Library, Astor, Lenox and Tilden Foundations.

early 1920s led by Marcus Garvey and the Universal Negro Improvement Association, and those organized by followers of Father Devine a decade later. The location of some of the most prominent Harlem churches along Seventh Avenue meant that it was the site for the funeral processions of many of the rich and famous. Mostly, though, it was where Harlemites both rich and poor donned their finest clothes and strolled down the avenue on Sunday afternoon.

Seventh Avenue also was home to a number of significant buildings in Harlem, including the area's finest

The Dunbar Apartments, Harlem. The six buildings of the Dunbar Apartments, built in 1926 at Eighth Avenue and 150th Street, housed 511 middle-class Negro families. W. E. B. Du Bois, A. Philip Randolph, and Paul Robeson were among the residents. Although specifically built for African Americans, they were beyond the means of poor southern migrants, who were segregated from middle-class and elite black neighborhoods.
General Research & Reference Division, Schomburg Center for Research in Black Culture, The New York Public Library.
Black America, 1929, pg. 235

hotel, the Hotel Theresa, and the headquarters of Garvey's UNIA. Dizzie Gillespie lived on Seventh avenue near 121st Street in the 1940s, while at the north end of the avenue stood the Dunbar Apartments, home of some of Harlem's most famous residents. While Seventh Avenue lacked the variety of entertainment outlets found on Lennox and Jungle Alley, it was the home of the Lafayette Theater and its two neighbors, Connie's Inn and the Rhythm Club. Connie's Inn, like the Cotton Club, served an all-white crowd. A block up the street, Small's Paradise had a more democratic admission policy. There, racially mixed crowds enjoyed first-rate musical and dancing acts as well as expensive liquor served by the Paradise's famous dancing waiters. Small's was a favorite of Harlem's literary crowd. Alain Locke, Countee Cullen, Harold Jackman, and Langston Hughes frequented the club. Even William Faulkner dropped by once. White novelist Carl Van Vechten used Small's as the model for the "Black Venus," the infamous Harlem club in *Nigger Heaven*. Displeased with the depiction, the proprietors banned Van Vechten from Small's for life.

Crossing both Lennox and Seventh Avenue, 135th Street provided a link between the two avenues in the heart of black Harlem. 135th Street was home to two major institutions that were important to the Harlem Renaissance, the 135th Street Branch of the New York Public Library, and the Harlem branch of the YMCA. The Y hosted poetry readings and other literary events, featuring Langston Hughes, Countee Cullen, and others. Several literary groups and book clubs met there. The Y also played a major role in the development of theater in Harlem. Beginning in 1919 one of the earliest theater groups, the Player's Guild, staged its first productions at the Y, including one featuring the acting debut of Paul Robeson. The Acme Players also used its stage for its theatrical performances.

The 135th Street Branch of the New York Public Library, the cultural center of Harlem, was deeply associated with the Harlem Renaissance. Regina Anderson and Nella Larsen were employed

Harlem, along Lenox Avenue within thirty second's walk of the 135th Street Branch of the New York Public Library. Photographs and Prints Division, Schomburg Center for Research in Black Culture, The New York Public Library Astor, Lenox and Tilden Foundations.

there; Gwendolyn Bennett, Ethel Ray Nance, and Jessie Fauset organized poetry readings and other literary events at the library. Countee Cullen participated in many of these readings. The library provided workspace for a number of writers, including Langston Hughes and Claude McKay. It organized art and literature programs for children featuring Langston Hughes, Jacob Lawrence, and Romare Bearden, among others. The first exhibit of African American art in Harlem was displayed at the library in 1921. This evolved into an annual art show and occasional solo exhibitions. Aaron Douglas had a one-man show there, and in 1934 he painted *Aspects of Negro Life*, one of his most important mural series, on the library's walls.

Ten blocks to the south, 125th Street served as Harlem's gateway and commercial hub. It stretched between two major subway stops, one on the Lennox Avenue line and the other on Eighth Avenue. Harlem's major department stores and retail establishments lined 125th street. Blumstein's Department Store at 125th near Eighth Avenue was the target of a 1934 boycott to protest the lack of black employees in the store. In the 1930s the opening of the Apollo Theater on 125th Street signaled the expansion of Harlem's entertainment district. The Apollo featured the finest acts and became the most prestigious African American performing stage in the country. The response of the Apollo's knowledgeable audience could make or break a performer's career.

By the 1920s wealthy and near wealthy African Americans occupied the most desirable housing in Harlem. Striver's Row was located on two adjacent tree-lined blocks, 138th Street and 139th Street, between Seventh and Eighth Avenues. The stately Italianate townhomes on these two blocks had been designed for wealthy whites, but the arrival of blacks in the neighborhood altered those plans. In the mid-1920s wealthy blacks moved in—not millionaires like the whites they displaced, but quite wealthy men of achievement, including bandleaders, dentists, physicians, and even a prizefighter. Wallace Thurman castigated the community for its snobbishness. Others noted that there seemed to be a color criterion for the neighborhood—most of the residents were quite light-skinned. Both Nella Larsen and Jesse Fauset depicted homes from this neighborhood in their fiction.

West of Striver's Row, atop the bluffs that rise just west of Eighth Avenue, Sugar Hill stretched along Edgecombe Avenue and nearby streets from 145th Street north to about 155th Street, overlooking the old Polo Grounds. From this perch above the city, luxurious apartment houses and brownstones overlooked Harlem. Prominent Harlemites including writer and journalist George Schuyler, artist Aaron Douglas, A'Lelia Walker, Duke Ellington, Paul Robeson, and Walter White lived there. Others, including W.E.B. Du Bois, Countee Cullen, Langston Hughes, Zora Neale Hurston, and James Weldon Johnson frequented the homes and parties there.

The apartment house on Sugar Hill that had the deepest connection with the Harlem Renaissance was 580 St. Nicholas Avenue. The building housed a number of Harlem notables including Ethel Waters, but most of the Harlem Renaissance activity occurred in the fifth-floor apartment shared by three young women: Ethel Ray Nance, who worked for Charles S. Johnson, the Urban League and *Opportunity* magazine, Regina Andrews, who worked as a librarian at the 135th Street Library, and Louella Tucker. Nance and Andrews were deeply embedded in the literary and artistic movement. Charles S. Johnson directed newly arrived artists to Nance, who housed them, sometimes for weeks, on the apartment's sofa, while Andrews provided a venue at the library for art exhibits and poetry readings. Artist Aaron Douglas was directed to 580 St. Nicholas when he arrived in Harlem, as was Zora Neale Hurston. Nance received special instructions to keep an eye on the flamboyant Ms. Hurston and make sure she kept the appointments that got her admitted to Barnard College and employed by Fannie Hurst.

Nance and Andrews also made their apartment a gathering place. Charles S. Johnson likely used this space to assemble the informal group of young Harlem writers and artists that formed in the months preceding the Civic Club dinner. Poets Countee Cullen and Langston Hughes spent many evenings there. Cullen was dragged from 580 to the Cat on the Saxophone (Nance, Andrews, and Tucker's favorite Harlem dive) for his first cabaret experience. Du Bois, Charles S. Johnson, Jessie Fauset, and James Weldon Johnson met with the young writers and artists at 580 as they attempted to guide the emerging Renaissance. Carl Van Vechten visited frequently, and he surprised his hostesses when he used both the apartment and Nance and Andrews as models for characters and events in *Nigger Heaven*. Andrews felt he had betrayed her hospitality.

This 1924 portrait taken on the roof of 580 St. Nicholas Ave., Harlem, after an all-night party honoring Langston Hughes in the apartment shared by Regina Andrews and Ethel Ray Nance captures, from left to right: Langston Hughes, Charles S. Johnson, E. Franklin Frazier, Rudolph Fisher, and Hubert T. Delany,.

Photographs and Prints Division, Schomburg Center for Research in Black Culture, The New York Public Library. Regina Andrews photo collection.

Far removed from Sugar Hill and 580 in both class and status, but no less important to the Harlem Renaissance, was Wallace Thurman's rent-free apartment at 267 136th Street. "267 House," sardonically christened "Niggerati Manor" by either Thurman or Hurston, was the abode of Thurman and Bruce Nugent and the gathering place of the radical group that produced the one-issue literary magazine, *FIRE!!* The dress and poverty of the habitués of 267 House reflected the bohemian side of the Harlem Renaissance. Life at 267 House was celebrated and satirized in two literary works—Thurman's *Infants of the Spring* and Nugent's unpublished "Gentleman Jigger." In dress, lifestyle, values, and literary and artistic tastes, the crowd at Niggerati Manor were far removed from the professionals at the NAACP and the Urban League and the more conventional literary gatherings at 580, James Weldon Johnson's Seventh Avenue apartment, or the very fashionable events at Walter White's home. Still,

Harlem on 136th Street (West) near Lenox Avenue in 1936. In 1928 this building was the site of A'Lelia Walker's
Dark Tower.
Milstein Division of United States History, Local History & Genealogy, Schomburg Center for Research in Black Cul-
ture, The New York Public Library, Astor, Lenox and Tilden Foundations

Harlem brought both groups (and others) together at its parties and
especially at its nightclubs.

One place where all Harlem artists and their editors and critics
gathered, along with artists and celebrities from downtown, was
A'Lelia Walker's Dark Tower. A'Lelia Walker was the heiress to the
fortune Madam C. J. Walker accumulated through her hair-straight-
ening and other African American beauty products, and her upscale
hair salons. A'Lelia Walker was a striking figure in Harlem. She was
a tall, large woman who frequently wore jewel-encrusted turbans and
sometimes carried a riding crop. After shedding two husbands in
quick succession, she surrounded herself with a cadre of attendants,
mostly women and gay men. In 1928 Walker opened the Dark Tower
in a twin townhouse she owned at 108–110 136th Street. Named
after a Countee Cullen poem, the Dark Tower was initially conceived
as a comfortable and informal gathering place for writers, artists, and
their friends. When it opened it was something quite different. It was

lavishly and expensively furnished, food and drink were priced beyond the means of most artists, and it attracted crowds from Harlem and downtown—including, now and again, visiting European royalty. Langston Hughes described A'Lelia as a "gorgeous dark Amazon in a silver turban," and "the joy-goddess of Harlem's 1920s." At the Dark Tower, he observed, "Negro poets and Negro numbers bankers mingled with downtown poets and seat-on-the-stock-exchange racketeers," and the parties were as "crowded as the New York subway at rush hour." It never became the literary salon she had envisioned, though, and Walker closed the Dark Tower after a year.

By the mid-1920s Harlem was noted for its nightlife. It provided entertainment and amusement not only for its own residents, but for white New Yorkers who traveled uptown for music, speakeasies, and a taste of exotic Harlem after dark. Carl Van Vechten helped popularize Harlem, both through *Nigger Heaven* and informal tours of Harlem's clubs and cabarets he organ-

Savoy Ballroom, 1935. The Savoy was one of Harlem's most popular night spots and the home of the "Lindy Hop." Beinecke Rare Book and Manuscript Library, Yale University.

ized for his white friends. By the second half of the decade the white crowds were coming on their own to mingle with blacks in the clubs of Jungle Alley or the Savoy, or to hear top entertainment in all-white establishments like the Cotton Club. Duke Ellington described the appeal of these clubs to white New Yorkers:

> Sunday night in the Cotton Club was the night. All the big New York stars in town, no matter where they were playing, showed up at the Cotton Club to take bows. . . . Somebody like Sophie Tucker would stand up, and we'd play her song "Some of These Days" as she made her way up the floor for a bow. It

was all done in pretty grand style. Harlem had a
tremendous reputation in those days and it was a
very colorful place. . . . "When you go to New York,"
people said, "you mustn't miss going to Harlem!"

In the fall of 1929 *Variety* reported that Harlem's nightlife surpassed that of Broadway, and that "from midnight until after dawn
it is a seething caldron of Nubian mirth and hilarity."

Of course, ordinary blacks did not rub elbows with white down-
towners at expensive nightclubs, even if they were in Harlem. For
the black working class there were some clubs that welcomed
patrons of both races, like the upscale Small's Paradise, featured in
Thurman's novel *The Blacker the Berry*. Most of the working class
frequented more affordable "black-and-tan" or all-black clubs. Many
of those that catered to mixed-race parties were considered disreputable by many middle-class African Americans for their open sexuality. Typical of these was Edmund's Cellar at 132nd and Fifth
Avenue, where Ethel Waters sang. In her memoirs, Waters described
the basement cabaret as having "a handkerchief-sized dance floor"
flanked by small tables seating up to 200 patrons. Three blocks up
Fifth Avenue at 135th Street, the Sugar Cane Club crowded so
many into its damp cellar that its customers, emboldened by bootleg
whiskey or sticks of marijuana, did the bump or the mess-around, or
as crowding increased simply shuffled in place—dancing on a dime.
Only the most daring whites made it to the Sugar Cane.

The distinguishing feature of Harlem nightlife was the house-rent
party. This egalitarian event originated as a way for cash-strapped
Harlemites to raise money for their inflated rent payments—$15 to
$30 more than white areas of Manhattan. Thursday and Saturday
nights were favored for these all-night parties. Saturday was payday
for laborers who usually had Sunday off, and Thursday was the night
off for sleep-in domestic workers. The would-be host printed up invitations through the Wayside Printer, an itinerate craftsman who
pushed his small wheeled press from block to block. He distributed
business-card-sized invitations to neighbors and strangers,

euphemistically announcing a "Parlor Social," a "Social Whist Party" or a "Tea Cup Party." He arranged music—usually a piano player or a small combo, but sometimes just a record player or a radio tuned in to the nightly broadcast from the Cotton Club—and cleared his flat of its furniture and carpet, perhaps bringing in folding chairs from a nearby funeral parlor. Food and drink were basic—bootleg whiskey or bathtub gin, with southern staples: fried chicken and fish, chitterlings, pig's feet, greens, and cornbread. The admission fee and the extra charges for food and drink paid for the entertainment, hopefully with enough left over for next month's rent.

The patrons of the house-rent party were primarily Harlem's working people—especially domestics, stevedores, and laborers—but all classes sometimes attended. Du Bois and others from Harlem's middle and upper classes pointedly stayed away, viewing them rowdy, disreputable, and destructive to the public image of African Americans. Many of the artists, writers, and musicians, including Wallace Thurman and Claude McKay, wrote about them. Bessie Smith celebrated them in her song, "Give Me a Beer and Another Pig's Foot," while Langston Hughes described them in his autobiography as a place where working-class blacks could drink and dance without a white tourist looking over their shoulder:

> Almost every Saturday night when I was in Harlem I went to a house-rent party. I wrote lots of poems about house-rent parties, and ate thereat many a fried fish and pig's foot—with liquid refreshment on the side. I met ladies' maids and truck drivers, laundry workers and shoe shine boys, seamstresses and porters. I can still hear their laughter in my ears, hear the soft slow music, and feel the floor shaking as the dancers danced.

Whites rarely gained admittance to these gatherings.

Not all Harlem residents lived on Striver's Row or Sugar Hill, or spent their nights at the parties and discussions at 580 St. Nicholas

Avenue. Most knew little or nothing of the Harlem Renaissance. Of the 140,000 or so living in Harlem in the mid-1920s, all but a few thousand were working class; many of these were underemployed or unemployed. For them Harlem was a different place. The reality of Harlem was changing in the 1920s; for most, conditions were getting worse.

Without question, Harlem was a rapidly growing black metropolis, but what kind of city was it becoming? Harlem historian Gilbert Osofsky argued that "the most profound change that Harlem experienced in the 1920s was its emergence as a slum. Largely within the space of a single decade Harlem was transformed from a potentially ideal community to a neighborhood with manifold social and economic problems called 'deplorable, unspeakable, incredible.'" Housing was overpriced, congested, and dilapidated. Jobs were hard to come by, in part because of the number of migrants competing for jobs, but also due to widespread job discrimination, even in the heart of Harlem. During the

A Negro doll factory in Harlem, circa 1929. With the influx of southern migrants, black-owned businesses flourished in the urban north. Those that emphasized racial pride, a popular Harlem Renaissance theme, were particularly in demand. Black dolls for African-American children were manufactured in Harlem.
General Research & Reference Division, Schomburg Center for Research in Black Culture, The New York Public Library Astor, Lenox and Tilden Foundations.

1920s the vast majority of Harlem's retail establishments, white owned and operated, would hire blacks only for menial jobs such as porter, maid, or elevator operator. As a result, most of Harlem's residents lived on the verge of poverty, a situation that contributed to the growth of vice, crime, juvenile delinquency, and drug addiction.

Even the quality housing that initially attracted blacks to Harlem proved to be illusory for most residents. Existing brownstones and roomy apartments were quickly subdivided. Developers threw up cheap tenements to cash in on the area's burgeoning growth. Rents and demand for housing remained so high that many black families were forced to take in boarders or hold rent parties in order to afford even low-quality housing. Overcrowding and segregation combined to undermine the neighborhood. Faulty maintenance, violation of municipal codes, and outright vandalism accelerated the process. By the late 1930s, 30 percent of the area's dwellings lacked bathing facilities.

In short, the day-to-day realities that most Harlemites faced differed dramatically from the image of Harlem life presented by James Weldon Johnson. Perhaps Johnson finally became aware of how far reality had diverged from his dream. In 1931, Harlem's greatest booster abandoned black Manhattan for a position at Fisk University in Nashville.

The frustration that some Harlem blacks felt was expressed by Carl Van Vechten in *Nigger Heaven*. Byron, frustrated by his failure as an artist, bitterly complained:

> "Nigger Heaven!" Byron moaned. "Nigger Heaven! That's what Harlem is. We sit in our places in the gallery in this New York theater and watch the white world sitting down below in the good seats in the orchestra. Occasionally they turn their faces up towards us, their hard, cruel faces, to laugh or sneer, but they never beckon. It never seems to occur to them that Nigger Heaven is crowded, that there isn't another seat, that something has to be done. . . . Harlem! The Mecca of the New Negro! My God!"

Harlem, then, represented different things to different blacks. It was their hope as well as their despair. More important, Harlem reflected the confusing and contradictory position of African Americans in the early twentieth century. It was the black migrant who left the South and went north with dreams of freedom and opportunity. It also was the shattered pieces of those dreams half-buried in a tenement room or down a garbage-filled alley. Harlem reflected the self-confidence, militancy, and pride of the New Negro in his or her demand for equality; it reflected the aspirations and creative genius of the talented young people of the Harlem Renaissance. But Harlem, like the black migrant, like the New Negro, and like the Renaissance writers, did not resolve its problems or fulfill its dreams.

It took a single event to bring clarity to these conflicting images and conflicting realities. On March 19, 1935, a young Puerto Rican boy was caught stealing a ten-cent pocketknife from the counter of a 135th Street five-and-dime store. The minor scuffle that broke out when the police were arresting the youth sparked rumors that the police had beaten a black child to death. Within moments, a large, angry crowd gathered, shouting charges of police of brutality and accusing the white merchants in the area of racial discrimination. Someone smashed a window, and the looting began. The riot spread into the night. By dawn, three blacks were dead, two hundred stores were trashed and burned, and more than $2,000,000 worth of property had been destroyed. Ironically, the boy whose deed triggered the riot had been released the previous evening when the merchant chose not to press charges.

Mayor Fiorello La Guardia organized an investigation of the riot and appointed E. Franklin Frazier, a professor of sociology at Howard University, to head the interracial committee that would carry out the study. They concluded the obvious: the riot resulted from general frustration with racial discrimination and poverty. What the committee did not report was that the riot shattered, once and for all, the illusion that Harlem was a near utopian African American city. The black metropolis, which only a few years earlier had been touted as the cultural center of black America, which as the black bohemia had thrilled Renaissance writers and entertained whites looking for exotic adventure, had been exposed for what it was—a ghetto, a slum, an area blighted by poverty and discrimination. Burned-out storefronts might be fertile ground for political action, but not for art, literature, and culture.

Harlem would see new black writers in the years to come. Musicians, poets, and artists would continue to make their home there, but Harlem never regained its position as the focal point of a creative movement with the national and international impact of the Harlem Renaissance.

PART TWO

To Make a Poet Black: Literature of the Harlem Renaissance

INTRODUCTION

The Harlem Renaissance was first and foremost a literary movement. Other arts, and politics, were extremely significant for
expanding the creative energies that inspired and enriched the
Harlem Renaissance, and for contributing to the rich artistic and
cultural milieu that made Harlem in the 1920s such a special place.
Literature, though—in the form of poems, short stories, novels, and
essays—formed the core of the movement. It was literature, not
music nor painting nor even musical theater, that the publishing
community celebrated at the 1924 Civic Club dinner. *FIRE!!*, the
one-issue magazine Wallace Thurman edited, was essentially a literary statement. Likewise, while culturally conservative political lead-

ers like W.E.B. Du Bois were not always happy with the popularity
of jazz and the blues, nor with the portrayal of blacks in musical theater and musical reviews, it was literature that most attracted their
critical eye and generated their sternest condemnations.

In terms of literary production, this aspect of the Harlem Renaissance was an astonishing success. The major writers, eighteen authors
who produced book-length literary works with major publishing
houses, produced almost fifty titles in the thirteen-year period
between 1922 and 1935. That compares to about a dozen books from
four major authors published in the preceding twenty-two years, most
by small presses with limited distribution. In addition to the major
authors of the Harlem Renaissance, scores of other black writers
wrote and published poems, short stories, or other literary works in
newspapers or magazines, and with small presses with local or
regional distribution. For example, in 1925 Bernice Love Wiggins of
El Paso, Texas, privately published a collection of her poems, *Tuneful
Tales*. Wiggins, whose body of work numbers at least 102 poems, also
published her verses in Texas newspapers and African American
newspapers like the *Chicago Defender*. The literary Renaissance was
centered in Harlem, but its effect spread across the country.

There was no common theme or style that characterized the
work of the major literary figures who were in, or associated with,
Harlem. Their backgrounds and their political and social views were
also diverse. They did share a determination to express their vision
in works that would be truthful and of high literary quality, and that
would give voice to the African American experience. It is important to note their insistence that there was no requirement that
restricted them to black issues and topics. Countee Cullen insisted
he was a poet, not a black poet. And, as Langston Hughes proclaimed, they wrote for themselves, notwithstanding the demands or
the agendas of the critics, black or white.

The resulting diversity of content and style is striking. Jessie
Fauset's four novels, set in upper-middle-class Philadelphia and
Harlem, described the lives and travails of the African American
"Talented Tenth," focusing largely on the efforts of women to take

charge of their lives. Her novels were stylish and restrained. Claude McKay, in contrast, set his novels among the black working class, in Harlem, Marseilles, and the West Indies. Amidst the labor, poverty, crime, sex, alcohol, gaiety, and suffering of lower-class life, his characters argued the nature of the black experience and the role of blacks in a white-dominated world. His novels were gritty, not refined. Wallace Thurman set his two novels in Harlem and attacked the foibles of the black middle class with satire—especially their intellectual pretensions and their own race and color prejudice. Langston Hughes set his only Harlem Renaissance novel in a small Kansas college town and tracked the "coming of age" of a black child raised by a succession of females.

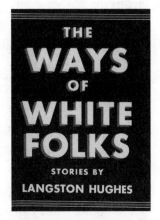

Langston Hughes's book jacket for *The Ways of White Folks*. This collection of Langston Hughes's short stories was published in 1934, and is notable for its exploration of race and the relationship between African American artists and white partons.
Beinecke Rare Book and Manuscript Library, Yale University.

Poetry is equally varied. Claude McKay and Countee Cullen utilized the sonnet and other classical poetic forms for their mix of racial and non-racial poetry. Langston Hughes was noted for adapting the forms and tone of the blues and jazz to his poems of urban black life. Sterling Brown applied blues and work songs to the African American rural experience. James Weldon Johnson wrote formal verse, such as his Negro national anthem ("Lift Every Voice and Sing"), but his most critically acclaimed work, *God's Trombones*, is a set of traditional black sermons set to verse.

The six African American writers featured in this section of the book represent only a sample of the larger group of writers who created the literary Renaissance of the 1920s. Langston Hughes and Countee Cullen represent the talented young poets, whose work in the early 1920s set new standards for African American poetry. Both were cited by black critics as the signal that a new level of literary creativity was emerging. Both lived up to their early promise and were central figures in the Harlem Renaissance. Nella Larsen and Zora Neale Hurston underscore the significance of black women in the Harlem Renaissance. They were known primarily for their prose. Larsen's two novels from the 1920s examined the complexities of race and mixed-race characters and their interactions with the black and white worlds. In contrast, Hurston's 1930s novels focused on life almost exclusively within rural southern black communities.

The last two writers framed the Harlem Renaissance; they also presented an outsider's perspective. Jamaican-born Claude McKay, a decade older than Cullen or Hughes, saw Harlem through the eyes of an immigrant with an international perspective. Richard Wright, about seven years younger than either Hughes or Cullen, was born in the southern United States and began his literary career in the 1930s. He was a transitional figure between the Harlem Renaissance and the literature of the post-Renaissance period. Also, he was one of several black artists and writers who chose an expatriate's life. He spent most of his career in France.

Together the six authors discussed in the chapters that follow provide a grand introduction to the range of Harlem Renaissance literature.

Langston Hughes

(1902-1967)

ARNOLD RAMPERSAD

If a Hollywood scriptwriter wanted to create a fictionalized Harlem Renaissance poet, Langston Hughes would be the perfect model for the part. Everybody liked Langston, and almost everyone liked his poetry. He was an inventive writer who, more than any of his contemporaries, brought the music of Harlem into his poetry. He was at the center of major literary events, including the creation of FIRE!!, the articulation of a manifesto for the Renaissance in "The Negro Artist and The Racial Mountain," and the struggle to maintain artistic integrity. Most importantly, he endured as a poet. As the majority of his literary colleagues fell silent in the 1930s, he continued to practice his craft for the next thirty years, creating short stories, novels, plays, and always poetry.

I f the Harlem Renaissance had an unofficial poet laureate, someone whose verse best captured the spirit of the age, Langston
Hughes almost certainly would have been that person. Although
he never married and had no children, he had a wide circle of
friends and acquaintances. Beloved both by fellow writers and ordinary black readers, he stirred and returned that affection in verse
that celebrated black life and culture as it had never been celebrated
before . Versatile and persistent, he continued to publish—in widely
different genres—long after every other important literary voice of
the era had fallen silent. He also left behind, in his memoir *The Big
Sea* (1940), the finest, most detailed account of the Renaissance
published by any of its participants.

James Langston Hughes was born on February 1, 1902, in Joplin,
Missouri. His father, James Nathaniel Hughes, was an aspiring
lawyer and bookkeeper. His mother, Carrie Mercer Langston
Hughes, was the only daughter of Charles Mercer Langston, once
prominent as a radical abolitionist, a black Republican politician,
and a businessman. During adulthood, she realized few of the goals
she might have imagined for herself while growing up, getting by as
a sometime city clerk, school teacher, actress, and writer.

Photograph of Langston Hughes at age 22.
Beinecke Rare Book and Manuscript Library, Yale
University. © Nickolas Muray Photo Archives.

After a few months in Joplin,
Langston moved with his mother
back to Kansas following the
breakup of her marriage. Fed up
with American racism, his father
settled in Mexico, where he lived
in relative prosperity as a businessman and landowner. With his
mother usually away in search of
work, Langston grew up in
Lawrence with his twice-widowed
maternal grandmother. Mary
Langston's first husband, Lois
Sheridan Leary, had been shot dead
in 1859 at Harpers Ferry as a mem-

ber of John Brown's insurrectionary band. Her second husband (Langston's grandfather) died before Langston was born. As a boy, Langston grew up with the legacy of political resistance and racial pride as family lore; however, he also grew up poor, and with a withdrawn, Bible-reading grandmother. Lonely, he found solace above all in "the wonderful world in books," as he put it. A good student, he also suffered from acts of racism in a city that had largely forgotten its abolitionist roots in the wake of *Plessy* v. *Ferguson* (1896) and other U.S. Supreme Court decisions upholding racial segregation.

After the death of his grandmother in 1915, Langston lived for a year with his mother in Lincoln, Illinois. There, according to him, he recited at his eighth-grade graduation ceremony his first poem, following his election as Class Poet by his fellow students (almost all of them white). In 1916, he moved to Cleveland, Ohio, where he spent four years as a student at Central High School. Once again, most of his schoolmates were white. Hughes excelled in the classroom and in extracurricular activities, including track and the writing of poetry and fiction published in the Central High *Monthly* magazine. Popular, he made many friends among the large number of children of immigrants from Eastern Europe, including Roman Catholics and Jews, who attended his school. He developed a love of cosmopolitanism and socialism that would shape his thinking for the rest of his life. Graduating in 1920 with excellent grades, he was elected Class Poet and edited the Central High annual magazine.

In the summer of 1919, and again for one year after his graduation, he lived with his father in the town of Toluca, Mexico. He learned to speak Spanish. Alienated by his father's materialism and disdain of his fellow blacks, whom he saw as shiftless and passive, Langston decided to move to New York City. That city, and especially the district of Harlem, had become mecca for many southern blacks seeking a new life. He convinced his father to let him study for a degree in mining at Columbia University in New York, after which he was to return to Mexico to help his father exploit abandoned silver mines on a large tract of land that he owned. However, Langston was far more interested in writing. Early in 1921, he sent "The Negro

Speaks of Rivers" (which he came to regard as his signature poem) to *The Crisis*, the magazine edited in New York by W.E.B. Du Bois as the official organ of the NAACP. Jessie Fauset, its literary editor and a future novelist, saw Hughes's promise at once. Linking the black past to some of the world's greatest rivers, such as the Congo and the Mississippi, this poem celebrates the spirituality and the historic importance of people of African descent. Thus began an association between Hughes and *The Crisis*, among the most important literary outlets controlled by black Americans in the 1920s.

Welcoming Hughes when he reached Manhattan later in 1921 to attend Columbia, Fauset introduced him to Du Bois at *The Crisis* offices. Finding the racial situation at Columbia difficult (school policy barred its three or four black students from living in its dormitories) but thrilled to be in Manhattan, Hughes spent most of his time in Harlem getting to know the people and their various institutions, and also at the theater both uptown and on Broadway. The smashing success of Eubie Blake and Noble Sissle's *Shuffle Along*, a landmark musical show by blacks, was one main reason that he'd been drawn to New York. (Sissle, too, had graduated from Central High.) The intense political and civil rights activity led by Du Bois and the NAACP, among others, during and immediately after World War I, also inspired him, as did Marcus Garvey, the flamboyant and wildly popular Jamaican immigrant often at odds with Du Bois. The leader of the United Negro Improvement Association (UNIA), Garvey rallied blacks with his Back-to-Africa slogan but also militantly affirmed the rights of blacks as citizens of the United States of America.

Leaving Columbia after his freshman year, Hughes also abandoned its upper-class associations by taking jobs first as a delivery boy for a Manhattan florist and then as a farm worker on Staten Island. His main aim now, however, was to become a seaman and see the world. At first he was assigned to serve on a large fleet of ships mothballed up the Hudson River following World War I. There, with much time to write, he concentrated on his poetry. When he published, he did so exclusively in *The Crisis*. By this time he had broken permanently with his father. He had also become close friends with the adopted son of a prominent Harlem minister, Countee Cullen, whose poetry would make him a star of the Harlem Renaissance.

In 1923, Hughes sailed to Africa on a freighter. Later, in *The Big Sea*, he would tell of dumping his schoolbooks overboard, in a gesture that underscored his rejection of middle-class ambitions and constraints. Working as a cook's helper, he traveled up and down the west coast of Africa, as his freighter took on and discharged cargo and passengers in ports such as Dakar and Accra. Reaching as far south as Angola, he gained firsthand knowledge of the effect of European colonialism, especially that of Great Britain, France, and Belgium, on the African peoples. Although he wrote few poems about Africa, this trip served as vital to his education as a black man, an American, a citizen of the world, and a writer.

He was hardly back in the United States before he returned to sea on another freighter, this time bound for Europe. Determined to see Paris (he had studied French in high school, and attributed his ambition to become a writer to the power of the French fiction writer Guy de Maupassant), he jumped ship on his second trip to Europe. Making his way to Paris, he spent several months there working in the kitchen of an American-owned nightclub, Le Grand Duc, where the irresistible rhythms of jazz bands left their mark on his verse. Visiting Italy, he was stranded in Genoa after losing his passport. Broke and in despair, rejected by the white crews of various American vessels, he wrote the often-anthologized poem "I Too" in a park in Genoa ("I too sing America. / I am the darker brother . . .").

Inspired by his experiences abroad, Hughes returned to the United States late in 1924. Still writing steadily, he spent the next year mainly in Washington, D.C., where his mother now lived. Again he worked in various menial occupations (in an oyster shop, for one) except for some weeks with the scholar Carter G. Woodson, the founder of Negro History Week (later Black History Month). Nevertheless, the year 1925 was decisive for him, as for several other younger black writers and artists. By this time his poetry in the *Cri-*

sis had secured him a wide following. Poems such as "The Negro Speaks of Rivers," "Mother to Son," Aunt Sue's Stories," "Danse Africaine," "My People," and "Dream Variation" raised his reputation as a black poet to new heights. In May, his poem, "The Weary Blues," about a blues singer in a Harlem nightclub and the strange power of his music, won first prize in poetry in a major literary competition organized by *Opportunity* magazine, the organ of the National Urban League. At the awards dinner he met the white novelist, critic, and rising champion of black artists Carl Van Vechten, who quickly arranged for Alfred A. Knopf, Inc., his own publisher, to bring out Hughes's first book, a collection of his poems.

The Weary Blues, book cover, 1926. Hughes's first book of poetry both angered and delighted critics.
Beinecke Rare Book and Manuscript Library, Yale University.

While he waited for *The Weary Blues* to appear, Hughes continued to work at odd jobs. He was busy as a busboy at the prominent Wardman Park Hotel in Washington when Vachel Lindsay, one of the best-known contemporary poets, announced publicly his "discovery" of a fine new poet. Boldly seeking publicity, Hughes had slipped Lindsay a few of his pieces just before Lindsay's own scheduled reading at the hotel. Newspapers soon carried photographs of the "busboy poet." His collection of verse, *The Weary Blues*, appeared in January 1926.

TRACK 6

Langston Hughes pioneered the adaptation of the blues to poetry. Here he reads his best known blues poem, *The Weary Blues*.

With good reviews, the volume helped to solidify his reputation, at least among blacks. In addition to Countee Cullen, Jessie Fauset, and Du Bois, Hughes was admired and liked (both for his poetry and for his generous nature) by other writers. These included Zora Neale Hurston, Wallace Thurman, Bruce Nugent, Rudolph Fisher, Helene Johnson, and Arna Bontemps. (His lifelong friendship with Arna Bontemps would result in thousands of personal letters and several published collaborations, including the story for children, *Popo and Fifina*, in 1932 and the landmark anthology, *Poetry of the Negro*, in 1949.) Key elders also admired him, including the poet and novelist James Weldon Johnson, the sociologist and editor of *Opportunity* Charles S. Johnson, and Alain Locke, the Howard University professor who had become perhaps the main theoretician of the Harlem Renaissance. Locke included some of Hughes's poems in *The New Negro* (1925), an anthology of poems, stories, essays, and drama hailed as the bible of the new cultural movement.

In January 1926, almost twenty-four years old, he used a loan from a wealthy white friend, Amy Spingarn, to enroll at the historically black—and elite—Lincoln University in Pennsylvania. His professors were white, but for the first time he lived on a daily basis with hundreds of other young black men. He found the experience exhilarating even as he made regular trips to New York to preserve his literary career. In New York, he was an important part of the initiative that resulted in the publishing of *FIRE!!* (edited by Wallace Thurman) in a direct challenge to the older, more staid leadership of the black literary world. The magazine, attacked for its sexual freedom by reviewers in the black press, folded after the appearance of its first issue. Hughes and most of his

Aaron Douglas illustration for a Langston Hughes poem; *Opportunity*, 1926. Hughes's poem, "Bound No'th Blues," addressed the plight of the black migrant. Aaron Douglas's dramatic illustrations appeared in both *Opportunity* and *The Crisis* in the 1920s. Beinecke Rare Book and Manuscript Library, Yale University.

young friends were not intimidated. In June, in the venerable *Nation* magazine, he published perhaps the single most important statement about black youths and the Harlem Renaissance, "The Negro Artist and the Racial Mountain." Younger black artists, he wrote, must recognize the beauty and authenticity of black American culture. Only then would they earn the right, crucial to them as artists and human beings, to write about any subject that they wished to explore in any form. The essay ends with a celebrated affirmation by "we" younger black artists of their twinned right and obligation to love black culture and to write with complete freedom on any topic they chose to address.

TRACKS 7 & 8

Langston Hughes reads his poem, "Mother to Son," which he first published in *The Crisis* in 1922 when he was 20 years old. It became one of his most popular poems. Langston Hughes reads his poem, "Dream Variation," which he wrote in 1923 during his first visit to the coast of West Africa. On this trip Hughes discovered both his connection and the disconnect with the continent of his ancestors.

The year 1926 also saw the heightened impact of the blues on Hughes's verse. Although he had known the blues for almost his entire life, he used the musical form in his poetry with growing intensity during his time in Harlem and Washington. Blues certainly dominated his second book of verse, *Fine Clothes to the Jew,* which Knopf brought out in 1927 and which suffered perhaps the most hostile reviews ever received by a poet in the black press. Because many of the poems dealt with the themes of sexuality and violence among so-called lower-class blacks, the New York *Amsterdam News* denounced Hughes as a "sewer dweller"; the *Chicago Tribune* called the book "a study in the perversions of the Negro." Nevertheless, along with the earlier *The Weary Blues,* this volume established Hughes as the most creative black poet of the age and also the one most deeply invested in vernacular black culture. Although many of his poems had nothing to do with race, his most acclaimed pieces paid tribute, in one form or another, to the beauty and humanity of blacks—as well as to the less conventional, less "respectable" aspects of their culture, which Hughes saw as an authentic expression of the genius of the people. He looked for poetic material in what others regarded as unsavory aspects of black urban culture, involving sex and violence. He experimented with the rich black vernacular language heard on Lenox Avenue or 125th Street in Harlem, or on black-dominated Seventh Street in Washington, D.C. Scorning the outdated "dialect tradition," with its links to minstrelsy, he nevertheless sought to revitalize the inclusion of uneducated black speech in formal poetry.

The most important personal feature of Hughes's life while he studied at Lincoln University was probably his relationship to his major patron of the period, Mrs. Charlotte Osgood Mason. A highly unusual, even eccentric white woman, the elderly Mrs. Mason believed in the spiritual and esthetic decline of the white world and in the corresponding regenerative power of the cultures of non-white peoples, especially Native Americans and, in the 1920s, African-Americans. Around 1927 (building on her friendship with Alain Locke), she began to give money systematically to both Hughes and Zora Neale Hurston. With the deepening national financial crisis after the Wall Street Crash of 1929, she offered the writers financial comfort even as she sought in return (with the best of intentions, no doubt) to control their artistic and even their personal lives. Hughes appears to have developed a genuine emotional attachment to the motherly aspects of Mason's personality, which led him to ignore far too long her domineering ways. Funded by her, he traveled in the South (memorably with Hurston in a car bought for her by "Godmother," as Mason liked to be called by her protégés) and also to Cuba, where he met younger artists and intellectuals in Havana.

Urged on by Mrs. Mason, Hughes wrote a novel, *Not Without Laughter* (1930). Its main character, the sensitive boy Sandy, is loosely based on Hughes himself as a child. Surrounding Sandy are a black woman and her three daughters. The daughters of the archetypal hardworking, loving matriarch and grandmother, Hagar, embody in different ways key strains of the black experience, from the middle-class Puritanism of one to the disreputable but highly creative blues-based brilliance of another. Hughes, who found the act of composing the novel difficult and uncomfortable, came to regard the form as not natural to him. Later he would also dislike the book because it reminded him of the bitter aspects of his relationship with Mrs. Mason.

Around 1930, that relationship ended. Despite his affection for Mrs. Mason and his appreciation of her generosity, he also saw her as too determined to control his art and his life. Their parting devastated him. While he sought an amicable farewell, the volatile Mrs. Mason expelled him with a ruthlessness encouraged by Hurston and Locke, who refused to jeopardize their access to Mrs. Mason's money by taking his side in any way. One fruit of the Hughes-Hurston friendship,

"For A'Leila," typewritten and signed poem by Langston Hughes, August 19, 1931, on the occasion of A'Lelia Walker's death, begins with the lines, "She did not die at home/ In her own bed at night./ She died where laughter was,/ And music, and gay delight." At her funeral Walker was eulogized by Adam Clayton Powell, Sr., Mary McLeod Bethune, and Langston Hughes, reading this poem.
Beinecke Rare Book and Manuscript Library, Yale University.

and one of the main factors in their breakup, was their work together on a musical play, *Mule Bone*. This drama is set in the rural Florida that was native to Hurston, who knew its folklore and folkways intimately. Distancing herself from Hughes, she denied that he had done any work whatsoever on the play. Hughes, in Cleveland, learned that Hurston was denying him any artistic credit and, feeling betrayed, broke completely with her. The play went unproduced until 1991.

This disaster, coupled with the spread of the Great Depression, ended any sense in Hughes that he was in the middle of a renaissance. With $400 and a gold medal from the Harmon Foundation as a prize for his novel, he traveled to the black republic of Haiti. After a few months there, he returned for a tour by car (in 1931–32) of the South and the West, to take his poetry to the black masses. Increasingly radicalized, he visited the Scottsboro Boys in prison in Alabama. In 1932, at the age of thirty, he cut short his tour and left for the Soviet Union in a band of twenty-two young African-Americans invited to help make a motion picture about race relations in America. Although the film was never produced, he stayed on for a year in the Soviet Union. He particularly enjoyed some months spent in Soviet Central Asia, among its mainly nonwhite peoples. During this year, Hughes wrote several ultra-radical poems, including "Good Morning Revolution" and "Goodbye Christ." Some of

Hughes and Dorothy West en route to the USSR, 1932, to participate in the ill-fated Soviet film project.
Beinecke Rare Book and Manuscript Library, Yale University.

these poems would come back to haunt him in later years when anticommunism ruled the United States.

In 1933 he returned home via China and Japan. Aided by another, more benevolent white patron, Noel Sullivan, he lived for a year in a cottage owned by Sullivan in Carmel, California. There he wrote the sardonic stories, fired by his bitterness at racism and the excesses of capitalism, collected as *The Ways of White Folk* (Knopf, 1934). The rest of the 1930s saw Hughes develop further as a radical poet. However, playwriting became his main literary activity in this decade. Working with the Cleveland-based Karamu Theater, he wrote and helped to stage entertaining comedies such as *Little Ham* (1936). His most successful play of the era was *Mulatto*, which sprang from his abiding, intimate interest in the theme of miscegenation. *Mulatto* had its Broadway debut in 1935. Although Hughes complained that its producer, a white man, contemptuously denied him his rightful share of the profits even as he sensationalized the play, *Mulatto* would hold the record for almost thirty years as the longest running play on Broadway written by a black American.

In 1937 he went to Spain to cover the civil war for the Pittsburgh *Courier*. Returning home early in 1938 with his radicalism revived, he quickly founded the Harlem Suitcase Theatre and launched it with his agit-prop play *Don't You Want to Be Free?* The play ran for over one hundred performances but made Hughes little money. Soon, in desperate need of money (not least of all for expenses for his mother's funeral), he took a job in Hollywood. His main task was to help write the screenplay, *Way Down South* (1939). Unfortunately, he was compelled to employ some of the more disliked racial stereotypes about blacks in the South common to Hollywood movies of that era. When the film appeared, the leftist press denounced him. In 1940, he published an autobiography, *The Big Sea*, which covered his life up to about 1931. To his dismay, some reviewers found its approach and style too simple; the book enjoyed only modest success.

Hounded by the right, and with World War II raging first in Europe, then in the Pacific, Hughes moved to the political middle by distancing himself publicly from radicalism and support for the Soviet Union. He stopped writing radical verse. Mainly he returned to the blues for inspiration, as in his book of poems, *Shakespeare in Harlem* (1942). He also zealously took up the cause of civil rights for American blacks. America's entry into World War II led to one of his major literary achievements. Having started in 1942 writing a weekly column in the Chicago *Defender* newspaper, in 1943 he introduced a comic fictional character, an insouciant Harlem barfly named Jesse B. Semple, or Simple. Hughes created Simple mainly to make the war effort more popular among blacks at a time when the armed forces were segregated and black soldiers poorly treated. However, Simple soon became the most successful aspect of the column, a comical and yet ultimately serious stroke of genius by Hughes. Eventually the Simple columns, published for about twenty years, yielded five collections of stories edited by Hughes, starting with *Simple Speaks His Mind* (1950).

In the 1940s Hughes published other collections of verse but achieved his long-awaited financial success by writing the lyrics for a

Broadway musical play, *Street Scene* (1947), based on Elmer Rice's prizewinning play of the same name, with music by the famed German émigré composer Kurt Weill. Now forty-five years old, Hughes was able at last to buy a home of his own, a townhouse in Harlem. This move inspired one of his liveliest books of verse, *Montage of a Dream Deferred* (1951). A collection of poems about Harlem life that Hughes declared to be, in fact, one long poem, *Montage* sought to capture the community's hopes and disappointments, its successes and its failures, its accomplishment but also its poverty, crime, and shiftlessness spawned largely by racism. Central to the book is its technical use of a musical form called bebop, the relatively new, sometimes harsh and discordant type of jazz (as in the music of Dizzy Gillespie) that reflected the gritty realties of modern black urban life.

In 1953, even as he prospered financially, Hughes suffered the indignity of a forced appearance before Sen. Joseph McCarthy's infamous anticommunist committee. Unlike some witnesses, he identified nobody as a communist or former communist. Nevertheless, he cooperated with McCarthy where other witnesses were defiant. He did so mainly to preserve his literary career and his links through it to the black masses (many artists who opposed McCarthy, such as the singer and movie star Paul Robeson, found their careers ruined). He conceded that his radical poetry had been a mistake. In return, McCarthy "exonerated" him, although right-wing attacks on Hughes did not end. In most ways, however, the 1950s was a decade of prosperity and intense productivity for Hughes, even if not all his work was of high quality. He wrote in a variety of forms. For example, he published a history of the NAACP, *Fight for Freedom;* volumes of "Simple" stories; a second, longer volume of autobiography, *I Wonder as I Wander* (1956), mainly about the Soviet Union; many small books aimed at children and young adults; and his *Selected Poems* (1959), in which he artfully culled what he took to be his best verse.

Hughes also continued to work in the theater, with his main achievement in the 1950s and 1960s being the development of the gospel musical play. In this form, a number of traditional and contemporary gospel songs are strung together with a loose plot, with the suc-

Langston Hughes and associates in the USSR, circa 1932.
Beinecke Rare Book and Manuscript Library, Yale University.

cess of the production depending largely on the virtuoso power of the gospel singers. Perhaps the most popular was *Black Nativity,* a perennial Christmas favorite. Hughes's book-length poem, *Ask Your Mama: 12 Moods for Jazz* (1961), an adventure in black avant-garde verse studded with musical cues and notes, prophetically exposed the rising social tensions that would explode into the Black Power movement in and after 1965. Thus, Hughes remained abreast of the changing fate of the black American world at the center of his art.

He continued to write and publish until his death, which came unexpectedly in 1967 in a New York hospital following an operation for a benign prostate condition. Later that year, his collection of old and new poems, *The Panther and the Lash,* captured the dramatic tensions that were starting to tear apart the fabric of American life as the dream of peaceful racial integration collapsed following the U.S. Supreme Court decision of 1954 against segregation.

Hughes was and remains black America's most beloved poet, and among its most versatile writers. The essence of his art is in its intimate connection to the evolving realities of black life, especially in the cities; to the music of black people, especially in the blues, jazz, and gospel forms, as it changed with the decades and the major transformations in black social and political reality; and to Hughes's

Langston Hughes and Carl Van Vechten in the1950s.
Beinecke Rare Book and Manuscript Library, Yale University.

unswerving love of and devotion to the black masses. He left behind an uneven but precious and large body of art, the product of more than forty years of ceaseless writing about African-American people and their culture in all of its variety. Some of the best of that writing came during the Harlem Renaissance, which both inspired and was inspired by his remarkable gifts.

Countee Cullen

(1903-1946)

LORENZO THOMAS

In a literary movement dominated by artists who came to New York from all corners of the country, Countee Cullen was Harlem's poet. This gave him a level of street popularity that no other writer attained in the 1920s. He grew up in Harlem and attended high school and college in the city, leaving only to take his MA from Harvard. Academic credentials in hand, he returned to Harlem, already recognized as a brilliant young poet. His book Color, the first volume of poetry published in the Renaissance, was highly acclaimed. Cullen's reputation was deserved. In addition to his poetry he helped define the literary renaissance as an anthologist, an editor, and the author of a literary column, "The Dark Tower." In 1926 Harlem's "Prince of Poetry" married Yolande Du Bois in a wedding that was Harlem's social event of the decade. However, the fairy tale marriage lasted less than a year, and Cullen's career as a poet also ended prematurely in the mid 1930s.

Countee Cullen's poetic career was typologically perfect: he enjoyed instant fame, popular adulation, and serious critical respect; he was prolific and he died young. *Color*, Cullen's first book of poems—which included works that had earned him several literary prizes—appeared in 1925, the same year that he graduated with honors from college. His accessible, articulate mastery of standard poetic diction, matched to a bold handling of controversial topics, made him one of the most prominent figures of the Harlem Renaissance.

Not much is known about Cullen's childhood. He was born on May 30, 1903 to Elizabeth Lucas but was apparently raised by a grandmother, Elizabeth Porter, in New York City, until he was fostered and adopted by Reverend Frederick Asbury Cullen and Carolyn Belle Mitchell Cullen. Rev. Cullen was pastor of the Salem Methodist Episcopal Church, the second largest congregation in Harlem, and Mrs. Cullen was a prominent civic leader involved in efforts to "uplift" the poor through culture and education.

Cullen began writing poetry for the student literary magazine while enrolled at the highly rated public DeWitt Clinton High

Portrait of Countee Cullen inscribed to Carl Van Vechten, 1925.
Beinecke Rare Book and Manuscript Library, Yale University.

School in New York. By the time he entered New York University in 1922, he had begun to publish his poems in magazines such as *Opportunity*, *The Crisis*, *Palms*, and *Poetry*. He'd also begun winning an astonishing string of poetry prizes.

Cullen's immediate success was the result of his unquestionable talent as a poet who chose to employ the traditional stanza forms of English-language poetry. He was a skilled versifier whose sonnets and ballads are fluent and flawless. This does not mean that Cullen did not value more recent vernacular forms. On a trip to

Rome in 1926, Cullen delighted in writing poems about visiting the graves of his Romantic poet heroes; yet he could also fully appreciate a "Colored Blues Singer" whose authentic lyrical skill enabled her to "make your grief a melody / and take it by the hand." Indeed, he made the experience of listening to the queen of the blues comparable to enjoying diva Maria Jeritza's performance of Giuseppe Verdi. Cullen himself—like Shelley, Keats, and Gertrude "Ma" Rainey—could also attune his artistry to the issues of his day, and had the ability to do so without creating a conflict between poetic diction and content.

In addition to his intellectual gifts, Cullen was a handsome and gregarious young man who enjoyed his celebrity. And Harlem revered the young writer as one of its own. As historian David Lewis noted, "with his high-pitched voice, nervous courtliness, and large Phi Beta Kappa key gleaming on the chain stretched across a vested, roly-poly middle, he was the proper poet with proper credentials." With a high school degree from DeWitt Clinton and his B.A. from NYU, he was embraced as a child of the city. His M.A. from Harvard in English and French established his literary credentials. Not even whispers about his preference for the company of beautiful young men diminished his popularity.

Cullen was much in demand as a speaker, a perfect example of the rising generation that Booker T. Washington and Dr. W.E.B. Du Bois described as the black community's "Talented Tenth." On April 9, 1928, it might have seemed preordained when Cullen, resplendent with Phi Beta Kappa key, a Harvard master's degree, and three books in print, married Nina Yolande Du Bois, the only daughter of the controversial scholar who was also a political activist and co-founder of the National Association for the Advancement of Colored People. As some two thousand Harlemites crowded the sidewalk to watch the parade of the three thousand invited wedding guests, the elaborate event undoubtedly qualified as "the wedding of the century." Harlem insiders wondered whether Miss Du Bois knew what she was doing, but the elaborate ceremony temporarily silenced the gossip. Reverend Cullen presided, with sixteen bridesmaids arriving from

Countee Cullen's *Caroling Dusk,* book cover, 1927. Cullen was not only one of the most highly regarded poets of the Harlem Renaissance, he also promoted literature by editing journals, and producing anthologies such as *Caroling Dusk.*
General Research & Reference Division, Schomburg Center for Research in Black Culture, The New York Public Library, Astor, Lenox and Tilden Foundations.

Baltimore in a private rail car, and groomsmen representing the most talented of the literary Renaissance.

Because Cullen had also won a Guggenheim Foundation fellowship to study in France, he departed for Europe following a brief honeymoon in Philadelphia, accompanied by his very dear friend, Harold Jackman. The new Mrs. Cullen was to sail two months later, accompanied by her parents. Harlem was stunned—the gossips had a field day. When the young couple reunited in Europe the marriage was already doomed. Soon enough, gossips were talking about the divorce of the century. While Mrs. Cullen had had enough of Paris, the poet would return to that city every summer until the European war in the late 1930s prevented travel.

Married life may have presented difficulties, but Cullen's literary career was firmly established. His books sold well, he wrote a literary column, "The Dark Tower," for *Opportunity,* and continued publishing poetry widely. Cullen also edited *Caroling Dusk: An Anthology of Verse by Negro Poets* (1927). Far more than James Weldon Johnson's pioneering *Book of American Negro Poetry* (1922), *Caroling Dusk* was a major showcase of contemporary African American literature. Cullen included the younger poets that had been represented in Johnson's earlier volume and many women poets.

Notably, however, while also including some of the more avant-garde experimental writers, *Caroling Dusk* emphasized African American poets' mastery of what Cullen called "the higher traditions of English verse." A clear implication of Cullen's editorial stance is that black Americans are, first and foremost, inheritors of the country's Anglo-American cultural heritage, not exotic outsiders or newcomers. That view was not shared by all of the artists involved in the "New Negro Movement" we recognize as the Harlem Renaissance, but it certainly was consistent with Dr. Alain Locke's program for the movement.

Following the appearance of Locke's groundbreaking anthology *The New Negro* (1925), which included Cullen's masterpiece "Heritage," the poets of the Harlem Renaissance received a great deal of national and international attention. As with Langston Hughes and Claude McKay, Cullen's poetry in translation became quickly known and loved by French-speaking readers in Africa, Europe, and the Caribbean. Ten of Cullen's poems appeared in German translation in the anthology

Countee Cullen's *Copper Sun*, book cover, 1927. *Copper Sun* was Cullen's second volume of poetry and contained his well-known piece, "From the Dark Tower."
General Research & Reference Division, Schomburg Center for Research in Black Culture, The New York Public Library, Astor, Lenox and Tilden Foundations.

Afrika Singt: Eine Auslese Neuer Afro-Amerikanischer Lyrik (1929), edited by Anna Nussbaum; and his poem "Totes braunes Mädel" ("A Brown Girl Dead") was set as part of an orchestral suite by Alexander Zemlinsky, the Viennese composer and conductor who was Arnold Schoenberg's teacher. Some of Cullen's work was also translated into Italian.

Portrait of Countee Cullen, by Winold Reiss, 1925. German artist Winold Reiss produced portraits of a number of Harlem Renaissance figures in the mid 1920s.
Manuscripts, Archives and Rare Books Division, Schomburg Center for Research in Black Culture, The New York Public Library, Astor, Lenox and Tilden Foundations.

Cullen's popular poem "Incident" (1925) succinctly depicts the power of racial prejudice that is the legacy of slavery. Perhaps because there is so little information about his childhood, the poem has been thought to be autobiographical. The speaker is an eight-year old boy who spends the summer in Baltimore, perhaps to stay with his grandmother. Encountering a white child his age, he is abruptly introduced to racism:

> I smiled, but he poked out
>   His tongue, and called me, "Nigger."

As intended, the offensive gesture makes an indelible mark on the speaker's self-esteem:

> I saw the whole of Baltimore
>   From May until December;
> Of all the things that happened there
>   That's all that I remember.

The poem simply reports this incident. But in doing so, Cullen voices his protest with quiet understated dignity.

Slavery depended upon a carefully policed structure of white supremacy. American slaveholders distorted religious doctrines and devised pseudoscientific theories to support a morally indefensible system. Their arguments were usually reinforced with the rationalization that the thousands of kidnapped and brutalized Africans belonged to an inferior species that deserved no better treatment.

African Americans devised many ways to counter such ideas. From Phillis Wheatley's *Poems on Various Subjects* (1773), literate black Americans attempted to demonstrate their creative genius, intellectual attainment, and cultural refinement. Following the abolition of slavery at the end of the Civil War, such demonstrations of essential humanity and fitness for citizenship became a general survival strategy for African Americans. But facing persistent white hostility would prove costly to blacks.

In *The Souls of Black Folk* (1903), W.E.B. Du Bois identified the crisis engulfing African Americans at the end of the Reconstruction era as a situation marked by "double consciousness," a medical term for a state of mental discomfort later known as schizophrenia. According to Du Bois, for black Americans in general, double consciousness was a distorted self-consciousness, a peculiar "sense of always looking at one's self through the eyes of others."

In *The Souls of Black Folk* Du Bois wrote, "One ever feels his twoness, an American, a Negro; two souls, two thoughts, two unreconciled strivings, two warring ideals in one dark body, whose dogged strength alone keeps it from being torn asunder."

Of course, the strictures of American society's racial policies were what defined the identities "American" and "Negro" as opposites and made them "warring ideals." Du Bois's perceptive analysis has been studied from political, economic, and sociological angles, but Cullen's magnificent poem, "Heritage," was a remarkable depiction of the personal impact of the psychological state described by the term double consciousness.

The persona, or character who spoke the words in this poem, is an educated young African American trying to understand how he might negotiate the Du Boisian dilemma of "two-ness." Africa, when thought of as an inheritance from biological ancestors, must be treasured. But perceived as backward and pagan, Africa was also seen as the opposite of the civilized Christian West. America, exemplar of the dynamism of industrial capitalism, is the speaker's current location, yet he is somehow emotionally attracted to the primitive, lush beauty of an imagined timeless Africa. Clearly both images here were idealized icons. But what is important—and literally crucial—was the fact that the speaker was required to embrace these extremes in his own being.

The poem begins with a powerful question: "What is Africa to me?" The speaker embarks on an inventory of what he has learned of his ancestral homeland through schoolbooks and the popular press. His imagination conjures up powerful and beautiful jungle scenes that tempt him to abandon the staid Victorian propriety of his everyday life. It is a dangerous exercise. "Heritage" describes a self-awareness so intense that "Though I cram against my ear / Both my thumbs, and keep them there" the speaker can hear his own heartbeat and the coursing of his blood as rival to the sounds of nature and ceremonial drums.

Though he is not a believer in "Quaint, outlandish heathen gods / Black men fashion out of rods, / Clay, and brittle bits of bone / In a likeness like their own," the speaker learns that this imaginary pagan Africa has the power to undermine his life as a modern American.

TRACK 9

Countee Cullen reads an excerpt from "Heritage." Although Cullen did not travel to Africa, he still explored the question of African heritage in this, his best known poem.

The major issues of Cullen's "Heritage" were finally framed as religious faith and self-identity. Which was more tenuous, his educated Western self or the atavistic traits identified with an African continent he had never seen? Cullen employed his considerable skills as a lyric poet to describe the persona's inner turmoil but he didn't stop there. The poem's edge of protest derived from the fact that American racism—in addition to portraying Jesus as a blond-haired, blue-eyed man—stubbornly refused to acknowledge Cullen's educated young African American speaker as the civilized man he, like everyone else, was struggling to be. That the poem's proposed image of a Jesus who looked like a black man—and, therefore, would truly understand what African Americans suffered—shocked readers. The extent to which the image of a Black Jesus disturbed white America became a measure of how thoroughly white supremacist ideas dominated our culture.

Similar examinations of the shortcomings of religion in ameliorating American social attitudes are found in poems such as "Pagan Prayer" (1926) and "Black Magdalens" (1926). Both poems contrast the compassionate biblical teachings of Jesus and the status quo of a two-faced, supposedly Christian, society.

In his ambitious long poem, "The Black Christ" (1929), Cullen stirred controversy and invited charges of sacrilege by depicting the resurrection of a black man lynched because of his romantic relationship with a white woman. While, as with "Heritage," the poem primarily raises questions about the efficacy of religious faith, it also affords an opportunity to make a blunt statement about a brutal, hypocritical society founded on racial inequity. "We are diseased, trunk, branch and shoot; / A sickness gathers at the root / Of us" (p. 208), Cullen writes. Nowhere else is he so stark in his judgment. Even here, however, Cullen remains a Keatsian "apostle of art," continuing to place great faith in the ability of art to lift the human soul above the events that mark a world of violence and hatred.

Cullen engaged in vigorous dialogue with other Harlem Renaissance writers in his insistence that he preferred to be evaluated as simply a poet, not a black poet. Nevertheless, much of his poetry—and all of his most powerful work—focused on issues of race. Cullen's focus, however, is often unique. In "At the Wailing Wall in Jerusalem" (1926), Cullen contemplated the condition of the Jewish people—oppressed for centuries, scattered across Europe. The relic of Solomon's temple drew his attention:

> ·This wall alone reminds a vanquished race,
> This brief remembrance still retained in stone,
> That sure foundations guard their given place
> To rehabilitate the overthrown.

Though he most likely did not think of African Americans as "a vanquished race," what cannot be fully determined is whether Cullen perceived useful similarities between the situation of the Jewish people and the African Diaspora.

These appropriately stately lines allude to cyclical theories of empire and cultural hegemony that have been proposed and debated since the 18th century. At the same time, it is clear that Cullen preferred to approach history, myth, or politics along the path of emotion manipulated by lyric poetry.

Cullen firmly believed in interracial harmony and his poem, "Any Human to Another," (1935) affirmed the humanistic creed alluded to in "Heritage." "Let no man be so proud / And confident," said the poet, as to ignore the fact that "Your grief and mine / Must intertwine / Like sea and river." It is a fine sentiment. But readers must wonder what the skilful Cullen intended to communicate when he chose to cast this poem in unsettling stanzas of four-syllable and five-syllable lines with dizzying, unpredictable periods between rhymes.

By 1935, the thirty-two-year-old Cullen had published five well-received books of poetry and the novel, *One Way to Heaven* (1932), and edited the poetry anthology, *Caroling Dusk: An Anthology of Verse by Negro Poets* (1927). The Depression having dimmed the lights of the Jazz Age and the Harlem Renaissance—especially for those relying on poetry for a living—Cullen became a junior high school teacher in New York where he taught French, English, and creative writing. One of his students was the young James Baldwin.

In 1940 Cullen married Ida Mae Roberson. This marriage was both more enduring and more successful than his first. He also continued writing, producing several poems, and he teamed up with his household pet, Mr. Christopher Cat, to co-author two children's books, *The Lost Zoo* (1940) and *My Lives and How I Lost Them* (1942). He also collaborated with poet and novelist Arna Bontemps on a project to adapt Bontemps's novel, *God Sends Sunday* (1931), for the stage. Originally conceived as an opera, the project eventually was reshaped as a musical, retitled *St. Louis Woman*, and the libretto by Bontemps and Cullen was complemented with songs by Harold Arlen and Johnny Mercer.

While involved in negotiations for the Broadway run of *St. Louis Woman* and working with Owen Dodson on *The Third Fourth of July*, a one-act play, Cullen succumbed to high blood pressure and uremia and died on January 9, 1946, a few months before his forty-third birthday.

For ten tears, beginning in 1925 with the publication of his first book of poems at the age of twenty-two, Cullen was one of the stars of the Harlem Renaissance. Beloved in Harlem, celebrated as its unofficial "poet laureate," recipient of one literary prize or honor after another, he established himself as a significant literary figure.

His last ten years, ending with his untimely death, were less productive. Nevertheless, Cullen remains without question an articulate voice of the African American experience, and its greatest lyric poet.

Nella Larsen

(1891–1964)

George Hutchinson

Women did not have an easy time in the Harlem Renaissance, especially women writers. The literary arena was largely a man's world. Nella Larsen challenged this tradition, both in her literature and in her life. Her two novels in the late 1920s established her as a gifted writer. Both novels, Quicksand and Passing, also challenged traditional concepts of race and gender. Larsen, more than any other Harlem Renaissance writer, addressed head on the psychological costs of racial and gender prejudice. Her characters suffered doubly as they struggled against society's rigidity. Tragically, Larsen's personal life mirrored that of her literary heroines, and she shared their fate—a victim of the same vulnerabilities that her fictional women of color faced. Larsen dropped out of sight and disappeared into New York City, but her two novels remain among the most compelling of the period.

No Harlem Renaissance author had a background more vexed by the color line than Nella Larsen, who lived her life in the shadows of America's great racial divide. She was born Nellie Walker in the spring of 1891 in one of the western hemisphere's most infamous red-light districts, Chicago's "Levee." Her mother, Mary, was a Danish immigrant and her father, Peter, a "colored" cook from the Danish West Indies (now the U. S. Virgin Islands). They applied for a marriage license in Chicago nine

months before Nellie was born, but no wedding is recorded; they may not have found anyone willing to perform the ceremony. Within a year, Peter Walker had either died or disappeared. Mary then wed a white Dane, a teamster named Peter Larsen, and gave birth to a second daughter, Anna Elizabeth. For years thereafter, the family suffered from the animosity against "mixed" families, and especially white women with "mulatto" daughters, while racial tensions escalated around them in the rapidly segregating near south side of Chicago.

Nella Larsen.
Beinecke Rare Book and Manuscript Library,
Yale University.

A tendency to inhabit and cross racial borderlines, by choice and by necessity, would remain a constant motif throughout Larsen's life and partly accounts for the mysteries surrounding it. She was acutely sensitive to the fact that mulattoes of working-class background with white mothers were assumed to be the illegitimate children of prostitutes. Many forces ensured the invisibility of persons and families who violated the law of the color line, which, after all, attempted to ensure that persons such as Nella Larsen literally could not exist. *La vie de Bohème*—the so-called "underworld" outside bourgeois morality, identified with ethnic or racial ambiguity and used by Modernist artists to signal their radical intentions—was intimate to Larsen from infancy, and it was not a life she was inclined to romanticize. Yet, always on the fringes of her fiction, it subtends the fairy-tale world of her white or New Negro elites and forms an invisible touchstone for everything she wrote.

In 1895, Peter moved to a white neighborhood outside of the Levee, and Mary took her daughters home to Denmark, possibly to escape the persecution directed at a white woman with a "black" daughter, for Nellie was light brown in complexion with distinctly negroid features. In Denmark Nellie met her extended family and learned the riddles, games, and songs she would recount years later in her first two publications. She returned to Chicago in 1898, and with Anna entered a school for German and Scandinavian children in the white immigrant neighborhood to which Peter had moved. Within months, however, the family moved back to a corner of the Levee—Twenty-second and State—that served literally as the intersection between black and white. By the time Larsen entered seventh grade, having moved to yet another mixed neighborhood further south on State Street, she and Anna were attending separate schools, no doubt to protect them from harassment, or possibly to protect Anna from suspicions that she might really be black, like her half-sister.

As both girls passed puberty it became clear that Nellie would have to assimilate to the Negro world to which her family could never belong. In the fall of 1907, almost certainly funded by her mother's dress-making, Nellie entered the "normal school" at Fisk University in Nashville, Tennessee, one of the most prestigious institutions of "the race," for training to be a teacher. Simultaneously, her family moved to an all-white neighborhood to escape the deteriorating conditions around them. For the rest of her life she was separated from them. Anna pretended to be an only child.

One of black America's most esteemed institutions, Fisk could prepare Larsen admirably to find a place in the black professional class. It provided her first experience of a nearly all-black environment. She found some comfort there, free of the stigma her mere existence brought on her family; but having no black kin or southern connections, being irreligious, and coming from an immigrant background, she never felt quite at home. The strict dress code, rules against wearing jewelry, and constant supervision of the girls' behavior grated on her. Then, in a devastating blow, at the end of her first year she was told not to return following a student protest against standards of dress and deportment for girls.

Stymied in the attempt to enter the African American elite, she sailed to Denmark to live with relatives on her mother's side—a move that was probably intended to be permanent. Living mainly in Copenhagen between 1908 and 1912 (visiting America in 1909), she absorbed the culture and literature of Scandinavia's "Modern Breakthrough," which often focused on the suppression of women's desires and the hypocrisies of the middle class. For reasons perhaps hinted at in her first novel, however, Larsen finally came back to the United States to enter a black nursing school attached to Lincoln Hospital and Home in the Bronx, a large general hospital serving chiefly white immigrants.

Larsen excelled at Lincoln and earned the rare distinction of "honor" on the State Board of Nursing examinations, then accepted the position of Head Nurse at Tuskegee Institute's hospital in Alabama. She quickly grew disillusioned with the school's poor treatment of student nurses and its hypocritical form of "race pride," which entailed suppression of individuality and rigidly conservative notions of proper dress and deportment. She resigned in protest after a year and returned to Lincoln Hospital, where she taught the history of nursing, a subject remarkable at the time for its strongly feminist bent and focus on women's history.

In 1918, at the age of twenty-seven, she joined the Bureau of Preventable Diseases as a public health nurse in the nearly all-white Bronx. Public health was a new field on the cutting edge of nursing at the time, emphasizing education and investigation. Nurses in Larsen's bureau circulated on their own in assigned districts, teaching hygiene and sanitation, investigating sources of infection, imposing quarantine, placarding buildings, and even closing down businesses. Larsen worked all through the harrowing "Spanish flu" pandemic of 1918–19—the most deadly in history—in which New

York suffered more flu cases than any other city but half the death rate of most because of the heroic work of Larsen's bureau. It was a pivotal event in the rise of public health, and Larsen's salary grew rapidly in consequence. She and her colleagues were also pioneers in sex education, actively addressing venereal disease, visiting families to teach women and girls, particularly how to talk knowledgably about sexual organs and functions and to claim control over their own sexuality. Few "female" occupations offered so much autonomy and public authority. Larsen's nursing background helps account for the fact that her fiction would be more "advanced" from a feminist standpoint than that of her college-educated peers.

Public health networks also gave Larsen entrée to black professional circles, where she met the New Negro elite and, along the way, the proverbial promising young man. In May 1919, at the age of 28, she married Dr. Elmer S. Imes, a Fisk graduate and recent University of Michigan PhD, the second black to obtain a doctorate in physics. A charming and sophisticated man ten years her senior, he shared Larsen's cosmopolitan tastes and love of books. He was well-connected to the African American elite but also had a strong bohemian streak and, like Larsen, liked to challenge racial taboos. Following the marriage, Nella Larsen Imes, as she now signed her name, began moving in circles that included W. E. B. Du Bois, Jessie Fauset, and James Weldon Johnson. She attended literary "teas" hosted by prominent matrons and events in the 135th Street branch of the New York Public Library, an incubator of the Harlem Renaissance, and in 1920 published two articles on Danish games and riddles for the first African American children's magazine, *The Brownies' Book*.

The next year she became the secretary of a committee organizing America's first public "Negro" art exhibit at the 135th Street branch of the New York Public Library. Encouraged by the branch librarian, she entered the school of the New York Public Library, the first black woman ever admitted for formal training in the library profession. Her education provided a superb background for a literary career and contacts in the publishing world. After working a year in the famed

Seward Park branch serving immigrant Jews, she took over the children's division at the 135th Street branch, where she excelled.

While Larsen had made her way into the black professional community, she remained marginal to it, lacking "background" and never fully assimilating to the mindset of the race-proud black bourgeoisie. Larsen had no intimate knowledge of her black father and had been raised by a white working-class family in a well-known red-light district. Moreover, she had been evicted from Fisk University, had left Tuskegee under a cloud, and had no diploma, making her ineligible for the sororities to which most women of her newly acquired class belonged. Evasive about her early life, she cultivated the manners of a modern sophisticate, smoking cigarettes, wearing short dresses and smart *cloche* hats, and decorating her homes in Greenwich Village fashion with "oriental" furnishings and plenty of up-to-date books.

Physically, Nella Larsen was a petite and very attractive woman, 5'2" in height and slender. Her complexion was light brown—the color of maple syrup according to one journalist, or of brown honey according to another—and she had jet-black hair, long and curly but always worn in a tight bun on the nape of her neck. She had a heart-shaped face, full lips, large dark eyes and unusually thick eyebrows that another woman might have chosen to pluck and trim, but Larsen was not that sort of woman. Her voice was low and sandy in texture, even somewhat husky—perhaps made so by her smoking habit. She liked rich colors, and she dressed fashionably, with her own style. The daughter of a dressmaker, Larsen was an expert at choosing material and altering dresses, which she often exchanged with friends. Chic, cosmopolitan, widely read, and critical, she observed the racial, sexual, and class mores around her with the eye of an ironist, a parvenu who took nothing for granted and resisted racial enclosure.

By 1924, she had developed friendships with a wide group of aspiring young black writers and intellectuals. She spent as much time in Greenwich Village as Harlem while living in Jersey City in the mid-1920s, for her closest friends either lived or socialized there. At a party hosted by one of them, Dorothy Peterson, Larsen met the well-known white novelist and music critic Carl Van Vechten, one of Elmer Imese's favorite authors. She quickly grew close to him and his wife, actress Fania Marinoff. Throughout the late 1920s, Larsen socialized constantly with them and their friends—editors at top publishing houses and literary reviews, actors, directors, writers, artists, dancers, and musicians. After she moved to Harlem in 1927, she was one of Van Vechten's best friends and chief hostesses there, and when his novel *Nigger Heaven* descended into the midst of black literary debates like an incendiary bomb—largely because of the title—she was implicated in the fracas. Van Vechten was accused by many middle-class blacks of caricaturing Harlem and exploiting his welcome there, but most of his friends, like Nella and Elmer, praised the novel. Indeed, Larsen courted criticism by becoming all the more intimate with Van Vechten and Marinoff, and defiantly dedicated her second novel to them.

Throughout the late 1920s, Larsen could frequently be seen in the company of white men, even dancing with them, without her husband present. This exposed her to accusations of racial self-hatred that continue even today. Yet it is important to understand why Larsen could never accede to the mentality of those who so accused her. Despite her love of black culture and comfort among black people, she believed that influential segments of the black bourgeoisie exploited the color line and even depended upon it psychologically. Like Tuskegee's leaders, they used the black "masses" as a constituency, clientele, and source of moral authority in order to gain position, security, and an inflated sense of their own importance. Yet they adopted the snobbish and Eurocentric attitudes of the white elites. Their attitudes only helped institutionalize an American ideology of race with which Larsen could never make peace, and which rendered her invisible and silent.

Larsen had been writing fiction and poetry since the early 1920s. Encouraged by friends, she resigned from the library in late 1925, and in the summer of 1926 her first published stories, "Freedom," and "The Wrong Man," appeared in *Young's Realistic Stories*, a pulp

magazine with a chiefly working-class audience. She used the pen
name "Allen Semi" (Nella Imes in reverse). Both stories focus on
white characters and reveal Larsen's concern with women's dependence, particularly the centrality of sexual subjection in their lives—
sexual allure being the lower-class woman's chief tool for achieving
security in a male-dominated universe, yet childbirth being a trap, a
source of profound dread. The stories' concern with the moral taint
that haunts vulnerable women of low-status origins would also
infuse the novels that made Larsen famous.

Quicksand (1928) and Passing (1929) ratcheted such themes up to
a new level while exploring basic requirements of color-line culture.
These novels center on how "outsiders" to the black-white opposition, always hidden at its center, must negotiate existence in the
chasm between the races. However, the point is less to explore a "bira-
cial psyche" than to question the psychological intricacies and moral
compromises by which both blacks and whites maintain an absolute
racial distinction developed originally to sustain white supremacy.

From the opening scene, Quicksand's lacerating attack on the
hypocrisy, racial sycophancy, and tyranny of the "race" leaders at
Naxos, a school transparently based on Tuskegee, would have
been immediately understood by Larsen's black readers. "The
dean was a woman from one of the 'first families'—a great 'race'
woman; she, Helga Crane, a despised mulatto, but something
intuitive, some unanalyzed driving spirit of loyalty to the inherent
racial need for gorgeousness told her that bright colors were fitting
and that dark-complexioned people should wear yellow, green, and
red." Helga Crane's protest against the school's efforts to cut the
students to "the white man's pattern" coincides with her sense of
being a partial outsider.

After leaving Naxos, Helga returns to Chicago, where her uncle's
new wife turns her away from the door with a completely specious
denial of their relationship, revealing with chilling precision how
race trumps family in the American context. Yet Larsen quickly
shifts Helga to an all-black environment in which the same underlying rule holds. When an elder "race woman," a well-known

speaker named Hayes-Rore who has taken her under her wing, asks Helga about her "people," and Helga begins to respond, the woman's face hardens and turns away: "The woman felt that the story, dealing as it did with race intermingling and possibly adultery, was beyond definite discussion. For among black people, as among white people, it is tacitly understood that these things are not mentioned—and therefore they do not exist." Larsen consistently depicts the space of interracial intimacy as a hidden location, crucial to the racial order but never to be honestly addressed.

Living in Harlem with the widowed, well-off, and race-proud Anne Grey, Helga must hide the truth of her origins. Grey histrionically disdains all white people, yet she "aped their clothes, their manners, and their gracious ways of living"—even preferred their music. Although Helga Crane has suffered far more from racism than Anne Grey, Anne's racial ardor feels oppressive to her. The two women's "sisterhood" is powerfully challenged by their different class positions and radically different relationships to the color line. As her feelings of alienation and racial entrapment grow, Helga sails to Denmark in the belief that there she might at last find the people with whom she belongs.

Denmark, however, does not offer an escape from racial subjection, only a different kind. Helga's aunt and uncle stress her exoticism to attract promising men whose connection with the Dahl family would enhance their status in the intensely class-conscious society of Copenhagen. However, to the consternation of the Danes, she fears the effects of mixed parentage upon her children, and suspects that eventually a white husband would come to hate her for being black. She carries a profound, specifically American dread of racism's power over relations of intimacy and family belonging. She becomes increasingly aware, as well, that while she had come to Denmark hoping to find her people, their interest in her is predicated on her racial difference.

When she returns to New York from Denmark, she is confronted once again with a kind of bourgeois black nationalism in relation to which her recent extended residence among "Nordics" makes her suspect. Elite African Americans like Helga's former fiancé both disdain social "mixing" among the races and feel a duty to marry and produce children to offset the fertility of the more "unfit" members of the race. Once again, Helga cannot fit in. The one man she feels might understand her has married Anne Grey, and after a brief, humiliating attempt at an affair with him, Helga seeks refuge from the demands of self-identity in a sudden conversion to Christianity, marriage to a preacher, and "uplift" in the rural South.

Veering sharply away from correspondence with her own life, Larsen plays off of a common pattern in earlier black fiction in which a "mulatto" heroine would achieve happiness by finally integrating into the black family, altruistically pledging her talents to the uplift of her poorer "brothers and sisters" in the south. *Quicksand's* denouement deliberately parodies such racial idealization.

Helga quickly recognizes that her efforts at "uplift" are presumptuous. The very women she had expected to "lift" her look down on her and pity her husband. After giving birth in rapid succession to four children—as if fulfilling her duty to enhance the gene pool of the race—and nearly dying in the fourth childbirth, Helga Crane loses all faith in Christianity and all interest in her husband. Bedridden, imperiled by the inexorable coming of a fifth child, she asks her nurse to read to her Anatole France's "The Procurator of Judaea," a story that reveals how concepts of racial difference connect with patrician practices of empire building, slavery, and national chauvinism, contributing to the oppression of women and the repression of sexuality except to produce racial subjects for the state. The theme pertains equally to Helga Crane and her white mother. Racial ideology, as Larsen presents it, requires the sacrifice of boundary figures, whose disappearance inheres in color-line culture.

In *Passing*, Larsen would explore such psychological dynamics more intensively in a new register. If *Quicksand* focused on the life and consciousness of a woman "neither white nor black" in the words of the novel's epigraph, *Passing* concerns the anxieties aroused by a woman both white and black. Clare Kendry is literally white in appearance, with blond hair and alabaster skin, and she lives as a white woman married to a white businessman, John Bellew. Yet she is black according to American racial norms, having been raised by her mulatto father (a janitor) before being taken in by white aunts, following his death, on Chicago's west side. When the novel opens, Clare Kendry has latched onto her childhood friend Irene Redfield as a means of reconnecting with the black world, provoking a deep disturbance in Irene's psyche, a phobic defense against the dissolution of racial and sexual boundaries upon which Irene's identity depends.

Most black-authored "passing" novels present passing as a means to get what white people have, and to be "free," but in Larsen's novel Clare Kendry passes in order to obtain what her more well-off black friends have, for her family background precluded her moving into their class position in the carefully policed boundaries of respectable black society. White society offers greater class mobility to those without family. Ultimately feeling trapped in the white world, Clare seeks to return to the black world, fearless about whether she will be found out by her racist husband; but in a striking reversal of the usual tropes connecting whiteness with freedom and blackness with repression, Irene decides she cannot allow Clare to be free—of her white identity, or her husband.

Irene's anxieties about racial difference parallel those of Clare's husband, who abhors the specter of "race-mixing." Yet his very repugnance for miscegenation—one reason he decided not to settle in Brazil, where he made his fortune—coincides with a fetishistic attraction to racial ambiguity, revealed in his pet name for his wife, "Nig."

Deriving from the invisible crossroads between blackness and whiteness, upper and lower classes, a place "out of bounds" in social terms, Clare inhabits a symbolically central position in the psyches of both her husband and Irene, who are the most insistently American characters in the novel. She dies at the hands of Irene at the end of the novel, pushed out of a black Christmas party in a sixth floor apartment, just after her husband breaks into the apartment where it is being held and accuses her of being a "damned, dirty nigger."

The text never tells us explicitly how Clare falls from the window, because Larsen has ingeniously used a third-person, limited point of view to filter all of our knowledge of events through Irene's consciousness, and Irene will not allow herself to remember what happened the moment after she rushed toward Clare at the open window and put a hand on her. When the black/white woman who threatens the racial boundary is done away with, no one will be to blame; her disappearance must remain a mystery, an absence on which the racial order depends.

Despite her exposure to various forms of white racism, both Nella Larsen and her husband expected her books to get a critical and derogatory reception in the black press for their negative portrait of black Christianity and attacks on powerful segments of the black bourgeoisie. However, the mere fact that the novels focused on upper-middle-class characters in mostly refined settings won the novels approval among some black readers seeking stories of racial uplift, and enthusiastic praise from W.E.B. Du Bois in *The Crisis*. The commercial success of Van Vechten's *Nigger Heaven* (1926), and especially Claude McKay's *Home to Harlem* (1928), overwhelmingly conditioned the reception of Larsen's first novel. Taking readers on a detailed tour of what McKay termed the "underworld" of black working-class life, with matter-of-fact treatment of carefree sex and casual prostitution, *Home to Harlem* earned McKay a reputation for staking out the "lowest" ground of the Negro Renaissance.

Quicksand seemed to many readers just the antidote they were looking for. The reaction against McKay so influenced responses to *Quicksand* that it blinded most readers to Larsen's main concerns. For the rest of the century she would be paired with Jessie Fauset as a genteel novelist of the light-skinned black elite, at best using issues of mulatto identity-conflict and passing as a disguise for sexual concerns she was too timid to confront openly.

Nonetheless, in 1929 and 1930, Nella Larsen was considered by many, both black and white, to be the best black novelist since Charles Chesnutt, the genteel yet distinguished author of *The House Behind the Cedars* (1900) and *The Marrow of Tradition* (1901). In 1930, at the peak of her celebrity, she was publicly accused of plagiarism in a story she had published in the prestigious magazine, *Forum*. It is clear that Larsen borrowed the basic elements of "Sanctuary" from Sheila Kaye-Smith's "Mrs. Adis," essentially transporting the story from the south of England to the south of the United States and turning a class drama into a racial one. The gossip was soon all over literary Harlem. Scholars have speculated that the scandal destroyed Larsen's literary career, but in fact she remained committed to being a novelist, and although her reputation was besmirched for some Harlemites, her friends and supporters stood by her and she came through the controversy rela-

Nella Larsen's first novel, *Quicksand*, published in 1928, examined the struggle of a mixed-race woman to deal with her heritage and her identity. Beinecke Rare Book and Manuscript Library, Yale University

tively unscathed. Soon after the scandal broke, nearing the age of thirty-nine, she was awarded a Guggenheim fellowship for work on a novel set in Europe concerning the different experiences of race that continent provided African Americans.

Much more devastating than the accusation of plagiarism was Larsen's discovery that her husband was having an affair with a popular white administrator at Fisk University, where Elmer was about to return as a professor. Losing out in a love triangle to a white woman raised the ghosts of her childhood, and Larsen never fully recovered from the blow. She left the question of what to do about the marriage up in the air while abroad, and felt free to indulge in affairs of her own. But after sixteen exciting months in Mallorca, Paris, and Málaga, during which she wrote at least two novels (never published), she returned to the United States, and after some prevarication reluctantly joined Elmer at the campus from which she had once been evicted. Everyone knew about the affair between Elmer and his paramour, discussed it, and even approved of it, for Ethel Gilbert and Elmer Imes were immensely popular with black faculty and students. Larsen, on the other hand, an outsider and considered a misfit, displayed increasingly erratic behavior that climaxed in a couple of feigned suicide attempts. Finally, after fourteen years of marriage, she sued for divorce and returned to New York.

After a series of further disappointments she interpreted as forms of abandonment—including a triangular affair involving two young white men she had met at Fisk—and failing to place her fiction for several years, Larsen cut off all her ties to the literary world and the Harlem elite. There were rumors of alcoholism and a drug habit.

From 1944 until 1961, she worked as a staff nurse and then nurse supervisor at Gouverneur Hospital on the Lower East Side, and from 1961 to 1963 at Metropolitan Hospital, serving East Harlem. Neither institution was strictly black or white; they served highly diverse populations, befitting Larsen's consistent resistance to racial exclusivity. Highly respected on the job, she quickly leap-frogged over her colleagues into the higher-paid supervisory positions, not entirely free of her alcohol and drug habits. She was forced to retire in June 1963, when authorities realized she had passed her seventieth birthday. (She was actually seventy-two.)

Feeling abandoned once again, she secluded herself in her eastside apartment. She died of a heart attack eight months later. The first person contacted after the remains were discovered, probably a former in-law, refused to claim the body. Finally the authorities tracked down her former nursing friend, who arranged for the funeral and buried Larsen in her own family plot. When informed that she was in line to inherit "Nellie Imes's" estate, Anna Larsen Gardner, her half-sister, replied, "Why I didn't know I had a sister."—which, of course, was a lie.

One of the greatest ironies of Larsen's career is that critics of later years frequently categorized her as a repressed apologist for black middle-class mores. Her treatment of mixed-race and "passing" characters also gave critics the impression that she had compromised her art in the desire to appeal to a white audience, and to prove to comfortable whites that there were refined and educated Negroes much like them. On the contrary, Larsen attends to the comfortable classes of whites (including Danes) as well as blacks only to critique their complicated hypocrisies and self-delusions, particularly in relation to race and sexuality.

Larsen's fiction reveals how modern black and white identities in America came to depend on the suppression of interracial intimacies, on controlling female sexuality in the interests of race, and on denying the possibility of being both black and white, or neither/nor. Her achievement was *sui generis*, and therefore largely misunderstood until the 1990s. Yet her novels, *Quicksand* (1928) and *Passing* (1929), are known today as the best novels of the Harlem Renaissance in the 1920s. They remain unmatched as explorations of the psychology of the color-line and the high cost of resisting it.

Advertisement for Nella Larsen's 1929 novel, *Passing*, her second and last published work. *Passing* addressed the theme of race and color within the black upper-middle class, and the controversial practice of "passing."
Beinecke Rare Book and Manuscript Library, Yale University.

Claude McKay

(1889–1948)

TYRONE TILLERY

Claude McKay was the "bad boy" of the Harlem Renaissance. A self-proclaimed "proletariat poet," he flirted with communism and visited the Soviet Union, where he was cast by the Soviet leadership as an unofficial spokesperson for the American Negro. Ultimately disillusioned in the "workers' paradise," he spent the 1920s in Europe and North Africa, living off his writings and, more often, the charity of friends, returning to Harlem in the declining years of the Renaissance. He was a talented and insightful writer. His sonnet, "If We Must Die," is the best-known poem of the Renaissance. His first novel, Home to Harlem, outraged the sometimes stodgy W.E.B. Du Bois with its vivid exposé of Harlem's lower classes, but became the best-selling novel by a black writer in the Harlem Renaissance.

Portrait of Claude McKay inscribed to James Weldon Johnson, 1937. Johnson was instrumental in getting McKay readmitted to the United States after his twelve-year stay in the Soviet Union, France, and North Africa.
Beinecke Rare Book and Manuscript Library, Yale University.

Few poems have expressed humanity's defiance more powerfully than Claude McKay's "If We Must Die." Forged out of the horrific interracial violence cascading through American cities in the summer of 1919, it exquisitely expressed the African American's rage toward a country that sacrificed so much to "save the world for democracy," but forgot to save it at home. A sonnet so threatening that Massachusetts' Senator Henry Cabot Lodge Jr. read it into the Congressional record as a dangerous example of what he called "Negro extremism."

A generation later Winston Churchill used the poem as a rallying cry for British resolve during World War II. When needed, it was there for the disciples of the 1960's black power movement—to be whispered among themselves and shouted to the world. A poem of remarkable durability, it was still there to inspire inmates at the notorious Attica prison in 1972 in the largest prison rebellion in American history. Over the decades many have forgotten or neglected to acknowledge the pioneering work of the Harlem Renaissance's Jamaican-born poet. But his power, as demonstrated by "If We Must Die," remains undiminished:

> If we must die, let it not be like hogs
> Hunted and penned in an inglorious spot,
> While round us bark the mad and hungry dogs,
> Making their mock at our accursèd lot.
> If we must die, O let us nobly die,
> So that our precious blood may not be shed
> In vain; then even the monsters we defy

Shall be constrained to honor us though dead!
O kinsmen! We must meet the common foe!
Though far outnumbered let us show us brave,
And for their thousand blows deal one deathblow!
What though before us lies the open grave?
Like men we'll face the murderous, cowardly pack,
Pressed to the wall, dying, but fighting back!

Claude McKay was born September 15, 1889, in the tiny village of Sunny Ville, nestled in the remote Jamaican hills of Clarendon parish. The youngest of Thomas Francis and Elizabeth McKay's eight children, Claude became one of the Harlem Renaissance's most gifted and enigmatic writers. The source of McKay's artistic gift can be traced to the paradoxical influences of his parents and the Jamaican environment. The product of a proud West African Ashanti heritage and Jamaican peasants, he based his faith less

TRACKS 10 & 11

Hear Claude McKay read and discuss his poem, "If We Must Die." The poem, written as a protest against the race riots and violence of 1919, became a universal statement of resistance against tyranny.

on peasant traditions and beliefs than on religion, reason, and a reverence for Anglo-Saxon justice. His contact with people tended to be formal, distant, almost aristocratic. Though Claude shared his father's patrician propensity, he found a greater emotional kinship with the contrasting personality of his mother.

Her roots could be traced to the island of Madagascar off the coast of East Africa. She was emotionally warm and more giving to her children and others in the peasant Jamaican community. Through her, Claude found the ability to appreciate the aesthetics in nature; closeness and, most importantly, love. Still, much like his father, throughout his life he had difficulty with interpersonal relationships. It proved to be an unsuccessful struggle to reconcile these two warring personalities. Claude would one moment mesmerize friends and audiences with his warmth and charm and in

the next suddenly lose control in a fit of anger, or become
detached and aloof.

But these were problems that manifested themselves in the adult
McKay. The youthful McKay was nourished by his mother, the
island of Jamaica, and several personal acquaintances. These influences helped him express in poems the beautiful and often harsh
aspects of Jamaican life. Composing in traditional English style, he
began to write poetry during his elementary school years. Some years
later while working as an apprentice wheelwright, he impulsively
departed from the English form and wrote a number of poems about
peasant life in the Jamaican dialect. The poems evoked vivid
descriptions of the colorful but often "hard times" scrabble of life for
the average Jamaican peasant. Most importantly they captured the
indomitable spirit of the *"Jamaican soul"*—one that embraced life's
uncertainties with a resignation that bordered on stoicism.

On the small island it was nearly impossible for such a gifted
young black Jamaican to fail to attract the attention of several
prominent literary whites. The most important was Walter Jekyll, an
English-born planter educated at Harrow, Trinity College, and Cambridge. Jekyll had retreated to Jamaica after renouncing religion following a debate over religion and science. Jekyll's interest in McKay
reflected a growing recognition among some white Jamaicans during
the early twentieth century that indigenous Jamaica constituted a
storehouse of material for artistic exploration and expression. Jekyll
became intrigued by the idea of this black peasant who not only
wrote poetry, but did so in the Jamaican dialect about Negro folk-
tales and tall tales typically shunned by the island's better educated
black community.

Jekyll proved vital to McKay's emerging talent, providing a
source of emotional, intellectual, and financial support. Through his
contacts McKay was able to publish some poems in the island's
largest newspaper, the *Daily Gleaner*. Eventually, with Jekyll's help,
McKay published a volume of his dialect poetry under the title *Songs
of Jamaica* (1912). A testament to the excitement generated by
McKay's dialect poetry, the volume sold over two thousand copies

and won the Mulgrave Silver Medal, a prize created by a British family for the best representation of Jamaican literature. In the same year he published *Constabulary Ballads*.

Both volumes were pioneering efforts by the black West Indian to visualize Jamaican life. Yet they too reflected a young black Jamaican's naïve infatuation with British culture. Indeed, in some respects *Songs of Jamaica* and *Constabulary Ballads* were as much a personal effort at self-discovery and identification as a literary representation of the peasant experience. Colonial British culture cast a long shadow over much of the indigenous black culture. Few Jamaicans, including McKay, escaped completely from the powerful influences to become "black Britons" first and indigenously Jamaican second. Still, it was a great formative period in McKay's life. An intellectual journey begun in his brother Uriah's library with the masters of Western literature continued under Jekyll as he introduced McKay to the German philosophers—Kant, Hegel, and Nietzsche.

By 1912, McKay, now twenty-three, had become something of a Jamaican Robert Burns and required a larger world to further his intellectual and creative ambitions. "Jamaica," he noted in his autobiography, *A Long Way From Home*, "was too small for high achievement. There, one was isolated, cut off from the great currents of life." McKay might well have added that despite the interest in Jamaica's indigenous culture and life of its inhabitants, a black Jamaican's future was severely limited, as the literary doors opened to white artists were closed to equally talented black writers.

Instead of sojourning to England, the sentimental motherland of his youth, McKay looked northward to the United States where, Alain Locke declared, "something beyond the watch and of statistics" was about to happen in the life of African Americans. In the midst of the American populace, black Americans were becoming more confident and vibrant; a new spirit gripped the growing urban masses. The vanguard of the "great migration," they heralded the metamorphosis of the new American landscape—the urbanization of black America, the rise of both a black proletariat and a new

Native African Union "Back to Africa" announcement, Harlem, c 1929. Harlem in the 1920s was home to many people of the African Diaspora; they had come from the American South, the Caribbean, Central and South America, and Africa. Movements to reclaim their African heritage and bring unity to the disparate groups had great appeal. General Research & Reference Division, Schomburg Center for Research in Black Culture, The New York Public Library, Astor, Lenox and Tilden Foundations.

intelligentsia. In a few years, critics would hail the emergence of the "New Negro" who took pride in the black race and its African heritage, and whose writings exposed and attacked discrimination, explored black folk culture, and strove to create a unique African American letters.

The epicenter of the extraordinary period of literary and artistic creativity was Harlem. Yet McKay's destination was not the "black metropolis," but Alabama's famous black industrial college, Tuskegee Institute. He arrived at Tuskegee in the midst of the sweltering Alabama summer of 1912. The choice had not been entirely his, but a concession to Walter Jekyll's disdain for modernism and industrialism. His benefactor worried that America's rapid industrialization threatened to destroy the world's equilibrium. Convincing Jekyll that Tuskegee would give him the proper education to return to Jamaica, make a good living (tilling the soil), and still pursue his poetry, a compromise was struck and McKay joined the South's black sons and daughters to study agronomy under Booker T. Washington.

McKay's initial introduction to America and his racial "cousins" did not end well, but the experience forced him to confront, if only in a conflicted way, questions of identity, vocation, and politics—questions submerged under layers of British colonialism. While McKay admired the fatherly strength and assurance that Booker T. Washington provided his students, he felt culturally and psychologically distant from his American brothers and sisters on the Tuskegee campus. He realized that racial kinship notwithstanding, differences existed between people of different countries and nationalities.

The lesson continued at Kansas State College in Manhattan, Kansas. After two years of taking courses ranging from sociology to the purchase of feed, and his uneasy movement among the small midwestern African American middle class, McKay set out for New York City and Harlem. The twenty-five-year-old McKay's decision to move, in 1914, could not have come at a better time. Already a poet of considerable success, he was in an ideal position to become a central figure in the blossoming intellectual and cultural center of black America. In a few years blacks from every corner of America and the world would descend upon Harlem to imbibe and partici- pate in the nascent arts movement. However, three years passed before McKay's poetic voice was heard again. A failed marriage and business, along with the birth of a child, Eulalie Ruth Hope, pro- vided distractions for the Jamaican poet. As it happened, these mar- ital and financial failures turned out to be a benefit to his literary future. In need of money, McKay drifted from place to place work- ing as a porter, houseman, janitor, butler, and waiter.

McKay drank deeply of Harlem's working class. "Their sponta- neous ways of acting and living for the moment, the physical and sensuous delights, the loose freedom ..." McKay wrote, had a cat- alytic effect on him. The intimacy, warmth, and native excitement of the cabarets located on 135th Street between Fifth and Seventh Avenues became the source of inspiration for much of McKay's poetry and prose. The African Americans of Harlem stood in stark contrast to the constrained patterns of his peasant origins and by his admission "served to feed the riotous sentiments smoldering in him." (Cooper, 135–36) McKay's involuntary vagabondage and life among Harlem's serving class renewed his literary pursuits.

His return to writing offered the literary community a glimpse of McKay's brilliant poetic gifts but also revealed the constraints and complexities he faced as a black Jamaican artist. This was particu- larly true for the period 1916–1919, when the older established schools of literature were being challenged by groups of literary rad- icals pushing different philosophies about style and content. Led by James Oppenheim, editor of *Seven Arts* magazine, his group believed that the triumph of socialism would reconstruct American society with a new culture, literature, and art. This new artistic approach, modernism, flew in the face of tradition. The modern poet would write without regard to form and style, using simpler language, even slang. Simultaneously, the new literary movement that began to appear in the black community was less concerned about social and revolutionary style than capturing and representing the broad expanse of the African American's racial heritage.

In spite of the opportunities offered to aspiring African American artists by *The Crisis* and, later, *Opportunity* magazines (*Opportunity* did not begin publication until 1922), publications of conservative and liberal persuasion, McKay preferred to try his hand with radical and leftist magazines. He sent a number of poems to *Seven Arts* only to suspect that they were primarily interested in publishing work from blacks that dealt exclusively with racial themes. And while the poems struck the proper spirit, its editor, Oppenheim, was troubled by the non-revolutionary traditional form on which McKay was weaned. Notwithstanding these reservations, *Seven Arts* published two of McKay's poems in its December 1917 issue. The poems, distinctly racial in subject, were noteworthy for McKay's ability to use folk material and indigenous racial literature. "Harlem Dancer" visually described the young black prostitutes of Harlem, whose "perfect half-clothed bodies swayed like a proudly swaying palm." On the other hand, "Invocation" reveled in the wonders of ancient Ethiopia, "before the white God said: Let there be light." The poem is also a reaffirmation of McKay's kinship with the "sable race" and prays that he is a "worthy singer of my world and race."

Still, McKay agonized over his suspicion that many publishers placed a premium on work treating racial themes. As a rule, racial issues had not exclusively inspired him. He had written many things whose subjects were not racial; art transcended race, and the "human feeling" transcended racial boundaries. This issue, and McKay's youthful fear of rejection, led him to publish his *Seven Arts* sonnets under the *nom de plume* "Eli Edwards" and to correspond with several writers between 1916 and 1919 with the pseudonym

"Rhonda Hope." Unfortunately, "misremembrance" would lead McKay to later deny racial themes were ever a major concern of his.

The issue of whether to write on subjects that addressed the universal qualities of life or yield to the pressure of writing exclusively on racial themes continued to dog McKay. An introduction to Frank Harris, editor of *Pearson's Magazine,* in 1918 only reinforced his fears. Harris was anxious to meet a "Negro who wrote poetry while waiting on tables for the railroad" and was impressed with McKay as a poet of rare talent. But in McKay's sonnet "The Lynching," later published in *Harlem Shadows,* he had yet to rise to the heights and storm heaven as Milton had done in "On the Late Massacre in Piedmont."

The following year McKay scaled those heights and stormed the heavens with his "If We Must Die." The sonnet captured the African American's state of mind during the 1919 orgy of interracial violence—defiance, despair, and bitterness. As scores of African American bodies lay strewn in the streets of America from Harlem , Chicago, and Washington, D.C., to Longview, Texas, they rallied to McKay's call that if they were to die, it would not be like hogs, "hunted and penned," but as men "pressed to the wall, dying, but fighting back." Instantly, the poem became the symbol of black America's new race militancy and unquestionably identified McKay's genius as a poet. Yet, as remarkable as the sonnet was in conveying the emotional state of mind of African Americans during this turbulent period in American race relations, it revealed again the ironies in McKay's life.

The poem did not signify a philosophical change in McKay's way of viewing man's experience from the universal rather than the racial and his commitment to concentrate on the black man's isolation and despair in the midst of Western society. McKay's class orientation as a British colonial made his interpretation of post World War I events solely in terms of race difficult if not impossible. McKay identified with a kinship greater and more complicated than simply race. Though black Harlem was his address, McKay found more common cause with white bohemia and the radical working-class ideologies of his day. He claimed that "If We Must Die" had not been written exclusively for African Americans but for all men who were being abused, brutalized, and murdered.

Since McKay's arrival in New York in 1914, he had persistently sought publication in white bohemian and radical literary magazines. The most important was *Masses*, a journalistic center of the white bohemian rebellion against middle-class America. Self-described as "frank, arrogant, and impertinent," it was a free-for-all proponent of social, political, and economic revolution. Under the editorship of Max Eastman, *Masses* reflected his belief that Marxism provided the underpinnings for the reconstruction of society along scientific lines. Moreover, McKay was drawn to the "freshness in its sympathetic and iconoclastic items about the Negro." The magazine folded following a zealous government witch hunt during World War I, but resurfaced in 1918 as the *Liberator*, edited by Eastman and his sister Crystal.

At the *Liberator* McKay met Eastman, and the two developed a relationship and kinship of mind as important as McKay's earlier one with Jekyll. It was telling that it was the *Liberator* and not *The Crisis* McKay sought for publication of "If We Must Die." Clearly more at home with the iconoclastic white bohemians of the *Liberator* staff than the race-conscious African Americans of the NAACP and other groups, McKay believed he had found a milieu that would nurture his intellectual temperament. The exploration was cut short when he suddenly left America for England in 1919. McKay's radical activities in the revolutionary IWW (Industrial Workers of the World), and the African Blood Brotherhood, the strident "If We Must Die," and his public encouragement of blacks in the *Negro World* to embrace Bolshevism brought him some unwelcome attention from the United States Justice Department. Two years later he returned to America and joined the staff of the *Liberator* magazine.

At first glance, a position as associate editor of the radical white *Liberator* magazine was a perfect fit for McKay. He brought to it the reputation of a poet recognized worldwide and the solid credentials of a radical committed to the working-class revolution. His reputation as a radical had further been enhanced by his activities as part of

an impressive group of Europe's international radicals and as a
reporter for Sylvia Pankhurst's *Workers' Dreadnought*, the organ of the
English working-class movement, during his two years in Britain.

For a while the *Liberator* provided McKay with the best of both
worlds. During the day he worked with a group of people who mirrored his radical and iconoclastic approach to literature and politics.
At day's end he returned to his old apartment on 131st Street in
Harlem and inhaled the black community's uniqueness, loitering
along Seventh Avenue enjoying the aroma of spareribs, corn pone,
sweet potatoes, and fried chicken.

McKay published *Harlem Shadows*
(1922) while at the *Liberator*. The volume
of verse received acclaim from conservative, liberal, and radical critics alike and
marked a milestone in his career as a poet.
Author and black theorist of the African
American literary movement James Weldon Johnson best captured the significance
of this work, declaring that no "Negro" had
sung more beautifully of his race than

TRACK 12

In his poem "The Tropics
in New York," McKay
reminds us that for many
residents of Harlem the
Caribbean, not the
South, was home.

McKay. He called upon African Americans to be proud of a poet so
capable of voicing with such power the bitterness that so often rose
in the heart of the race.

Ironically, the days on the *Liberator* also proved to be the proverbial "best of times and the worse of times" for McKay. While many
blacks paid tribute as Johnson suggested to McKay's poetic power and
contribution to the rapidly emerging "Harlem Renaissance" movement, he beat a steady drumbeat of criticism of African Americans'
approach to art and politics. During his two years in England he had
published one criticism after another of black leadership's failure to
reject "bourgeoisie economic capitalism" and racial reform in favor of
Marxism and the Communist revolutions sweeping the world. Indeed
McKay's relationship with American blacks had always been distinctly synthetic. Arriving in Harlem at such a propitious moment in
the birth of the black cultural movement, McKay made little attempt

to become a part of the growing group of black artisans moving daily in the black metropolis. Ironically, McKay was a gifted "outside observer" with the ability to describe his experience with Harlem's black folk, but he remained voluntarily estranged from any significant personal or close relationships with either its artists or leaders.

The creation of such a relationship may have allowed McKay a safe haven until his halcyon days at the *Liberator* abruptly came to an end. Acting as the *Liberator*'s literary critic, McKay and William Gropper, the magazine's artist, attended Leonid Andreyev's *He Who Gets Slapped*, a play about an inventor who, suffering betrayal in life, makes a career of it by becoming a clown whose act consists of getting slapped by all the other clowns. He falls in love with another circus performer, and those who betrayed him enter his life yet again. When McKay arrived at the New York theater he was told that the complimentary "first-row" tickets for drama reviewers were intended only for whites. While Gropper was offered a seat near the stage, McKay was shunted upstairs to the balcony. He was emotionally devastated by the theater's racial "slap in the face" and even more by the dismissal of the incident's importance by his radical comrades at the *Liberator*. They organized no boycott or demonstration against the theater's humiliation of a gifted black poet. The inaction forced McKay to reevaluate his ideas on the relationship between blacks and white radicals. Betrayed, bitter, and disillusioned, he was convinced that the subtle bigotry of white radicals would have to be addressed before they could hope to persuade the black masses to join in any revolutionary effort.

McKay traveled to the Soviet Union late in 1922, determined to place the issue of race and its relationship to the class struggle before the Fourth Congress of the Third International. Despite his enthusiastic reception by officials of the Communist Party and the opportunity to set the issue squarely before leaders like Gregory Zinoviev, president of the International, and Leon Trotsky, in the end the Comintern failed to adequately and substantively address race and radicalism. In June of the following year a disappointed McKay left

the Soviet Union along with many of the ideals he had so strongly
held of Communism's future for blacks worldwide. Though black
radicals in America generally believed that his appearance before
the Third International reflected favorably on the new crop of
Marxists who were the latest development in racial leadership,
McKay did not return to the United States.

His immediate destina-
tion was Germany, where
he arrived in early 1923 to
seek medical attention for
syphilis. Without much
improvement he went to
Paris for additional treatment and convalescence.
However, the "dreadful
disease" and the long
period of literary inactiv-
ity in the USSR had
sapped much of his cre-
ative energy. McKay
found himself struggling

Claude McKay in the Throne Room, the Kremlin, circa 1923.
McKay traveled to the Soviet Union in 1922 to attend the Fourth
Congress of the Third International. He was feted by the Krem-
lin leadership, but McKay claimed that he left the Soviet Union
as he arrived, an artist and a free spirit, not a member of the
Communist Party.
Beinecke Rare Book and Manuscript Library, Yale University.

again to make ends meet while trying to revive his flagging literary
career. With *Harlem Shadows* returning so little in royalties he was
reduced to odd jobs, nude modeling, and imploring financial support
from friends and past supporters of his work. The self-imposed exile
was made even more painful as news that the much anticipated
"Negro literary movement" was well under way.

By 1924 McKay had virtually abandoned poetry for the greater
financial rewards of prose and begun to write stories and explore a possible manuscript on his Harlem experience between 1914–1919.
When word that noted white writer Carl Van Vechten was on the
verge of being the first to get a provocative novel about "Harlem
Negroes" published, McKay beseeched Walter White, NAACP
national executive secretary and movement participant, to use his
influence to secure an advance on his manuscript. It was of little

comfort when White counseled him to be more optimistic, that Countee Cullen had a book of verse accepted by Harper; Langston Hughes, a volume of poetry accepted by Knopf; Rudolph Fisher, a number of short stories published in *Atlantic Monthly*; and that James Weldon Johnson was working on a book on Negro spirituals. McKay's fear that Van Vechten's novel on Harlem blacks would hurt his chances to get his novel published proved unfounded. Though criticized by the more conservative black writers and critics as legitimizing a "vogue of Negro primitivism," *Nigger Heaven*'s (1925) acceptance was probably the most important factor in creating a milieu receptive to McKay's imminent portrayal of black life in Harlem.

In 1928 McKay's novel *Home to Harlem*, the story of Jake, a black soldier who goes AWOL during World War I and returns "home to Harlem," was released. The plot unfolds around Jake's search for a "tantalizing brown prostitute" whose services he procured on his first night home and who touches something in Jake when she returns his money as a gift after leaving him during the night. Financially it was a much needed success, and the first novel by a black writer to make the bestseller list. It was also a lightning rod for the debates already swirling among the Harlem Renaissance's participants. The debates revealed deep divisions within the black community about the nature of the movement. No question was more emotionally debated than "How shall the Negro be portrayed?" Because McKay had written about the lower class of Harlem's black community, *Home to Harlem* placed him squarely in the center of the controversy. Reviews reflected cultural and class splits within the literary movement. Some critics dismissed it as a cheap attempt to glorify the lowest class of Negro life to peddle sexual sensationalism to white bohemia. Others saw it differently, viewing it as a love story, somewhat crude, but not without a genuine element of romance and a significant social documentary.

McKay remained in France to publish two additional novels, neither with Harlem or the United States as the central location: *Banjo* (1929) and *Banana Bottom* (1929). In 1932 McKay's *Gingertown*, a collection of his earlier short stories about Harlem, was published. From a literary and financial perspective all failed. By the early thirties McKay was, for the third time in his life, destitute. In the midst of the global depression, few of McKay's friends or literary admirers could come to his aid. More than a decade had passed since he had lived in the United States. But forced by exigencies of survival, the Jamaican immigrant ignominiously returned to America in 1934 to find that the confidence, enthusiasm, and excitement so characteristic of the Renaissance had given way to economic fear, despair, and pessimism. The "Negro" was no longer in vogue, and few could disagree with the observation that the movement was "dead now."

Home to Harlem book cover by artist Aaron Douglas. *Home to Harlem* was McKay's first novel. It was a bestseller, but Du Bois and some other black critics condemned it for perpetrating negative stereotypes of blacks.
Beinecke Rare Book and Manuscript Library, Yale University.

In the same year McKay finally applied for American citizenship, something he had refused to do since his first arrival in the United States. Citizenship did not immediately improve his economic situation. With support from the Federal Writers Program, McKay was able to eke out a living, producing several socio-historical publications during the late thirties. In 1937 he wrote his autobiography, *A Long Way From Home*, a chronicle of his odyssey from Jamaica to Harlem, Europe, Russia, and back to America. Three years later McKay published his last work, *Harlem: A Negro Metropolis*, a non-fiction account of Harlem during the twenties and thirties. While much of it was devoted to McKay's perception of communist influence among blacks, in the process it was a fascinating examination of the interplay of social, political, and economic movements at war for the leadership and direction of African Americans during the depression years. From Father Divine and Marcus Garvey to Sufi Abul Hamid, McKay skillfully described the interplay of race chauvinism and working-class and radical ideology in the country's largest black community.

From the late thirties through the early forties, McKay believed that the Communist Party conspired to sabotage his literary reputation because of his rejection of their insincere approach to the problems of race and radicalism going back to the 1920s. From 1944 to his death on May 22, 1948, at the age of fifty-nine, he spent his last years in Chicago as a personal advisor on Communism to Bishop Sheil, senior auxiliary of the archdiocese of Chicago. Laid to rest in Queens, New York, the Jamaican poet and critical figure in the Harlem Renaissance was still "a long way from home."

Claude McKay at Smalls Paradise, April 1945. Smalls was one of Harlem's most popular nightclubs.
Beinecke Rare Book and Manuscript Library, Yale University.

Perhaps more than any other Harlem Renaissance figure, Claude McKay embodied the extraordinary emergence of a "New Negro" who took pride in the rediscovery of the black race and its African heritage. His writings, along with many others', exposed and attacked discrimination, explored the vitality of black folk culture, and strove to create a unique African American literature. Even more, he symbolized the complexity of a cultural movement fraught with tensions: between the ideal of Africa and the reality of America; between the allure of a romanticized rural past and the demands of an alien urban present, whether on the peasantry in rural Jamaica or the blacks in southern American states; and between the dictate to affirm the uniqueness of African American culture and the need to achieve acceptance by the majority white culture.

Zora Neale Hurston

(1891–1960)

M. GENEVIEVE WEST

Zora Neale Hurston emerged in the late twentieth century as the most highly acclaimed novelist of the Harlem Renaissance. This literary stardom stands in contrast to her reputation in the 1920s and 1930s. Although acknowledged for the short stories she wrote in the 1920s, most black critics dismissed her major body of work in the 1930s. Some saw her work as self-indulgent; some criticized her as a clown who performed for the entertainment of whites. Much of this criticism derived from her gender and the fact that she defied convention. Moreover, trained as a folklorist she approached her work differently from her contemporaries. This training and her keen observations of black life enriched her writings and led to her success.

Zora Neale Hurston—playwright, novelist, essayist, short story writer, and folklorist—"had the map of Dixie on [her] tongue." Her gift for language and her portraits of black culture have made her one of the central figures of twentieth-century American literature. She surfaced during the Harlem Renaissance as one of the best-known African American short story writers. Although she published seven books, as well as numerous short stories and essays, her black contemporaries were often critical of her work and her reluctance to engage the politics of race in America. At the time of her death she was an out-of-print literary has-been. The recovery of Hurston's work began in the decade following her death. Popular readers and scholars alike have rediscovered her work. Today, Hurston is everywhere—in book stores, on U.S. postage stamps, and in high school and college classrooms. Hurston's legacy of fiction, folklore, and essays challenge race, class, and gender stereotypes to assert the value of rural African American folk culture.

Charcoal drawing of Zora Neale Hurston by an unknown artist, probably in the late 1920s.
Beinecke Rare Book and Manuscript Library, Yale University.

Hurston was born in 1891 in Notasulga, Alabama. Although she claimed to have been born in years ranging from 1901 to 1903 in the all-black community of Eatonville, Florida, census records indicate that Hurston actually arrived a decade earlier, before the family relocated to Florida. Her father was a preacher, and his complex relationship with her mother forms the foundation for her first novel, *Jonah's Gourd Vine* (1934). Hurston suggests in her 1942 autobiography, *Dust Tracks on a Road*, that her mother was the most profound positive influence in her life. Lucy Hurston always encouraged her daughter to "jump at de sun."

When Lucy Hurston died in 1904, her daughter's childhood ended. Hurston's father married a woman she passionately hated, and at fourteen she began a period of wandering, bouncing between relatives and jobs. Scholars know nothing about her life between 1905 and 1912. By 1915, however, she was living in Memphis, Tennessee, with her brother Robert. From there she accepted a position as a lady's maid with a traveling Gilbert and Sullivan troupe that took her to Baltimore, Maryland, where she returned to high school at age twenty-six. Biographer Valerie Boyd suggests that it may have been at this time that Hurston began taking a decade off of her life, passing for much younger than she was in order to return to school. In 1918, she moved to Washington, D.C., with hopes of entering Howard University.

Working as a maid and manicurist, Hurston was able to support herself while she earned an associates degree at Howard. There she joined Zeta Phi Beta Sorority. As she worked with Alain Locke, a powerful Harlem Renaissance gatekeeper, in the student literary club and with Lorenzo Dow Turner, an important linguist, she also wrote poetry and short stories. That work provided an entrée into the city's literary salons, where Zora met fellow Harlem Renaissance luminaries Jean Toomer, Georgia Douglas Johnson, W.E.B. Du Bois, and Jessie Fauset.

When she ran out of money for school in 1925, Hurston moved to New York in hope of becoming a writer. There she was at the center of the Harlem Renaissance. She was renowned both as a storyteller and as the subject of stories herself. Hurston biographer Robert Hemenway tells us that "'Zora stories' circulated widely." She often transgressed gender and class norms, and reveled in the attention it brought her. For instance, she once walked the streets of New York smoking a cigarette, which was considered inappropriate for a lady, just to watch the reactions of others. A classic tale told by Langston Hughes recounts Hurston taking a nickel for car fare from a blind beggar's cup, promising to repay it later. With the help of white writers Fannie Hurst and Annie Nathan Meyer, Hurston completed her education at Barnard College. She graduated in 1927 and began supporting herself. She collected folklore for Carter G. Woodson and a private patron, created several critically successful dramatic productions, and wrote. In the years that followed she traveled a great deal and moved frequently between New York and Florida.

Hurston was an unconventional woman for her time. She was strong willed and independent. Although she did not address marriage in her autobiography, her fiction and her relationships with men suggest a deep ambivalence. She wed three times to younger men—in 1927, 1939, and 1944. Each time, however, the marriage lasted less than a year. Married life, it seems, did not suit Zora. Unlike the conventional wife of the period, she refused to give up her writing and research. She never worked anywhere for long. For instance, in 1938 she worked on the Florida Writers Project, a state division of the Works Progress Administration. The following year she taught drama at the North Carolina College for Negroes, and by 1940 she was living in Hollywood and consulting for Paramount Pictures. Starting in 1942, she called Wanago, a houseboat (which she often anchored in Daytona), home.

Perhaps the greatest tragedy of Hurston's life came in 1948 when she was charged with molesting a young boy. When word of her arrest leaked from the courts, the accusations became front-page news in black weekly papers. Although Hurston proved that she was out of the country when the events allegedly took place, it was nearly a year before the district attorney dropped the charges. The ordeal devastated Hurston psychologically and financially. When the saga ended, she retreated to Florida, where in 1950 for a short time she took a position as a maid in a Miami home to make ends meet. Over the next decade, her professional opportunities and her health declined. Although Hurston continued to write, she was unable to find publishers for her final manuscripts, and they remain unpublished today.

Hurston's opposition to court-ordered desegregation again returned her to the spotlight in 1955, but the hostility she engendered was largely unexpected. Her response to *Brown vs. Board of Education* was complicated. In a 1955 letter to the editor of the *Orlando Sentinel* she wrote on the topic. In the letter, "Court Order

Can't Make Races Mix," she argued that there was nothing inher-
ently better about attending school with white children, that
Florida's black schools were improving, and that the courts should
have used their influence to enforce compulsory education. She
would have welcomed voluntary desegregation but understood that
legally enforcing desegregation would do little to change peoples'
hearts and minds. Her ideas, however, were imperfectly expressed,
and her letter to the editor brought sharp condemnations from
around the country.

Although she had taught, conducted anthropological research,
consulted in Hollywood, served as a guide for other anthropologists
working in the South, and published seven books, Hurston failed to
find financial security. At the end of her life, friends and family who
might have provided financial assistance did not know where she
was. She would not have wanted their pity. In 1959, at the age of
sixty-eight, a stroke forced her into the St. Lucie County welfare
home, where she died, in debt, in 1960. Members of the community
solicited donations to pay for her funeral and her interment in an
unmarked grave in a segregated cemetery, Genesee Memorial Gardens [Hemenway 347–48]. Today, a headstone donated by writer
Alice Walker marks Hurston's resting place.

Among her contemporaries, Hurston's work was controversial. She
did not focus on conflicts between blacks and whites, as many
expected her to do. Instead she delved into black communities where
whites were peripheral or entirely absent. Alice Walker has suggested
that "Zora's pride in black people was so pronounced . . . that it made
other blacks suspicious and perhaps uncomfortable." In the 1920s,
while W.E.B. Du Bois was encouraging artists to create "positive propaganda" to combat racist depictions of African Americans, many of
the younger artists took another path. Hurston—like Langston
Hughes, Sterling Brown, Claude McKay, and Rudolph Fisher—resisted middle-class concerns about whites stereotyping the folk. Later, in
the 1930s, when the protest novel dominated American fiction, she
resisted that trend as well. In her essay "Art and Such" she argued that
conforming to the "line of least resistance" would limit "originality."

Some were concerned that white readers would use the images in Hurston's work to erase class differences within the race and to perpetuate racism. Zora understood those concerns. In her art as in her life, however, Hurston refused to bow to convention. She treasured black folk traditions—despite their manipulation and distortion by white writers. Hurston rehabilitated those traditions to create authentic, affirmative portraits of black life.

TRACK 13, 14 & 15

Zora Neale Hurston was both a writer of fiction and an accomplished anthropologist and folklorist. While working for the Works Progress Administration, Ms. Hurston contributed these folklore recordings to the Florida Folklife project. In these selections, she sings "*Mama Don't Want No Peas No Rice,*" and explains how she learned the songs. Track 15: "*Uncle Bud*" was relatively bawdy for the day. You can hear Hurston laughing as she recites the amusing lyrics.

One controversial choice Hurston made was to use dialect, which had a long, exploitative history. Dialect had been central to minstrelsy and popular in literature since the local color movement following the Civil War, but she believed that language and the characters that used it were terrible distortions. In the essay "Characteristics of Negro Expression" Hurston wondered "why the black-face comedians are black-face; it is a good puzzle—good comedians but darn poor niggers. Gershwin and the other 'Negro' rhapsodists come under this same ax. Just about as Negro as caviar." She wanted to reclaim, to reconstruct traditions that had been repeatedly exploited for white audiences, and she did so in part by using the idiom of the folk, rather than simply distorting the spelling of words.

Hurston also worked to reclaim traditions like the "cake walk" dance, which is central to the plot of her one act play, *Color Struck*. The cake walk originated among slaves on the plantation who mimicked the whites dancing inside. This cultural tradition, too, had become a staple of minstrel shows, but in *Color Struck* she returned it to an authentic context within the black community. She used other strategies as well, like incorporating humor and critiquing indirectly, which were similarly complicated for her contemporaries. In the 1960s, however, readers interested in celebrating folk life and reconnecting with past traditions rediscovered Hurston's work. They reveled in her use of humor and idiom. Today a great deal of scholarship examines Hurston's sophisticated use of these rhetorical strategies.

Only later in her career, in the 1940s, did Hurston begin to address the politics of race and art in America. In drafting her autobiography, *Dust Tracks on a Road*, Zora was forced to remove her criticisms of American political practices, creating a distorted image of the author. This may have prompted her to address more directly the interracial realities of life in America. After her publisher rejected a manuscript about a black woman doctor, she complained to an interviewer that "material is controlled by publishers . . . who think of the Negro as picturesque."

Periodicals, then, became an outlet for Hurston's ideas. In the *Negro Digest* article, "My Most Humiliating Jim Crow Experience," she recounts a visit to a New York physician's office where she was treated in a closet filled with soiled linen. "Crazy for This Democracy" addresses the irony that America had been promoting democracy abroad while failing to practice it at home. That idea had been central to early versions of her autobiography, but she had been forced to remove it.

Hurston's use of language was linked to her training as a folklorist, which stressed the importance of authenticity and accuracy. At Barnard, she studied anthropology with influential and renowned Columbia University scholars Franz Boas and Ruth Benedict. Although she grew up knowing "about the capers Brer Rabbit is apt to cut," her education gave her "the spy-glass of Anthropology" with which to examine black cultures, first in the South and then in Jamaica and Haiti.

She undertook her first attempt to collect folklore in 1927 after graduating Barnard. With the aid of a $1,400 grant from Carter G. Woodson's Association for the Study of Negro Life and History, Hurston traveled south from New York to Eatonville to collect lore. While the trip was less successful than she hoped, it aided her when she met patron Charlotte Osgood Mason. Mason was a wealthy white woman who was interested in black art. During the Harlem Renaissance she supported Langston Hughes, Claude McKay, Aaron Douglas, and others. She provided Zora a car and monthly stipend for collecting folklore. In exchange, the folklorist returned the fruits of her labor to Mason, who controlled the material. Their legal contract began one of the most complex relationships of Hurston's life. Mason had a penchant for the primitive and restricted her protégées' work, prohibiting Hurston from writing and dictating how and when Hurston could use the material she collected. The contract did, however, permit Hurston to collect the material that would become her first book on folklore, *Mules and Men* (1935), and scholarly articles in the *Journal of American Folklore* and *The Journal of Negro History*.

Mules and Men chronicles Hurston's search for folklore—tall tales, myths, legends, quips, games, songs, and hoodoo in the South, both in Florida and in New Orleans. In order to appeal to a broad readership, Lippincott, her publisher, encouraged Zora to insert narrative between the lore. Thus, unlike a traditional, scholarly volume of tales, Hurston's became a narrative of her search for folklore in which readers could see the contexts for the stories and their exchange. It was an important innovation that anticipated contemporary folklorists' interests in context and folklore as performance.

At the time, however, Hurston's fellow anthropologists were not impressed. And in general, black critics were less enthusiastic than white critics. Former mentor Alain Locke in his review of the book criticized her portrait of black life as too pastoral. Others were particularly troubled by the title of the volume, *Mules and Men*, believing it degrading. In contrast, readers today see the title as based in African American folklore, indicating the duality of black life in the South during the 1920s—to be a man and yet to be perceived as a mule. Alice Walker remembers that by sharing the book with friends "a kind of paradise was regained." Hurston's presentation of black communities and folk traditions has been central to reevaluations of her work and her current place in the canon.

Hurston's second volume of folk-lore, *Tell My Horse* (1938), was the product of two prestigious Guggenheim Fellowships that permitted her to study Haitian voodoo and the processes for making zombies. Hurston believed zombies were real because she saw one, a woman whose brain had been severely damaged, perhaps by a drug created from plants, so she could be used as a slave. During Hurston's second year in Haiti, however, she became violently ill and believed that she had been poisoned because of her research. As a result, she was unable to uncover the means used to create zombies.

In writing about her experiences, Hurston tried to target both scientific readers and popular audiences with a

Tell My Horse: Voodoo & Life in Haiti & Jamaica, dust jacket, 1938. Hurston was and accomplished collector of folklore, and her study of voodoo rites are especially impressive. However, neither her folklore nor her novels were well received by critics in the 1930s.
Beinecke Rare Book and Manuscript Library, Yale University. Reproduced with permission of Harper Collins Publishers.

single volume, and the results were less satisfactory than they had been in *Mules and Men*. Voodoo is easily sensationalized, and critics were not quite certain how to address Hurston's acceptance of zombies as real or her detailed descriptions of ceremonies. One reader described it as one of only two scholarly books on voodoo "worth reading," but again, Alain Locke was highly critical, claiming, "Scientific folklore it surely is not." Today *Tell My Horse* is a respected resource on Haitian voodoo, but Lippincott marketed it as a travel book, which could only have contributed to concerns that Hurston was not a serious scientist but an exploiter of black culture.

Hurston also transferred her love of black culture to the stage. Most of her dramas remain unknown, but *Mule Bone* is an important exception. In 1930 Hurston and Langston Hughes collaborated on *Mule Bone* in an effort to bring authentic black folklore to the theater. They based the plot on "The Bone of Contention," a story Hurston had collected in Florida, and created a comedy that follows the conflict between two Eatonville friends who have both fallen for the same woman. At some point, however, Hurston changed her mind about wanting to collaborate. Without telling Hughes, she worked to remove his contributions and shared her version with Carl Van Vechten, a friend and advisor to both who was a well-known white authority on black culture. Van Vechten shared the play with a contact, and eventually the play arrived (without Hurston's knowledge) in Cleveland, where a community theater group wanted to produce it. At the same time, Hughes was in Cleveland and learned of the new play by Zora—and Zora alone. It appeared to Hughes that Hurston was trying to sell the play without his knowledge and without giving him artistic credit. The result was a now infamous literary feud that ended their friendship and left the play unproduced until 1991.

Portrait of Zora Neale Hurston, 1937, the year she published her most famous novel, *Their Eyes Were Watching God*.
Beinecke Rare Book and Manuscript Library, Yale University.

In 1932 Hurston produced *The Great Day*, a dramatization of a full day in a sawmill camp. The production was well received, but ticket sales did not cover the cost of the loan Hurston had taken out to pay for production costs. The following year Zora was living in the South and adapted her idea to *From Sun to Sun*, taking the dramatic musical program to Florida schools and to the National Folklife Festival. Again, response was positive but offered little means of financial support. Since her death, Hurston's dramatic works have not received the critical or popular attention her other writings have attracted. "From Luababa to Polk County: Zora Neale Hurston Plays at the Library of Congress" (2005) may finally bring this genre of her work much-deserved attention.

Hurston's best-known treatments of black culture appear in her fiction. Her short stories range across rural and urban settings. Her treatments of urban life, including "She Rock" and "Story in Harlem Slang," humorously depict life in Harlem. More often, readers associate her with the Florida folk, which she depicted in her first published story, "John Redding Goes to Sea." Here she uses the argot of the folk to introduce hoodoo or conjure as a powerful force to be taken seriously rather than dismissed, and she returns to that theme in "Spunk" and "Black Death." "Drenched in Light" and "The Conscience of the Court" are often read biographically as depicting Hurston's desire to see the world and her near destruction at the hands of a false accuser. More recent interpretations by Susan Meisenhelder, however, suggest the stories are more complex than they initially appear and undermine white male power. Other stories—like "Under the Bridge," "Muttsy," and "The Gilded Six-Bits" (one of Hurston's best)—explore the theme that dominates the body of her work: the complexities of relationships between men and women, particularly in marriage.

Hurston treats similar issues in her 1926 contributions to the now famous one-issue magazine *FIRE!!*. To create a new outlet for black artists, Hurston collaborated with the era's more rebellious writers, Langston Hughes, Gwendolyn Bennett, Richard Bruce Nugent, and Wallace Thurman, and artist Aaron Douglass. While *Opportunity* and *The Crisis* offered important outlets for the young writers, both were published by social organizations. In contrast, *FIRE!!* was intended to be controversial, and Nugent's contribution of a stream-of-consciousness story about a gay man and Thurman's story detailing the emergence of a young prostitute guaranteed it would be.

Hurston included two of her best pieces from the period, "Sweat" and *Color Struck*. "Sweat," frequently anthologized today, chronicles Delia and Sykes' abusive marriage. Hurston layers biblical imagery to create a complex tale that provides readers a sense of poetic justice and yet challenges the Christian values by which the protagonist lives her life. *Color Struck* also explores a relationship between a man and a woman, but the one-act play exposes the warping impact colorism and white standards of beauty have when internalized by a black woman. The protagonist can love neither herself nor her child.

Hurston's first novel, *Jonah's Gourd Vine*, appeared in 1934. Inspired by her parents' relationship, the novel chronicles the rise and fall of John Buddy Pearson, a preacher whose lack of self-knowledge leads to his neglecting his family, infidelity, and ultimately death. It demonstrates Hurston's maturing use of folk materials, including powerful sermons based on those she collected in Florida. As she explored marriage from a male perspective, she crafted four very different unions that debunk negative stereotypes of black womanhood and black preachers. Her contemporaries appreciated Hurston's treatment of folk characters and her use of language, both in narration and in dialogue. Hurston's former mentor, Alain Locke, echoed many reviewers in describing the novel as an objective look at the folk.

Two years later *Their Eyes Were Watching God* (1937) appeared. The plot follows the trials of a thrice-married woman looking for a loving romantic relationship that will not smother her sense of self. Zora was struggling with a relationship when she wrote the novel. In her autobiography she explained, "The plot was far from the circumstances, but I tried to embalm all the tenderness of my passion for him in *Their Eyes Were Watching God*."

Today considered Hurston's best, the novel has elicited a remarkable array of contradictory responses from critics. In 1937 black critics were divided. Author George Schuyler liked the story of the "brown feminist," but Alain Locke and Richard Wright were highly critical. Writing for the left-wing magazine *New Masses*, Wright even accused Hurston of minstrelsy in an attack so harsh that references to it have become pro forma in contemporary scholarship: "The sensory sweep of her novel carries no theme, no message, no thought. In the main her novel is not addressed to the Negro, but to the white audience whose chauvinistic tastes she knows how to satisfy."

In sharp contrast, Alice Walker has said that "no book is more important to [her]." Today many critics see the novel as a feminist one that charts Janie's emerging sense of self, and while not all agree, such feminist perspectives of the novel have been central to her recovery. A flood of scholarship over the last twenty-five years covers Hurston's treatments of gender, class, colorism, language, and folklore in the novel. Readers continue to find Janie's story compelling, and this novel, more than any book by Hurston, is responsible for her current stature in the canons of American literature.

Hurston's next novel, *Moses, Man of the Mountain* (1939), takes a folkloric approach to the *Pentateuch*, drawing from oral traditions in her treatment of Moses and treating the nature of oral tradition as a theme. An exploration of the psychology of slavery and freedom, the novel satirizes "race leaders" who selfishly promote themselves. Through Moses's imperfections, Hurston plumbs the complexities of leadership, even when that leader is divinely sanctioned. In general, critics were intrigued by the novel but did not heartily endorse it. Among black readers, women tended to be more positive than men, who were again her harshest critics. Alain Locke accused her of stereotyping, and Ralph Ellison, then an emerging author and commentator, said the novel "did nothing" for "Negro Fiction." However, more recent assessments by John Lowe and Susan Meisenhelder have successfully argued that *Moses* plumbs the same issues as her other fiction: race, class, and gender. Although inconsistencies in language pose problems for readers, the ambitious novel is an important extension of the literary tradition of paralleling the African American experience to that of the Hebrews escaping bondage in Egypt.

Hurston's fourth and final novel surprises many readers: it focuses on white Florida crackers. *Seraph on the Suwannee* (1948) contributes to the trend from the 1940s of black authors writing about white characters. Fiction about whites was seen as "raceless." Many believed that such fiction, by authors such an Ann Petry, Richard Wright, and Willard Motley, demonstrated an author's prowess, an ability to transcend race to create "universal" art. In this genre, Hurston uses Freudian psychology to explore relationships between men and women, focusing on the marriage of an ambitious, self-made man from an old southern family and an insecure, poor woman. Reviews in white periodicals were generally positive, but the novel went unreviewed in the black press, perhaps because Hurston had recently been accused of child molestation.

Photograph of Zora Neale Hurston, 1934. Beinecke Rare Book and Manuscript Library, Yale University.

Decades after her death, all seven of Hurston's books are in print—in multiple editions. Her stories and shorter folkloric writings have been collected for readers, as have her letters and some of her plays. And previously unknown works are still surfacing. Three contributions to her sorority magazine and several previously unknown stories that appeared in black newspapers have been located. The biggest find, however, has been *Every Tongue Got to Confess: Negro Folk-Tales from the Gulf States*, which was discovered in papers at the Smithsonian. The volume provides a look at the folklore Zora collected in the late 1920s in a more traditional format, without the narrative and context of the tales found in *Mules and Men*. She wrote prolifically, and her letters and papers mention writings that remain undiscovered. No doubt, more of her work will find its way out of dusty attic trunks and basement boxes and into bookstores.

Today many see Zora Neale Hurston as a central link in the tradition of black women's writings. Alice Walker has claimed Hurston as an important foremother, and critical constructions of a black women's literary tradition often treat her work as pivotal and groundbreaking. New approaches to Hurston's work continue to spur scholarship, and the discovery of her works promises to keep her in the public eye. Readers today want to know more about this woman who, in the words of contemporary author Michelle Cliff, "broke the white man's rules" to produce an enduring body of work that not only entertains but also challenges readers to confront traditional American constructions of art, race, gender, and class.

Richard Wright

(1908–1960)

Amritjit Singh

Richard Wright publicly separated himself from the Harlem Renaissance in his noted 1937 literary essay, "Blueprint for Negro Writing." His early literary writings with their strong socio-political content were seen by many critics as a clear break with the Renaissance. However, in spite of his own protests and those of the critics, Wright's early career had connections to the Renaissance, and his writing fit easily into the broad spectrum of its literature. Like artists Jacob Lawrence and Romare Bearden, Wright was a transitional figure, connecting the Renaissance to post-Renaissance African American writing. Wright also received a degree of critical acclaim and financial success that eluded earlier writers. Native Son was a featured selection of the prestigious Book-of-the-Month Club, and the resulting sales brought him a level of financial security unheard of among black writers. 2008 will be the centennial of Richard Wright's birth.

Richard Wright remains a central figure in twentieth-century African American literature. Starting his life in the Jim Crow South, he wrote about black life in both the South and the North. During the 1950s, when he lived in Paris, Wright developed a strong interest in Pan-Africanism and in the political and economic struggles of African and Asian peoples. While some critics see his later nonfiction as a kind of aberration in his career as a novelist, works such as *Black Power* (1955), *The Color Curtain* (1956), *Pagan Spain* (1957), and *White Man, Listen* (1957) explored the same themes of power and participation (or lack thereof) in global circles of meaning that Wright's early works had examined in relation to race within the United States. Wright's work is often represented in literary history as a radical break with the Harlem Renaissance, and yet he was essentially of the same generation as many younger writers of the Renaissance. When examined closely, it becomes evident that he was engaged in a critical conversation with some of them regarding the intricate link between race and art.

Richard Nathaniel Wright was born on September 4, 1908, at Rucker's plantation, about twenty miles east of Natchez, Mississippi. Ella Wilson Wright, Richard's mother, had been a school-

teacher before her marriage to Nathan Wright, an illiterate sharecropper. Poverty and instability characterized Wright's childhood. In 1911 Ella Wright took her son Richard and his newborn brother Leon to Natchez, where they lived with her family. Nathan joined his wife and children in Natchez and briefly found employment in a sawmill. When Richard was five, the family moved again, this time to Memphis. Within a year Nathan Wright deserted his family. Ella Wright struggled to raise her children working as a cook, but illness, poverty, and racism plagued the family.

Portrait of Richard Wright.
Beinecke Rare Book and Manuscript
Library, Yale University.

Ella's illness in 1916 forced the Wright children to spend some time in a Memphis orphanage before moving with their mother to a succession of relatives. Later that year, while the Wrights lived in Elaine, Arkansas, with Richard's favorite aunt, Maggie Hoskins, and her husband Silas, local whites murdered the prosperous Silas Hoskins to take over his liquor business. The family, along with Aunt Maggie, fled again, first to West Helena, Arkansas, and then to Jackson, Mississippi.

His mother's chronic health problems, the family's nomadic life, and, as he grew older, the need to work interfered with Wright's education. It was not until 1921, when he enrolled in the fifth grade in Jackson, that he enjoyed consistent schooling. Wright became a good scholar and avid reader, and graduated from the ninth grade four years later. This ended his formal education.

In December 1927 Wright, along with his aunt Maggie, moved to Chicago, where she hoped to open a beauty salon. Chicago was a revelation for the young Richard Wright, enabling him to observe black urban life closely at his many odd jobs even as he struggled with his own writing. In the 1920s, like some younger Harlem Renaissance writers, Wright was fascinated with a variety of political figures and movements, including Marcus Garvey and his United Negro Improvement Association. In commenting on the Garveyites in *American Hunger* (1977), his posthumously published sequel to *Black Boy* (1945), Wright admits that "theirs was a passionate rejection of America, for they sensed ... that they had no chance to live a full human life in America. ... I understood their emotions, for I partly shared them." At the South Side Boys' Club, where he worked in the mid-1930s, he had an opportunity to meet the urban versions of the various Bigger Thomas types that he had first encountered in the South—fearful, restless, alienated, and volatile. He later recounted this in his essay, "How Bigger Was Born," first published in June 1940 as a defense of *Native Son*.

Wright's political evolution continued in depression-era Chicago. Soon after the John Reed Club was organized in 1932, Wright became the executive secretary of its Chicago chapter and experienced for the first time a sense of fellowship with black and white artists. Joining the Communist Party in 1933, Wright began to receive attention for his literary talents, publishing several revolutionary poems, including "I Have Seen Black Hands" and "Between the World and Me," in leftist literary magazines such as *Left Front, New Masses, The Rebel Poet,* and *Partisan Review.* In 1937 Wright moved to Harlem, where he encountered the Harlem Renaissance in its waning years. Still involved in the Communist Party and leftist literary activities, he served as the Harlem editor of *The Daily Worker* and joined Dorothy West and Marian Minus to co-edit the radical literary journal, *New Challenge.*

It was in New York that his literary career took off. In 1938, *Uncle Tom's Children,* his collection of five stories, was published to critical acclaim. In depicting his male and female protagonists in life-or-death struggles in the Jim Crow South, Wright displayed a full awareness of his artistic aspirations, as well as his commitment to a powerful theme that he explored passionately in varying contexts and in different genres until his death in Paris in mid-career on November 28, 1960.

Throughout his career, Wright had one persistent theme: the difficulties that millions of individuals around the globe faced in trying to live "a full human life" and cultivate the most cherished values of Western civilization within the truncated spaces defined by the realities of factors such as race, class, and national origin. In Wright's fiction, African Americans remained marginalized by the white supremacist structures that had evolved out of slavery and Jim Crow; in most of his non-fiction, Asian and African masses were weighed down not only by custom and superstition in their traditional societies but also by centuries of colonial exploitation. As Harold T. McCarthy puts it, "In African, Asian, and Spanish life [Wright] found a universal significance for the Negro, which had been America's Metaphor" (Macksey and Moorer, 69). In writing *Native Son* (1940), the book that, according to Irving Howe, changed "American culture...forever" (100), Wright fashioned a Marxian, almost Brechtian, aesthetic that denied his readers the cathartic satisfaction of empathy with Bigger Thomas, the novel's alienated and violent young protagonist. Extended sections in *Native Son* connect us powerfully to its protagonist's sharp sense of the limited spaces that American society allows him to define and pursue his ordinary human desires and aspirations. In the process, Wright compels his readers to focus on the urgent need to change the conditions that would create even more Bigger Thomases.

Although *Native Son* is situated in Chicago, Wright wrote most of his novel after moving to New York in June 1937. In June 1939, when he sent his completed manuscript to Harper and Row, he was still a member of the Communist Party, but his relationship with the party had begun to deteriorate. The novel, centered in its young black protagonist's point of view, pleased neither the Communists nor the liberals. However, the novel, chosen as a Book-of-the-Month Club Selection, was a great critical and financial success and won Wright much attention in the New York literary circles. In March 1941, he married Ellen Poplowitz (Poplar), a Jewish American woman whom he had known for about two years through the party. In 1945, they bought a large house at 13 Charles Street in Greenwich Village, where the couple settled with their daughter, Julia, who was born in April 1942. But even in this bastion of liberal thought and bohemianism, the Wrights frequently experienced racism directed at interracial couples, and Wright worried about bringing up his daughter in such a milieu.

TRACK 16

In 1951, Argentina Sono Film produced a movie based on *Native Son*. Richard Wright was cast as the 25-year-old Bigger Thomas, despite being 42 at the time. Still, Wright conveys Bigger's fear and anger in the audio of this scene from the film.

In 1946, the Wrights went for an extended eight-month visit to Europe—mostly Paris, which attracted Wright as an artist. In August 1947, he felt quite justified in removing himself permanently, along with his wife and daughter, from a racist United States, experiencing, as he asserted, "more freedom in one block of Paris than in all of America." In 1949, his second daughter, Rachel, was born at the American Hospital in Paris.

In an unpublished essay, "I Choose Exile" (1950), Wright strongly defended his choice of living outside the States by claiming that his perspective as an exile represented the essence of Americanness, and he wondered in his correspondence why the exile of many white writers (such as Gertrude Stein and Ernest Hemingway) never received the kind of negative attention that his own did. While Wright was fully cognizant of racist and colonialist elements in the European psyche and conduct, his doubts about the American ability to overcome institutional racism completely were perhaps exacerbated by his own concern about the lingering specters of McCarthyism.

Wright's sojourn as an exile in Europe and his travels in Africa and Asia provided him a new freedom as an artist to explore "race" in the larger global context that included not only the African Diaspora but also the exploited masses in Asia and elsewhere. Many readers would recognize how the existentialist, extra-racial undertones of Wright's 1942 novella, *The Man Who Lived Underground*, became a major theme in his 1953 novel, *The Outsider*, which was widely viewed as his response to French and German existentialist writings on human alienation and self-determination. The novel's ambiguous ending was hardly an endorsement of Nietzschean existentialism. And its critique of fascism, communism, and existentialism was achieved through the incredible career of its protagonist, Cross Damon, who filtered these Western ideologies through his black American experience. As a "man gifted with double vision," as a center of "*knowing*, being both *inside* and *outside* of our culture at the same time," Damon found the communists' desire to hold "absolute power over others … [to be] a sensuality that made sexual passion look pale by comparison."

According to Michel Fabre, 1953 marked Wright's spiritual departure from Paris, as Wright became invested in a more global view of his "purely American pre-occupations…his own situation in particular, of the black situation in general, and the situation of contemporary man." As Wright acknowledged in a July 1953 *Ebony* piece, leaving the United States was "a break with my former attitudes as a Negro and a Communist—an attempt to think over and redefine my attitude and my thinking." The distance he gained in Paris from the U.S. racial situation helped him to become a "citizen of the world." In "I Choose Exile," he had already underscored the need for Americans to break away from narrow provincialism and to inject an awareness of African and Asian realities into a renewed pursuit of the highest American and Western ideals. As part of his own pursuit of such ideals, Wright published, between 1954 and 1957, four major non-fiction works in genres as diverse as the ideological essay, journalistic reporting, and travelogue. These works represent in Wright's career a deeply personal movement toward connection and renewal, away from the nihilism of the Nietzschean existentialism that destroys Cross Damon.

Black Power recorded his firsthand observations in the Gold Coast as it was about to emerge as Ghana under Kwame Nkrumah's leadership as the first African nation to free itself from British colonialism. *The Color Curtain*, a "companion volume" to *Black Power*, was his report of the first major conference of Afro-Asian nations in Bandung, Indonesia. Even more than *Black Power* and *The Color Curtain*, *Pagan Spain* was a personal, provocative narrative, not a book of mere reporting. As Hazel Rowley notes, *Pagan Spain* anticipated "New Journalism," and I would add, also the kind of subjective, idiosyncratic narrative that we associate today with V.S. Naipaul and Paul Theroux. As the title suggests, the book exposed the "pagan" underbelly of a Catholic Spain where religion had roots buried deep in sexuality and the unconscious. Through his use of engaging dialogue, fascinating characters, and gripping stories, Wright explored the relationship between superstition and modernity that unifies all of his nonfiction in the 1950s.

By 1956, Wright had read or reviewed Frantz Fanon's *Black Skins, White Masks* and Dominique O. Mannoni's *Prospero and Caliban*. Like them, in *White Man, Listen!* he examined colonialism and its psychological effects upon ordinary people throughout the world and expressed the hope that the Westernized leadership of new African and Asian nations, the "tragic elite," would help their masses to disengage from "the irrational ties" of religion, custom, tradition, and superstition to empower themselves through the same processes of modernization and industrialization that had provided the foundations of democracy and individual freedom in the West. *Savage Holiday* (1954), his only novel with all white characters, was characterized by the same psycho-sexual elements that readers had encountered in his other major novels. In *The Long Dream* (1958), Wright returned painfully and powerfully to his Mississippi experience. These two novels and the stories published posthumously in *Eight Men* (1961) are ample evidence that Wright never abandoned fictional forms of expression. Considering the convergence of motifs in his writings of all genres—for example, the abuse of power by and for the individual and the community—his later nonfiction must be regarded as an integral part of his intellectual and artistic growth.

It is a truism of African American literary criticism that the publication in March 1940 of Wright's *Native Son* represented a radical break with the debates that the younger Harlem Renaissance writers raised in relation to both the didactic aesthetic of middle-class leaders such as W.E.B. Du Bois (as expressed, for example, in his 1925 article, "Criteria for Negro Art"), as well as Alain Locke's cultural pluralism (as reflected in his essay "The New Negro"). In several places in his writings and interviews, most memorably in "Blueprint for Negro Writing" (1937), Wright defined his relationship to African American literary history. In "Blueprint," Wright asserted that "Negro writing in the past has been confined to humble novels, poems, and plays, prim and decorous ambassadors who went a-begging to white America." He went on to suggest that these "artistic ambassadors...dressed in the knee-pants of servility...were received as though they were French poodles who do clever tricks" (37). Since Wright did not separate the Harlem Renaissance as a distinct stage in the development of African American writing that preceded him, he was apparently painting with the same tar brush all of "Negro writing in the past," including Harlem Renaissance novels and poems.

Toward the end of "Blueprint," Wright made his plea for a social realism that would transcend nationalism and even Marxism to allow an African American writer to rely on "perspective" to shape his or her writing. He defined "perspective" as "that fixed point in intellectual space where a writer stands to view the struggles, hopes, and sufferings of his people." For Wright in 1937, the "theme for Negro writers will emerge when they have begun to feel the meaning of the history of their race as though they in one lifetime had lived it themselves throughout all the long centuries." He further argued that "for the Negro writer to depict this new reality requires a greater discipline and consciousness than was necessary for the so-called Harlem school of expression."

Such statements, when combined with denials by both him and Ralph Ellison of any strongly felt literary link to the works of the Harlem Renaissance, leaves one wondering about the attitudes of these two major writers toward their predecessors in the African American literary tradition. Were they simply in denial about their knowledge of Harlem Renaissance writing, or did they indeed miss out on the major works of the Harlem Renaissance because these works were already out of print and/or unavailable in libraries? Or else, were Wright and Ellison exhibiting an extreme form of the "anxiety of influence" that all writers feel in relation to the existing tradition, but whose pressure was felt much more intensely by black American writers in view of their very limited publication opportunities and the fierce competition that until the 1970s accommodated only one black American writer at a time in the mainstream literary culture? Maybe Alice Walker's 1975 discovery of a "literary mother" in Zora Neale Hurston established a new trend, a "major development," as Henry Louis Gates, Jr. noted, "that heralds the refinement of our notion of tradition" against the ardent denial of "black male paternity" by black writers (Afterword to the 1990 Harper Perennial edition of *Their Eyes Were Watching God*).

Regardless of the conclusions we might reach regarding such questions, we can begin by acknowledging that while Wright is often viewed today as the representative of the next generation after the

Wallace Thurman.
Beinecke Rare Book and Manuscript
Library, Yale University.

Harlem Renaissance, he was not much younger than several important Harlem Renaissance artists. In fact he was only six years younger than Wallace Thurman, Langston Hughes, Marion Anderson, and Arna Bontemps, all of whom were born in 1902. Dorothy West (with whom he worked briefly in 1937–38 as editor of *New Challenge*), Countee Cullen, Bruce Nugent, and Josephine Baker were even closer in age to Wright. By 1929, the year in which Wright turned twenty-one (and he had been a voracious reader long before that), quite a few of the major literary works associated with the Harlem Renaissance had already been published, including many that were well reviewed and/or widely circulated. These would include Jean Toomer's *Cane* (1923); Alain Locke's *The New Negro* (1925); Charles S. Johnson's, *Ebony and Topaz* (1927); Walter White's *Fire in the Flint* (1924) and *Flight* (1926); Du Bois's *Dark Princess* (1928); Hughes's *The Weary Blues* (1926) and *Fine Clothes to a Jew* (1927); Rudolph Fisher's *The Walls of Jericho* (1928); Countee Cullen's *Color* (1926) and *Caroling Dusk* (1927); Carl Van Vechten's *Nigger Heaven* (1926); Claude McKay's *Home to Harlem* (1928) and *Banjo* (1929); Thurman's *The Blacker the Berry* (1929); Jessie Fauset's *There Is Confusion* (1924) and *Plum Bun* (1929); and Nella Larsen's *Quicksand* (1928) and *Passing* (1929). Besides the growing influence of *The Crisis* and *Opportunity,* the black American literary scene had already experienced the short-lived but powerful impact of small magazines such as *FIRE!!* (1926) and *Harlem* (1928).

And while Wright had close interaction at various points in his life with both Hughes and Bontemps (both visited him in Paris in the fall of 1960; Hughes was in fact the last visitor from the States to see Wright just before his death), Wallace Thurman would appear to be the most legitimate precursor to Wright based on the striking resemblances between their views on art and literary expression, their shared personal attitudes toward organized religion, and their alienation from their fathers, who had abandoned their respective families during their childhoods. Both Thurman and Wright also achieved a level of unusual comfort with their white collaborators— Thurman with William Jourdan Rapp on two full-length plays, *Harlem* (1929) and *Jeremiah the Magnificent* (1933), and Wright with Paul Green in 1940 on the stage version of *Native Son*. Both were brilliant minds, largely self-taught, and obsessive readers. Both were inspired by H.L. Mencken's iconoclasm and emulated his authorial impulses and styles in different ways.

Although Thurman did not start the "hegira" of his life in the harsh racism of the deep South that seared Wright's imagination, his beginnings in Salt Lake City, Utah, and Boise, Idaho, gave him Wright-like perceptions and insights into the African American experience that were shaped by a strong sense of his permanent outsider status. In different ways, both of them displayed a level of ambivalence toward folk culture. An unflinching secularist like Wright, Thurman's early and strong rejection of the church parallels that of young Richard in *Black Boy*. While Thurman felt much closer to his Baptist grandmother, Ma Jack, all his life than Wright ever did to his Seventh Day Adventist Grandmother Wilson, both women failed miserably in their attempts to convert their precocious, rebellious grandsons to their belief systems. Thurman's description in his correspondence with Hughes about the only meeting he had as an adult with his estranged father bears a striking resemblance to Wright's later description of a similar event in his life at the end of Chapter I in *Black Boy*.

But beyond these fascinating personal parallels, one is struck by even stronger similarities between the views expressed by Thurman and Wright in their literary and social essays, book reviews, interviews, and correspondence on how the social constructions of "race" have long plagued the work of both white and black writers and critics. Once we acknowledge Wright to be in such meaningful "conversation" with Thurman, the Renaissance's *enfant terrible*, we have to reconsider the idea of his work being the kind of radical break with the Harlem Renaissance that it has often been represented to be in African American literary history.

Both Thurman and Wright fashioned richly nuanced answers to the aesthetic challenges faced by African American writers in a racially divided society as they struggled to find their true voices and artistic independence against what Hughes described in his well-known 1926 essay, "The Negro Artist and the Racial Mountain," as "the undertow of sharp criticism and misunderstanding from his own group and unintended bribes from the whites." But Thurman's 1927 essays such as "Nephews of Uncle Remus" and "Negro Artists and the Negro" go much further beyond Hughes's assertions of independence to claim for himself the voice of an early literary theorist and public intellectual. For example, in "Negro Artists," noting how the provincialism of *all* Americans affects black and white artists alike, Thurman deftly interlinked the cultural complexes of blacks and whites: "Those American Negroes who would not appreciate the spirituals until white critics sang their praises have their counterparts in the American whites who would not appreciate Poe and Whitman until European critics classed them as immortals." In his many witty and acerbic essays and reviews (gathered for the first time in his *Collected Writings* in 2003), Thurman defended Carl Van Vechten's *Nigger Heaven* and took Du Bois to task for his negative review of Fisher's *The Walls of Jericho*, but more importantly he attempted to articulate his theory of a "black aesthetic"—in especially positive terms in "Nephews"—anticipating not only Wright but also in some ways the extensive writings on the subject in the 1970s.

In "Blueprint," Wright declared, "White America never offered these Negro writers [of the past] any serious criticism. The mere fact that a Negro could write was astonishing. Nor was there any deep concern on the part of white America with the role Negro writing should play in American culture." On the other hand, he continued, "a majority of literate Negroes" took pride in these writers' "often technically brilliant performances" without ever questioning seriously how their writings might serve as "something of a guide in their daily living." With regard to Hughes's *The Weary Blues*, Thurman observed in "Negro Artists" how the young poet had fashioned his art by selecting and preserving "such autonomous values as were being rapidly eradicated in order to speed the Negro assimilation," and yet the book "did not evoke much caustic public comment from Mr. Hughes' people. Negroes were too thrilled at the novelty of having a poet who could gain the attention of a white publisher to pay attention to what he wrote." Describing the "Negro renaissance" of the 1920s as a fad in which whites were fast losing interest, Thurman noted that some Negroes had "quietly" begun to deplore Hughes's "jazz predilections, his unconventional poetic forms, and his preoccupation with the proletariat. But they were hopeful that he would reform and write in a conventional form about the 'best people.'"

Both Thurman and Wright were suspicious of uncritical uses of Black Nationalism as a source or inspiration for writing, and both wanted African American writers to master their craft. For Wright, "The Negro writer's new position demands a sharper definition of the status of his craft, and a sharper emphasis upon its functional autonomy." Like Thurman, Wright rejected the pressure of the didactic in African American writing, suggesting that "if the sensory vehicle of imaginative writing is required to carry too great a load of didactic material, the artistic sense is submerged." As a lifelong Marxist and in 1937 still a member of the Communist Party, Wright ended his "Blueprint" with a short section entitled "The Necessity for Collective Work" that argued against the isolation of black writers from one another and from white writers. For both Thurman and Wright, "tradition" could not be relied upon as a guide, and as Wright put it, "Surely this is the moment to ask questions, to theorize, to speculate, to wonder out of what materials can a human world be built ... with thought, care, self-consciousness, and deliberation."

Unlike Wright, Thurman did not go through a communist phase, yet in his essay "The Coming Revolution" (1929) we find the following declaration, which Wright would have probably endorsed: "[G]ladly would I urge the Negro masses to take an active part in the revolution, just to see them, for one moment emerge from their innate sluggishness, massacre their ministers, and perhaps, in the interim, give birth to a few exceptional individuals capable of arising above the mob, Communism, Christianity, and all such other doctrines to become master intellects and creative giants."

Staunchly individualist and sounding more like the Wright of *White Man, Listen* (1957) than of "Blueprint," Thurman rejected all group ideologies (including too much reliance on civil rights), as he urged his fellow writers freely to pursue their imagination and creativity. In the "Author's Preface" to his unpublished collection of essays, *Aunt Hagar's Children* (1929), Thurman acknowledged that writers had "no panaceas to offer, no sure fire theories for the solution of the race problem." Viewing the old guard's jeremiad for social justice as wasteful of both time and creative energy, he stressed the need for responding to racial insults through a rigorous cultivation of individuality. Wright would most likely have endorsed Thurman's literary manifesto in the "Author's Preface" that it was "the duty of those who have the will to power in artistic and intellectual fields to shake off psychological shackles, deliberately formulate an egoistic philosophy, develop a cosmopolitan perspective, and soar where they may, blaming only themselves if they fail to reach their goal. Individual salvation may prove a more efficacious emancipating agent for his [the Negro's] generation and for those following than self-sacrifice and morbid resentment."

While the style and aesthetic of *Native Son* as a novel of social protest have been viewed as a radical break with the Harlem Renaissance, Wright's literary career in its entirety signified in many ways an extension of the many contributions made by Harlem Renaissance artists such as Jean Toomer, Rudolph Fisher, Countee Cullen, Claude McKay, Langston Hughes, Zora Neale Hurston, Wallace Thurman, John P. Davis, and Dorothy West. In the 1920s and 1930s, these writers passionately debated issues of "black aesthetic" and thus opened spaces for a sharper articulation of differences, as well as intertexual responses, among their African American successors such as Wright, Ellison, James Baldwin, Toni Morrison, Alice

Walker, Ishmael Reed, Amiri Baraka, and Audre Lorde. In fact, by 1937, Wright had joined the late-day Harlem Renaissance debates by suggesting, in his review of *Their Eyes Were Watching God*, that while Hurston's novel showed facility with dialogue, it perpetuated the "minstrel show tradition and the clichés about black life so dear to the white reading public." However, since 1978, when *Their Eyes* first became available in a reliable reprint, millions of readers have belied Wright's assertion that Hurston's novel had "no theme, no message, no thought." As Mary Helen Washington noted in her introduction to the 1990 Harper Perennial reprint of *Their Eyes*, in a period of literary history dominated by Wright and the "stormy fiction of social realism, the quieter voice of a woman searching for self-realization could not, or would not, be heard."

Before Wright, many Harlem Renaissance writers had also developed cross-cultural interests through their travels to Europe and elsewhere. Surely, a book such as McKay's *Banjo* anticipated the examination of identity and politics in transnational contexts that Wright attempted in his later nonfiction. Additionally, Hughes, Locke, and Du Bois were very aware in the 1920s of the pressure of the global in their own work as opinion-makers dedicated to African American culture and citizenship. In 1923, Hughes was the first among the Harlem Renaissance writers to visit West Africa. In fact, the African American voice in Hughes's first published poem, "The Negro Speaks of Rivers," embraced not just Africa but all human civilization by invoking the Euphrates along with the Nile and Mississippi rivers. George Schuyler's Liberian visit in 1931 resulted in his documentary novel, *Slaves Today*. Through their firsthand contact with African realities, both learned, like Wright in 1954, the dangers of romanticizing the "Dark Continent." In his 1925 anthology, *The New Negro*, Locke did not link African American artists directly to the African arts that had influenced the works of European painters such as Picasso. For Locke, what the African American artist could derive from African art was "not cultural inspiration or technical innovations, but the lesson of a classic background, the lesson of discipline, of style, of technical control." More than once in his anthology, Locke highlighted the national and international scope of the New Negro movement by comparing it, in a postcolonial vein, with the "nascent movements of folk expression and selfdetermination" that were taking place "in India, in China, in Egypt, Ireland, Russia, Bohemia, Palestine and Mexico." Du Bois reported regularly in *The Crisis* on the stirrings of freedom and social change around the world, publishing, among other items, "messages for the Negro" from both M. K. Gandhi and Nobel Laureate Rabindranath Tagore. A quarter of a century later, Wright continued this mission of expanding a global, cross-cultural awareness of race and power relations through his work as a public intellectual, especially through his non-fiction writings from the 1950s.

A self-taught maverick, Wright attempted throughout his life to satisfy his almost insatiable intellectual curiosity in many areas of human knowledge through his disciplined reading projects. (For example, in the 1930s in Chicago, he read searchingly in Alfred Adler, Sigmund Freud, Carl Jung, and other psychologists.) At the same time, his career as an artist and man of letters displays a certain level of unity and design, marked by his intense interest in the emerging patterns of modernity against the background of the many disenfranchising forces at work and the socio-economic and psychic consequences they created for millions around the world. His work was published to critical acclaim against the odds of the many disenfranchising forces at work and the socio-economic and psychic consequences they created for millions around the world. This figure in the carpet shaped all his work, and his writings in the 1950s are very much of a piece with early works such as *Uncle Tom's Children, Native Son, Black Boy,* and his WPA-supported documentary history, *Twelve Million Black Voices* (1941). The perspectives he fashioned in the 1950s in his self-chosen new role as a global intellectual resonated well with his earlier perspectives. By the late forties, he had apparently been thinking about the relationship between racism at home and the global realities of colonialism and capitalism, viewing the African American as more than "America's metaphor." In 1946, he described the problem of 15 million black

Americans as "symbolic" of the situation faced by over 1.5 billion people of color throughout the world. In a 1947 interview, Wright boldly declared the African American to be "intrinsically a colonial subject, but one who lives not in China, India, or Africa but next door to his conquerors, attending their schools, fighting their wars, and laboring in their factories. The American Negro problem, therefore, is but a facet of the global problem that splits the world in two: Handicraft vs. Mass Production; Family vs. the Individual; Tradition vs. Progress; Personality vs. Collectivity; the East (the colonial peoples) vs. the West (exploiters of the world)."

In the 1950s, Wright observed from Paris the slowly changing realities of American life, but remained unconvinced that they represented "qualitative" changes in public policy or social attitude. Wright's interest in matters racial and American was still intense, and he wondered if, "armed with these gloomy insights from an exiled life, I could aid my country in its clumsy grappling with alien realities." These realities included the "naked and shivering world" of Asian and African nations just awakening to freedom. For him, the struggle for Civil Rights in the U.S. was inextricably linked to the full freedom for peoples of color throughout the world. So, while others participated in the boycotts and marches at home, Wright was convinced that he was fighting the same battles in a global context by participating in debates on Negritude and Pan-Africanism and supporting movements for freedom in Africa and Asia. These new interests of Wright's had been partly shaped by his friendship with George Padmore, a West Indian exile who lived in London, and through his involvement in the journal *Présence Africaine*. Although Wright learned much from his conversations with Léopold Senghor, the Senegalese poet, about the different factors affecting the psychology of Africans and African Americans (for example, Africans were much less prone to self-hatred), he distanced himself from the essentialism and Afrocentrism ("the African personality") of Senghor's definition of *Négritude*. Like Fanon, Wright felt closer to Aimé Césaire's version of *Négritude*, which focused more clearly on issues of politics, modernity, and social change.

In September 1956, at the first congress of world black writers organized by *Présence Africaine*, in a presentation entitled "Tradition and Industrialization," Wright clarified his "split" position: "I'm black. I'm a man of the West. These hard facts condition, to some degree, my outlook. I see and understand the West; but I also see and understand the non- or anti-Western point of view. . . . How can the spirit of the Enlightenment and the Reformation be extended now to all men? How can this boon be made global in effect? That is the task that history now imposes upon us." The contextual critique of the West—combined with his sometimes unabashed admiration for Western ideals and traditions—that Wright offered throughout his oeuvre undoubtedly fell short of the epistemological perspectives from postcolonial studies and critical race theory that we associate today with the work of thinkers such as Edward Said, Homi Bhabha, Derrick Bell, Richard Delgado, and Patricia Williams. But Wright remains, along with Du Bois, an important precursor to developments such as transnationalism, the Black Atlantic, and African Diaspora studies.

In the late 1950s, from his exile in Paris, Wright observed the death of his Aunt Maggie in 1957; his mother died two years later. By this time he was also suffering from ill health and from nagging financial problems. He was also worried about his career and struggling with what would be his final novel. By this time he had grown disillusioned with life in France, especially following his eldest daughter's admission to Cambridge. In 1959, his wife and youngest daughter relocated to London. Wright prepared to join them; however, his application for a resident visa was rejected. He also began suffering from intestinal problems that several hospital visits failed to resolve.

On November 26, 1960, after a morning visit in his Paris apartment with Langston Hughes, Wright checked into a small French clinic for diagnostic tests and convalescence. He died there two days later from a heart attack. For many, his sudden and unexpected death remains shrouded in mystery.

PART THREE

Music and Musicians and the Harlem Renaissance

INTRODUCTION

It is impossible to imagine the Harlem Renaissance without its music. Jazz and the blues provided the background music for almost every event in the Harlem Renaissance. Gatherings of writers and poets at 580 St. Nicholas generally moved to one of Ethel Ray Nance and Regina Andrews's favorite basement clubs for an evening of dancing, drinking, and music. Less formal gatherings at "Niggerati Manor" reconvened to a Harlem dive, or perhaps a house rent party where a blues pianist provided entertainment and dance music. Langston Hughes reported in his autobiography that he spent much of his freshman year (and only year) at Columbia at *Shuffle Along*, where he was enchanted by the music and fell in love with singer

Shuffle Along sheet music cover, circa 1921. Shuffle Along revolutionized African American musical theater and was one of the milestones marking the emergence of the Harlem Renaissance.
Beinecke Rare Book and Manuscript Library, Yale University.

and dancer Florence Mills. Poets and writers depicted jazz joints, musicians, and blues singers in their writing, while artists painted them. Music was everywhere.

African American music differed from literature and art in several significant ways. First, African Americans had already proven their creativity in music long before the onset of the literary Renaissance. Rising out of minstrel shows, vaudeville, and the so-called "coon shows" of the late nineteenth century, songwriting and performing acts like Cole and Johnson (plus, for a time, James Weldon Johnson) and Will Marion Cook, dominated the popular music industry of Tin Pan Alley in the early years of the twentieth century. At the same time, the new musical sound of jazz emerged from the black sections of New Orleans, and W. C. Handy gave birth to the blues in Memphis. Unlike literature, black musical innovations like jazz and the blues were first developed in other parts of the country and then exported to New York.

In the years prior to World War I the new musical sounds came to New York and to Harlem. Ragtime first hit the black clubs of the Tenderloin and San Juan Hill districts, and ragtime creator Scott Joplin relocated to New York in 1907. W.C. Handy followed in 1918. By that time James Reese Europe's band had assumed the title of the first jazz band in New York City. Another ragtime pianist, composer, and former vaudevillian, Eubie Blake, teamed with his vaudeville partner Noble Sissle in 1921 to produce Shuffle Along, the first all-black musical on Broadway. By this time Harlem's musical scene was in full swing. Blues singers accompanied jazz bands or sang as headliners and in the early 1920s began recording and selling phonograph records. By the end of the decade the Duke Ellington orchestra and other musical acts were broadcast nightly from coast to coast.

Black music and the black music industry also differed from black writers and artists in terms of their audience. First, the top musicians made much more money than did writers and authors. While black writers struggled to make a living, blues singers and jazz musicians did well economically, and some made a fortune. In the 1920s Bessie Smith recorded over 200 songs, and Ethel Waters and Duke Ellington made enough money to live in luxury apartments on Sugar Hill. Music also attracted a larger and more diverse audience. Among blacks, far more people knew who Ma Rainey was than James Weldon Johnson or even Langston Hughes. Singers and the top musicians became celebrities. Black music and black performers were also more readily accepted by white audiences. By the 1930s Duke Ellington and his all-black band were making regular concert tours through the South where they performed to enthusiastic white audiences. Even in the North they broke the color line in concert halls in Chicago and other cities—at least on the performance stage, though usually not in the audience. Radio broadcasts and recordings also brought the music, but not the music makers, into white homes.

The chapters that follow in this section examine only a few of the many great singers, musicians, and composers who created African American music during the Harlem Renaissance. Eubie Blake, a talented pianist and composer, pioneered black musical reviews on Broadway and helped create a popular new musical genre for the Harlem Renaissance. Blues singers Bessie Smith and Ethel Waters stand out for the intensity and emotion of their music and their impact on audiences. Louis Armstrong and Duke Ellington are notable for both their talent as musicians and composers and their role in bringing jazz into the mainstream and establishing it as a national and international force in music.

Eubie Blake

(1883–1983)

TERRY WALDO

Langston Hughes credits Shuffle Along, *and by inference Eubie Blake and its creators, with launching the Harlem Renaissance. This may be an exaggeration, but Blake and his associates redefined African American musical theater and took it to Broadway, and in doing so laid the foundation for the Harlem vogue that was the basis for the 1920s fascination with black writing, art, music, and theater. Blake began his career in music and entertainment at the beginning of the century, and made his last show business appearance on* Saturday Night Live *at age ninety-eight. In the interim he played vaudeville and clubs as a singer and piano player, wrote songs, wrote and produced musical reviews, and appeared in films and on television. In the process he helped assure that African Americans would enter the mainstream of American music and entertainment.*

It could be said that the Harlem Renaissance actually began when a remarkable, all-black Broadway show called *Shuffle Along* began a hugely successful run on May 23, 1921, at the Sixty-Third Street Theater. This show, produced, written, and performed by blacks, grabbed the attention of the general public and created an interest in and awareness of African American music and entertainment. This was the beginning of the "Jazz Age" and for the following decade its cultural and spiritual center would be Harlem. The musical genius behind this achievement was Eubie Blake.

Blake was one of the most influential figures ever to emerge from the black entertainment world. Born James Hubert Blake on February 7, 1883, in Baltimore, Maryland, Eubie died five days after his one-hundredth birthday on February 12, 1983. During that century he managed to rise out of the economic poverty of the Baltimore ghettos and became one of the most influential and honored figures of American entertainment. He was a true superstar who not only conquered Broadway but also became a film and television favorite when he was well into his eighties. Physically, Eubie was a somewhat short, very slender man with long, spidery fingers who maintained a completely shaved head. On the surface he appeared to be extremely frail, but even in his tenth decade he had the energy and intensity of a man in his thirties. Add to this a remarkably facile mind, quick wit, and incredible musical dexterity and it was obvious why he became such a heavily booked TV performer. The old pro with some seventy years of show business experience knew how to entertain.

Eubie's history was remarkable right from the beginning. He was born in Baltimore, Maryland, to two ex-slaves. His father, John Sumner Blake, worked as a stevedore. His mother, Emily Johnson Blake, John's second wife, was a laundress. Eubie was the only one of twenty-one children born to John's two wives to reach adulthood, although he must have had countless half-siblings owing to the fact that his father was forced to breed in the custom of the old Southern plantations.

Eubie, at the age of six, while visiting a local music store, demonstrated an aptitude for playing the organ. His mother purchased one for $75 on an installment plan—25¢ per week—and managed to get him music lessons. Although he quit school in the third grade, Eubie's musical aptitude would soon provide him with gainful employment. By 1899, only sixteen years old, he would regularly sneak out his bedroom window to play piano at one of Baltimore's finer brothels, Aggie Shelton's Bawdy House; although strongly disapproved of by his religious mother, this rather classy "house of ill repute" allowed the teenager to support his family.

Piano players in such establishments played the popular music of the day. In 1899 that included the tender ballads of the Victorian Age, ever-popular Stephen Foster tunes, and a brand-new fad that was sweeping the country, now called "ragtime." Scott Joplin, the "Father of Classic Ragtime," had just published his magnificent syncopated opus, "The Maple Leaf Rag." The same year, the young Blake composed his own rag that would years later be recognized as a masterpiece to rival Joplin's. It was called "Sounds of Africa" when Eubie first recorded it in 1921, but in due course it became known as "The Charleston Rag."

It is an enormously difficult work of startling originality. "The Charleston Rag" contains an amazing array of pianistic devices (or "tricks" as Eubie called them) that have not been duplicated in any other work. These include a unique left-hand melody in the opening strain and a series of dazzling pianistic breaks and acrobatic hand stretches that occur throughout in both hands. Although copyrighted in 1917, it was not transcribed until the 1970s, when I did so with Eubie's guidance for a folio of his rags called *Sincerely, Eubie Blake*.

Eubie said that he got his first real job in show business when he was eighteen. On July 1, 1901, he joined Dr. Frazier's Medicine Show as a melodeon player and buck dancer (a term for all young black dancers who performed in such shows). By the end of the following year, Eubie made his final appearance as a dancer in a New York production of *In Old Kentucky*. During the ensuing years he played in various saloons and sportin' houses along the East Coast. In 1907 Blake finally settled into the new Goldfield Hotel, built by his childhood friend, the lightweight boxing champion of the world,

Joe Gans. Working here and in Atlantic City during the summers, Eubie attracted a clientele of celebrities who would often travel from New York to catch his spectacular piano playing.

In his later years Eubie was the only living contact to a world of masterful piano players who moved from town to town in the beginning years of the twentieth century and invented a variety of individual styles. But for his remarkable memory and ability to imitate their playing, this would all be lost. This colorful list of unrecorded ticklers includes "Cat Eye" Harry, "Big Head" Wilbur, and "One Leg" Willie Gant, who Eubie claimed was the best of them all. Willie, the son of a domestic servant, had been given, with the support of one of his mother's clients, extensive training in classical music at the prestigious Boston Conservatory of Music. Near graduation he had participated in a class competition in which he performed a difficult Liszt work.

TRACK 17

Eubie Blake wrote "Troublesome Ivories" in 1911 but did not record the song until much later. This 1974 recording includes Blake's spoken introduction to the song.

All the contestants played behind a curtain. He was awarded first place by the judges, but the school refused him first prize because he was black. Willie was so hurt that he left the classical world and spent the rest of his days playing ragtime in the clubs. He could take any music and turn it into ragtime. Eubie played his grandiose and syncopated version of John Philip Sousa's "Stars & Stripes Forever."

Another favorite of Eubie's from those early years was Jesse Pickett's "Bull Dyke's Dream," which Eubie later renamed "The Dream Rag." Pickett played this singular work, with its Latin American rhythms, at the Chicago World's Fair of 1893, but Eubie dated it as a pre-Civil War creation.

Even the great Scott Joplin, the king of ragtime composers, made no recordings, but Eubie heard him around 1915 and was able to demonstrate how he played. As Eubie told the story, he and Joplin were at a big dinner party at a hotel in Washington D.C. near the White House. In attendance were some of the greatest ragtime piano players in the country, and they urged Joplin to perform. Joplin, never a great piano player, was now in the tertiary stages of syphilis. Still the attendees hounded him with chants of "We want Joplin! We want Joplin!" until he reluctantly got up and played "The Maple Leaf Rag." Eubie recalled, "It was pitiful. The man was dead. These guys were a bunch of sharks and they turned up their noses at Joplin. I spoke up for him and told them that if it hadn't been for this man having the *nerve* to publish this music, none of us would be working!"

As Eubie was a connection to this lost world of the pioneers of ragtime, he was also a mentor to many of the later jazz stars. Duke Ellington listed Eubie as one of his two primary teachers. He and a host of other jazz piano giants, including James P. Johnson, Willie "the Lion" Smith, and "Luckey" Roberts learned as teenagers from the master when they used to hear him during the summers at Atlantic City. They, along with the younger "Fats" Waller, would later be known as the legendary kings of "Harlem Stride Piano." But Eubie was more than just a piano player. He would prove to be one of America's greatest composers.

In 1915 Eubie, age thirty-two, teamed up with singer and lyricist Noble Sissle. Unlike Blake, Sissle had been born into a well-to-do family and had received a college education. He met Eubie while leading Joe Porter's Serenaders, a band at Riverside Park in Baltimore. They persuaded the vaudeville headliner, Sophie Tucker, to perform one of their tunes, "It's All Your Fault." This was their first big break and launched them in the music business. Eubie recalled that they were able to break down racial stereotypes by refusing to bow to custom and perform in tattered costumes or use degrading "colored dialect." The sophisticated Sissle and Blake dressed in fine white tuxedos and worked

Photograph of Eubie Blake, 1924. Handwritten along the left side is: "It was through you that I met the wonderful Prince of Dahouney. To my Friend L. Lyon. From Eubie Blake 1924." The Maryland Historical Society, Baltimore, Maryland.

with grand pianos. They became the first successful black American musical act that did not have to use burnt cork.

Thanks largely to one of Sissle's connections, they soon became part of New York's High Society musi-cal scene. Sissle introduced Eubie to James Reese Europe, who would have a significant influence both on Blake and on the professionalization of the black music industry. Europe was a conductor, composer, promoter, and band organizer, but he was much more. As Eubie said, "He was to col-ored musicians what Martin Luther King was to the rest of Negro people. He did more for African American musicians than anyone else before or since." In 1910 Europe created the Clef Club in New York as a combina-tion social organization and booking agency for black musicians. He created and marketed orchestras and bands that played for high-end social events for the "bluebloods." In doing so he raised respect—and fees—for African American musicians. Among his many accomplishments he established a unique form of black music by creating orchestras that featured banjos and other string instru-ments. He introduced the works of the great African American composers of the day at groundbreaking concerts held at Carnegie Hall. He also provided music for the famous dance couple, Irene and Vernon Castle, who introduced the Fox Trot and the One Step. Both would become American dance crazes.

Eubie Blake and friends in the country. Blake and six unidentified African-Ameri-can women pose in a field in 1925. The woman in front appears to be holding a small stringed instrument, perhaps a man-dolin or a banjo.
The Maryland Historical Society, Baltimore, Maryland.

When World War I broke out James Europe served as an officer in a machine gun company of the first all-black fighting unit to see action in France. This unit, the 369th Hellfighters, was decorated for bravery in combat. In addition, Europe organized and led the unit's band that introduced African American music to Europe. When the 369th returned to New York after the war on February 19,

1919, they were given a tickertape parade that progressed up Fifth Avenue to Harlem. A few months later, on May 9, 1919, tragedy struck Europe. He was stabbed in the neck during an argument with a member of a drumming act that was touring with the band. Europe bled to death from a severed jugular.

Had he lived, it is hard to imagine what James Reese Europe would have accomplished. Eubie had been his assistant conductor, co-composer, and business partner and during the war, being too old to be drafted, Eubie had remained in New York and taken charge of Europe's musical organizations, but he could never replace him.

After the war, Sissle and Blake dressed up their vaudeville act, renaming it "The Dixie Duo." In 1919 they opened in Bridgeport, Connecticut, moved to the Harlem Opera House and soon performed in the top-flight Palace Theater in New York. At this time they signed on as songwriters for Witmark Music and soon began work on a musical that would present African Americans on Broadway on the same level as their white contemporaries.

As Eubie explained in later years, Negroes had appeared on Broadway before, notably in several Bert Williams and George Walker shows such as *In Dahomey*, which opened in 1903. However, they could only perform in theaters in the summer when the heat— air conditioners did not exist then—made lower prices for tickets mandatory. After George Walker and several other key black performers died around 1909, no African American-centered show appeared on Broadway until the 20s. Also at this time, a white backlash against black heavyweight boxing champion Jack Johnson translated into a drastic reduction in work for all black entertainers.

A chance encounter at an NAACP fundraiser in Philadelphia in 1920 introduced Sissle and Blake to Flournoy Miller and Aubrey Lyles. The following year these four partners would create the first full-priced black Broadway musical. Miller and Lyles, both graduates of Fisk University, had been writing and honing their comedy routines in Black Theater productions since 1910. They, like Sissle and Blake, believed that the only way blacks could get into the white entertainment world in a dignified manner was through musical comedy. It was decided that they would use one of their comedy routines, *The Mayor of Jimtown*, as the plot for their new musical. The title was later changed to *Shuffle Along*.

The road to Broadway was not an easy one. The show was put together on a shoestring. During the pre-Broadway out-of-town tour the cast often went without pay. When the musical finally reached Broadway in a rather dilapidated theater called The 63rd Street Hall, it had the disadvantage of being located some distance from the majority of Broadway houses. And of course, there was no money for promotion or publicity. Beat-up costumes and sets were borrowed from other already closed productions. But despite all the obstacles, Eubie *knew* the show could not fail. And he was right. *Shuffle Along* would be the most successful and socially important black show of all time.

Shuffle Along opened on May 23, 1921, and on the strength of word-of-mouth audiences and critics were soon making their way uptown to 63rd Street to catch the new Negro sensation. This energetic "hot jazz" musical became so popular that extra midnight shows were added. Audiences had never seen anything like it before.

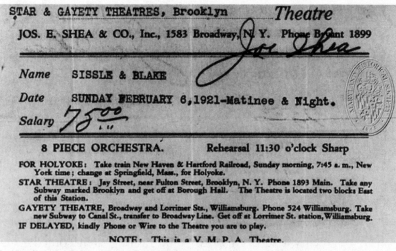

Booking slip by Jos. E. Shea & Co. for Sissle & Blake to perform at the Star & Gayety Theatres in Brooklyn on February 6, 1921, for the matinee and night shows. They were engaged at a salary of $75. This booking was made about three months before they opened *Shuffle Along* on Broadway.
The Maryland Historical Society, Baltimore, Maryland.

When the musical opened, there were no well-known performers other than the four principles. But *Shuffle Along* launched the careers of many black stars, including Josephine Baker, Adelaide Hall, Paul Robeson, and the legendary Florence Mills. It ran for 504 performances on Broadway and had three successful touring companies. One could even claim the Sissle and Blake musical became the genesis of the Harlem Renaissance. For, suddenly, black entertainment and culture was in vogue. Thanks to *Shuffle Along,* the Jazz Age had begun. For at least a decade colored shows on Broadway and in Harlem would become big hits for black and white audiences.

"I'm Just Wild About Harry" sheet music. This song was one of the hit songs from *Shuffle Along* and remained a standard throughout the first half of the twentieth century. Digitized from an original handwritten score with "Sissle and Blake" ink stamp.
The Maryland Historical Society, Baltimore, Maryland.

Ten hit songs were sung in *Shuffle Along,* including the American standard, "I'm Just Wild About Harry," which later had a big revival as Harry Truman's campaign song. This marvelously ingenious number might never have been remembered if Eubie had had his way. He originally composed it as a waltz in the style of Victor Herbert. Leading lady Lottie Gee had refused to sing it unless Eubie changed it into a lively one-step, which people expected in a colored show. Against his will he converted it into the familiar 2/4 time and it became an all-time hit. Eubie thanked Paul Whiteman, who commissioned at least five different arrangements that kept the number alive. Another song from the show, "Love Will Find a Way," was not only a beautiful and original composition, it has the historical significance of being the first theatrical musical number in which blacks could express real feelings of love free of egregious racial caricatures.

Spin-offs followed. Sissle and Blake created another musical, *The Chocolate Dandies.* Miller and Lyles teamed up with stride pianist and composer James P. Johnson to produce a show in 1923 called *Runnin'*

Front and rear covers of the program for Noble Sissle's and Eubie Blake's musical, *The Chocolate Dandies*, appearing at the Metropolitan Theatre in St. Paul, Minnesota. The program features black and white photographs of the cast, chorus, orchestra, and Sissle and Blake. *The Chocolate Dandies* was their second hit following *Shuffle Along*.
The Maryland Historical Society, Baltimore, Maryland.

Wild. This show featured "The Charleston," the dance that became emblematic of the "Roaring 20s."

Meanwhile Sissle and Blake were in their prime as performers. Most people believe that the first sound film was the Warner Brothers' Al Jolson vehicle, *The Jazz Singer,* but Eubie and Noble appeared in sound films for Dr. Lee De Forrest in 1923, the first African American act to do so. They would later appear in a short film for Vitaphone called *The Dream of the Big Parade* in 1927. Unfortunately, no copies exist of that film. In 1932 Eubie appeared in *Harlem Is Heaven* with Bill Robinson and in the same year another Vitaphone short called *Pie Pie Blackbird* with the very young child dancing stars, the Nicholas Brothers. In these last two films Eubie appears as a conductor. His next and last film appearance did not occur until 1976. In a movie about Scott Joplin, Eubie portrayed the owner of the Maple Leaf Club where Joplin played.

TRACK 18

"You Ought To Know" was from the 1924 Sissle and Blake musical, *The Chocolate Dandies*. This 1926 recording features Eubie Blake on piano and Noble Sissle on vocals.

In addition to being enormously popular in the United States, Sissle and Blake also successfully toured England. Sissle wanted to remain there, but Eubie was homesick. They parted when, at the suggestion of Cole Porter, Sissle became a bandleader in Paris. Beginning in 1927, Eubie teamed up with lyricist Henry Creamer to write songs. He also wrote and conducted numerous floorshows in Harlem. Actually, Eubie's musical directing skills were prodigious. By the 1940s, even though he was considered an old man in his sixties, he was often brought in to conduct the more difficult scores.

Eubie had several Broadway successes. Most notable was *Lew Leslie's Blackbirds of 1930*. Eubie joined forces with Andy Razaf, Fats Waller's lyricist, for this singing and danc-ing spectacle, which featured Ethel Waters, Buck and Bubbles, and Mantan Moreland. Eubie's theme song, "Memories of You," as well as "You're Lucky to Me," appeared in this production. The former has become a "Great American Song-book" classic. Both Ethel Waters and Andy Razaf described "You're Lucky to Me" as one of the most harmonically innovative songs ever written. That same year Eubie penned, with the white lyricist Jack Scholl, "Loving You the Way I Do" for another show, Will Morrissey's *Hot Rhythm*. It was named Broadway's hit song of the year and resulted in Scholl's being sent to Hollywood. But no one asked Eubie to head west.

Poster advertising Sissle and Blake at the Victoria Palace, London, 1925. The Maryland Historical Society, Bal-timore, Maryland.

In 1933 an attempt to revive *Shuffle Along* failed because it seemed too dated. However, it did mark the first appearance of the young Nat King Cole. The 30s proved to be hostile to black shows. The fad had passed. When the depression hit, blacks were first to be cut out. As Eubie explained, this didn't happen all at once, but lit-tle by little. Black performers and writers disappeared from Broad-way. Fortunately, Eubie was able to join with lyricist Milton Reddie and write a number of shows—Eubie couldn't remember how many—subsidized by the WPA (Works Progress Administration). Blake considered Reddie to be the best lyricist he ever worked with, reminding him of Cole Porter.

As the depression wore on, Eubie found himself working less and less and playing a lot of pool during the day. He was not alone. Many other performers and writers were in the same boat, including Jelly Roll Morton and Willie "the Lion" Smith. Many of these gentlemen had time to become pool sharks.

Finally, in 1940 Eubie teamed up again with lyricist Andy Razaf to create one more show. The result was *Tan Manhattan*, which Eubie maintained was his best score. It was, however, a commercial failure. After a short run in the Howard Theater in Washington D.C. the show came to Harlem's Apollo Theater, where it played for only a week. With great reviews and a huge cast that included such African American luminaries as Nina Mae McKinney (who previously starred in the King Vidor film, *Hallelujah*), Cotton Club star Avon Long, and comedian and book writer of *Shuffle Along*, Flournoy Miller, Eubie had thought that the show would surely move to Broadway, but it never took off. The musical arrangements were finally reconstructed and the show was given a well-deserved concert performance at the Chicago Festival for the Humanities in 2004. The score turned out to be an amazing combination of numbers that reflected a broad spectrum of black musical heritage, including swing, blues, and gospel. Racial pride and protest were reflected in such songs as "We Are Americans, Too," and one of its ballads, "I'd Give A Dollar for a Dime," is now recognized as a classic in the Great American Song Book.

Eubie Blake performing on stage in the 1930s, with Noble Sissle standing near a white piano in the background. Both men wear straw hats, and Eubie appears to be dancing and singing.
The Maryland Historical Society, Baltimore, Maryland.

In the 40s Eubie continued to conduct for the Apollo Theater. Although he had spent most of his career playing for whites, he took great pride in playing for his own people and did so whenever possible. He wrote music and played for shows for the USO, primarily for black troops, during World War II.

Eubie's first wife, Avis, whom he married in 1910, died in 1939. On Dec 27, 1945, he married Marion Gant Tyler, an ex-chorus girl and daughter of the man who invented the potato chip. As Eubie put it, "he got the coop with the chicken." She owned the five-story brownstone on Stuyvesant Avenue in Brooklyn where he lived the rest of his life. As a result of this marriage he also acquired a manager. Marion attended to all his business dealings, beginning with getting money long owed to him from ASCAP for his compositions. She also made sure he ate well and practiced the piano every day.

In 1946, at the age of sixty-three, Eubie enrolled at New York University. There he studied the highly advanced Schillinger system of music composition with Professor Rudolph Schramm. Eubie did well in the course, but not without conflict. Never shy about expressing his opinion, he complained in class that he did not like modern classical compositions. He thought Stravinsky was "lousy" and he certainly had no love for the serial or atonal music that Schramm favored. Schramm told Eubie that he was afraid that Eubie, being the experienced and famous professional in the class, would dissuade younger students from appreciating recent musical innovations. To which Eubie replied, "Good! I hope they don't like it!" But in spite of their disagreements, Blake and Schramm respected each other. When Eubie graduated in 1950, his thesis equivalent was a harmonically advanced modern ragtime composition called "Dictys on Seventh Avenue." Schramm, for his part, composed a "Eubie Concerto" as a Christmas present for Eubie in 1979. I had the honor of performing it on piano at its world premiere at Carnegie Hall with Skitch Henderson and the New York Pops in March 2005.

Harry Truman's 1948 presidential campaign revived interest in Sissle and Blake's "I'm Just Wild About Harry." The two old partners started seeing each other again. In 1952, they attempted once again to revive *Shuffle Along*. But last-minute ill-conceived changes in the show—and perhaps the material being outdated—resulted in the show closing after only four performances. Eubie referred to 1952 as "the year of the turkey."

The 1950s saw a renewal of interest in ragtime. Eubie would become the central figure in a revival of the music that would reach a peak in the early 1970s. A book first published in 1950 by historians Rudi Blesh and Harriet Janis, *They All Played Ragtime*, influenced a new generation of ragtime fans and performers. This was the first serious book about ragtime and its inventors, including Eubie and Scott Joplin. It set the stage for a few of the still-living early ragtime masters to begin recording. In 1958 and 1959 Eubie made two albums for Twentieth Century Fox: *The Wizard of the Ragtime Piano* and *Marches I Played on the Old Ragtime Piano*. In 1960 he appeared on an NBC television special, *Those Ragtime Years*, hosted by Hoagy Carmichael. A few years later, in 1962, ragtime entertainer and historian Bob Darch produced an album, *Golden Reunion in Ragtime* (for the Stereoddities label) that featured Eubie along with two other pioneers of the ragtime era: Joe Jordan and Charlie Thompson.

In 1969 Columbia Records released a double album, *The 86 Years of Eubie Blake*. It was newly recorded under the supervision of legendary producer John Hammond in three days in a Columbia studio with a small audience. Eubie chose Horowitz's piano for the session and dazzled the onlookers with selections covering the entire span of his career, from "The Charleston Rag" of 1899 to his most recent new compositions. This marked the beginning of a new career for the elderly man. In a few years he was appearing on *The Tonight Show* as one of Johnny Carson's favorite guests. During 1973 Eubie, at the age of ninety, made forty appearances. They included a concert with the Boston Pops on May 27. When the 105 musicians of the orchestra joined him on "Memories of You" Eubie was crying tears of joy. Eubie, now considered a national treasure, was given honorary degrees from prestigious universities, including the New England Conservatory in 1974 and Harvard in 1975. In 1979 a new Broadway show called *Eubie!* featured Gregory and Maurice Hines, the astounding dancers who had been raised on shows at Harlem's famed Apollo Theater. And in 1981 he was given the nation's highest civilian honor, the Medal of Freedom Award, by President Reagan.

That year Eubie also made what would be his last major TV performing appearance at the age of ninety-eight on *Saturday Night Live*. In November 1982 he made the trek to Washington to attend a star-studded gala taped at the Kennedy Center to honor his one-hundredth birthday, which would occur on February 7, 1983. Eubie's health did not permit him to attend the celebration held on his birthday at the Paramount Theater in New York, but he was able to hear it by way of a direct hookup to his home in Brooklyn. He died five days later on February 12, 1983.

Eubie Blake was not only the musical father of the Harlem Renaissance, but also a primary figure in the seminal musical events that led up to its flowering in the 20s. Since the beginning of the twentieth century, he was at the center of the struggle to bring black music into the mainstream of American culture. His success at that effort was a grand and historic triumph. We can only marvel and be thankful that he lived long enough to share so much of his talent and accumulated wisdom with a late-twentieth-century worldwide audience.

Bessie Smith

(1894?–1937)

CHIP DEFFAA

Bessie Smith, celebrated as "The Empress of the Blues" and eulogized as "The Greatest Blues Singer in the World," epitomized the Harlem Renaissance blues singer in the minds of most Americans. Bessie was larger than life. Physically she was a large woman, almost six feet tall; she was also a woman of insatiable appetites, as her notorious love life attested. Most significantly, she was a singer who communicated her soul through song. Throughout the 1920s, audiences could not get enough of her. Her live performances were packed, and her record sales were outstanding. More than any other singer's, her career was tied to the Harlem Renaissance. Her fame soared as the Renaissance emerged and faded as the Renaissance declined. Fate denied her the opportunity for a comeback.

Bessie Smith, "the Empress of the Blues." This photo of Bessie was taken by Carl Van Vechten in 1936. Van Vechten made photo portraits of many black and white celebrities, beginning in the early 1930s.
The Yale Collection of American Literature, The Beinecke Rare Book and Manuscript Library.

In a cemetery outside of Philadelphia, you'll find a gravestone with an inscription that reads: "The Greatest Blues Singer in the World Will Never Stop Singing—Bessie Smith—1895–1937."

That epitaph isn't hype. It was the consensus of most musicians, singers, and general audience members that Smith— billed in her day as "The Empress of the Blues"—was indeed the greatest of all. The best recordings made by Smith in the 1920s and early 1930s, unlike those of most of her contemporaries, continue to speak powerfully to today's listeners. Smith's ripe, heavy voice remains compelling, her authority unshakeable.

Smith was the most influential woman in the history of the blues. And her impact on music was far ranging. Louis Armstrong, of course, loved her and learned from her. Billie Holiday, the most influential of female jazz singers—an artist whose recording career began just as Smith's was ending—cited Smith and Armstrong as her two prime influences. Dinah Washington, billed in the 1950s and early 1960s as the "Queen of the Blues," recorded numbers in tribute to Smith— as, over the years, did LaVern Baker, Ruth Brown, Carrie Smith, Valerie Wellington, and others from the worlds of blues and rhythm-and-blues. She was also an influence on such jazz and pop artists as Jack Teagarden, Connee Boswell, Jimmy Rushing, and Bobby Short. Gutsy rock icon Janis Joplin idolized Smith, and found her a key source of inspiration. It was Joplin who, in 1970, helped pay for Smith's gravestone; Smith's grave had previously gone unmarked. Smith's influence may also be heard in the work of folk/blues singing star Odetta and in such dramatic, hard-to-classify song stylists as Baby Jane Dexter and Judy Henske. Mahalia Jackson, the sublime, world-renowned gospel artist, said "Bessie was my favorite, but I never let people know I listened to her." Bessie Smith sang what many religious folk termed "the Devil's music."

As a jazz critic, I've met a number of musicians who, in their early days, recorded with Bessie Smith (such as Elmer Snowden and Benny Goodman), performed with her live (such as Bill Dillard and Doc Cheatham), or simply had the pleasure of witnessing her work.

Bud Freeman, the tenor sax master who—along with the likes of cornetist Jimmy McPartland, clarinetist Frank Teschemacher, and guitarist Eddie Condon—helped put "Chicago-style" jazz on the map, explained to me in 1985 that seeing Bessie Smith live in her prime essentially spoiled him for all subsequent singers; he found her a transcendent artist. He told me that in the mid 1920s, "Bix, the great Bix [Beiderbecke, the famed cornetist], took me and Teschemacher to hear Bessie Smith in a little bit of a place. Jimmie Noone had the group, a little quartet, and ohhhhh, it was just magnificent. And Bix would get drunk and throw all his money at her." Listening to Smith, Freeman recounted, was akin to "listening to a symphony." For him there was no competition: "She was the greatest blues singer that ever lived."

Freddie Moore, who would later work with such jazz notables as King Oliver and Sidney Bechet, was the house drummer in a black theater, The Gaiety, in Birmingham, Alabama, for seven years beginning around 1917. He told me: "Way back in the 'teens, I played for all of them: Sara Martin, Butterbeans and Susie, Ida Cox, Ma Rainey—she's the oldest one—Bessie Smith. The best blues singer was Bessie Smith. She could really sing the blues. The rest of them sang, but not like Bessie Smith...The others was popular, but not like Bessie Smith. She was her own."

Bud Freeman, whose voice grew hushed with respect as he recalled Smith's "soulful singing," told me he believed that at heart "Bessie Smith was a church singer. And Ethel Waters. They learned that in their churches." It did not matter to him that Smith's repertoire—reflective of the uninhibited life she led—included lyrics far earthier, bawdier, and more profane than might ever be heard in any church. The glory of her artistry, he felt—the honesty, the depth, and the commanding sense of swing; all those qualities, he believed, had their roots in the black church. And indeed Smith always was a loyal churchgoer; so was Ma Rainey. As Smith insisted in one of her signature numbers, if she went to church on Sunday, but cabareted all day Monday, "t'ain't nobody's bizness if I do..."

Mahalia Jackson once reflected: "Mamie Smith, the other famous blues singer, had a prettier voice, but Bessie's had more soul in it. She dug right down and kept it in you. Her music haunted you, even after she stopped singing."

Her life was not easy. From her birth in Chattanooga, Tennessee, to her death in Clarksdale, Mississippi, Smith felt the harsh effects of poverty and racism. She was exploited financially, more thoroughly than she realized. But she lived as fully as she knew how, without complaining, compromising, or apologizing. Along the way, she gratified her strong appetites for food, liquor, and sexual partners both male and female. Street-smart, she fought vigorously for what she wanted. (And standing about six feet tall, weighing about two hundred pounds, she had a formidable physical presence.) Her pride, strength, and sheer gusto inform the 160 vivid recordings and one short film that she has left behind.

Where did this one-of-a-kind talent come from?

Smith was most likely born April 15, 1894, in Chattanooga; at least that is the birth date she gave on her 1923 marriage-license application. (No birth certificate has been found. Information on Smith's early years is extremely scant.) We know that she was born into dire poverty in a totally segregated society. Her father, William Smith, a part-time Baptist minister, died soon after she was born. By the time she was nine, her mother, Laura, and a brother, Bud, were dead as well. An older sister, Viola, cared for the surviving Smith children (Bessie, Tinnie, Lulu, Andrew, and Clarence) in the run-down family cabin, soon raising babies of her own there, as well. The family barely managed to stay afloat. The schooling offered blacks was, needless to say, substandard compared to that offered whites, and it seems doubtful that Bessie received much formal education. (In later years, Smith offered vague, idealized recollections of childhood, saying for example that she enjoyed roller-skating.) Job opportunities for blacks in the region were also severely limited—the main legal options back then included becoming a manual laborer, a domestic, or a performer.

Beginning when she was about nine (around 1903), Bessie and a brother, Andrew, began entertaining passersby on Ninth Street for spare change. He would play guitar; she would dance and sing. Another brother, Clarence, also busked when he could as a self-taught entertainer. At this time, radio and talking pictures were still many years in the future. Phonograph records were in their infancy. To the average American back then, entertainment almost exclusively meant live entertainment. By 1912, Clarence Smith was singing and dancing in Moses Stokes's show, one of many touring black shows; Bessie soon joined her brother as an entertainer in the show—her first full-time, professional gig. She was hired primarily as a dancer.

Significantly, the company included among its featured entertainers Gertrude "Ma" Rainey (1886–1939). Eight years older than the novice Smith, Rainey was a seasoned pro who knew how to hold an audience. Smith—who of course never attended any kind of school for performing and never took a voice lesson in her life—got an invaluable education while touring with the masterly Rainey. The tradition of great female blues singing, in which Smith would ultimately rise to pre-eminence, begins with Rainey. Billed as "the Mother of the Blues," Rainey had no predecessors. She was the primary model for all who followed.

Rainey knew how to project her voice powerfully to fill any size theater—a priceless skill in that pre-microphone era. She knew how to modify songs so as to stay most often on the notes she could project in the strongest and most attractive manner. She knew how to concentrate emotion, so as to create maximum impact while only varying tempo or pitch slightly. Her songs reflected her own experiences and occasionally included references to the down-home folk magic that her fellow southern blacks would understand. (Rainey and Smith were also, it should be noted, dark-skinned black women with African features at a time when lighter-skinned black women with Caucasianlooking features were given far more opportunities in show business.)

Ma Rainey always, proudly, dressed liked a diva. The way she walked, talked, and held herself on stage demanded respect; whether she was singing, moaning, or simply gazing at the audience, people felt her presence. She took her time when she performed. Moreover, whatever she chose to sing about—hard times, disappointing men, loneliness, longing, passion—felt real. Every one of these traits that made Rainey a star would in time be found—and even more fully and powerfully realized—in Smith.

Through a process of osmosis—just being around the first female blues star over a period of months—eighteen-year-old Bessie Smith undoubtedly learned lessons in showmanship, musicianship, and how to carry oneself, onstage and off. There's always been a bit of Rainey's singing in Smith's. And the two women got along well. There was warmth between them.

Several months later, Rainey was working in a different traveling show, and Smith was working with her there, too. One story that later circulated claimed that Rainey was so fond of Smith that she kidnapped her, forcing her to join her in the new show. (Although Rainey was married to fellow entertainer Will "Pa" Rainey, her sexual and emotional interest in women was well known. Over the years, Rainey had affairs with women she worked with, as did Smith.) Both Rainey and Smith reportedly got a good laugh out of the story that Rainey once kidnapped Smith; no one ever forced either of those two exceptionally strong women to do anything they didn't want to do.

Throughout her career, not surprisingly, Rainey would clash with various other singers. So, too, would Bessie Smith clash with various would-be pretenders to her throne; she did not welcome competition. Yet Ma Rainey and Bessie Smith stayed on good terms with one another. They even wrote lyrics together. In that early period when they worked together, were they ever lovers, as some speculated? No one knows. But when Rainey, in the mid 20s, was arrested in Chicago for running a disorderly all-female party, it was Smith whom Rainey called to bail her out. Which Smith gladly did.

In the late teens and early 1920s, Smith and Rainey were major stars to the black audience members who packed their personal appearances (and they were especially well known and well loved in their native South). They earned their fame and following through word-of-mouth (aided by write-ups in the black press); audiences packed the theaters where they played because people knew they were powerful performers. They earned their stardom in black vaudeville simply by the quality of their live performances. They were established as headliners before the arrival of radio, and before they were ever given any chances to record. But these extraordinary artists were unknown to most of white America. They became stars on the T.O.B.A. circuit—a chain of theaters which provided black entertainment to black audiences in the teens and 20s. Officially, the initials stood for "Theater Owners Booking Association," although black show folk often maintained they really stood for "Tough On Black Asses"; performers typically worked harder, for less compensation—and in less well-maintained theaters—than did their white vaudeville counterparts.

We have no documentation of Bessie Smith's growth as a singer in her early years. In the first two decades of the twentieth century, blacks—with a few exceptions, like pioneering black Broadway star Bert Williams and bandleader James Reese Europe—simply were not being recorded. Not much is known of Bessie Smith's formative years, except for the scattered recollections of people who chanced to work with her. White impresario Irvin C. Miller, for example, recalled ordering his manager to fire young Bessie Smith from one of his traveling shows because she did not measure up to his standard of physical beauty; to Miller, whose slogan was "Glorifying the Brownskin Girl," Smith appeared too black.

The first solo black female artist to record was New York vaudevillian Mamie Smith (no relation to Bessie), in 1920. Her rendition of Perry Bradford's "Crazy Blues" (the first blues recording by any female, August 10, 1920) was a surprise hit. There was enough pent-up demand among blacks who loved the blues to ensure its success. And it "crossed over" to a fair number of white record buyers, too, introducing many to the blues. Mamie Smith's follow-up records in 1921 and 1922 included a half-dozen hits. Record companies began to realize there was a market for black entertainment. Record companies set up "race records" divisions to cater to blacks. (The term "race records," coined in the early 1920s by Ralph Peer of Okeh Records, was soon being used by Paramount, Columbia, Victor, and other labels.) In 1923, Bessie Smith, Ma Rainey, and Clara Smith (also no relation to Bessie)—who for years had proven their appeal in live performances—were finally given a chance to release records. These mature, time-tested artists could now reach many who'd never heard them live. Smith, who'd had more than a decade's worth of experience singing to demanding live audiences before she made her recording debut, was more than ready.

The first recording of Bessie Smith ever to be released, "Down-Hearted Blues" (February 15, 1923), became one of the year's biggest hits, selling an astonishing 780,000 copies within six months. For four weeks, it was the nation's number-one seller. It brought Columbia Records, then on the verge of bankruptcy, a welcome infusion of much-needed cash. From the very first line ("Gee, but it's hard to love someone when that someone don't love you"), it was a magnificent debut recording; Smith's tone was beautiful, her majestic, chantlike delivery of the song (written in 1922 by Alberta Hunter and Lovie Austin) was perfect. The only money that Smith was ever paid for that blockbuster recording, however, was $250. For Smith's work throughout 1923, Columbia paid her a flat fee of $125 per usable side (thus, $250 for a two-sided 78 rpm record).

Smith was grateful for being paid so "well," as it seemed to her; she had no idea how much white recording stars were making. In fact, she naively declared that Columbia's Frank Walker, who supervised her recordings from then up through 1931, was the first and only white man she ever trusted. While the terms of her successive contracts with Columbia eventually raised her fee per usable side to $150, and then for a while to $200, she was never paid royalties as a recording artist. She had no idea how thoroughly recording companies took advantage of her.

Had she been paid any reasonable royalty for recording, she'd have made tens of thousands of dollars for that first release in 1923, rather than $250. For example, Al Jolson, the leading entertainer of the era, received a royalty of $.075 per disc for the recordings he made for Brunswick in the 1920s. Jolson's top-selling Brunswick record, the 1928 coupling of "There's a Rainbow Around My Shoulder" and "Sonny Boy," sold 938,466 copies, for which Jolson received royalties of $70,384.95.

Neither Smith nor her boyfriend (and soon-to-be-husband) Jack Gee, who promised her he'd look after her, realized just how badly she was being exploited. And the exploitation would continue. When Columbia, for example, began reissuing Smith's recordings on double-LP sets in 1970, the first four sets sold more than 200,000 units within two years; Smith's only son and heir, Jack Gee Jr., could certainly have used artist's royalties. But no royalties were ever paid to Smith or to her estate for her work as a recording artist. Thus not only Smith, but her son as well, years later suffered as a result of the contracts she signed in the 1920s. (When Smith began recording songs that she also wrote, she did receive royalties for her songwriting—but not her singing—on those particular numbers; however, most songs she recorded were written by others.)

The blues originated in the black South. After World War I, so many blacks migrated from the South to northern cities like Chicago (which Ma Rainey made her base) and New York (which Bessie Smith made her base) that there was a guaranteed receptive core audience for the great blues singers. Harlem nightclubs and theaters featuring jazz and blues artists attracted Harlem residents as well as white thrill-seekers and admirers from downtown.

Record companies marketed "race records" primarily to blacks, placing ads for them in the black press and distributing them primarily in black neighborhoods.

Through the '20s Smith continued to turn out records that sold well (due in large part to the fervent support of black record buyers), such as "Baby Won't You Please Come Home?" (1923), "T'ain't Nobody's Bizness If I Do" (1923), "Careless Love Blues" (1925), "The St. Louis

TRACK 19

Hear Bessie Smith sing
"Mean Old Bed Bug
Blues," as recorded in
September 1927.

Blues" (with Louis Armstrong on cornet, 1925), "I Ain't Got Nobody" (1926), "Lost Your Head Blues" (1927), "A Good Man is Hard to Find" (1928), "Empty Bed Blues" (1928), and "Nobody Knows You When You're Down and Out" (1929). By 1924–25 Smith was commanding, for her personal appearances, the highest fees of any female black performer—$2,000 a week, out of which she paid the others in her shows. (Smith traveled with a full troupe, so audiences could enjoy attractive young dancing showgirls and some comedy before Smith herself–in a striking gown and wig—finally made her appearance on stage.)

In her songs, Bessie Smith pretty much expressed the feelings of a generation of black listeners. She might sing of unfaithful men, of financial struggles, of flooding rivers destroying homes, of the unfairness of life, of having a loved one incarcerated; she sang with understanding, forbearance, and strength. And also at times with great, spirit-lifting zest—jubilation was to be found despite adversity and oppression.

Frank Schiffman, who ran Harlem's famed Apollo Theater for nearly four decades, commented in 1971 to Chris Albertson (by far the most thorough of Smith's biographers): "In all my long, long years, I don't remember any artist who could evoke the response from her listeners that Bessie did."

Noted arranger Sy Oliver once recalled witnessing Smith "hypnotize" and then "walk" an audience member during a show: "The man was completely mesmerized by Bessie's singing, and as she slowly walked backwards, looking straight at him, he followed." Guitarist Danny Barker said: "She could bring about mass hypnotism." Indeed, her unusually slow, steady beat, her repetitive lyrics and rhythms, and her intense, sonorous delivery were ideal for creating trancelike states among listeners.

Word-of-mouth won Smith her share of white fans, some of them downtown New Yorkers who ventured into Harlem's clubs and theaters (and their counterparts in other northern cities); many more in the South, where she gave some shows exclusively for white audiences and made some radio appearances. In the South, the popularity of the blues always crossed racial lines. But many white northerners, especially outside of big cities like New York, never really were exposed to Bessie Smith during her lifetime. They never saw a black newspaper, never went to a record store or club or theater in a black neighborhood; if she was wowing audiences in stage shows in Harlem, they had no idea. Smith's sole film, the 1929 two-reeler *St. Louis Blues*, was shown primarily in black neighborhoods. She was not doing network radio shows.

Smith didn't care if, in her heyday, she was a far bigger star in black America than in white America. She was singing for her people—mostly working-class black Americans. Throughout her life, she moved in almost all-black circles and had no particular interest in gaining the approval of white society. That there were white intellectuals like Van Vechten who admired her and wanted to introduce her to upper-crust friends, and champion her as an artist, was of little importance to her. When Van Vechten invited her to one of his soirees in 1928, giving her a chance to network with promi-

Bessie Smith,1936. Another Carl Van Vechten photograph of Bessie Smith. In this image Smith holds a cluster of feathers, or perhaps a large feather hat.
The Yale Collection of American Literature, The Beinecke Rare Book and Manuscript Library.

nent, well-connected friends (including, that night, George Gershwin, Adelle Astaire, and Constance Collier), she went reluctantly. She wanted to please her pal, Porter Grainger (co-author of one of her most enduring numbers, "Tain't Nobody's Bizness If I Do"); Grainger realized that Van Vechten and his friends could potentially help his career. But the evening ended disastrously, with Smith knocking down Van Vechten's wife. She felt out of place at Van Vechten's get-together, felt she was being patronized—viewed as some kind of a "singing monkey" rather than as a peer. And she did not suffer fools gladly.

Smith drank heavily. She always had a short fuse. When she lost her temper, she was quick to curse out—loudly and thoroughly—anyone who crossed her. If provoked, she was ready to brawl. Her reputation for abrasiveness cost her some jobs. She was difficult; some producers—both white and black—simply didn't want the aggravation. She was fired from one all-black Broadway-bound show in the early 1920s after cursing out its creator. She might well have had more opportunities in the theater and in film had she been more diplomatic.

However, she was making what to her seemed to be very good money, and spending freely. (She also, it should be noted, spent freely on family members, always trying to do what she could for her sisters Viola, Lulu, and Tinnie.) She was singing what she wanted to sing, working a lot; and she was partying with whomever she chose. Life was good.

Smith's bohemian reputation, especially involving her love life, was the subject of some gossip in the business. Her niece, Ruby Walker Smith, who toured in her shows for years, recalled her saying—with her characteristic mix of pride and defiance—that she could have, sexually, any of the dozen chorus girls in her show she wanted, any night she wanted them. And she certainly had the personal charisma to attract partner after partner. Ruby recalled one woman who was involved with Bessie for a while in the mid '20s attempting suicide at a rough point in their relationship. The company hushed it up. Bessie did not want her husband, Jack Gee, knowing details of her sexual involvements with either sex.

Bessie had a strong sex drive. She wasn't shy about fulfilling her needs with assorted partners—everyone from legendary jazz soprano saxophonist Sidney Bechet (who wrote in his autobiography that he and Smith were lovers for a while) to pianist/songwriter Porter Grainger (who, according to Albertson, once had sex with her even though he was gay; she simply wasn't the sort of person people refused). When she sang on records of "needing some lovin'," it sounded far more adult than the holding-hands kind of love white recording artists were singing about back then. Smith could record double-entendre songs like "Kitchen Man," "Empty Bed Blues," and "Need a Little Sugar in My Bowl" that white pop singers of the time would never dare.

In "My Man Blues," which she wrote and recorded with blues-singing rival Clara Smith, she and Clara agree at the record's end to share the two-timing man they've both been with. (In real life, Bessie Smith and Clara Smith got into a fight over a woman they both were attracted to and stopped speaking to one another, according to Ruby Smith.)

Bessie sang, in her recording of her own composition, "Soft Pedal Blues," of a woman "who runs a buffet flat." At a "buffet flat," party-goers could observe, and perhaps participate in, all sorts of sexual activities, on display the way all sorts of food might be available at an ordinary buffet. Bessie's open attitude toward sex is a key part of her identity; we feel a "take me as I am" kind of integrity in her singing. A line of very powerful, very vital female singers—Ma Rainey, Bessie Smith, Billie Holiday, Dinah Washington, and Janis Joplin, all giants in their field—enjoyed liaisons with partners of both sexes.

Bessie Smith's artistry, it might be noted, was not quite for everyone. Black jazz orchestra leader and recording artist Sam Wooding (who achieved success in the U.S.—first in New York clubs—and then abroad in the 1920s) associated Smith and her slow, repetitive blues with Southern blacks. He personally liked snappy black New York vaudeville singers who could put over the latest pop songs and show tunes (like "Button Up Your Overcoat" and "Singing in the Rain") with showbiz flair. To him, such slick professional singers (even if they offered little emotional nourishment) were more up-to-date, more sophisticated. Smith may have sung with more soul, but to him too much of her blues sounded the same.

For many upper-class blacks in the 1920s and '30s, Smith was too much "of the streets," a rough-edged reminder of lower-class roots they wanted to forget. Looking back, we can see Smith as one of the standout artists of her time. Her recordings of "St. Louis Blues," "Nobody Knows You," "You've Been a Good Old Wagon," "Beale Street Mama," "Oh Daddy," "I've Got What It Takes," and others, are definitive. They have stood the test of time. But to some black intellectuals during the Harlem Renaissance—equating "culture" with European-style operas and classical music—Smith was a crude, primitive "blues shouter" to be ignored.

Poet Langston Hughes was a major exception to this point of view. Hughes wrote in "The Negro Artist and the Racial Mountain": "Let the blare of Negro jazz bands and the bellowing voice of Bessie Smith singing Blues penetrate the closed ears of the colored near-intellectuals until they listen and perhaps understand." In "Songs Called the Blues," he argued that the blues and spirituals were the "two great Negro gifts to American music." He listed the three greatest blues singers as Mamie Smith, Clara Smith, and "the astounding Bessie Smith."

In the 1920s, Bessie Smith, Ma Rainey, Clara Smith, and Mamie Smith recorded prolifically. The disdain of the more fastidious black critics did not faze them. (Indeed it is doubtful they were even aware of them.) But by the early 1930s, their recording careers were over—victims of changing tastes and a Depression that left most of their diehard fans with little money for luxuries like records. Bessie Smith went out with a bang, though. Her final session in 1933, with such jazzmen as Buck Washington, Jack Teagarden, Chu Berry, Benny Goodman, and Frankie Newton, was one of her most satisfying, yielding "Do Your Duty," "Take Me for a Buggy Ride," and the masterly, irresistibly exuberant "Gimme a Pigfoot."

The collapse of the T.O.B.A. vaudeville circuit in 1930—due to the combined effects of the Depression and increased competition from talking pictures and network radio—hurt Smith's career. She continued to work where she could, touring when she could, playing an occasional big booking in Harlem at the new Apollo Theater or Connie's Inn. And if she no longer commanded anywhere near the fees she once had, she lost none of her fiercely independent spirit.

When told by one Harlem theater manager that some of the chorus girls she had touring with her were too black and would have to be replaced, she told him that he would hire the whole troupe or she would not perform. He gave in.

But times had changed. The rising younger generation was more interested in seeing a good-looking young singer like Ivie Anderson perform numbers in the latest style (like "It Don't Mean a Thing If It Ain't Got That Swing") than in watching a portly, fortyish blues shouter declaim her time-tested material.

When she headlined a cast of fifty at the Harlem Opera House in October 1934, the reviewer for the *New York Age* panned the show, noting, "Bessie Smith is undoubtedly a good blues singer—but blues singers don't seem to rate as highly as they used to." Smith's fans warmed to her personality, he noted; but they did not call her back for an encore. She quietly sold off the fabulous jewelry she'd acquired in high times. And she worked on adding newer styles of songs into her act.

Smith was looking forward to performing downtown at Carnegie Hall in 1938 in a major concert that John Hammond was organizing, "Spirituals to Swing." It was to be the highest-profile booking she'd had in years. Hammond was sure that, working with some of the greatest—and most popular—current swing musicians, she'd be a sensation at Carnegie Hall and would find a new audience. He told her that after the concert he would begin recording her again, using jazz greats of the day like Count Basie, Buck Clayton, Jack Teagarden, and Chu Berry. Lionel Hampton planned to record her, too. There was talk of her doing a film in Hollywood.

Then came the car crash, late one night in 1937 in Clarksdale, Mississippi. She was touring the South in a tent show. The big old Packard in which she was riding—a relic of headier days—hit a truck. Her arm was nearly sheared off. A doctor stopped to administer first aid; then a car hit his car, crushing it into Smith's car and injuring its two occupants in the process as well. Smith was eventually taken to a hospital for Negroes, which, her son said, was not as well equipped as the hospital for whites; he said the doctors "had to run all over town to get the proper equipment" to try to help her. She died in that hospital for Negroes in the Deep South. He believed she would have received better treatment—and conceivably even been saved—had she been white. (Some publications reported that she was taken first to a white hospital that refused to treat her. Although that story has been proven false—no ambulance would have taken her to a whites-only hospital because they would have known she would not be admitted—it has circulated for many years, and even inspired a play.)

John Hammond, the noted record producer and jazz writer, commented simply after her passing: "Bessie Smith was the greatest artist American jazz ever produced...She was one of those rare beings—a completely integrated artist capable of projecting the whole personality into music." He dedicated the "Spirituals to Swing" concert, which he had hoped would lead to her comeback, to her memory. He invited her niece, Ruby, to sing in her stead at the concert; he got Ruby recording deals and tried (without much success) to build her up as Bessie Smith's musical successor.

Lionel Hampton (the longtime "King of the Vibes") remarked to me in 1993 that it seemed unfair that, in Smith's final years, she was without a recording contract, that she did not have the status in the Swing Era that Benny Goodman enjoyed, or that he himself had enjoyed. With her enormous talent she should have been right on top in her last years, he felt. In the mid 1920s Smith had been the highest-paid female black entertainer in the world. But with the onset of the Depression and the passing of the vogue for the blues, she fell on hard times. Hampton believed she was due for a comeback when she died in 1937. (And the next few years saw a significant revival of interest in older jazz and blues artists, as young fans began to look into the roots of current music.)

The driver of Smith's car the night that she died—her companion in her final years, Richard Morgan—happened to be Hampton's uncle. Hampton added that following Smith's passing, Morgan grieved himself to death.

Smith's death received rather perfunctory attention from the white press; the *New York Times*, while acknowledging that she was the "Blues Singers' Queen," gave her passing fewer than one hundred words. However, some 10,000 black fans paid their respects at the huge memorial service in Philadelphia. Over time, articles, books, and plays about Smith were written, raising her public profile again. Her timeless recordings have continued to be reissued—many actually selling far better and reaching a broader audience in modern times than they did when they were originally released.

Louis Armstrong

(1901–1971)

Dan Morgenstern

In many ways, Louis Armstrong exemplified the stereotyped version of the life of a jazz musician. He was born in New Orleans and absorbed the rich musical heritage of that city as a child. He survived an impoverished childhood that included a stint in the Colored Waifs' Home. He began his professional career playing in a brothel. He arrived in New York City, via Chicago, at the onset of the Harlem Renaissance and established himself as a gifted musician through recordings, a spot in a hit Broadway musical, Hot Chocolates, and a stint at one of Harlem's hottest clubs, Connie's Inn.

However, what distinguished Armstrong was not his background but his musical genius, his special touch that caused other musicians, singers, and songwriters to flock to him and made him an international star.

The Harlem Renaissance was in full swing when Louis Armstrong arrived in New York in September 1924 to join the Fletcher Henderson Orchestra, in residence at the Roseland Ballroom in Manhattan's theater district. The young New Orleans-born trumpeter would remain for thirteen months, but no notice was taken of his presence by the artistic and intellectual movers and shakers uptown.

One might think that this was due to the fact that the Henderson band performed for white dancers, miles away from Harlem's throbbing nightlife, but the Hendersonians frequently guested there, and

This photograph of Louis Armstrong relaxing was taken on his tour in Paris in 1934.
Courtesy of the Institute of Jazz Studies.

also recorded prolifically. The real reason was that jazz, while recognized as a music in which African Americans played a major role, was not highly regarded by the black intelligentsia. Langston Hughes, a recent arrival, was one of the rare exceptions, and ironically it was a white man, Carl Van Vechten, who proselytized for jazz and blues as artistically significant. Van Vechten introduced Eugene O'Neil to Armstrong, presenting him with a recording of "St. James Infirmary"; in his note of thanks, the great playwright described Armstrong as "a darl."

For musicians, black and white, it was a different story. As a notable acolyte, Rex Stewart (whom Armstrong would recommend as his replacement) remarked, trumpeters attempted to replicate not only Armstrong's instrumental traits but also his characteristic vocal inflections. Stewart claimed that some even attempted to catch colds in order to capture the Armstrong hoarseness. His impact on his bandmates, and on Henderson's chief arranger, saxophonist Don Redman, was profound. In terms of rhythmic freedom (what would become known as swing) and the ability to construct musically and emotionally meaningful solo statements, Armstrong was miles ahead of his predecessors and contemporaries. When it comes to jazz, he wrote the book. The young man had come a long, long way by the time of his arrival in New York.

Born August 6, 1901 out of wedlock in one of New Orleans's roughest and most deprived neighborhoods, out of school and helping to support himself and his mother before finishing fifth grade, Little Louis, as his friends had already nicknamed him (fully grown he would stand at 5'6"), was not a likely candidate for success, but against all odds he not only survived but thrived. (Throughout his life and for more than a decade after his death in 1971, Louis and the world considered July 4, 1900, his birthday, but researcher Tad Jones discovered a baptismal certificate in a New Orleans church that recorded August 6, 1901, as his date of birth.)

Armstrong was blessed with a strong constitution and the perfect physique for playing an instrument as demanding as his chosen horn. His marvelous teeth defined his trademark smile and anchored his embouchure, the setting of muscles and flesh that governs the trumpet mouthpiece. He credited his maternal grandmother, who mainly raised him to the age of five, and his mother, a mere nineteen when she gave birth and to whom he was deeply attached, with instilling in him the system of values that would carry him through his extraordinary life, enabling him to confront with confidence, even serenity, experiences and situations that he could not have imagined in his wildest childhood dreams. As he himself described them in his charming autobiography, *Satchmo: My Life in New Orleans*, published in 1954, these values were deceptively simple: "I didn't go any further than fifth grade in school myself. But with my good sense and mother-wit, and knowing how to treat and respect the feelings of other people, that's all I've needed through life."

In a variation on this same basic theme (and variations are of interest in the work of a great improviser) he tells us, speaking of his adopted son, Clarence, who was mentally handicapped: "I managed to teach him the necessary things in life, such as being courteous, having respect for other people, and last but not least, having good common sense."

Elsewhere in *Satchmo*, Louis alludes to another gift that would stand him in good stead: "Ever since I was a small kid, I have always been a great observer." That gift contributed to making him such a vivid writer of prose, in his own, pre-Celine, mainly three-dot style. (*Satchmo* was edited into "proper" sentence structure, but the original manuscript, as well as the many letters and impromptu writings that have survived from his prolific output, show that characteristic.) He acquired his first typewriter shortly after leaving New Orleans for good in 1922, and his earliest surviving letter complains that the recipient has failed to answer a previous one. (Much of this material has been collected in *Louis Armstrong, in His Own Words*, 1999.)

But while he loved words, it was of course music that was his passion. He was exposed to it early, and in abundance, for the New Orleans of his childhood and youth was one of the world's most musically oriented cities. There was, early on, music in church, and most appealingly, the sounds and sights of the brass bands that paraded on holidays and also provided the music for the unique New Orleans funerals. There were free Sunday concerts in the parks, also mainly brass bands. And it was possible for a kid, sneaking out late, to catch from the outside music made in the taverns and joints close to his clapboard home (with not even an outhouse) in an alley.

Before long he was making music with the first of all instruments, the human voice. With three neighborhood friends he organized a quartet that performed for pennies in the street, supplementing his income from various odd jobs. Among the better ones was working for a family of Russian Jewish immigrants, the Karnofskys, who operated a junkyard; Little Louis would ride on a wagon with one of the sons, calling out for and collecting rags, bottles, and other items, and blowing on a tin horn. And thereby hangs a tale: for decades, ever since the publication of Louis's first biography, *Swing That Music*, published in 1936, and on the basis of many interviews, it was assumed that Louis acquired his first trumpet while placed in the Colored Waifs' Home, actually a reform school for wayward boys to which he had been sentenced after shooting off a pistol in the street on New Year's Eve of 1912. But in a memoir written in 1969–70, Louis claims that, after polishing his skills on the tin horn and wanting something better, he spotted an old cornet in a pawnshop window and raised the required $5 with an advance as a down payment.

What he did get at the Waifs' Home, however, was his first proper music instruction, and before long he had advanced to leader of the school's brass band, feeling great pride when parading through his old neighborhood while the assorted "gamblers, hustlers, cheap pimps, thieves and prostitutes" among whom he was raised but whom he never judged (he had no problems admitting that his mother might have turned a few tricks) cheered him.

In June 1914 he was released from the Home to the care of his father, hitherto a distant figure but now in need of Little Louis's services. Both he and his wife, who was expecting, were working, and thirteen-year-old Louis was put in charge of his two half-brothers and cooked for the entire family—tasks that he discharged with aplomb, though the older of the two boys was a constant troublemaker. This rite of passage ended when his mother, who by now was taking care of her second child, a daughter, pleaded that she was in greater need of Louis. There seems to have been no further close contact with his father, but he always spoke well of the man.

Back with his beloved mother and young sister, the boy now applied himself with great energy to various jobs, including loading a coal cart and as a longshoreman, from morning to night, and then, very soon and to his great joy, his first paid work as a musician. It was in what he described as a honky-tonk on the outskirts of the red-light district known as Storyville.

(To briefly digress: Much has been made of the connection between jazz and the only legalized site for prostitution in the history of the United States, but while the better bordellos did hire ragtime pianists, such as Jelly Roll Morton, or string trios, the music to become known as jazz was heard in saloons and dancehalls, not houses of ill repute. In 1917, shortly after the U.S. entered the first World War, Storyville was shut down, considered too much of a temptation for members of the armed forces.)

Run by a white man of French extraction named Henry Ponce, this rough tavern catered in the main to ladies of the night, who would "come in with a big stack of money for their pimps. When you play the blues they will call you sweet names and buy you drinks and give you tips," as Armstrong put it in *Satchmo*. On Saturdays, Ponce's would stay open all night, and sometimes things could get rough, but not as rough as in a joint in nearby Gretna, where Armstrong worked a bit later on: "Levee workers...would drink and fight each other like circle saws. Bottles would come flying over the bandstand like crazy, and there was lots of just plain shooting and cutting. But somehow all that jive didn't faze me at all, I was so happy to have some place to blow my horn."

There was indeed not much that ever fazed Armstrong, who met his first wife, Daisy Parker, in that very Gretna joint. She was a prostitute and at twenty-one, at least three years older than he. At the onset of their relationship, he was a customer, but they were soon in love. For a month, they had daily telephone conversations, and one fine Sunday, Armstrong dressed up in his "sharpest vine" to pay a visit. But almost as soon as he had arrived at Daisy's, her "old man" pushed in the door and knocked her down. Louis ran for his life, barely retrieving his prized hat, and made it to the New Orleans ferry.

Armstrong had decided to give Daisy up when she came looking for him—on her very first trip to the big city. (He would later discover that she was truly a country girl with almost no schooling, unable to read or write.) They spent the night at a hotel and got married the next morning—with his mother's blessings, though she knew of Daisy's profession. They found an apartment, Armstrong's first of his own, and settled in. In addition to a wife, the young man had taken on another responsibility, adopting his cousin Clarence, whose mother had recently died. And he was still the sole support of his mother and sister.

Around this same time, the young musician's idol, King Oliver, recommended him to trombonist Kid Ory when he left New Orleans for Chicago in the fall of 1918. Among all the great cornetists active in his home town, Oliver was the one Armstrong most admired, and in exchange for running errands for Mrs. Oliver, he had received informal lessons. Armstrong joined Ory's band, which then signed a contract for a steady weekend job at a white country club in New Orleans.

Despite his added responsibilities, the new job provided enough "wherewithal" to enable Armstrong to acquire his first phonograph. His earliest records included the Caruso recordings that came free with every Victrola in those days, and the Original Dixieland Jazz Band discs—the first jazz discs, still quite new in 1918. But he soon branched out, and what he listened to (and in many cases kept for the rest of his life) included opera (very popular in New Orleans, with its French Opera still of international caliber in the early twentieth century) and cornet virtuoso Herbert Clark, long featured with Sousa's famous brass band. "I had Caruso . . . and Henry Burr, Galli-Curci, Tetrazzini—they were all my favorites. Then there was the Irish tenor, McCormack—beautiful phrasing." Galli-Curci and Tetrazzini were coloratura specialists with tremendous upper range, and it is not far-fetched to consider them an influence on Armstrong's unprecedented extension of the trumpet's compass, or operatic cadenzas a model for the startling ones he would create.

By now, though still fondly known to his colleagues as "Little Louis," Armstrong had established himself as the city's leading trumpet voice, and indeed as someone quite special. The Creole clarinet master Sidney Bechet was stunned when hearing Armstrong's flawless rendition of the intricate clarinet solo on "High Society." This local specialty, itself derived from a piccolo part, was something no other trumpeter could have managed then, and few could manage today.

While still in Ory's popular band, he had also formed his own band with contemporaries (Ory was fifteen years older), and was no longer in need of non-musical jobs. In 1919, Fate Marable, the leader of the band featured on the Mississippi River excursion steamers, came looking for Armstrong to offer him a job. It was the best-paid and most prestigious employment open to black musicians in New Orleans, so it did not take Armstrong long to accept. Characteristically, he told the well-educated and much respected Marable that his music reading skills were not extensive, but

Marable wasn't concerned. He assigned one of his musicians, Davey Jones, a multi-instrumentalist, to bring the youngster up to snuff. A man of rather dour disposition, Jones did not take too kindly to this task (his pupil later described him as "one of those erect fellows who think they know everything"), but the Armstrong charm eventually brought him around. Jones did, however, manage to teach Armstrong something quite different. The older man was practically starving himself to invest all his earnings in cotton farming. But the boll weevils devoured his crop, and he almost became suicidal.

"I'll never be rich," Armstrong concluded from this, "but I'll be a fat man." He managed to be both, though his girth hardly became excessive, but he never spent much on himself. He saw no need for "a flock of suits," though his ladies were well provided for, and perhaps because he never forgot the generosity his early playing had inspired from his audiences of whores, pimps, and hustlers, he gave away all he could afford throughout his life, but not indiscriminately.

It was another lesson learned early on. When Armstrong returned from a six-month stint on the steamer St. Paul, with more money in his pocket than ever before, he headed straight for the old neighborhood. The first familiar face he encountered was that of Black Benny, gifted part-time drummer and full-time hustler, a man of great physical strength and courage, who early on became one of "Little Louis's" many protectors. He was one of the most strongly drawn figures in *Satchmo,* and clearly someone the youngster admired. Benny, happy to see his protégé, immediately made him aware that he knew about the money:

> He asked me to stand him a drink, and who was I
> to refuse the great Black Benny . . . When the drinks
> came, I noticed that everybody had ordered. I threw
> down a twenty-dollar bill to pay for the round which
> cost about six or seven bucks. When the bartender
> counted out my change Black Benny immediately
> reached for it, saying, 'I'll take it.' I smiled all over my
> face. What else could I do? Benny wanted the money

and that was that. Besides I was so fond of Benny it did not matter anyway. I do believe, however, if he had not strong-armed that money out of me I would have given him lots more. I had been thinking about it on the train coming home…But since Benny did it the hard way I gave the idea up. I sort of felt he should have treated me like a man, and I did not like the way he cut under me…So I disgustedly waited for an opening to leave, and did.

Worth quoting at length, this episode showed that Armstrong was distancing himself from his early environment. He did not pass judgment on the people among whom he was raised, but his values, even early on, clearly differed from theirs. The key difference was what used to be called character, perhaps an old-fashioned term. This also expressed itself in his lifelong adherence to an almost Calvinist work ethic, a fierce loyalty to his public, and total dedication to his music. But always in a complex manner, just as his commitment to hard work did not include self-deprivation. The music always came first, as when he explained that his fourth wife, Lucille, was the only one who understood that she could not compete with his beloved horn, and that was why their marriage was the one that lasted, for almost thirty years.

The union with Daisy was dissolving by the time Armstrong returned from that six-month riverboat trip. It had been fragile almost from the start due to Daisy's unbridled jealousy, which expressed itself in ways that threatened his livelihood, as when she threw bricks at him (a hit in the face could well have split his lips and ruined his embouchure), or his life, as when she attacked him with a kitchen knife. As luck would have it, in 1922 King Oliver sent him a telegram asking him to join the already famous Creole Jazz Band he was leading at Chicago's Lincoln Gardens.

At twenty-one years of age, Armstrong had seen a good deal of the world outside New Orleans and environs during his riverboat years. The biggest city he'd visited was St. Louis. Chicago was of another magnitude. When his train arrived late and there was no one to meet him, he was tempted to turn around and go back home, but a redcap, instructed by Oliver, spotted him and directed him to a taxi stand. When he arrived at the Lincoln Gardens and heard the band, he almost turned around again, but the doorman ushered him in, and before he knew it he was on the bandstand, horn in hand.

Louis Armstrong with Homer Hobson on the way from Chicago to New York in 1929.
Courtesy of the Institute of Jazz Studies.

King Oliver's Creole Jazz Band were not all strangers; aside from the leader, there were the Dodds Brothers, clarinetist Johnny, and drummer Baby, who had been his fellow bandsmen on the river-boats. Indeed, everyone was from New Orleans, except the pianist, Lillian Hardin. Lil, as she was known, was from Memphis, where she had studied music at Fisk University for three years, moving to Chicago in 1917 with her family and soon finding work with the transplanted New Orleanians who already were dominating the city's jazz scene. Three years older than Armstrong, pretty, lively, and up-to-date in flapper fashion (she drove her own car, which impressed Armstrong greatly, among other things) she at first saw him as a hick, but soon became aware that there was something special about him, not least from the way his colleagues viewed him.

Hiring Armstrong was a wise move by Oliver, who was aware that his protégé was better off under his wing than as a potential rival; furthermore, the two-trumpet teamwork that he initiated brought the already popular band to new musical heights. A favorite with dancers, it also attracted musicians, black and white, famous and novice, local or visiting. Among them were many who would become prime movers in the next decade, when jazz, now marketed as swing, became the dominant popular music. A case could be made for the Oliver band as the first that really did swing, not least due to the rhythmic breakthroughs of Armstrong, who also, slowly but very surely, was developing the vocabulary and syntax of jazz as a truly expressive musical art.

The year 1923 was a watershed for black jazz musicians. To be sure, they had been recorded before—the band of James Reese Europe, still primarily in the ragtime idiom, as early as 1913—but not at their most representative. But now, King Oliver, Jelly Roll Morton, and the great Bessie Smith (known as "The Empress of the Blues" but very much a jazz spirit), as well as Sidney Bechet, all came to bat. The recording process was still acoustic, with electrical just about to take over, so we will never hear what the classic Oliver band really sounded like. What we get is an inkling, but there *are* moments: Armstrong's very first solo, on "Chimes Blues"; the marvelous duet passages by him and Oliver; and, in the clearest indication of things to come, Armstrong's inspired breaks (interludes when the rest of the band drops out and only the solo voice is heard) on his own tune called "Tears," with Lil Hardin credited as co-composer.

Armstrong, never a composer on the scale of Duke Ellington, did write a number of fine pieces. The first, while still in New Orleans, he gave the strictly non-commercial title of "Get Off Katie's Head"; it was bought outright for $50—a goodly sum in 1917, but not nearly what it would earn as a hit under its published title, "I Wish I Could Shimmy Like My Sister Kate," by the local partnership of pianist-publisher Clarence Williams and violinist-bandleader Armand Piron. The composer learned his lesson, and later works were properly registered for copyright with the Library of Congress.

These early compositions are in Armstrong's hand, undoubtedly developed under the tutelage of Lil Hardin, who in February 1924 became the second Mrs. Louis Armstrong. They had been a couple for some time before that, and Lil was a significant influence. Her first goal was to get her man out from under Oliver, but Armstrong was nothing if not loyal, and it was only when she was able to prove that Oliver had been underpaying his men and, more to the point, had stated that he was keeping Louis under wraps, that he left the man amateur psychologists have suggested was a father figure. Even so, Armstrong never said a critical word about Oliver,

and steadfastly sang his praises as the most important role model of
his musical life.

Lil quickly got Armstrong a good local job, but had bigger plans
for him. She knew that Fletcher Henderson, by then the most
prominent black bandleader in New York, had met and heard Armstrong while on tour as Ethel Waters' musical director and accompa-
nist in 1922 and had tried to persuade him to join them—an offer
Armstrong refused unless his friend, drummer Zutty Singleton,
could come along. Lil now let Henderson know that Louis was available, and he was promptly sent for.

He had been instructed to join his new colleagues at a band
rehearsal, in full swing when he arrived. Henderson greeted him and
pointed to his chair in the trumpet section; finding his part and place
in the medley of Irish waltzes in progress, all went well until a passage
where the rest of the band played softly but he blasted away. Henderson stopped the music and asked the newcomer how this passage was
marked on his part. "Pp," was the answer. "Well," said the leader,
"don't you know that means pianissimo?" Without missing a beat,
Armstrong answered: "I thought it meant 'pound plenty'!"

Pandemonium ensued, and the newcomer's quick wit earned him
the respect that his attire had called into question at first glance:
though Lil had done her best to improve his provincial taste in
clothing, he still favored the thick-soled so-called policeman's shoes
popular in his hometown, while the Hendersonians were noted for
sartorial sophistication.

As previously noted, Armstrong's effect on the band's music was
profound, but only a few of the many recordings he would make with
it during his thirteen-month tenure gave him the exposure one would
have expected. This was one of the factors that eventually caused
Armstrong to give his notice, but there were others. The reason he
would usually give in later years was that his colleagues were not sufficiently serious about their music and that discipline was lax—something that affected Henderson's bands throughout his career.

But when I visited Armstrong at his home some seven months
before his death, and talk turned to Henderson, he let go with the

bitterness that shows in other late-in-life utterances. Henderson played favorites, giving trumpeter Elmer Chambers, "with his nanny-goat tone" (and here Armstrong offered a devastating but accurate vocal imitation) an equal amount of solo space; he refused to let Armstrong sing, except when the band performed for black audiences, though when given the chance, people loved it; and he was "dicty," 1920s Harlem slang for high-toned. There was a class distinction here; the son of teachers, Henderson was a college graduate who had initially come to New York to pursue graduate studies in chemistry but was soon sidetracked into music.

The singing was what particularly rubbed Armstrong the wrong way. Back in Chicago, he was in a recording studio the day after his arrival, backing a blues singer, as he had done in New York, with, among others, Bessie Smith. These freelance recordings featured him more prominently than with Henderson, and included notable encounters with Sidney Bechet, the sole instrumentalist then on a comparable level.

More significantly, he now began to record under his own name as leader of His Hot Five, a studio band (it performed live only at a couple of benefits) made up of familiar faces, all from New Orleans except Lil: Kid Ory, now in Chicago with Oliver; Johnny Dodds; and banjo and guitar player Johnny St. Cyr, who'd been a riverboat colleague. On their first session, Louis confined himself to spoken introductions of the musicians, but soon he was singing, and coming up with his first big hit, "Heebie Jeebies," on which he scatted (singing wordlessly), a style that he popularized.

Many of the numbers recorded by the Hot Five (sometimes expanded to seven with the addition of Baby Dodds's drums and a tuba) were original compositions by Armstrong and/or Lil (who had further pursued her musical studies), and they were soon also distributed in Europe. Immensely influential, they established Armstrong as the major voice, instrumental and vocal, in

TRACK 20

Louis Armstrong leads His Hot Five and sings on this 1927 recording of "I'm Not Rough."

the music called jazz that was beginning to attract worldwide attention, not only as something to dance to or be entertained by, but to be taken seriously as something new in the art of music. To be sure, Armstrong was not alone in bringing this about, but almost everyone who contributed significantly was influenced by him, now that his music could be heard (and studied, since the phonograph allowed for repetition) in all its glory.

As noted, the Hot Five/Seven were a recording unit, and most of Armstrong's time was spent in other musical environments. He was a member of the pit band at the Vendome Theater, the South Side's premiere movie palace, which also performed as a stage attraction— his feature was the "Intermezzo" from *Cavalaria Rusticana*. After the last show, he would make his way to the Sunset Cafe, where the band was under the nominal leadership of violinist Carrol Dickerson but Armstrong was the star, along with the brilliant pianist Earl Hines, who by 1928 would partner the trumpeter in a new and more modern edition of the Hot Five/Seven, producing such masterpieces as "West End Blues" and the astonishing duet on "Weather Bird," a piece Armstrong had contributed to the Oliver band.

The Sunset was managed by a man who would play a major role in Armstrong's life a bit later on. Joe Glaser came from a well-to-do Jewish family but was more interested in boxing, horse racing, and the thriving nightlife fostered by Prohibition than in studying medicine as his parents had hoped. For a while, Armstrong, Hines, and Zutty Singleton tried their hand at operating a ballroom of their own, but the result was financial disaster, and the Sunset soon had them back.

Armstrong's records were becoming sufficiently popular to give his label's artist manager, Tommy Rockwell, the bright idea of bringing him to New York to be featured in a musical slated for Broadway called *Great Day*, with an African American theme; the composer was the well-known Vincent Youmans, and Fletcher Henderson's augmented band was also involved. A few months before, Rockwell had brought Armstrong to New York to make some records, including his first of a mainstream popular song, "I Can't Give You

Anything But Love," in a departure from the repertoire usually assigned to black singers, and it was successful.

For the *Great Day* rehearsals, Rockwell wanted Armstrong alone, but characteristically, loyalty and friendship won out, and the whole band came along. As they made their way, in a little caravan of individual cars loaded with instruments, they found to their surprise that people knew and welcomed them wherever they went, which included a detour to view Niagara Falls. With proper management they could have turned the trip into a successful tour, but as it was they arrived broke in New York, with one of the cars a casualty.

Entering Rockwell's office, Armstrong cheerfully announced that he and his band had arrived and needed food, drink, lodging, and a job. Once he regained his composure Rockwell pieced together some one-night stands, but as things turned out, bringing the band along was a good move.

Great Day was a costly flop, with a paltry thirty-six performances on Broadway. By the time it opened, Armstrong was long gone from its embattled ranks. But he was on Broadway nonetheless, in the cast of a show by then well into its fourth month of a successful run. *Hot Chocolates* racked up 219 performances and could have extended that if its producers had not been so eager to take it on the road.

With a score by the already notable team of Fats Waller and Andy Razaf, *Hot Chocolates* was born at Connie's Inn, a Harlem night spot second only to the Cotton Club in the lavishness of its floorshows. It was there that Rockwell had found a spot for Armstrong and his band, in relief of the much more sedate LeRoy Smith band. When the show proved good enough for Broadway, Smith's crew was in the pit, but with the addition of Armstrong.

Originally he was featured only as an entr'acte, playing the show's hit song "Ain't Misbehavin" from the pit, but after the *New York Times*'s anonymous reviewer noted that the song's "rendition between the acts by an unnamed member of the orchestra was a high light of the premiere," he was listed in the program and soon also seen on stage as part of a trio, The Thousand Pounds of Harmony, with Waller and leading lady Edith Wilson.

Three weeks into the show's run, Armstrong was in the Okeh stu-
dios recording "Ain't Misbehavin'"; it became his first big hit, issued
not only in the "race" but also in the general series—as would all his
records from then on. Its backing, also from *Hot Chocolates*, was
"Black and Blue," sung in the show by Edith Wilson as a dark-
skinned woman's lovelorn lament but transformed by Armstrong
into what has been called the first black protest song. As such, it
(and Armstrong) is famously made emblematic of the hero's plight
in Ralph Ellison's masterful novel *Invisible Man*.

After each night's show, Armstrong taxied to Harlem to lead his
band at Connie's, and he was now in such demand that he also did
a spot in the late show at the Lafayette Theater (predecessor of the
Apollo), fortunately next door to Connie's. "Had to get my sleep
coming through the park in a cab," he recalled years later—his gift
for catnapping would stand him in good stead throughout his career.
"I was only twenty-nine years old [actually twenty-eight]. Didn't
exactly feel I had the world at my feet, but it was very nice that
everyone was picking up on the things I was doing."

Indeed, everyone was becoming aware of the genius of Louis Armstrong. His special touch caused songwriters and publishers to bring
him their wares, and for decades to come he put his stamp on what
were to become "evergreens." (Bing Crosby, who listened well, would
later call him "the beginning and the end of music in America.")

The road would appear to lead straight ahead, but there were
some bumps. He did not go on the road with *Hot Chocolates* (his
replacement was an ingénue named Cab Calloway), but in the summer of 1930 made his first visit to California, where the West Coast
version of the Cotton Club, near Hollywood, had made him a good
offer. Doing fine, making more records and becoming popular with
the movie colony, he suddenly found himself in a jam. He was fond
of marijuana, which was not yet illegal in most states but was
banned in California; and when he and the white drummer Vic
Berton shared a joint in the club's parking lot, they were busted.
Rockwell promptly sent an aide to get his star off the hook. Johnny
Collins, a bit of a roughneck, succeeded in getting the charges

dropped, but also seized the opportunity to double-cross Rockwell, convincing Armstrong to sign an exclusive management contract in order to get the job done.

While in California, Armstrong appeared as himself in *Ex-Flame*, the first of many film appearances. By early 1931, he was back in Chicago. He and his second wife were not getting along, and when he met a pretty young woman, Alpha Smith, who made it very clear that she was more than casually interested in Armstrong, the trumpeter soon set up housekeeping with Alpha and her mother, who was, he later wrote, much nicer to Clarence than were Lil and her mother.

In Chicago, Collins and Armstrong put together the first Armstrong big band proper—the previous ensembles had all been pre-existing units that he had fronted. This one included a number of fellow New Orleanians and would be remembered by its leader as the happiest of all his bands. They were having fun in a Chicago club known as the Cellar when an unwelcome visitor from New York made a sudden appearance in Armstrong's dressing room, demanding, on behalf of Rockwell and the owners of Connie's Inn, that he return promptly to fulfill a supposed contract. Armstrong demurred, but the visitor pulled a pistol and made him call Connie's and promise to take the next train to New York. Meanwhile, Collins, alerted, had enlisted some local strong-arm aid and neutralized the visitor.

The band wasted no time in leaving Chicago behind, and in what was to prove his best managerial move, Collins arranged a booking in New Orleans. Armstrong's first visit to his hometown in nine years was a triumph. It included a welcoming parade (an uncommon honor accorded at that time and place to an African American) and a cigar named for him (the Louis Armstrong Special). He sponsored a baseball team, Armstrong's Secret Nine, and of course paid a visit, with his band, to his alma mater, the Colored Waifs' Home. In a typical quick response, he did his own announcing on radio when the bigoted station employee refused to introduce him; he was so effective that he continued in that role throughout the long engagement.

There were many such breakthroughs to follow. Armstrong would break the color barrier in many venues all over the United States in the 1930s, for it was by no means only in the South that such lines were still drawn. He would also, in 1937, become the first of his race to land a sponsored radio program, *The Fleishmann Yeast Show.*

When Armstrong made his first transatlantic foray, in July 1932, he was the first jazz artist to appear as an individual star— not a bandleader or featured act in a show. He also became the first black artist to front an otherwise all-white band. That first European visit, of some three months duration, was confined to Britain, with a non-playing trip to Paris, no doubt at Alpha's behest. He received a mixed reception: enthusiasm from musicians and jazz fans (of which there was a substantial number), and puzzlement and sometimes outrage (primarily from older conservative reviewers). An amusing sidelight was a backstage visit from a delegation of classical musicians who politely asked to examine his trumpet to ascertain if it, and its mouthpiece, had not been doctored in some fashion. His virtuosity was still something not quite fathomable.

The next European interlude was of a different order. It began in August 1933, again in London, where Armstrong soon had his final break with Collins, whose crude behavior was a particular embarrassment in well-mannered England. Collins departed with Armstrong's passport (readily replaced) and dire threats that he would never work in his homeland again. (Collins had meanwhile managed to make his peace with the New Yorkers). Under a new banner, Armstrong now performed in Denmark, Sweden, Norway, and Holland to great acclaim; in Copenhagen, he was met by thousands inside and outside the train station; there was a band, a sea of flowers, and a motorcade to his hotel (in London the year before, the hotel where reservations had been made refused to honor them). He appeared in a Danish feature film, and in Stockholm there was a reception honoring him and Marian Anderson, who also happened to be in town. This was a prelude to what would become almost routine when Armstrong started touring worldwide in the 1950s.

After more British performances, Armstrong, with Alpha, took the longest vacation of his life, from April to October 1934. The couple

rented a flat in Paris and did
much "hanging out" with fellow
Americans in Paris and the
locals, such as Gypsy guitarist
Django Reinhardt, who idolized
Armstrong. Work resumed with
concerts in Paris; at the opening
show, he had to take so many
curtain calls that he had
changed into his bathrobe by the
time of the last. (An Armstrong

Louis Armstrong. Library of Congress.

performance was intensely physical; he perspired profusely and made
certain that a stack of handkerchiefs was within easy reach on stage;
there would be a complete change of clothing at intermission).

There were further concerts in Belgium and Switzerland, and
then in Italy, where, unlike Hitler's Germany, jazz was still welcomed. Then, quite suddenly, Louis and Alpha returned home in
late January 1935. There, trouble awaited. Lil sued for back maintenance, and Collins threw a wrench into a contract for a tour. The
official excuse for the lack of anticipated appearances was lip
trouble, but Armstrong was fearful that Collins, with his gangster
connections, would really damage his lips and teeth. It was then that
he decided to look up Joe Glaser, his old acquaintance from the
Sunset Cafe. Post-Prohibition, Glaser was not doing all that well,
mainly managing second-string prizefighters. There was an immediate rapport between the two men.

No contract was signed; a handshake sufficed. Glaser had ties to
Rockwell; his career as a talent agent began at a desk rented in the
office of Rockwell-O'Keefe, with Armstrong as his sole client. There
was a new band, another welcoming parade in New Orleans, setting
of salary and attendance records at Harlem's Apollo Theater, and
then a long booking at Connie's Inn and a contract with the newly
formed Decca record label, in which old admirer Bing Crosby had a
stake. When the band toured down south, Glaser was on the bus,
next to the driver, ready to handle trouble.

But there wasn't much of that any more; Armstrong was now reaching a level of recognition shared by few. The sound of his unique voice was heard on jukeboxes and radio, and his visage was becoming familiar on the movie screen. A steady stream of records, some with songs especially written for him, such as Hoagy Carmichael's "Jubilee" (featured in the 1938 Mae West film *Every Day's a Holiday*), kept fans at home and abroad happy.

Already, Armstrong kept a tough schedule. Glaser, by now with his own company, Associated Booking Corporation, specialized in black artists and soon had an impressive roster of clients, but Armstrong always came first. Glaser found it difficult to turn down any good offer, even when Armstrong and the band could clearly do with a rest, and Armstrong was committed to his public. So there were prestigious and comfortable engagements, such as record-breaking appearances at first-run movie palaces, but also stretches of one-night stands, including outdoor dances like the one Armstrong remembered because no one stopped dancing when a thunderstorm erupted.

Meanwhile, Alpha was not happy with Armstrong's long absences from the apartment they had taken on Harlem's Sugar Hill. They had married when Lil's divorce became final, in 1938, but Armstrong would later complain that all Alpha seemed to want now was furs and jewels. Thus he was not exactly devastated when she disappeared one fine day with a drummer; he had no trouble ending the relationship, legally and emotionally. Soon he met the woman who would become his fourth and final wife, dancer Lucille Wilson. They were married in 1942, and in that year Lucille surprised him with a present—a house she had bought for them in Queens. It was the first real home he'd had since Lil and Chicago, and here he would remain, even when Lucille and Glaser conspired to find something fancier.

He would agree to only a few modifications, such as modernizing the kitchen. He had his beloved upstairs den, where he would entertain friends on his rare stays at home. When you paid your first visit, he would make sure that you used the bathroom, which Lucille had outfitted with mirrors and gold-plated fixtures. He would wait for his

guest to emerge and solicit an opinion, and then offer the observation that the house in which he spent his early childhood had no
convenience to offer except the backyard. To a man who all his life
was focused on this aspect of existence—he was a firm believer in
and enthusiastic exponent of a daily laxative—this fancy bathroom
was symbolic of his rise, but with tongue firmly in cheek.

When America entered the Second World War, Armstrong
insisted on playing as many free concerts as possible for the troops—
especially for black contingents. Quite a few such performances were
recorded by Armed Forces Radio, and the enthusiastic response is
palpable. But something new was brewing in jazz, and it would go
hand in hand with changes in social attitudes, nurtured to no small
degree by the disappointing home front results of the war fought to
make the world safe for democracy.

What with travel restrictions, inroads in personnel made by the
draft, and most of all the growing popularity of singers like Frank
Sinatra and their sentimental ballads, the war years took their toll
on the big bands. The recording ban imposed by the Musicians'
Union in the summer of 1942, lasting almost two years, was anything but helpful. By 1946, many bandleaders had thrown in the
towel, at least temporarily, but Armstrong soldiered on, loathe, as he
said, to put sixteen musicians and one singer out of work.

But he was now also caught in the middle of the vociferous critical sniping in the jazz world caused by the—ironically—contempo-
raneous rise of modern jazz (soon called bebop) and rediscovery of
the music's past. One might have thought that Armstrong, given his
stature and spanning both poles, would be above the fray. But extra-
musical factors were also at work. Armstrong had never changed his
public persona of genial entertainer; it was, after all, his nature as
well as his meal ticket, and now many younger musicians and their
journalistic spokesmen were branding him an Uncle Tom, ignoring,
or ignorant of, the many doors he had opened, and dismissing his
music as passé.

Deeply wounded by what he called "the modern malice," Armstrong gave as good as he got, but outside the narrow world of jazz,

these debates had little resonance, and career changes were afoot.
Cast as himself in the film *New Orleans*, a somewhat hokey but well-
meant story based on the rise of jazz (it also starred Billie Holiday,
one of his most loyal fans), he was featured at the helm of a small
traditional band, and in a Carnegie Hall concert, presented in a similar setting. The critical response was so positive that another New
York concert was organized, this time with a hand-picked all-star
group, and again the reception was enthusiastic.

The big band was now jettisoned, and Armstrong and Glaser set
about forming what would be called the Louis Armstrong All Stars.
In the initial lineup was the great white trombonist Jack Teagarden,
who'd also just scuttled his big band. Their partnership would last
four years; the All-Star format, as long as Armstrong's life.

He applied himself to the new task, more demanding than the
big-band setting, with ferocious energy. From start to finish, he was
the star and sparkplug of the show, instrumentally and vocally, and
also as master of ceremonies. Before the group's initial year was up
he had become the first jazz musician to be featured on the cover of
Time magazine, and had been selected as King of the Zulus in his
hometown, with another warm welcome, this time for his racially
integrated band—another first, though much of the black press was
critical of Armstrong identifying himself with the traditional Mardi
Gras culture of the Zulu crowning. (This would certainly not be the
case today).

In early 1948, the All Stars made their first European visit, as the
centerpiece of the first International Jazz Festival, a new breed of
musical venue, held in Nice. By 1950, the group embarked on the
busiest touring and performing schedule of any band in the history
of jazz—or of any music, for that matter. Armstrong's worldwide
popularity rose to a level matched by few; at the time, perhaps only
by Charlie Chaplin, with Elvis and the Beatles still waiting in the
wings. The live performances, invariably sold out, were reinforced
by frequent film and television appearances and a string of hit
records, including such seemingly unlikely material as "Mack the
Knife" from the *Threepenny Opera;* "Blueberry Hill," crossing over to

country music before Fats Domino or Ray Charles; Edith Piaf's signature "La Vie en Rose," and finally and most decisively, in 1964,
"Hello Dolly," which booted the Beatles from first place on the trade
magazine charts. And there were such artistic triumphs as selections
from *Porgy and Bess*, in partnership with Ella Fitzgerald (moving Ira
Gershwin to tears); the first (and only) joint venture with Duke
Ellington, taking the piano chair with the All Stars for the occasion,
in 1962; and *The Real Ambassadors*, a kind of jazz oratorio with a
political message composed for him and the All Stars, with guests,
by Dave Brubeck in 1961.

By then, Armstrong had become so widely known as Ambassador
Satch that a New Yorker cartoon showed politicians debating
whether to send "Satchmo or John Foster Dulles" on an important
diplomatic mission. He had made his first visit to Africa in 1956, to
Ghana, where he and the All Stars were greeted by a crowd of more
than a hundred thousand, and Armstrong was delighted to encounter
a woman who reminded him of his mother; highlights were incorporated in the documentary *Satchmo the Great*, narrated by Edward R.
Murrow. (On a later African visit, civil strife was suspended in the
Congo to allow both factions to attend a huge outdoor concert.)

But in 1957, the man who had spread so much international
goodwill for his country caused the biggest headlines of his career.
Interviewed shortly after having watched, on television, the ugly
spectacle of the school crisis in Little Rock, Arkansas, Armstrong
lashed out, not only at Governor Orville Faubus, but also at President Dwight Eisenhower. At this very time, he had been frequently
mentioned as the most likely candidate for the first U.S. State
Department-sponsored visit by a jazz artist to the Soviet Union, but
now he questioned how he could defend his country to the Russians
if asked about civil rights for his people.

This was big news. Armstrong had long supported such organizations as the NAACP and the Urban League, but with checks rather
than public statements. Glaser immediately asked for a retraction;
Armstrong adamantly refused. Some right-wing columnists and
editorialists made dire predictions about the effect of this outburst

on Armstrong's career, but just a single cancelled date resulted. The Russians never did get to see Armstrong, though he would tour behind the Iron Curtain to great acclaim. Five years later, Benny Goodman, whose parents had been born there, became the first official American jazzman to tour the USSR, with an integrated band.

Armstrong's legendary capacity for work (many All Star sidemen, though well paid, could not stand the pace for more than a few years) failed him briefly in 1959. Touring Italy, he suffered what was almost certainly a heart attack, but Glaser managed to pass it off as acute indigestion, and Armstrong, quite possibly refusing to accept the facts, was soon back in harness. His dedication to his profession did not stop with the last curtain call; no matter where he performed, a table would be set up back stage, and there, having made a quick change, Armstrong would preside over a stack of photographs, armed with a green felt pen. The ritual that ensued was fascinating to watch: every fan who approached would be asked his name, and how to spell it, often resulting in jocular exchanges (Armstrong, in his prolific writings and in conversation, loved wordplay), and would leave with a personally autographed photo. Children were special favorites—Armstrong remained devoted to Clarence, had seen to that he married someone who would take good care of him, and of course supported the couple, but he longed for a child of his own and was occasionally almost fooled; Glaser sometimes had to resort to blood tests.

Armstrong's loyalty to his public expressed itself in other ways. Once, when a rainstorm had reduced the audience arriving for a Sunday afternoon performance from a potential fifteen hundred to a mere seventy-five, the house manager suggested a cancellation. Armstrong, relaxing in his dressing room, jumped to his feet. "What?" he shouted, "These folks came miles to see us in this weather and you want to send them away? We'll do a show just as if we had a full house." And that is exactly what he did. In fact, he was at his best, and his fellow musicians followed suit.

It was this dedication that caused Armstrong to make his last stand, against the advice of even his closest friends—and, unprecedentedly, some of the All Stars as well. In 1968, he had been hospitalized several times for circulatory problems; during the last of these stays, Glaser suffered a massive stroke and died in the same hospital. Not allowed to play the trumpet, he of course was able to sing, as he did at a glorious tribute at the Newport Jazz Festival on his seventieth birthday. For this milestone, there had been an outpouring of tributes, now from every corner of the jazz world, including voices that had once scorned him.

Soon after the Newport birthday party, capped by a duet with Mahalia Jackson, Armstrong took up his beloved horn again; according to a member of the All Stars, he played like a demon at the first rehearsal. His final trip abroad, fittingly to England, came late in 1970. Though not feeling well, he took on a March engagement at New York's Waldorf-Astoria, after which he suffered a heart attack. On what he believed to be his seventy-first birthday, he was seen on television, sitting up in bed at home, looking frail but sporting that smile, fingering his trumpet, singing a few bars of "Sleepy Time Down South," and promising that he would be back in action soon.

Two days later—on the morning of July 6, 1971—Louis Armstrong died in his sleep at home. Lucille did not want a big funeral, opting for the local church in Corona, Queens, but she did agree to have her husband's body lie in state at the Park Avenue Armory in Manhattan. Thousands came, from all over, to have a final look. Thousands more gathered outside the church, including musicians who had brought their horns; Armstrong had always said that when he died, he'd want "the cats to have a little blow over me." But at the service, only singing could be heard. In New Orleans, however, musicians and fans decided to have their own outdoor service, complete with parading brass bands, making the kind of music Armstrong had been so proud to participate in as a young man.

Ten years later, another young man with a horn emerged from New Orleans, coming to sudden fame with his combined jazz and classical and entrepreneurial skills. From the start, Wynton Marsalis invoked the Armstrong name with reverence and performed Armstrong music; and in his wake there were once again young black trumpeters who not only could but wanted to express the Armstrong legacy. Nothing could have pleased Louis more.

Duke Ellington

(1899–1974)

Cary D. Wintz

Duke Ellington was not raised in poverty; instead he enjoyed a stable, comfortable, and loving childhood. Ellington did not grow up in New Orleans, Memphis, Kansas City, or one of the other fabled, fertile birth- places of black music; instead he was raised in Washington, D.C., a city with little in the way of a musical tradition. He did not cut his teeth play- ing in a brothel or bar room; his first gigs were playing for private parties in Washington and its suburbs. Nevertheless, Ellington became one of the giants of jazz. Unlike Armstrong, his genius was in composition and arrangement. He had the ability to construct a song or a more complex composition around the talents of each of his orchestra members and to create a complex and original sound. More than any other musician of his day, he elevated jazz from the basement gin joint to the concert hall and made it one of the world's great musical forms.

Duke Ellington was a musician and entertainer unsurpassed in his accomplishments. He was the pianist and a bandleader for one of them most artistically creative and commercially successful jazz orchestras in the world. He was a composer of over one thousand orchestra arrangements, an opera, and several jazz concertos, as well as film scores, television productions, and even sacred music. Although born and raised in Washington, D.C., he became thoroughly a New Yorker whose music expressed the soul and the life of the city— "Take the 'A' Train," his four-year stint at the Cotton Club, and "Harlem Air Shaft" bound him to his adopted city. Ellington stood at the forefront of the cultural upheaval that was the Harlem Renaissance.

Edward Kennedy Ellington was born in Washington, D.C. into a working-class/middle-class family on April 29, 1899. Daisy Kennedy Ellington worked at times as a domestic, but devoted much of her time to her son; apparently, she had lost an earlier child at birth. His father, James Edward Ellington, was a butler, a waiter, operated a catering business, and worked as a blueprint maker. His only sibling was a sister, Ruth, born when he was sixteen years old. The Elling-

This photograph was a publicity shot of Duke Ellington taken in the early 1930s.
Courtesy of the Institute of Jazz Studies.

tons lived in the northeast section of Washington that housed "the lighter complexioned people with better type jobs" in contrast to southeast Washington, where the black working class and under classes lived. The family occupied fourteen residences in northwest Washington between 1899 and 1921, and at times money was tight, but that does not seem to have affected Ellington's childhood. Instead, he recalls that his father "always acted as though he had money, whether he had it or not. . . and he raised his family as though he were a millionaire." He also recalls that he was doted on by the women in the family. Aunts and cousins pampered and spoiled him, while his mother never took her eyes off him. So, money or not, Ellington enjoyed a childhood in a warm and loving family and had a secure home life.

Ellington's childhood was fairly typical. He did all right in school, but not great. His house was filled with music—both parents played the piano well—and he began piano lessons at about the age of seven, but was not the prodigy some say he was. Of his music lessons, Ellington admits that he "missed more than I took." His love was baseball, not music, and when the inevitable recital came, he was the only student who could not play his part. As a youth, art interested him more than music, and instead of an academic high school program, he enrolled in, but did not graduate from, the commercial art program at the Armstrong Manual Training School. Other youthful activities were fairly typical, although they likely would have shocked his conservative mother. At the age of twelve Ellington and his friends began to sneak into the local burlesque house, an activity Ellington maintained provided him his first instruction in the methods of the entertainment industry. Two years later he became a regular at the neighborhood pool hall, learning skills that years later helped him survive in New York. Typical of Ellington, even his small sins had a practical aspect to them.

About this time, Ellington gained the nickname "Duke" from his schoolmates, likely because of his self-assurance and regal bearing. Also, his attention returned to music, especially the new ragtime sound that was popular among the younger set. When he was fourteen, he heard pianist Harvey Brooks play in Philadelphia and was enthralled. He again took up the piano, determined to imitate his idol. He had no formal training. Instead he hung around and watched piano players, picked the brains of local musicians, and tried to copy their techniques. Ellington recalled that "back in those days, if you were a constant listener and hanger-on like I was, any piano player in D.C. was wide open and approachable. If you were to ask any one of them something like, 'How did you do that, that you just played?' they would stop doing whatever they were doing and play it again while I watched and listened to it and its explanation." Then he spent time at home playing around on the piano, trying to remember his old lessons and attempting to replicate the techniques and sounds he heard around town.

As he improved, his friends cajoled him into playing at their parties, and he discovered that the piano player was popular, especially with the girls. There was always a pretty girl hanging around the piano. Now that he was playing in public, he had to learn more so he would not embarrass himself. Always in a hurry to get better, he tried to learn through shortcuts, looking for ways to create impressive effects without extensive study. Music took up more and more of his time. He put together a small band with his friends, and by the age of sixteen or seventeen he began playing an occasional professional job, usually at someone's party; not jazz (still largely unknown), but rags and popular songs.

At seventeen he composed his first song, playing around on the piano at home. "The Soda Fountain Rag" (he had worked for a time as a soda jerk) reflected his interest in ragtime and especially the influence of the work of his favorite musicians, James P. Johnson and Will Marion Cook. One of Ellington's friends invited him over and put a roll of Johnson's new hit, "Carolina Shout," on his player piano. They slowed the apparatus down so Ellington "could see which keys on the piano were going down as I digested Johnson's wonderful sounds. I played with it until I had his 'Carolina Shout' down pat." Ellington then performed the song around town. When Johnson came to do a concert at the Washington Convention Hall, Ellington was pushed on stage by his friend to challenge Johnson with his own song. Johnson played along and applauded Ellington's efforts and after the concert took Ellington as his guide as he made the rounds of Washington's joints.

By 1918, Ellington's first professional band, The Duke's Serenaders, Colored Syncopaters, was getting steady work playing jobs around Washington. As his reputation grew, he worked harder to hone his skills and he learned to read music. As steady money began to come in he dropped out of the Armstrong Manual Trade School to pursue music full time. He also operated a sign-painting business, often painting and printing the posters and announcements for the customers who hired his band. In 1918, he moved out of his parents' home into his own apartment and even installed a telephone to hustle business for the band. In July 1918 he married his neighborhood sweetheart Edna Thompson (both sets of parents thought their child had married beneath their status); in March 1919, Edna gave birth to their only surviving child, Mercer Kennedy Ellington.

With a family to support, the business side of music became essential. Music was an occupation where blacks, especially those like Ellison who did not have a college education, could earn fame and a good living. The band at this time consisted of saxophonist Otto (Toby) Hardwick and trumpet player Arthur Whetsol, both friends from Washington; New Jersey drummer Sonny Greer, with whom Ellington had played during his high school years; and Baltimore banjoist Elmer Snowden, who was the leader of the band. This group would be the nucleus of Ellington's later bands, including the Washingtonians who played at the Kentucky Club in New York. This band emerged from his playing at high school parties when he was in his early teens and evolved into a moneymaking enterprise under Snowden's leadership. By 1919 Ellington was doing well enough to buy a house and a car.

The year 1923 was a major turning point for Duke Ellington and the band. In February, Sonny Greer received a job offer in vaudeville that included Ellington and Otto Hardwick. Ellington took the gamble. He left his wife and son, his home, his secure income, and the contacts he had made for the uncertainties and the possibilities of New York. On March 3, 1923, they joined vaudeville entertainer Wilber Sweatman's band for a one-week show at Harlem's Lafayette Theater as part of an "all-star" vaudeville show. After several other gigs with Sweatman's band, they declined his offer to join a multicity tour. They would seek their fortune in New York.

Lacking contacts, work was almost impossible to find. Ellington recalled that he and Sonny Greer spent their days mostly hustling pool games for money. "We might start with a quarter. The minute we got two dollars, we'd quit, go home, dress up, order two steak dinners, give the girl a quarter, and have a quarter left for tomorrow." In the evenings they hunted for work in the clusters of nightclubs that had opened in Harlem, and went cabareting. At night they slept in the apartment of one or another of their relatives or family friends.

While they failed to find work, Ellington's charm, snappy dress, and good looks made the group popular among the more established musicians. One of Harlem's top pianists, Willie "The Lion" Smith befriended Ellington and his band and showed them the ropes—taking them along on his jobs, and to the bars and joints and all-night parties that always followed the gigs. Ellington learned more about the music business and sharpened his musical skills, but steady work eluded the band. Smith also introduced them to the house rent party scene. This brought them some work. As Ellington recalled, every Saturday night they could play a house rent party, get all the food they could eat, and earn one dollar.

After a month or so with no steady work, growing bored rather than desperate, Ellington found fifteen dollars lying on the street. "We had a square meal, got on the train, and went back to Washington to get ourselves together before we tried it again."

The New York that Ellington visited in the spring of 1923 was just entering the Harlem Renaissance. Already it was becoming a center of black music, entertainment, and literature. In 1921 Noble Sissle and Eubie Blake's *Shuffle Along* had launched the African American musical review and taken black shows to Broadway. By 1923, contemporaries of Ellington like Langston Hughes and Countee Cullen were making a name for themselves in poetry.

Music was a fundamental part of the Harlem Renaissance. It touched almost all aspects of the literary and artistic creativity of the period. Black writers and artists frequented the clubs and joints, and also events like the house rent parties where musicians worked and played. Some, like Langston Hughes, James Weldon Johnson, and Wallace Thurman, used music in their art, as either the background or setting for their writing or incorporated in the subject and structure of their art. Without question the writers and artists knew

Harlem's musicians and entertainers, and the majority of them were great fans of their work.

However, the relationship between the musicians and the literary side of the Renaissance was not so close. As Cab Calloway wrote in his autobiography, "Those of us in the music and entertainment business were vaguely aware that something exciting was happening, but we weren't directly involved . . . the two worlds, literature and entertainment, rarely crossed."

By June 1923, Ellington and his group were back in Harlem. This time the promised job had come to them through Fats Waller, but when they arrived, it too had fallen through. Again they hit the streets looking for work. Their break came when they got a job at Barron Wilkin's Exclusive Club on 134th Street and Seventh Avenue. Barron's was a swanky private club that catered to blacks and whites equally, provided that they had money and were willing to spend it. Ellington and the band were hired to play "under conversation" music—quiet music that would not interfere with conversation—certainly not jazz. Because the 6'1" Ellington was a "handsome and commanding" figure and the band were nice middle-class boys, they were well liked by the well-heeled upper-class clientele. With salary and tips they were making enough money for Ellington to rent a room and send for Edna, his wife.

In the summer of 1923, Ellington learned much about the music business in New York, especially how to make money from it. The ambitious Ellington had good business sense, and worked hard to sell himself and his talent. First, he discovered that anyone could submit a song to the music publishers. Ellington teamed up with a lyricist, Joe Trent, and they spent their afternoons going from office to office auditioning their songs. Although their efforts rarely paid off, they did sell a song or two, and overnight they wrote an entire show, *Chocolate Kiddies*, which became a hit in Germany. These experiences fueled Ellington's determination to become a songwriter.

In July 1923 Ellington made his first record, as a member of Elmer Snowden's five-piece Novelty Orchestra. The recording was never released, but it opened another opportunity for the ambitious

This is an early photograph of Duke Ellington and the Washingtonians taken circa 1923 while the band was playing at the Kentucky Club at 49th and Broadway in Manhattan. Left to right, the band members are Sonny Greer, Charlie Irvis, Otto Hardwicke, Elmer Snowden, Bubber Miley, and Duke Ellington.
Courtesy of Institute of Jazz Studies.

Ellington. A month later, this time leading his own band, he made his first radio broadcast, on station WDT, playing backup for a blues singer. He also cashed in on the growing popularity of black nightclubs. While continuing to play for Barron's, Ellington took a daytime job as a rehearsal pianist at the newly opened Connie's Inn, another swanky club that catered to a white clientele, and was famous for the elaborate musical revues that it staged—several of which, like its 1929 hit *Hot Chocolates*, moved on to Broadway. Ellington paid close attention and learned everything he could about musical revues.

The band's success at Barron's brought them a job at the Kentucky Club, a new spot in the theater district at 49th and Broadway. The band, still headed by Snowden, received a lucrative six-month contract. They opened in September 1923, and would play there almost continuously for four years. Significantly for the development of the band, this job was not to play under conversation music, but the new hot music—jazz. This required the band to develop a new sound, which they borrowed from other bands and imported through new personnel.

The most notable addition to the band was trumpet player James "Bubber" Miley, who had adapted his technique from "King" Oliver of New Orleans. Miley set the style for the new band with his use of the plunger for the wah-wah technique, and the unique growl sound he produced through his throat. Under his influence the band changed from a sweet-sounding dance band to a hard-driving, soulful blues sound. Miley didn't use his distinctive effects as a novelty; he made them central to the melody, producing what Ellington termed the band's jungle style.

Through late 1923 and early 1924, the band continued to grow as it added personnel and instruments, including a trombone and a tuba, which gave them a still more robust sound. The most important personnel change came in February 1924 when the band's leader, Elmer Snowden, was forced out for cheating the band out of a portion of their money. Ellington was elected the new bandleader.

The Kentucky Club, originally the Hollywood Club, was a very good place for the band to build its reputation. The club, located in a basement, was rather dingy but it was strategically located near Times Square and the major Broadway theaters. Because it was open all night it became an after-hours hangout for musicians and those interested in music. The band worked very hard, generally playing dance music until midnight, then playing backup at midnight and again at 2:00 a.m. for comedians and vocalists. After the rest of the band departed, Ellington and drummer and vocalist Greer would remain, Ellington playing the piano and Greer working the tables for tips. In this setting Ellington became expert in knowing how to please his audience.

During the four years at the Kentucky Club, the band grew, evolved, and expanded its audience. In 1924, it added trombonist Charlie Irvis, an accomplished musician with a sound that matched well with Miley's trumpet techniques. Two years later Ellington replaced Irvis with another trombonist, Joe "Tricky Sam" Nanton, who applied growl sounds and muting techniques similar to those used by Miley.

As the band evolved, Ellington's control over it increased to the point that it ceased to be a band of equals that Ellington led, and became instead Ellington's band. As he assumed control, two elements in his leadership style emerged that became central to the band's success and its character.

Ellington was far more talented as a composer than as a piano player, but it was as a piano player that he first achieved musical success in Washington. This photograph was a publicity shot taken for the 1929 movie *Black and Tan*, which featured Duke Ellington playing himself. Courtesy of the Institute of Jazz Studies.

The first element was discipline. This could be seen in the band from its earliest days in New York when the players were noted for being meticulously and fashionably dressed. Any member who diverged from that style was quickly brought into line. More importantly, the band was always well rehearsed. Most other small bands played from published standardized arrangements, or played loose, improvising on the spot. Ellington's performances were always carefully arranged through a collaborative give-and-take, until each participant was satisfied with the sound and understood his role in the arrangement. Finally, Ellington exerted discipline over individual behavior. He expected band members to be as committed as he was. This meant that they had to be punctual for rehearsals, performances, and recording sessions, and their drinking and other personal behavior could not interfere with the band's performance or its relationship to its audience or its employers. Ellington did not seem to fire anyone directly. But anyone whose behavior became detrimental to the band did not last long.

TRACK 21

Under Irving Mills' management, Duke Ellington and the Kentucky Club Orchestra grew famous and recorded dozens of songs including this November 1926 recording of "The Creeper," with Bubber Miley on trumpet and Sonny Greer on drums.

Ellington's second characteristic was collaboration. While he was the band's leader, and as time passed more and more in control, and while he received most of the credit and fame from the band's success, working with Ellington was a collaborative process. Ellington had the ability as a bandleader to structure his compositions and arrangements to bring out the strengths and best qualities of each band member. As the personnel of the band changed, so did its sound and its flavor. This was clearly evident in the way that Miley altered the sound of the band, as did trombonists Irvis and Nanton in turn. It was also true in the composition of original music. Ellington usually received the credit, but the details of a composition, and sometimes the original idea, involved one or more band members.

The exact nature of this relationship was complex and difficult to analyze. As record producer Irving Townsend described it, "all who were close to Duke [became] extensions of himself...Each, in an odd way, personified a part of the Ellington personality." Biographer John Edward Hasse suggested that perhaps it was the band members and associates who completed Ellington or balanced his personality traits, like the earthy sounds of Miley and Nanton balanced Ellington's urbane smoothness.

The band's reputation grew from its performances at the Kentucky Club as well as from performances in other venues, either before their nightly show, or touring during the summers, or during the frequent hiatuses when the club closed for several weeks for repairs following one of its "insurance fires," or when it was padlocked for a month or so by the city for liquor or other violations. Ellington took advantage of these opportunities to play in New England or at other New York spots. His band's growing reputation filled the Kentucky Club. On most nights at 3:00 a.m. it was impossible to get a seat, and the standing-room-only crowds made it impossible to dance.

By the mid 1920s, the Washingtonians was a good band, but not a great one. Likewise, their recordings were good but not great. During the second half of the decade changes occurred that elevated the band into the top ranks. Central to the band's ascension was Ellington's relationship with Irving Mills.

Irving Mills began working in New York's music world prior to World War I. By 1919, he had partnered with his brother and established a music publishing house. Mills was noted for finding and identifying unknown but talented composers. Ellington recalled that he operated a business buying blues songs from composers who could find no other buyers.

"He was known as the last resort for getting some money by those who had been peddling songs all day without success. I first heard of him secondhand, and one day I joined a group of five or six songwriters. The personnel varied, but they would get together, each with a lead sheet of what they considered rather ordinary blues under his arm, and head for Mills Music." The procedure, Ellington explained, "was to sell those blues outright to Irving Mills for fifteen or twenty dollars. It was very simple—no hassle. Just give him the lead sheet, sign the outright release, pick up the money, and go."

Of course musicians exploited the system, sometimes repeatedly selling the same composition. However, when Mills recorded one of the blues songs he had bought and made money on it, the seller inevitably protested that Mills had cheated him.

Ellington recalled that he first met Mills in 1923 within the first six months following his arrival in New York. Mills frequented the Kentucky Club. One night, Ellington recalled, Mills said "he didn't know what we were doing with our music, but he liked it and would like to record some of it with our band. We jumped at the chance."

The process was very simple. Mills would request that Ellington have four numbers ready for recording the next morning at 9:00 a.m., and Ellington would stay up at night composing. This happened about once a week, but sometimes three or four times in a week. Ellington loved the arrangement. He enjoyed composing and recording, he liked the fame and publicity it generated, and of course he liked the royalties it generated. Most of all, as Ellington observed, "I was getting my kicks writing and recording, and some of my tunes were beginning to show up well in the sales department . . . I was in the environment I wanted to live in."

For the first recording, Mills signed the group to a contract with Vocalion, a major record label. Mills insisted that Ellington record his own compositions. Some critics have suggested that Ellington's band performed best when working on their own compositions, and this may have influenced Mills's position, but both also made more money when Ellington recorded his own music. For the first Vocalion project in late November 1926, Ellington used four of his own compositions, including one of his standards, "East St. Louis Toodle-Oo." This is considered the most significant of his early recordings.

The Vocalion contract was just the beginning. Mills negotiated other record contracts for Ellington with major companies such as Victor and Columbia, and he published Ellington's songs through

Mills Music. In 1927 Mills arranged thirty-one recordings for Ellington, more than twice as many as he had previously recorded. In 1928 Ellington and Mills formalized their relationship. After leading the band and managing its affairs for four years, Ellington negotiated a management deal with Mills. Mills would assume responsibility for promoting, booking, and managing Ellington and the band. In return he received 45 percent of the earnings, and his attorney received another 10 percent.

While the percent of the earnings that went to Mills was unusual, the deal was not as one-sided as it appears. First, Ellington received a share of some of Mills's other operations, although it is clear that Ellington did not make as much money from Mills as Mills did from Ellington's activities. Second, the contract consolidated Ellington's control over the band. Ellington and Mills negotiated the contract and all business communication was between the two of them. Other band members either accepted the arrangement or left the band. While there was significant change in band personnel during the late 1920s and 1930s, the contractual relationship does not seem to have been a factor.

Most importantly, Mills guided Ellington's career during the key period during the late 1920s and the 1930s when Duke Ellington emerged as one of the most highly acclaimed musicians and orchestra leaders in the world, and also one of the greatest and most successful entertainers. In addition to the record contracts, Mills arranged a series of very lucrative tours. Both of these activities increased the band's visibility and the market for its music. Mills also brought a high level of professionalism to the band's operations. The tours were well organized; each band member had a full itinerary of transportation arrangements, hotels, and rehearsal and performance times. Mills also worked effectively to break down color barriers and provide the band with opportunities heretofore unavailable to blacks.

Another contribution that Mills made was as a master of publicity. He was one of the very early flacks in the entertainment industry. He excelled in bringing Ellington to public attention and getting him visibility and press coverage. One phase of this campaign was to recast both Ellington and jazz, taking jazz out of the basement joints and brothels, altering its reputation as lower-class black musical form and promoting it as sophisticated, serious music, and transforming Ellington into a composer of equal talent and accomplishment as the European classical composers. Jazz would be America's contribution to the musical world, and Ellington would be its Beethoven.

Of course, none of this would have been possible if Ellington had lacked the talent, the determination, or the character necessary for success. Both men profited. Ellington would face criticism for his reliance on Mills (the Reverend Adam Clayton Powell called Ellington a "musical sharecropper"), and the two parted ways in 1939. Ellington never provided any details on the breakup, but he did acknowledge that Mills had served him well: "In spite of how much he made on me, I respected the way he had operated. He always preserved the dignity of my name. Duke Ellington had an unblemished image, and that is the most anybody can do for anyone." Mercer Ellington credited Mills with guiding his father well during the formative years of his career.

Perhaps the most significant change that occurred early in Mills's association with Ellington was the shift of the band's home base from the Kentucky Club uptown to Harlem and the Cotton Club. After four years at the Kentucky Club, Ellington and his band did not return there after their summer tour. Instead, perhaps because of Mills's influence, they took a series of engagements at other performance venues and for several musical revues. These performances raised their visibility and generated increasingly favorable reviews by the New York press. Then, in late fall, the Cotton Club hired Ellington and his band as their house band.

Exactly how this happened is not clear. One story argued that following a performance at Harlem's Lafayette Theater, the general manager of the Cotton Club persuaded Ellington to fill the vacancy there. Other sources suggest that Mills arranged the job. Others suggest that the gangsters who ran the club made Ellington "an offer he could not refuse." Ellington himself reported that the band was required to audition for the job along with six other bands. Whatever the process, Ellington and his band opened at the Cotton Club on December 4, 1927, and stayed there for four years.

In 1927, the Cotton Club was the most famous nightclub in New York City, if not the entire United States. It was noted for three things: its mobster owner Owen Madden, who opened the club after serving a prison term for manslaughter and made it the star of New York nightlife and the hub of his distribution center for bootleg beer and whiskey; the strict "whites only" policy that imposed a color line in the heart of Harlem; and the quality of the music and entertainment, which not only included Ellington's band but also a chorus line of beautiful, light-skinned African American women.

During Ellington's time there the club featured a jungle look and Africa-inspired sets, which together with the jungle sounds that Ellington brought to his music offended some black leaders. While Ellington's band featured a wild and raucous form of jazz and performed songs like "The Harlem River Quiver" that incorporated the club's jungle theme, the tuxedo-clad musicians and the stately, impeccably dressed Ellington clearly set themselves apart from the Africa-inspired ambiance.

The Cotton Club also required changes to Ellington's band. The contract required a band of at least eleven musicians (instead of the six or seven the band had used previously). This led to richer, more complex orchestration, with the addition of clarinet, trombone, saxophone, and a singer. It also triggered changes in band personnel, both to improve the sound and increase its professionalism. Most notably, in early 1929, Ellington replaced lead trumpet player Bubber Miley with Cootie Williams, reportedly because of Miley's drinking and absenteeism, especially at critical times. Although Miley had been central to the band's sound and its early success, Williams brought a similar sound, including the throaty growl, and became one of the band's most reliable, serious, and sober members.

Rather than stereotyping or tainting him as the "white man's musician," the Cotton Club engagement accelerated Ellington's development as a premier bandleader and composer, and made the band the most popular jazz band in the United States—among both whites and blacks. The band expanded its audience base by continuing to turn out records under the direction of Irving Mills, and by capitalizing on the fame and recognition that radio broadcasts brought to them. In 1927, Columbia Broadcasting System (CBS) began broadcasting Cotton Club shows. By the end of the decade, these nightly half-hour broadcasts were carried coast to coast by the emerging CBS network. The Cotton Club, already the most famous Harlem cabaret, now became all of America's entertainment as it entered homes across the country. Duke Ellington became a broadcast celebrity among both black and white jazz lovers—the Cotton Club was segregated, but the radio broadcasts were colorblind.

The Cotton Club era stimulated some of Ellington and the band's most notable compositions. Earlier compositions like "East St. Louis Toodle-Oo," which became a standard, and especially "Black and Tan Fantasy," which around 1928 became the band's unofficial theme song, became closely associated with the Cotton Club act. New compositions were added to the band's play list: "The Mooch," "Cotton Club Stomp," "Creole Love Call" (a hit vocal for the band's singer, Adelaide Hall), and most of all "Mood Indigo" typified the growing sophistication and popularity of Ellington's music. Music critics began to take notice.

Ellington's method for creating music was distinctive. He did not follow the standard process for musical composition. Instead he would come to the recording studio or rehearsal session with unfinished ideas, small pieces of music, and together with the band play around with them until the sound he was after emerged. The process was one of collaboration between Ellington and the band, and it linked composition to the particular skills of each band member. The result was a structured composition—one in which even the spaces for individual improvisation, spontaneity, and solos, so central to jazz performance, were constructed into the piece that in turn was custom-designed for the players in the band.

This process evolved during the late 1920s into what some have termed composition by controlled or directed improvisation. The group's compositions and recordings in the late 1920s, written specifically for their personnel, established their distinctive sound. For example, the sound of "East St. Louis Toodle-Oo" was defined largely by Bubber Miley, whose trumpet work provided the minor theme. "Black and Tan Fantasy" again used Miley in the minor key. This work, which utilizes a small segment of Chopin's "Funeral March," was cited by music critics for elevating jazz to a more sophisticated level and as an example of complex and intentional composition rather than improvising. It was one of the pieces that caused scholars to begin to look more seriously at Ellington as an artist rather than a mere jazz musician or leader of a dance band.

As Ellington approached his thirtieth birthday he was on top of the world. His career was advancing spectacularly, and he was earning enough money to move his family into a luxury apartment at 381 Edgecombe Avenue, in the heart of Sugar Hill.

His personal life was not going so smoothly. Ellington was always a ladies' man, and never had any problem finding a willing lover. In the late 1920s, his marriage with Edna faded away. They had been drifting apart for years, and both had affairs. The precipitating event was a fight in 1929 that ended when Edna slashed Ellington's cheek with a knife or a razor. The couple separated, but never divorced or remarried. Although Ellington would declare "music is my mistress," he had long-term relationships with two women over the years, and countless short-term affairs. Ellington biographer Hasse quoted Mercer Ellington about the breakup of his parents' marriage: "I came home from school one day and there was a strange woman living with my father and taking care of me and Ruth. My mother it turned out had moved . . . They separated without telling us." Mercer was ten years old at the time; Ruth, Ellington's young sister, was fourteen and living in the household. Ellington's new lover was Mildred Dixon, a member of one of the Cotton Club's featured dance duos.

Nine years later, as he neared the age of forty, Ellington again changed his household. In 1938 he took up with Beatrice (Evie)

Ellis, another younger beauty from the Cotton Club. This time he moved out, leaving behind the apartment at 381 Edgecombe Avenue that he shared with Mildred, Mercer (who was now in high school), and Ruth (who was attending Columbia Teachers College). He also left behind all of his clothes and the furniture and moved into Evie's apartment on St. Nicholas Place. Ruth and Mercer, realizing their father was not coming back, took their own place at 409 Edgecombe; Evie and Duke moved around the corner in 1939 to the apartment at 935 St. Nicholas Avenue that they would occupy until 1953. Although Ellington would take several lovers over the years, he would live with Evie until his death at the age of seventy-five.

In the 1930s, Ellington reached the pinnacle of his success as a musician, orchestra leader, and composer. By 1930, Ellington's relationship with the Cotton Club began to change. In 1927, when Ellington arrived at the Cotton Club, the club itself was the draw; Ellington was simply part of the entertainment. By 1930, however, it was Ellington the crowds came to see, at the Cotton Club or wherever he played. With this popularity as a base, Ellington and Mills moved to expand Ellington's career and especially to broaden the type of music that they produced. Mills set the stage for this process with a sophisticated marketing and publicity campaign that downplayed race and emphasized the classical and artistic quality of Ellington's music. They dropped references to "primitive" and "race" music, and instead marketed Ellington as a genius whose music was of the same artistic quality as that of classical European composers.

The results of this campaign were spectacular. In 1931, Ellington left the Cotton Club, and for the rest of his career he would work as a touring artist and recording star. On the road he performed some one-night stands, but the typical engagement was a week or more, usually in theaters, nightclubs, or hotel ballrooms. Mills arranged the bookings and the itinerary and traveled with the band, taking care of all details. One of their first major engagements was in Chicago for a week at the Oriental Theater. Ellington sold out the 3,200 seat theater (which grossed $49,000 for the week, a near record), and the band received rave reviews from the Chicago press. The band then went on a fourteen-week tour for the Publix Theater chain for $3,500 a week plus travel expenses (that is $46,398 per week in 2006 dollars). The National Broadcasting System (NBC) followed with a ten-week tour of the central states, with live broadcasts wherever possible. Before the year was up the band did three more stints at Chicago's Oriental Theater, performing to an estimated 400,000 there during the year.

Clearly, 1931 was a breakthrough year for the band. Not only were their audiences and earnings up, but they also had undermined racial barriers, opening the door for other African American performers. *The Chicago Defender*, one of the most prestigious African American newspapers, noted that Ellington performed throughout Chicago before enthusiastic audiences in venues previously reserved for white performers.

While Ellington continued to make recordings during this period, and his recordings sold well, they did not capture the evolution of Ellington's music or Ellington as an entertainer as effectively as did the live performances. With the help of Mills, Ellington created stage performances that combined elements of a concert with those of a musical revue. The band was always carefully dressed, often in white tuxedos. Ellington brought forth the dignity of an orchestral conductor. Always handsome, he dressed exquisitely. In February 1932, a San Francisco newspaper reporter described him as "handsome in his square shouldered double breasted blue suit, with maroon tie and pencil striped soft shirt, glistening black hair slicked back, a wisp of a mustache, diamond ring and gold cuff links as his only bits of flash." The stage shows included the band and its music (many compositions were performed live for years before they were recorded) and other acts. Popular dancer Earl "Snake Hips" Tucker and dancer and later actress Fredi Washington were regulars, as were tap dancing acts, and of course, vocalists. In 1932, *Fortune* magazine noted the incredible popular success of Ellington, especially in light of the fact that jazz did not generally have a large popular audience. The magazine credited Ivie Anderson, the band's regular vocalist, and acts like

"Snake Hips" Tucker for part of the success, but concluded "there can be little doubt Ellington's success is mainly due to his music itself."

In 1933 Mills arranged for the band's first European tour—to England, Holland, and France. The tour was a success. English audiences and critics were savvier about jazz than were Americans, and they were enthusiastic about the quality of Ellington's music. Music scholars wrote about Ellington and American jazz in their journals as a serious music form. All of this reinforced Mills's efforts to cast Ellington as a serious musical talent, and the accolades the band received in Europe helped establish this. Even before Ellington left for Europe, some American scholars had begun to take his music seriously. A year earlier, Percy Grainger, a prominent composer and professor of music at New York University, invited Ellington to perform for his music appreciation class and compared his music to that of Delius and Bach; a year later the New York School of Music named Ellington's "Creole Rhapsody" the best composition of the year.

During the 1930s and 1940s, as Ellington pursued more serious music, his compositions became longer and more complex. His 1931 composition, "Creole Rhapsody," was his first effort at a symphonic piece. In the mid 1930s he also began to record a series of concertos he composed featuring various instrumentalists from his orchestra. Among the best were "Echoes of Harlem" (1935), featuring Cootie Williams, and the following year, "Clarinet Lament," with Barney Bigard. This process would culminate when he premiered his forty-four-minute opus, "Black, Brown, and Beige" at Carnegie Hall in 1943. The piece celebrated the history of African Americans. While the concert was sold out and there was great fanfare leading up to the performance, the piece received mixed reviews. Some critics argued that Ellington lacked the formal training in music theory and composition needed to tie together all the themes in a symphonic piece. "Black, Brown, and Beige" was never performed again in its entirety. Ellington, though disappointed by this reception, continued his pursuit of "serious" music.

The band also altered its personnel during the 1930s. The first major change was the addition of Ivie Anderson as a vocalist when the band left the Cotton Club. Until then the band had consisted only of instrumentalists. However, while at the Cotton Club they had regularly worked with female singers, and band members were pressed into singing when vocals were required. More personnel changes occurred in 1939. Following the death of bassist Jimmy Blanton, Ellington brought in tenor saxophonist Ben Webster—the first time he had a major tenor soloist in the band. Ellington and Irving Mills also ended their business relationship that year. More significantly Billy Strayhorn, a young composer with formal training, joined the entourage. Strayhorn's first contribution was one of the orchestra's signature pieces, "Take the 'A' Train." Ellington and Strayhorn would become close friends, and from this point until the composer's death in 1967, most of Ellington's body of work would be written in collaboration with Strayhorn.

In many ways Ellington and his band hit their peak in the 1930s. While the band, under Ellington's direction, would continue to perform until 1974, and while they would remain successful by both commercial and artistic measures, they gradually lost their cutting edge and dropped back into the pack of popular bands. This would begin in the late 1930s when swing music elevated other bands to higher levels of popularity. Following World War II other changes in musical tastes, especially in popular music, left Ellington behind. Time also took a toll on the band itself as age, death, retirement, or simply road-weariness removed key musicians from the mix.

Throughout the 1950s and 1960s Ellington continued to compose, record, and tour. His career enjoyed something of a comeback following an inspired performance at the 1956 Newport Jazz Festival, and the album that followed, *Ellington at Newport*, became the bestselling album of his career. For the next decade he composed and recorded over 200 songs, worked on movie soundtracks, and continued a grueling schedule of live performances and television appearances. In addition to continuing to expand on his traditional repertoire and explore more classically oriented composition, he also branched out into a new genre, sacred music. On September 16, 1965, he premiered work commissioned by the Grace Cathedral of San Francisco. The resulting

"Concert of Sacred Music" was largely drawn from his earlier "Black, Brown, and Beige," but the new opening section, "In the Beginning, God," won the Grammy that year for best original jazz composition.

Over the next several years Ellington experienced both triumph and loss. In 1966, Edna Ellington, still his legal wife, died and was buried in Washington, D.C. A year later, Billy Strayhorn, only fifty-one years old, died after a two-year struggle with cancer. This loss of his close friend and collaborator impacted Ellington more than any deaths other than those of his parents. In 1965, financial constraints had forced him to furlough half of his band while the other half performed on the small stage at Rainbow Grill in New York's Rockefeller Center. This was the first time band members were removed from the payroll for financial reasons. Also in 1965, Ellington and his orchestra had performed at the White House Festival of the Arts, the following year he received the President's Gold Medal, and in 1968 President Johnson named him to the National Council on the Arts. In all, Ellington visited the Johnson White House seven times. In 1969, President Nixon hosted a White House party celebrating Ellington's seventieth birthday, and capped the evening by awarding Ellington the Presidential Medal of Freedom, the highest honor that the United States government can bestow on a civilian.

In January 1973, Ellington was diagnosed with lung cancer. He continued to tour with the band throughout the year. In March 1974, he had to leave the band while it was on tour and check into a hospital. He continued to work on several projects from his hospital bed, including the composition of an opera and editing his "Third Sacred Concert." Duke Ellington died on May 24, 1974, just after his seventy-fifth birthday.

Ellington's funeral brought out thousands of fans and friends. Sixty-five thousand viewed his body, and more than 12,000 crowded into his funeral at the Cathedral of St. John the Devine. Statements of grief came from across the country. President Nixon referred to him as "America's greatest composer."

Following his father's death, Mercer Ellington took over the band and directed it for more than two decades until his own death in

1996. He worked diligently to keep his father's name and music alive. His efforts, though laudable, were not necessary. Accolades and awards continued to bring honor to Duke Ellington and his music. In 1999, a worldwide celebration of Ellington commemorated the centennial of his birth. A year later he won two Grammies, including one presented to *The Duke Ellington Centennial Edition— The Complete RCA Victor Recordings, 1927–1973* as best historical jazz album.

What was Ellington's impact on the Harlem Renaissance? Like Claude McKay, Langston Hughes, Jacob Lawrence, and other Harlem Renaissance writers and artists, Ellington used his creativity to express the black experience, and in doing so he used Harlem as a setting for his work and celebrated Harlem as the African American metropolis. Of his many works about Harlem that Ellington and his band played, none expressed his personal connection to Harlem better than "Take the 'A' Train," (which was written by his collaborator Billy Strayhorn) celebrating the express subway from downtown to Harlem:

> You must take the "A" train
> To get to Sugar Hill way up in Harlem

However, Ellington's influence extended far beyond the Harlem Renaissance, Harlem, and even the United States. Ellington was an internationally acclaimed musician and composer whose talents and accomplishments were recognized around the world. But perhaps his greatest influence was on African American youth. Novelist Ralph Ellison, who had gone to college at Tuskegee on a music scholarship, had a clear and thoughtful understanding of exactly what Ellington brought to music, as well as his significance to the African American community. In an essay that he wrote in 1969, "Homage to Duke Ellington on His Birthday," Ellison recalled being a black teenager in Oklahoma City listening to Ellington's music on a scratchy old phonograph. The music was both familiar and strange.

Familiar because beneath the stylized jungle sounds (the like of which no African jungle had ever heard) there sounded the blues, and strange because the mutes, toilet plungers, and derby hats with which I was acquainted as a musician had been given a stylized elegance and extension of effect unheard of even in the music of Louis Armstrong. It was as though Ellington had taken the traditional instruments of Negro American music and modified them, extended their range, enriched their tonal possibilities.

Ellison noted that he and his friends loved jazz and the blues even though in school their teachers critiqued it as inferior to the great European musical tradition. Jazz and the blues spoke directly to his soul, but "it was not until the discovery of Ellington that we had any hint that jazz possessed possibilities of a range of expressiveness comparable to that of classical European music."

Ethel Waters

(1896–1977)

GENE JONES

Ethel Waters was a woman with an enormous range of talents. Her career began as a tall, lanky, blues singer. Billed as "Sweet Mama Stringbean," she was a skinny Bessie Smith who excelled as a singer and recording artist. In the 1930s, heavier and more mature, she became active in film and on Broadway, ultimately emerging as a successful dramatic actor. By the 1950s, Sweet Mama Stringbean had morphed into Beulah, a stereotypically overweight black maid working in a white household as the lead character on a television sitcom. Behind these public personas was a determined woman and talented singer who worked her way out of poverty to become a powerful blues singer in the Harlem Renaissance.

Ethel Waters did not think that she was beginning a career as an entertainer in 1917 when she accepted the offer to perform at the Lincoln Theatre in Baltimore. She was twenty-one years old, a winner of talent shows in neighborhood bars, and she was leaving the best job she ever had to work two weeks in vaudeville. She was earning her living as a maid in a Philadelphia hotel, making $3.50 a week plus an extra $1.25 for helping out in the laundry room. The Baltimore job paid $10 a week, plus the coins that the Lincoln's patrons might toss onto the stage during her act. To ensure that the hotel job would be there for her when she returned, she talked her mother into working in her place.

It would be over a year before she came back to Philadelphia, returning as a featured performer at the Standard Theatre, the city's biggest black vaudeville house. During that year away, she had learned much about her new profession and about herself. Besides the mechanics of cobbling together an act, she discovered that she loved to perform, how tough show life could be, and how tough she herself was. And audiences had taught her that she was good. She was as yet unknown to whites, but black audiences had doled out

This photograph illustrates the composed beauty of "Sweet Mama Stringbean." The photograph, taken in the late 1920s, was signed to Mary Lou Williams, another very prominent African American jazz singer. Courtesy of the Institute of Jazz Studies.

thousands of hard-earned dimes and quarters to see her. She had studied other vaudevillians, black and white, not to steal their material or to get performing tips, but to understand what set her apart from them. She discerned the difference: it was that innate touch of class, that tantalizing restraint that she applied to the lowdown songs and dances she used in her act. The word "Miss" had already attached itself to her billing.

Ethel Waters began her performing life in the persona of "Sweet Mama Stringbean," a big-boned, gap-toothed temptress who sang smutty songs and danced without using her feet. During her last years in the public eye, she was Saint Ethel, the morbidly obese, hymn-singing totem of the Billy Graham Crusades. In middle age, with only a handful of stage and film roles to her credit, she became one of the most acclaimed actors of her generation. But in her thirties, she was one of the three or four best singers of popular songs who ever lived, as well as one of the most influential. She had nearly two dozen big-selling records, half a dozen of them huge hits, starting in the earliest days of race records and going into the swing era. Several of the best pop composers of the time wrote songs for her.

When Ethel Waters began recording in 1921, nobody on records sounded like her. By 1930, almost every female singer, black or white, had at least a touch of Waters in their recorded performances. Only Louis Armstrong, Bessie Smith, and, later, Sinatra and Elvis had as many outright imitators. Edith Wilson, Mildred Bailey, Connie Boswell, Josephine Baker, Lee Wiley, Lena Horne, Dinah Washington, Peggy Lee, and Doris Day (along with almost every female cabaret singer working today) were all her disciples. She was the one who figured out what post-vaudeville popular singing should be. She delivered the goods, both the sad and the happy, without overselling them. As is usually the case with genius, there is no accounting for hers; no amount of biographical detail or musical archaeology can explain where it came from. Waters simply knew what to do every time she stepped before an audience, a microphone, or a camera, including when she stepped before each of them for the first time.

Ethel Waters was a thorny character: bulldog-tough in negotiation, dismissive of her rivals, and fiercely protective of her stardom. She was not allowed to skip a rung up the ladder in her climb from mud shows to stardom, and she never offered a hand to anyone below her. In her autobiography, written when she was fifty-five, there is not one mention of an enduring friendship. Anyone in her professional or personal life who crossed her—managers, producers, directors, writers, husbands, boyfriends, girlfriends—did so at their peril. (Bill Robinson taught his wirehaired terrier to growl at the mention of Waters' name.) She badmouthed rival singers—Alberta Hunter, Adelaide Hall, Josephine Baker, Billie Holiday, Lena

Horne—as they rose in turn to challenge her. She earned everything she got, and she knew the worth of what she had to offer.

Like several other pop music innovators of her day, Ethel Waters led a desperately bleak early life. She was born in the poorest neighborhood of Chester, Pennsylvania, a southwestern suburb of Philadelphia, on Halloween night in 1896. Her very conception marked her for trouble: her mother, Louise Anderson, was raped at knifepoint when she was twelve years old. Ethel's father, John Waters, was a few years older than his victim, and, since he was a family acquaintance, there was some discussion about his marrying Louise . But his mother, who was white, forbade it, so it didn't happen. He quickly disappeared from the lives of Louise and Ethel, and he died when Ethel was three.

Louise Anderson carried the trauma of her rape throughout her life. She lived into old age as if in shock, not blaming Ethel for what happened but never accepting her either. In her mid-teens, Louise married Norman Howard, but he deserted her. She got occasional jobs as a maid or a laundress, but could not keep them. Her only solace came from the hope induced in her by the Bible-banging preachers who held tent revivals in the neighborhood.

The only reliable adult in Ethel's family was her grandmother, Sally Anderson. She took on the responsibility of raising Ethel, so Ethel called her "Mom." Sally Anderson's intentions were good, but when the money didn't stretch far enough, she sent Ethel and/or her mother to another poor relation's house. In her autobiography, Waters wrote: "My whole childhood was almost like a series of one-night stands. I was shuttled about among relatives . . . continually being moved around to Camden, Chester and Philadelphia homes." The homes had many things in common, all of them bad.

By age six, Ethel was living with her grandmother on Clifton Street, in the heart of Philadelphia's red-light district. Her "Mom" was a laundress for whores, and Ethel got a close look at both trades. She helped Sally wash countless bundles of sheets and underwear, and she ran errands for the hookers, pimps, and thieves who were her neighbors. She saw turmoil, drugs, and violence all around her and drew moral lessons from what she saw. She resolved never to drink, smoke, or gamble, and she never did.

Big for her age, and the proud possessor of the foulest mouth in Philadelphia, Ethel was the natural leader of neighborhood children whose lives were as low as her own. She organized a gang of kids to steal things, mostly food, from any merchants foolish enough to turn their backs on them. Ethel was strong and not afraid to fight, but she seldom had to. She warded off bullying, muggings, and attempted rapes with her "vile tongue [which] was my shield, my toughness, my armor."

Miraculously, during her tumultuous childhood, Ethel managed to spend a bit of time, off and on, in school. While staying with her Aunt Ide in North Chester, she lasted through almost an entire year at an elementary school. She quickly learned to read and to count, and found her favorite subject to be elocution, with its memorizing and reciting. At age eight, Ethel was taken out of school by her mother and put to work as a domestic servant. When she was nine, her grandmother took charge of her again and enrolled her in an integrated Catholic school at Ninth and Pine Streets in Philadelphia. This was the beginning of Ethel's longest stint as a student— nearly two years—and she loved it. At three o'clock every afternoon she resumed her role as the toughest urchin in town, but from eight until three she behaved herself and soaked up everything the nuns had to teach her. She thrived on the books and the discipline, and she liked the way that the hushed gravity of the confessional made her feel. Of course, necessity took her out of this school and put her back into domestic service. She would receive only a few more haphazard months of education before she left Philadelphia.

In her adolescence, a full-time domestic now, Ethel began to frequent neighborhood dancehalls on her evenings off. At one of these she met a small, dapper man named Merritt Purnsley. He was twenty-three when she married him; she was thirteen. She endured nearly a year of his beatings and neglect before she left him. Her beloved grandmother, Sally, died shortly after their breakup, and, aching with sorrow, Ethel allowed herself to be "saved" at a "children's revival" in Chester. Religion did not become the center of her life, as it had for her mother. Ethel would never be a regular churchgoer, even during her Billy Graham years, but she took comfort in church when she needed it.

Dancing was not at the center of Ethel's life either. Work was, but she got her first taste of public recognition when she began to win dance contests. She especially liked the waltz and the schottische, a popular dance similar to the polka that became linked with ragtime in the early twentieth-century United States. She could acquit herself gracefully at them, but she could also outdo the crassest exhibitionists in the kind of hip-shaking, muscle-rolling, improvised dancing that took prizes in rough bars. Enjoying her dancehall fame, she began to enter amateur talent contests as well. She had never considered herself a singer, but songs would add variety to her dancing presentation, so she learned a few. One of these was "When You're a Long, Long Way from Home," a song which had its brief popularity in the winter of 1914–15. Two small-time actor-producers saw her win a contest with it in a place called Jack's Rathskeller, and they offered her two weeks in Baltimore with their show. By accepting their offer, the amateur turned professional.

To listen to Ethel Waters's best recordings today, to hear the rightness of her phrasing, her precise diction, and pitch-perfect intonation, while thinking about her beginnings is to wonder, "Where did that come from?" This paragon of popular singing, who grew up in hell, somehow transcended everything without losing the capacity to feel. There was enough pain left in her to endow a ballad with honest feeling, and a puckish spirit shone through her sassy tales of two-timing papas and hard-to-please mamas.

Most of Waters' autobiography is taken up with these nightmarish early years, and music (hearing it or making it) barely figures in her early memories. But two anecdotes in the book seem at least to hint at the sensibility that shaped her artistry. In one of them, her staid, Catholic grandmother admonishes her mother, who was bellowing hymns as she went about her chores. Ethel remembered Sally Anderson saying to Louise: "You don't have to holler so. God has very big ears. He can hear you even if you whisper." Another story concerns the fact that she had few friends as a child. Waters wrote: "I wanted other people to like me but never made the slightest effort to win them over. I felt it was up to them to discover my remarkable qualities."

In 1917, Ethel Waters arrived in Baltimore to begin two weeks at the Lincoln Theater. One of the acts in the Braxton & Nugent show was a duo called the Hill Sisters, and Ethel Waters's brief turn was spliced into their longer one. She was billed as the third Hill Sister, given a featured spot and the nickname "Sweet Mama Stringbean," a name that was based on her tall, thin physique. Waters was amazed by her first audience's response to her. They yelled their approval of her singing, and they screamed with delight as she danced. When her part of the act was over, they showered the stage with coins. Before the first week was out, Waters had a following, people who came back to see her.

She knew that she needed more material, and she was taken with a number that Charlie Anderson, the show's female impersonator, was singing. He gave it to her and it became her signature song. It was W. C. Handy's "Saint Louis Blues," and her commitment to it shows Waters, for the first time, reaching beyond the repertoire that was expected of her. The song was still new (copyrighted in 1914), and it was more often used as dance accompaniment than as a vocal selection. Urban blacks liked to fox-trot to it, but its gritty lyrics reminded them of the South that they had come north to forget. It was authentic, a true blues, unlike the blues-tinged joke songs that were the currency of black vaudeville. With its wailing verse, its middle-section tango, and a stompdown for a chorus, it is musically the richest song of its time. A singer cannot toss off "The Saint Louis Blues"; it demands involvement and interpretation. Ethel Waters would stop shows with it for fifteen years. (She claimed to have been the first female singer to feature the song, and she probably was. She never recorded her original version. She finally made a recording in 1932. For this recording she chose an odd arrangement that centers on her trading vocal lines—using altered lyrics—with the Cecil Mack Choir.)

Waters made another useful discovery during her first week in show business: she learned how crooked managers can be. One of her producers, Braxton, began stepping onto the stage during her bows to pick up the coins that the audience invariably threw. Ethel thought he was saving them to give to her with her second and final week's salary. Of course, in plain sight of the audience, he was robbing her. Braxton refused to part with the coins, but he did offer Ethel a contract to extend her stay. After giving her bosses a tongue-lashing, she and the Hill Sisters left them to book themselves wherever they could. The Braxton & Nugent operation was low, but it was not the lowest. Over the next year, Ethel and the Hills would touch the muddy bottom of show business.

Besides the vagaries of their profession, black touring performers faced a dozen hassles a day over the barest necessities of life—eating, sleeping, washing. Most restaurants wouldn't serve them, and most hotels wouldn't house them. They carried sandwiches and apples in their pockets, never knowing whether sandwiches or apples could be had in the next town. They slept in theater basements, in public parks, in sheds, in train stations. At many small-time theaters the workday lasted from 9:00 a.m. until midnight, with everyone on the bill in a continuous loop of performances. When Ethel and the Hills were stranded without bookings in Lexington, Kentucky, they signed on with a carnival there. Like everybody else in Bob White's Greater Shows, they occasionally slept in stables, with the horses. Maggie Hill left the act in Savannah, Georgia, after finding the theater owner's teenage son hiding under her bed in the boarding house. Ethel and Jo Hill soldiered on without her.

On arriving at Atlanta's 91 Theatre (at 91 Decatur Street), Ethel found that she was to be on a bill with Bessie Smith, the Empress herself, the most famous blues singer of the day. Smith summoned Waters to her dressing room and demanded a private audition of the numbers she would be doing. She dismissed Ethel as "a long goody" and told the manager that Ethel was forbidden to sing any blues at the 91. At Ethel's first show, the audience yelled for her blues, but she did not depart from her blues-less program. After several people had asked for their money back, the manager told Ethel that, in the second show, she could sing a blues as an encore if she got one. She got the encore, and, as she launched into "Saint Louis Blues," she could hear Bessie storming in the wings, railing about "these northern bitches" invading her territory.

In Anniston, Alabama, Ethel went on a joyride with her show's cast in a borrowed car. The driver swerved to avoid hitting a horse and buggy in the road, and the car flipped over. Shards of glass from the windshield littered Ethel with cuts, and her right leg was severed almost to the bone. Neglectful care in the black ward of a white hospital left her with gangrene. A black doctor finally arrived to clean the wound, but he told her it would be slow to heal. In the meantime, Ethel had to keep working. She couldn't walk, so, at her next engagement, in Birmingham, she arranged for two men on the stage crew to carry her out and place her in front of a backdrop before the curtain rose. After she had sung and the curtain fell, they carried her off. A pool of blood marked the place where she had stood.

Ethel resolved to "sing her way home" to Philadelphia. Six weeks later, she walked onto the stage of the Standard Theatre, the neighborhood girl who had made good. This flash of local fame did not pay her bills, however, and she soon found herself singing in the same bars she had sung in before she left. By day, she bused tables at the Automat.

In 1919, Waters received a wire offering her two weeks' work at Harlem's Lincoln Theatre. A successful engagement there led to a permanent job at Edmond's Cellar, a basement club at 132nd Street and Fifth Avenue. Edmond's was a lowlife hangout, with 150 seats jostling each other, a three-piece band, and faded paper flowers straggling from its ceiling. Ethel got $2 a night, plus tips, and was expected to do three or four shows between the hours of 9:00 p.m. and 9:00 a.m. The raunchy songs of her vaudeville days were still the core of her repertoire, but Lou Henley, the club's pianist, advised her to learn some pop tunes as well. She was reluctant at first, but found that she could hold boisterous customers with "My Buddy," "Dear Old Pal of Mine," and "Rose of Washington Square." Other Harlem entertainers began coming in to see her, and Edmond even hosted the occasional white "slumming party." In Waters' words, she had changed the Cellar from a dump into "a high-class dump."

After a year or so at Edmond's, she began to play bigger, better places, including several clubs in Atlantic City. She toured again, this time in a rickety revue called *Hello, 1919!* When she returned, although she did not know it, she was perfectly poised—in the right place (New York), at the right time (1920), of the right sex, of the right color (for once), doing precisely the right thing, singing the blues—to ride the wave of the revolution that would increase her professional options a thousandfold: the recording industry's blues boom.

In February 1920, a black songwriter-vaudevillian named Perry Bradford bullyragged an Okeh record executive into recording a singer named Mamie Smith in two of Bradford's songs. The solo voice of a black woman had never before been heard on a commercial recording, and Smith's record sold like crazy. The industry had discovered a new commodity, blues, and, even better, a hitherto untapped market for records, blacks. Every label, large and small, scrambled to sign black female blues singers.

Cardinal Records got to Ethel first, and she made two sides for that small company in March 1921. Within a month she was signed to Black Swan, the first black-owned record label. Her first record for Black Swan held a hit on each side, "Oh, Daddy" and "Down Home Blues." Her second session produced a third hit, "There'll Be Some Changes Made." The company sent her on a promotional tour as its first and biggest star, and, in doing so, clinched her reputation as a singer. When Black Swan folded in 1924, Ethel did not. She made a few sides for Paramount and Vocalion, then, in April 1925, at twenty-nine, signed a contract with Columbia, the label that would be her home for seven years. There are many fine things in her early recordings, but the essential Waters library begins with her term at Columbia. She was a supremely confident and adventurous singer by then, there is greater variety in her choice of material, her accompaniments are better, and—not the least of it—Columbia's electric recording equipment lets us hear her more naturally than did the cardboard horns that she had sung into at Black Swan.

Waters' Columbia work (nearly fifty of her total of 259 sides) still shines with her effortless musicality. No singer of the late 1920s, with Armstrong as the sole exception, seemed to be trying so little and doing so much. She had a middle-range soprano voice, bell-clear and capable of seamless leaps to near-coloratura heights or to masculine depths. Her diction was perfect and accent-free. Unlike the other blues women of her generation, she did not shout or growl or muddy her lyrics. She was respectful of melodies and words, but would improvise on either. Because she had not modeled herself on anyone during her vaudeville days, she had no stagy habits to break to accommodate a new medium. Years before Armstrong or Crosby, Waters was the epitome of ease in the recording studio. Even now, eighty years later, we can hear the fun in her singing. She poked fun at others, too, leaving us deft and funny impersonations of Bessie Smith, Clara Smith, Rudy Vallee, and, in the early thirties, Armstrong and Mae West.

Choosing a couple of Waters songs to represent her "best" or "most important" of this period is like trying to select the best two cherries from a basketful of them. Two sessions in August 1928, however, yielded some mighty tasty cherries. The first paired Waters, for the only time, with her favorite pianist, stride master James P. Johnson. The rapport between them is palpable, as they serve up Andy Razaf's salacious "My Handy Man" and "Do What You Did Last Night." They did a hipster-sly "Guess Who's in Town?" and, best of all, a tender and nearly unadorned ballad, "Lonesome Swallow." Two days later (on August 23), Waters was back in the Columbia studio, with Clarence Williams as her pianist. The gem from that session was "West End Blues," a King Oliver tune that Louis Armstrong had recorded definitively only two months ear-

TRACK 22

This 1928 recording of "Do What You Did Last Night" is one of the few times Ethel Waters recorded with James P. Johnson, widely regarded at the time as the best piano player on the East coast.

lier. Armstrong's version, with its wordless singing and majestic playing, is considered by many to be the best jazz record ever made.

Like Armstrong, Waters knew exactly what to do with "West End Blues," but her record is different from his in everything except its effect. She sings the words, no moaning or wailing. Without a trace of melodrama, it is deep, honest blues singing. After a straight-forward chorus, she scats a bit in homage to Armstrong, and that, too, is sorrowful and perfect. Most of the Waters songs recorded before 1930 are of the sassy-naughty vaudeville sort. But after her success with "Dinah," in 1925, pop songs began to dot her reper-toire. She had hits with "Sugar" (1926), "Am I Blue?" (1929), "I Got Rhythm" (1930), and "Three Little Words" (1930).

In 1927 Ethel Waters finally made it to Broadway in a short-lived revue called *Africana*. It was a black show, but it was white New

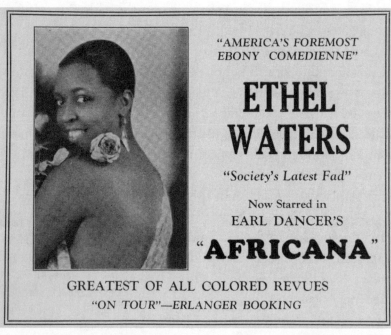

Ethel Waters, marketed herself as "America's Foremost Ebony Comedienne," in this advertisement placed in *The Official Theatrical World of Colored Artists: National Directory and Guide*, published in 1928.
Photographs and Prints Division, Schomburg Center for Research in Black Culture, The New York Public Library Astor, Lenox and Tilden Foundations.

York's first look at her. Columbia was
still advertising her as an "Ebony Comedienne," but critics, black and white,
were beginning to call her an artist, possibly the greatest of her race and generation. James Weldon Johnson observed
simply that she "dominated the show."
He compared her stage presence with
that of Florence Mills, but stressed their
physical and stylistic difference: "Miss
Waters is tall, almost statuesque, with a
head of hair so beautiful that Antonio
Salemmi asked the privilege of doing it
in bronze . . . Miss Waters gets her audiences, and she does get them completely,
through an innate poise that she pos-
sesses . . . her bodily movements, when
she makes them, are almost languorous."

Ethel Waters in feather skirt. This photograph from the 1920s or early 1930s
was inscribed to Carl Van Vechten.
Beinecke Rare Book and Manuscript
Library, Yale University.

In 1929, Waters made her first film, an inconsequential revue
called *On with the Show* (in which she sang "Am I Blue?"), and later
that year she made triumphant appearances in London, at the Pal-
ladium and at the Café de Paris. Two more Broadway shows followed: *Blackbirds of 1930* and, in 1931, *Rhapsody in Black*.

In 1933, after hearing Waters' powerful singing of "Stormy
Weather" at Harlem's Cotton Club, Irving Berlin signed her for his
own revue, *As Thousands Cheer*, which was to be built around the
idea of a "living newspaper." Introduced by a headline that read
"UNKNOWN NEGRO LYNCHED BY FRENZIED MOB," Waters
(the only black performer in the cast) sang "Supper Time" in the
character of the lynching victim's wife, who must break the news to
their children and must also prepare supper. There had never been
such a dramatic risk taken in a musical revue, and audiences were
stunned by Waters's performance. In the same show, she introduced
the hip-flipping "Heat Wave" and parodied Josephine Baker with a
song called "Harlem on My Mind." There was no more "Ebony

Comedienne" nonsense after "Supper Time." Ethel Waters was an artist, all right, and, in the pit of the Depression, she was earning the biggest salary on Broadway—$5,000 a week.

But Waters, whose "Supper Time" was considered more a dramatic landmark than a musical one, was offered no dramatic roles after singing it, nor even offered any songs of the theatrical caliber of "Supper Time." She toured with *As Thousands Cheer*, confident that something good would come from her work in it, but nothing did. She made three all-black short films: *Rufus Jones for President*, which was hijacked by the dazzling presence of eight-year-old Sammy Davis Jr., *Hot and Bothered*, and *Bubbling Over*, in which she sang "Darkies Never Cry." Her only feature film of this time was *Gift of Gab* (1934), an oddball, unfunny comedy that co-starred Ruth Etting, Alexander Woollcott, and Bela Lugosi. Her next Broadway show was another revue, *At Home Abroad* (1935), in which she sang "Hottentot Potentate" and "Thief in the Night." She dutifully recorded her two *At Home Abroad* songs, but they made no stir. She hit the road for over two years, touring with then-boyfriend Eddie Mallory's band.

The next Broadway offer came late in 1938, for a leading role in a non-musical show. This play would energize her stagnant career and alter the direction of her professional life. The play, *Mamba's Daughters*, was written by DuBose Heyward and based on his novel. In it forty-two-year-old Ethel Waters played the avenging mother of a rape victim, and the ferocity of her performance established her as a non-musical star. After her triumph in *Mamba's Daughters*, she began to think of herself as an actress who sang, not the other way around. She would present herself in concert and would continue to make records throughout her life, but she now saw singing as something profitable to do while she waited for dramatic roles.

Waters had gained weight for *Mamba's Daughters*, and her singing got a little fatter, too. She never lost her pure tones nor her crisp enunciation, but a certain stodginess, the sound of deliberation, crept into her musical work. There would be no more flirtatious, scatty flights of improvisation, no more easy riding over toddling tempos, no more glancing off rhymes or playing hide-and-seek with downbeats. Like the rapist in *Mamba's Daughters*, "Sweet Mama Stringbean" was killed by Ethel Waters onstage in 1939.

Ethel Waters would have no more hit records, but she would put two more standards into the American songbook. The first, "Taking a Chance on Love," came from *Cabin in the Sky* (1940), the Broadway musical she took when no non-musical roles came to her. When this charming piece of *faux* folklore was filmed in 1943, she introduced "Happiness Is a Thing Called Joe." One of her co-stars in the film was young Lena Horne, whose talent and beauty and preferential treatment by MGM drove Waters into tsunami-like rages. Her tantrums on the set were the stuff of Hollywood legend, and the experience probably had something to do with her not making another film for six years.

Waters' next film was *Pinky* (1949), during the rehearsals for which she, the actress, directed Elia Kazan, the director. ("God is my director," she would tell Fred Zinnemann on a movie set a few years later.) *Pinky* doesn't keep its promise to be the last, blistering word on race relations in postwar America, but Waters's performance as the dignified, long-suffering grandmother of the "half-white" Jeanne Crain is undeniably a terrific piece of acting. She held her own in scenes with Ethel Barrymore, and won an Oscar nomination for her work.

Pinky's notoriety brought Ethel Waters back to Broadway for her last great stage role, as Berenice Sadie Brown, the housekeeper who is the pillar of Carson McCullers's *The Member of the Wedding* (1950). Just as she had told Kazan how to direct, she told McCullers what to write. The playwright had conceived the housekeeper as a cigarette-smoking, gin-sipping agnostic who sang a Russian lullaby to her charges at bedtime. Waters would have none of it. She wanted piety written into Berenice Sadie Brown, and she got it. She got the lullaby changed, too. When the frustrated McCullers asked Waters to suggest a more appropriate song, she sang "His Eye Is on the Sparrow" a cappella and brought the creative team to tears. The song went into the play, of course, and it would be associated with Waters for the rest of her life. She took its title for the title of her autobiography, co-written with Charles Samuels in 1951. (The song is not a folk hymn, as many assume, but was written in 1905 by Charles H. Gabriel and Mrs. C. D. Martin. Waters remembered it because it had been one of her grandmother's favorites.)

Noble Sissle and Eubie Blake with Ethel Waters, 1952.
The Maryland Historical Society, Baltimore, Maryland.

Ethel Waters's performance in *The Member of the Wedding* is, along with Laurette Taylor's in *The Glass Menagerie* and Marlon Brando's in *A Streetcar Named Desire*, one of the best-remembered and most-praised performances of the so-called Golden Age of theater. But again, as had been the case with "Supper Time" and *Mamba's Daughters*, a perfect performance was not enough to bring a black, middle-aged actress another dramatic role. There were no such roles being written. Her portrayal of Berenice brought Waters the chance to repeat it on film, in 1953, but that was all. (Perhaps knowing what awaited her in films and television, she played the lead in CBS-TV's black-maid sitcom, *Beulah*, during the Broadway run of *The Member of the Wedding*.) The mayor of New York City proclaimed an "Ethel Waters Day" in 1953, but it didn't pay her bills.

In 1955 she began to take roles in anthology television shows. (*Climax* and *General Electric Theatre* were the first, and they were followed by many others over the next few years.) The following year, she went on a game show, NBC-TV's *Break the Bank*, telling the host, Bert Parks, that she was broke and owed back taxes. (She won $10,000.)

In 1957, sixty-one years old and needing money, she was back on Broadway in a concert called *An Evening with Ethel Waters*. One night after the show she was in her hotel room alone, scanning the radio dial, when she heard the announcement that a Billy Graham Crusade was coming to Madison Square Garden. Although getting around was painful for her (she weighed nearly 400 pounds by then), she felt she had to go. She was both comforted and exhilarated by Graham's preaching, so much so that she made the effort to go again that same week. After several visits, she was finally recognized by a Graham staffer and asked to join the choir. She spent a few evenings singing with the choir, sitting in a chair that had had its arms ripped off to accommodate her size. Finally the obvious question was asked: Would she please sing "His Eye Is on the Sparrow"? She sang it, and she held the Garden in her hand.

Waters would be a stalwart of the Crusades for the rest of her life, accompanying Graham to Honolulu, London, Winnipeg, Chicago, and Cleveland, among many other locales. Her show business past was completely obliterated now, as she had willed it to be, and the pop music industry had long since forgotten her. She made two LPs of hymns for the Word label, but they were sold mostly at Crusade souvenir tables. Few record stores stocked them. When President Nixon presented her at a Sunday morning worship service at the White House in January 1971, he introduced her as "the most out-standing gospel singer in the world today." On September 1, 1977, two months before her eighty-first birthday, Ethel Waters died of cancer in her Chatsworth, California, apartment.

Literature, not music, was at the core of the Harlem Renaissance, and however hard Carl Van Vechten tried to weld them to each other, the match was never really made. There is no evidence that Ethel Waters or other singers and musicians of the period took much notice of the writing of Claude McKay or Jean Toomer; black writers, how-ever were quite aware of Waters and of her art. Certainly Waters's presence at Edmond's Cellar, and then on Broadway, helped make Harlem what it was. Like the dark poets and novelists of 1920s Harlem, Waters brought something extraordinary to the American scene: a vocal style so fresh, so intimate and appealing, that other singers, black and white, wanted to sing like her. The good ones still do.

PART FOUR

The Visual
and
Performing Arts

INTRODUCTION

If literature is the core of the Harlem Renaissance, and if it is not possible to imagine the Harlem Renaissance without music, what can we say about the visual and performing arts? Traditionally we have said relatively little. Even the most famous artists of the period, Aaron Douglas or Jacob Lawrence, for example, are not as well known as poet Langston Hughes or blues singer Bessie Smith. There are several reasons for this. First, unlike music or even books, works of art are less accessible to the general public. Furthermore, the tradition of the visual arts was not as well developed prior to the Harlem Renaissance as was that of music and literature. The most prominent pre-Renaissance artist was Henry Ossawa Tanner. While accomplished in the naturalistic style that dominated American art in the late nineteenth century, only a few of his paintings depicted African Americans or African American themes. Also, he spent most of his career in Paris. Nevertheless his example stimulated the following generation of black artists.

In many ways, African American art emerged out of the Harlem Renaissance as artists explored African and African American themes in their paintings, prints, and sculpture. Art tended to lag behind literature and music chronologically. The first stirrings of black art did not occur until the mid 1920s; much of the most significant painting took place in the 1930s or even the 1940s. For example, most of the illustrations in the 1925 Harlem issue of *Survey Graphic*, which helped launch the Harlem Renaissance, were done by Winold Reiss, a German-born artist who specialized in drawing African Americans and incorporating African-based motifs in his illustrations. The following year, when Alain Locke brought out the expanded book version of the Harlem issue, African American artist

Book cover for *The Blacker the Berry,* by Wallace Thurman; artwork by Aaron Douglas, 1929. This connection between the writer and the artist was common during the Harlem Renaissance.
Beinecke Rare Book and Manuscript Library, Yale University.

Aaron Douglas, newly arrived from Kansas, took over much of the illustration. Douglas, incidentally, had studied under Reiss when he came to Harlem, and he credits the German artist with encouraging him to begin to draw in the heritage of African and African Americans in his work.

By the late 1920s, a growing number of artists were working in Harlem. Many, like Douglas, found employment doing illustrations for black journals like *The Crisis* or *Opportunity*, and working with publishers illustrating and producing advertising material for books by black writers. In this context collaboration developed between black writers and black artists. In 1926,

Douglas was a member of the group that produced *FIRE!!*, and along with Bruce Nugent did most of its illustrations. He also created drawings to illustrate each of the sermons in James Weldon Johnson's *God's Trombones*.

Other black artists practicing in Harlem during the 1920s included sculptor Augusta Savage and painter Palmer Hayden. Both received funding that enabled them to study in Paris; Hayden received the Harmon Foundation's Gold Medal for art in 1926. The accompanying stipend financed his studies. Augusta Savage's first effort to study art in Paris in 1923 ended when the French government denied her a position in an art study program because of her race. In 1930 she made it to Paris, supported by a Rosenwald Foundation fellowship.

In the 1930s, the art community expanded. Formal and informal organizations in Harlem provided art instruction and contact with practicing artists to help develop the talented youth of the community. By the mid 1930s, the Federal Arts Project of the Works Project Administration began a program in Harlem for black artists. Romare Bearden recalled that at one organizational meeting almost one hundred prospective artists turned out.

In the chapters that follow, three artists and one performing artist are featured. Aaron Douglas was in many ways the most significant artist of the Harlem Renaissance. In addition to his talent and the quality of his work, he was in Harlem during most of the 1920s and was closely associated with the writers of the movement. Romare Bearden and Jacob Lawrence were respectively thirteen and eighteen years younger than Douglas. Both spent much of their youth in Harlem, where they were nurtured by Augusta Savage and other black artists. Both did most of their work in the late 1930s and 1940s. Their work, however, was very different.

The fourth chapter in this section examines the life and career of Josephine Baker. Baker first achieved notoriety as a member of the chorus line of the touring production of *Shuffle Along*. She immediately attracted attention with her distinctive animal-like moves and her comedic skills. Her talent was unique. Her performances involved singing, dancing, and a little acting, but it was her stage presence that wooed her audience. By the late 1920s she was an international star with her own Paris nightclub.

The four chapters that follow also illustrate that the range of talent and creativity in the Harlem Renaissance extends beyond music and literature.

Aaron Douglas

(1899–1979)

AMY KIRSCHKE

Aaron Douglas was the African American artist most directly associated with the Harlem Renaissance. He arrived in Harlem in 1925 as the Renaissance was in full swing, and he executed the major body of his work from the mid 1920s to the mid 1930s, within the chronological limits of the movement. Thematically and stylistically his work addressed major concerns of the Renaissance—the African heritage and the historical identity of African Americans. And, more than any other artist, he worked and lived among Harlem's literary community. He was connected with the group that hung out at Wallace Thurman's "Niggerati Manor," and he was an illustrator and associate editor of FIRE!!. Much of his early work illustrated or promoted various Harlem Renaissance publications. Douglas's major artistic triumphs were public works—murals at Fisk University and the Harlem branch of the New York Public Library that chronicled the course of African American history, from Africa to bondage to emancipation to urban America.

As the most prominent and active visual artist in the Harlem Renaissance, Aaron Douglas has been renowned for his magnificent journal and book illustrations and for his murals, *Aspects of Negro Life*, now at the Schomburg Center for Research in Black Culture, in Harlem. A recent restoration of the Fisk University murals has illuminated Douglas's lifelong commitment to revealing the strong connection of black Americans to Africa and his involvement in issues of African American identity, and historical memory.

Aaron Douglas was born in Topeka, Kansas, on May 26, 1899. His father, Aaron Douglas Sr., was a laborer. His mother, Elizabeth, remained at home with the children, Aaron's half brothers and sisters—Aaron was the only child of her union with his father, who was twenty-two years her senior. His parents originally came from Tennessee and Alabama; they were "exodusters," the 10,000 to 15,000 Southern blacks who migrated to Kansas in the 1870s and 1880s in search of a life free from the racial oppression of the post-

Restoration of Aaron Douglas mural at Fisk Library, 1969. The restoration was done under the supervision of Aaron Douglas. This image shows workers on scaffolding restoring the upper portions of a large mural.
Photo courtesy of George W. Adams.

Reconstruction South. Topeka was the final destination of many exodusters. It had a thriving African American community—almost 10 percent of the city's population of 80,000, in a state where blacks numbered only about 3 percent of the total population. Although it had its share of racism, Topeka was a relatively progressive city with an active black church and black organizations, including cultural and political groups.

Aaron Douglas, New York, 1933. This photo was taken by Carl Van Vechten in the bathroom of Van Vechten's New York apartment. At the request of Van Vechten, Douglas had painted an "African" design, similar to motifs he had used in his murals, on the bathroom wall. In the photo, Douglas stands in front of the decorated wall. Beinecke Rare Book and Manuscript Library, Yale University.

Elizabeth enjoyed drawing and painting, and studied with the itinerate artists who passed through the Topeka area. Aaron watched her draw and as a child began to paint and draw as well. His parents lacked any formal education, but provided him with encouragement and support. Douglas demonstrated ability and determination in school and graduated Topeka High School in 1917. Although the school was overwhelmingly white, the yearbook praised Douglas as "one of the most talented artists in school." He had clearly flourished there, providing illustrations for his school publications on a regular basis. Although Douglas later recalled thinking about becoming a lawyer, he already knew that art was his passion, and planned to go to college to study commercial art.

Too poor to attend college, Douglas, like many blacks of this era, took a train north to find work, ending up in a machine-tool factory in Detroit. The work was onerous, and he and fellow black laborers were treated harshly, but Aaron was determined to raise the money for college. "Detroit, the money Mecca of every young Negro youth who yearned to escape the oppressive conditions of his life, was the place where my journey came to a temporary halt. I was not quite sure of myself at this time and willingly chose every opportunity to test my strength and prove my manhood," he recalled in his unpublished autobiography. Only seventeen years old, Douglas lived in Detroit for two months, and attended free art classes at night at the Detroit Museum of Art, his first formal training. He went on to Dunkirk, New York, for more work, before returning to Kansas later that year.

His brief experience with factory work would remain with him throughout his lifetime. It influenced his images of labor, his artistic work, and his leftist political sensibilities as he illustrated journals, flirted with radical politics, and painted large-scale murals of black labor. Despite the hardships of the work, including sweeping broken pieces of glass from the floor in a glass factory, Douglas later recalled the time as positive and informative. "In spite of the tension and anxiety of the first few weeks from home, I found some moments of this period as delightful as any that I have ever experienced before or since." Douglas took risks throughout his life, starting with leaving home to work in the factories and continuing on through college and into adulthood. In an intensely segregated society, Douglas was brave and audacious in his efforts to better himself as a student and artist.

With new clothes and three hundred dollars in his pocket, Douglas headed to Lincoln, Nebraska, to attend the University of Nebraska. In fact he arrived in Lincoln ten days into the term with no transcripts or diploma in hand. The Lincoln faculty, perhaps sensing his determination, creativity, and earnestness, allowed him conditional admittance. Douglas continued to work as a busboy to finance his education, but found time to pursue his art and soon won several awards, gradually winning the respect of the faculty at the University of Nebraska.

Douglas's studies were interrupted by the outbreak of World War I, and in anticipation of the draft, he joined the Student Army Training Corps (SATC) and looked forward to "proudly drilling through the streets of Lincoln." Shortly after he volunteered, he was called in by the Nebraska commander and told his services would not be needed, a rejection he found "a deeply humiliating experience." He understood that racial prejudice was at the core of this decision, but fought that prejudice by going north and joining the

SATC at the University of Minnesota, after spending a summer working at a Minnesota steel company. He remained there until after the armistice was signed in November 1918.

Douglas later recalled that "Patriotism was as Afro-American as religion." He had followed the writings of W.E.B. Du Bois, editor of the NAACP's *The Crisis* magazine. Du Bois urged black Americans to close ranks and serve in the military, believing this service would lead to full civic equality. Although Du Bois's hopes were not realized—the end of the war brought renewed racial oppression and segregation—his words inspired Douglas, a "constant reader" of *The Crisis*. Douglas also drew hope from the Urban League's *Opportunity* magazine. In his autobiography he recalled that: "The poems and stories, and to a lesser degree the pictures and illustrations were different. The poems and other creative works were *by* Negroes and *about* Negroes. And in the case of one poet, Langston Hughes, they seemed to have been created in a form and technique that was in some way to consonant or harmonize with the ebb and flow of Negro Life."

Douglas went back to Lincoln and graduated from the University of Nebraska in 1922 with a Bachelor of Fine Arts. He was listed in the yearbook as a member of the Art Club, the only black pictured in the club photo of fifty-three students. He had worked hard through college, taking risks as one of a small minority of blacks at Nebraska and one of the only black studio art majors. In 1923, he was hired by Lincoln High School in Kansas City, Missouri, to teach art, one of two black faculty members at the school. He made a close friend of the only other black faculty member, William L. Dawson, who taught music.

In Kansas City the young artist also renewed acquaintances—and a romance—with his future wife, Alta Sawyer, who had been his high school sweetheart. Sawyer was now trapped in an unhappy marriage, and Douglas's letters to her during this time and over the following years expressed both his personal love and feelings, and his evolving artistic, political, and racial sensibilities. During this time, Douglas read voraciously about the history of art, exploring the diversity of artistic traditions. Still, the only black artist he made reference to was Henry O. Tanner, who had lived and painted in Paris and remained firmly within conventional European traditions, working in the style of Impressionism and focusing primarily on biblical subjects. Tanner's depictions of African Americans numbered only a few.

Douglas soon took another huge risk, a step that became a milestone in his career. In his readings, Douglas came across a spectacular issue of *Survey Graphic,* a special Harlem issue featuring the work of Bavarian artist Winold Reiss on its cover. The cover was a respectful and forthright depiction of the black actor Roland Hayes. Like many artists of his time, Douglas had planned to travel to Paris to study, but after seeing the journal—which would eventually be developed into Alan Locke's book, *The New Negro*—Douglas decided first to go to Harlem and try his luck there. The *Survey Graphic* issue had provided a fascinating insight into that all-black world, with detailed discussions of political developments, the artistic scene, and the social problems that this urban black community faced. Douglas, wanting to be part of it, departed for Harlem, leaving the security of his teaching job behind him. He hoped to find other artists who shared his growing consciousness of his race, his burgeoning interest in African American identity, and his desire to create a record of this history of blacks in America. He would not be disappointed.

Opportunity magazine holds a special place in the heart of the Urban League movement. It is the organization's oldest official publication. First published in 1923, *Opportunity* captured the thoughts and opinions of the leading artists, scholars, activists, historians, and opinion makers of the day. Today, the magazine continues as one of the most highly anticipated publications in the civil rights movement, offering in-depth and scholarly analysis of the issues of the day. Beinecke Rare Book and Manuscript Library, Yale University.

Douglas arrived in Harlem a handsome man of medium build; he had intense brown eyes and wore glasses. He had full lips and always wore a mustache, and, as a young artist, a goatee for a short time. He was very soft spoken. He was introduced to W.E.B. Du Bois, the towering black intellectual leader of the time, and was hired to do illustrations for *The Crisis*. Douglas would also soon meet Charles S. Johnson and provide images for *Opportunity*, and he met the *Survey Graphic* artist he had so admired, Winold Reiss, who offered him a scholarship to study in his atelier.

Douglas's artistic work before Harlem had not been race-based, but upon his arrival in Harlem he changed the focus of his endeavors. He immediately became interested in African art, which he could view in museums, galleries, at the 135th Street Library, and in private collections of prominent Harlem leaders, including that of Alain Locke. Winold Reiss strongly urged Douglas to paint what he knew best, his own life, people, and experiences. He found support from journal and book editors who learned of his illustrations, black patrons, and white patrons too, including Carl Van Vechten and Charlotte Mason. Nevertheless, Douglas was able to make the situation work for him. Organizations such as the Harmon Foundation provided support as well, by including Douglas in their traveling exhibitions.

Douglas soon met poet Langston Hughes, with whom he would develop a lifelong friendship and collaboration. Of Douglas's style, Langston observed: "Aaron Douglas drawing strange black fantasies causes the smug Negro middle class to turn from their white, respectable, ordinary books and papers to catch a glimmer of their own beauty."

As Douglas began to receive commissions in Harlem, he had to confront the growing interest in "primitivism." He viewed Africa as a source of cultural and visual inspiration, not as an escape, and used it as a starting point to interpret contemporary black life. Perhaps because of its close ties to African American history, Douglas was particularly drawn to West African masks of the Ivory Coast, including the Dan tribe. He also embraced elements of African culture through the use of Egyptian art in his work. The discovery of Tutankhamen's tomb inspired a fascination for all things Egyptian. Douglas studied Cubism and embraced the flat, cut-out style of Synthetic Cubism, as well as the work of the

European Orphists, including Delaunay and Kupka, and American Stanton MacDonald-Wright.

Douglas had only a few contacts when he first moved to Harlem, but soon found himself surrounded by a social network of writers, editors, musicians, and artists. Of this group he later wrote, "I had the good fortune to be one of a small group of eight, ten perhaps a dozen young men and women who met in the streets, the libraries, the churches and the cabarets of Harlem, which was at that time the Mecca, the intellectual and artistic focal point of the black world of the twenties." Soon, the home of Aaron and his new wife Alta—who had left her husband and joined Aaron in New York—would become an artistic meeting place in Harlem.

Douglas wanted to celebrate black culture, but understood the challenge ahead of him to create images that did so. As he wrote to his wife, "We are possessed, you know, with the idea that it is necessary to be white, to be beautiful. Nine times out of ten it is just the reverse. It takes lots of training or a tremendous effort to down the

Pen and ink drawing by Aaron Douglas. Never previously reprinted. Provided by an anonymous donor.

idea that thin lips and straight nose is the apogee
of beauty. But once free you can look back with
a sigh of relief and wonder how anyone could be
so deluded." When Douglas collaborated with
Langston Hughes on illustrations for some of his
poetry and books, he wrote Hughes of his vision
of black art:

> Your problem, Langston, my problem,
> no our problem is to conceive, develop,
> establish an art era. Not white art painted
> black ... Let's bare our arms and plunge
> them deep through laughter, through

"Forest Fear," by Aaron
Douglas, was an illustra-
tion for *The Emperor
Jones.* Provided by an
anonymous donor.

> pain, through sorrow, through hope, through disap-
> pointment, into the very depths of the souls of our
> people and drag forth material crude, rough, neg-
> lected. Then let's sing it, dance it, write it, paint it.
> Let's do the impossible. Let's create something tran-
> scendentally material, mystically objective. Earthy.
> Spiritually earthy. Dynamic.

Several fascinating Douglas illustrations chronicle black life during this time. One of the most interesting appeared on the cover of
The Crisis in September 1927, *The Burden of Black Womanhood.* The
woman featured in the center of the cover illustration is clad in an
Egyptian-inspired garment, with her shoulders parallel to the picture
plan, her hips to the side. The flatness of the figure shows the influences of Synthetic Cubism, Matisse, Egyptian art, and art of the Ivory
Coast. The woman's profile appears to be that of a Dan mask; she
looks heavenward, with her Deco-patterned hair flowing down her
back, while she carries the burdens of the world in her strong arms, a
world framed by Orphist-inspired concentric circles. Below her,
mountains that resemble pyramids, a tulip that represents papyrus,
precisionist skyscrapers to show modern urban life, a factory, and a
log cabin showing rural roots cross the base of the composition. The

date and price of the magazine are encased by a river lining the bottom of the cover, perhaps representing the Nile River, as Douglas often did. This visually striking cover attracted a substantial female audience and addressed Du Bois's commitment to include women's issues regularly in *The Crisis*, including parenting issues, birth control, education, and in the early years, suffrage rights.

Douglas's magazine illustrations extended to the covers of two new magazines. The elite among Harlem's talented young artists and writers collaborated on the first issue of *FIRE!!* The group included Douglas, writer Zora Neale Hurston, poet Langston Hughes, writer Bruce Nugent, artist/writer Gwendolyn Bennett, and Wallace Thurman, who served as editor. Douglas was deeply involved in this venture, providing the place for meetings at his home, and penning the artistic statement on stationery he designed. The organizers hoped to break from the traditional narrow leadership of Harlem's intellectual elite and found a more radical, youth-oriented publication. Douglas's statement captures this youthful defiance:

> We are all under thirty. We have no get-rich-quick complexes. We espouse no new theories of racial advancement, socially, economically or politically. We have no axes to grind. We are group conscious. We believe that the Negro is fundamentally, essentially different from their Nordic neighbors. We are proud of that difference. We believe these differences to be greater spiritual endowment, greater sensitivity, greater power for artistic expression and appreciation. We believe Negro art should be trained and developed rather than capitalized and exploited. We believe finally that Negro art without Negro patronage is an impossibility ... if there is any one thing more than another that we ask of our friends it is that they remove their Nordic (White folks) spectacles before they criticize or even praise our work.

Douglas served as *FIRE!!*'s chief artist; his cover design was particularly striking. The cover, in black and red, provided an original expression of the influences of African identity and memory. It was so simple in its clean, plain design, it seemed almost abstract. The cover was a profile of a mask-like face. On the left were eyes, nose, lips, and chin, created by simple geometric voids. On the right were an ear and an earring. Below, a sphinx lined the base of the cover. Again, Douglas took a risk. To become involved in the venture, he risked alienating the mainstream Harlem leadership, including Du Bois and Charles S. Johnson, and he risked his own finances. Despite pooling their finances to publish it, only one issue of *FIRE!!* ever appeared. Later in life he called the venture, proudly, "daring ... outrageous ... outlandish" and said the magazine's title captured "the uninhibited spirit that is behind life."

Douglas also designed a very creative cover for a magazine that never made it into production, *Spark: Organ of the Vanguard.* (His original drawing is in the Schomburg Center for Research in Black Culture.) The cover, signed at the bottom and dated 1934, was a black and white drawing dominated by a black fist, strong and sure, complete with shackle and broken chain, crossed by Orphist-Cubist rays and a curving Orphist line. The faceted composition contained many smaller scenes, including a lynch mob, with clubs poised to attack, a steeple representing the black church, skyscrapers representing modern life, war ships, a lynching victim, marching troops and artillery, an enraged soldier with a swastika on his chest, and the letters "DEMO," which represent the unfinished, unfulfilled, broken promise of democracy. The fist was particularly bold, and presaged the future symbol of black power long before that icon had been developed. The cover showed Douglas firmly ensconced in contemporary political issues in Harlem life, at a time when he became interested in the tenets of Marxism. Like many black intellectuals who were radicalized by the Depression, Douglas was willing to take risks and was anxious to express the political needs and agenda of his people in a daring and audacious manner.

Douglas spent the year 1928 at the Albert C. Barnes Foundation in Merion, Pennsylvania, along with Gwendolyn Bennett. He hoped the year would establish his reputation further and help him find financial support to live and study in Paris. It did not lead directly to that result, but it did expose him to many of the modern art masters in Barnes's collection, including Matisse, Picasso, Modigliani, and a fantastic African art collection. The African art pieces at the Barnes numbered over two hundred. Barnes believed African sculpture was the highest form of sculpture attained in the history of art. His collection came primarily from present-day Mali, Gabon, Congo, and Ivory Coast, as he felt those four countries produced the strongest works.

Douglas received numerous commissions to illustrate books and provide journal illustrations, including for James Weldon Johnson's *God's Trombones*, Paul Morand's *Black Magic*, Wallace Thurman's *The Blacker the Berry*, and the journal *Theatre Arts Monthly*. Perhaps his most moving and revealing commission was the Fisk University murals, restored only recently. Douglas was commissioned in 1930 by the president of Fisk University, Henry Jones, to create a large mural cycle for the relatively new library, a neo-gothic step-back structure, Cravath Hall. In the original commission, he was hired to decorate the catalogue room, the north reading room, and the south room on the second floor, and the periodical room and Negro Collection room on the third floor. The third-floor murals did not survive.

In some ways, the murals appear to be disjointed because they are spread throughout several rooms and are interrupted by windows; it is hard to see a continuous narrative. The recent restoration, painstakingly executed by the Washington, D.C.-based team Cunningham-Adams, has revealed that the rooms and the mural program are indeed connected and inter-related. Through the discovery of four missing end wall murals in two rooms, and decorative frescoing of ceilings and supports, the entire program now appears as one cohesive story, all carefully planned by Douglas. In the catalogue room, Douglas planned seven panels, which included representations of Day, Philosophy, Drama, Music, Poetry, Science, and Night.

In the reading rooms, Douglas planned an ambitious cycle, which he described as the "Pageant of the Negro" from Central Africa to contemporary America. In the north room, he showed the Negro in Africa, beginning in the jungle where the slaves had originally lived, followed by the men who bore burdens down to Egypt, represented by pyramids. Hunters and warriors lead the viewer to the magic fetish located in the center of the wall, where its worshippers are depicted as well. A tom-tom player beats a war-dance rhythm; the enslaved are taken down to a slave ship in the corner.

"Defiance" was one of Douglas' illustrations for *The Emperor Jones*. Provided by an anonymous donor.

Douglas considered the two greatest contributions of the Negro in America to be music and labor. On the north wall between the windows, opposite the "Negro in Africa," he included murals to represent the spirituals. From the left to right are pictured "Gabriel blow your horn," "Four and twenty elders knelt down to pray," "I want two wings," "Arise, shine for thy light is a comin,'" "Steal away," "Go down Moses," and "My ship is on the ocean."

In the south room, Douglas chronicled the Negro in America. "The African slaver...is sufficient to recall that magnificent picture of terror and death which thousands of slaves endured in the middle passage." Douglas pictured slaves moving in step, dragging their burdens, while one kneels on the auction block. Christianity, the first great source of spiritual light for the American Negro, is symbolized by a skull, Golgotha, over which is spread outstretched wings. Religion helped to ease the burdens of the enslaved, and the second light, a giant star of Emancipation, is held aloft by human hands. The third great light was the light of Education, symbolized by Fisk's Jubilee Hall, shown in silhouette against the light. (This mural no longer exists.) On the south wall of the south room, laborers are represented by railroad builders, farmers, cotton pickers, road builders, and miners. Douglas recounted, "At the end of the wall a small figure turns a questioning glance toward the city...is the Negro to become a machine-tending city dweller or is he to remain rural?" The final two mural cycles on the third floor were destroyed.

The destroyed murals included those in the periodical room, which showed important countries across the world, symbolized by famous buildings, and the Negro Collection room, which chronicled phases of African life. The Cunningham-Adams team found a few small areas with paintings still remaining, including the light image of the Lincoln Memorial, but they were unable to restore the few remaining fragments.

After Douglas created the Fisk mural series he returned to Harlem, where he executed his famous 135th Street Library murals, *Aspects of Negro Life*. He then returned to Fisk University in 1937 to become the founding chairman of the art department, where he would spend the next forty years. He was asked by Fisk to refurbish the murals in 1969, and did so. When the restoration team of Cunningham-Adams removed several layers of dirt from the murals (which turned out to be coal dust) they discovered that during the 1969 restoration Douglas had actually repainted the entire cycle. In fact, his 1969 restoration is more fully credited to Douglas than the original 1930 project, for which he had substantial help from assistants. Douglas had once said that he knew very little about color as a young artist. But over time, he had developed strong ideas about color. Although he suffered from serious vision impairment in 1969, he knew the project well enough to restore it successfully himself.

The Fisk murals originally were dominated by muted, light blues; later, in the restoration, Douglas repainted the entire series with a much bolder palette including deep greens and mauves. It is possible that the colors had faded during the forty years, but most likely he purposefully employed a strikingly different palette when he repainted it. The new color scheme reflected Douglas's maturation as an artist; as an older man, he wanted to make a more forceful statement. Douglas had thirty years to look at his art and think about it before he repainted it. He may have been critiquing his work in his mind for decades, and decided that cleaning his own murals was a chance to rectify any shortcomings. Douglas also may have seen such drastic changes to his work over the years, given the accumulation of dirt and the damage suffered by his murals, that he felt he needed to recover his own aesthetic intent given these irreversible depredations.

As a young artist in the 1920s, Douglas had worked with W.E.B. Du Bois and shared his interest in issues of identity and collective memory. Douglas took the Fisk commission very seriously. He hoped to provide the Fisk students with a visual source of race pride, a depiction of the historical struggle of African Americans from slavery to freedom, and of course, the inspiration of education within the hallowed halls of Cravath Library. He sought a connection with Africa and an African identity, the memory of slavery as well as the ultimate survival and success of African Americans. He honored Africa as a source of identity and inspiration, and the entire program culminated in the promise of a brighter future through Fisk's opportunities in education.

Not content with his growing commissions in Harlem, Douglas wanted to fulfill a lifelong dream of studying in Paris. After the 1930 completion of the massive Fisk project, he finally got his chance. After a brief stint at the Academie Grand Chaumiere he studied at the Academie Scandinave. Douglas worked hard at traditional life drawing classes, and made drawings of cubist-inspired circles as he pursued a brief interest in modernist painting.

Upon his return to Harlem, Douglas found more commissions awaiting him. He had become an accomplished muralist, providing murals for Bennett College, the College Inn in Chicago, and others. The Fisk murals would provide the background for his smaller but extremely important series for the 135th Street Library, now the Schomburg Center for Research in Black Culture, *Aspects of Negro Life*. Here Douglas experimented with color in a much more sophisticated way, in large-scale images that chronicle black life. *The Negro in an African Setting* depicts a joyful life before slavery. *Slavery Through Reconstruction* features life after the Emancipation Proclamation, not all of it in a positive light. *An Idyll of the Deep South* evokes the toil of labor and the realities of lynching. *Song of the Towers* brings home the realities of Depression era America, with hope residing in the creativity of black Americans. The murals include Douglas's signature style, influenced again by Cubism, African Art (including Egyptian), and Orphism as well. This series was executed at a time when Douglas was exploring Marxism, but he feared he could not make these influences too obviously felt in the murals because of the possibility of censorship.

Following the completion of the Schomburg murals, Douglas devoted himself primarily to revisiting his old works and painting a number of unexceptional portraits. In 1937 and 1938 he won Rosenwald Fellowships that allowed him to travel through the South and to the Caribbean. In 1940 he left Harlem and joined the faculty at Fisk, where he taught art courses and organized the institution's art department. In 1944 he received his MFA degree from the Teacher's College at Columbia University.

Douglas spent the rest of his career at Fisk, teaching and chairing the art department until his retirement in 1964. He continued to paint portraits and participated in a number of art exhibits around the country. He also lectured on the history of African American art and on the Harlem Renaissance.

Aaron Douglas died in Nashville, Tennessee, on February 3, 1979, at the age of eighty. Fisk University held a memorial celebration of his life, which was attended by many close friends and colleagues. Douglas left instructions to have his ashes scattered.

Douglas had a lifelong commitment to reclaiming African American identity, the joy of African American art, culture, and the jazz age, with a strong influence of the historical memory of Africa. Douglas had a rich career, highlighted by numerous group exhibitions and one-man shows. But his passion was to create a black-made image of African American life from the vantage point of a man deeply interested in the identity of his people. He recognized that he had a unique power as an artist, and he was always willing to take risks to relay his message. Through his illustrations, murals, paintings, and teaching, Aaron Douglas inspired both the public and his students to explore and celebrate African American history and culture.

Jacob Lawrence

(1917–2000)

ALVIA WARDLAW

Chronologically, Jacob Lawrence was born into the post-Harlem Renaissance generation. He was fifteen years younger than poet Langston Hughes or jazz great Duke Ellington. Spiritually, he was deeply connected to the Renaissance. He arrived in Harlem in 1930 at age thirteen and immediately immersed himself in the youth arts movement there. Because visual arts lagged behind literature and music, Lawrence's emergence as a significant artist in the late 1930s still placed him in the Renaissance period. More important, Lawrence was something of a prodigy. He began his first major work, his series of forty-one paintings, The Life of Toussaint L'Ouverture, *when he was still a teenager. By 1941, he had completed a large body of his major work, including the series on L'Overture, a similar biographical series on Harriet Tubman and John Brown, and his masterpiece, a sixty-painting series,* The Migration of the Negro. *At just twenty-four years of age, Lawrence had established himself as one of the great twentieth-century African American painters.*

Jacob Lawrence, 1941. Photograph taken by Carl Van Vechten. Lawrence was only twenty-four when this photo was taken, but he had already produced a body of work that established him as one of the top-ranked African American artists.
Beinecke Rare Book and Manuscript Library, Yale University.

Jacob Lawrence was a child of the Harlem Renaissance. He was born in Atlantic City, New Jersey, in 1917 and when he was thirteen moved with his mother and siblings to Harlem. At this impressionable and watershed age, Lawrence was enthralled by the vibrancy and complexity of New York City. The images of everyday life, combined with his deep interest in African American history, would provide him with the subjects and material that would make him the most influential artist to emerge from Harlem during the Renaissance.

Lawrence's mother possessed the foresight to provide him an environment that was both intellectually challenging and safe for her young son. A single working mother of three, Rosa Lee Lawrence enrolled her son Jacob in an after-school program at Utopia Children's Center. There, at 170 West 130th Street, Lawrence would spend many hours creating art projects. Solemn and quiet, he showed great concentration and focus. At sixteen Lawrence won a prize in Sunday school at the Abyssinian Baptist Church for a map depicting the travels of the apostle Peter.

Soon after he enrolled in the after-school program at Utopia, Lawrence was befriended by Charles Alston, a young artist and recent graduate of Columbia University. In an interview years later, Alston said that the precocious Lawrence needed no instruction, only the challenge inherent in any new projects. As Alston put it, he simply "let Lawrence paint." This unfailing recognition of the unique quality of Lawrence's talents would accompany him throughout his career. Lawrence was fortunate to be embraced by a teacher like Alston who permitted the serious young boy to work at his own pace, undisturbed, manipulating color and form that would later evolve into his signature style. Alston's permissive role as a mentor reflected the creative climate in Harlem, where many elders supported young talent such as Lawrence—often to the point of personal sacrifice. New York City was a great laboratory of creativity for the artist to explore, and Harlem was the young Lawrence's lively incubator.

Several adults in Harlem would shape Lawrence's life forever. Two of the artist's favorite mentors were Charles Seifert and Augusta Savage, both major figures in the Harlem Renaissance. Professor Seifert, a self-taught historian and bibliophile, had read almost everything that had been published on black history. He then passed that information on to the quiet and serious Lawrence. Seifert's guidance and the resources available at the 135th Street Library enabled Lawrence to became an independent researcher who sought out little-known stories of African American life not to be found in traditional and mainstream publications.

Another major figure, Augusta Savage, had her own artist workshop, teaching studio art courses in sculpture and painting. Both as teacher and mentor, Savage supported and promoted Lawrence's career. In 1934, when Lawrence was seventeen and still a student at the High School of Commerce, he was forced to give up his education to work three jobs when his mother lost her job. Fortunately, Lawrence managed to attend his art classes during this period. It was also at Augusta Savage's workshop that Lawrence met his future wife, Gwendolyn Knight, a beautiful young artist from Barbados.

Through the synthesis of his training in design from Alston and Savage and his sense of African American history from Seifert, Lawrence was able at a very young age to create works that celebrated the lives of African American icons: *Toussaint L'Ouverture* (1937), *Frederick Douglass* (1938–39), and *Harriet Tubman* (1939–1940). These works, created in series of multiple images, developed a new visual language in American art. Military strategist and leader Toussaint L'Ouverture was unknown to most Americans, both black and white, during that period that coincided with the unleashing of Jim Crow laws and the massive numbers of lynchings throughout the South. Lawrence saw the play *Haiti*, written by W. E. B Du Bois, at the Lafayette Theater in 1936 and soon after began his own research at the Division of Negro History, Literature, and Prints at the 135th Street Library.

The Life of Toussaint L'Ouverture, completed in 1938 when Lawrence was twenty-one, consisted of forty-one pictures depicting L'Ouverture's role in establishing Haiti as the first black republic in the western hemisphere. The series was exhibited at the opening of the DePorres Interracial Center in Harlem in 1939, then at the Baltimore Museum and the following year at Columbia University and the Chicago Negro Exposition.

The Life of Toussaint L'Ouverture, 1938, visually documented the genius of the general who struggled and fought to bring Haiti to freedom. The determination of a people to fight hand-to-hand battles for their freedom, the specific logistics of military battle with the French, and the later downfall of General L'Ouverture was vividly documented by Lawrence. During this period before television and the advent of mass media, when African American history was not discussed in schools or documented in publications produced for non-black audiences, Lawrence consciously strove to bring the name and deeds of Toussaint L'Ouverture into the mainstream of African American history. In the process he developed a genre of multi-canvas artworks that brought forth a historical narrative.

All of Lawrence's instructors at the time recognized the unique dynamic of the young artist's design style. It displayed a self-assurance that matched the ambitious, audacious magnitude of his themes. His geometricized forms, combined with just enough visual tension, allowed the viewer to explore the composition. At the same time Lawrence always included unexpected elements that intrigued. The sharply defined quality of many elements was heightened by a strong sense of color. The result was an interlocking style that provided visual satisfaction of the highest degree.

While studying with Charles Alston and Augusta Savage, Lawrence witnessed the creation of the epic mural series by Aaron Douglas, *Aspects of Negro Life*, that was created for the 135th Street

Library. He watched while, across the street from the library, Charles Alston completed the murals *Magic and Medicine* at Harlem Hospital. As a witness to such cultural history, Lawrence received an extraordinary education outside the classroom.

Charles Alston would become like a father to the artist. Indeed, Lawrence followed Alston to his new center for classes at the Harlem Artist's Guild. In turn Alston welcomed Lawrence into the circle of artists that gathered at his studio at 306 Edgecombe. "306" was a meeting ground for African Americans, just as "291" downtown was a meeting place for contemporary white artists such as Alfred Stieglitz and Georgia O'Keefe. Indeed, 306 was often referred to as the "uptown 291." At 306, Lawrence was able to meet with and talk to artists like Romare Bearden, Alston's young cousin, and the brothers Joseph and Buford Delaney, as well as the philosopher, professor, and cultural critic Alain Locke. It was Locke, after an introduction by Alston, who in 1938 arranged the first exhibition of Lawrence's art at the 135th Street YMCA. The exhibition was sponsored by the James Weldon Johnson Literary Guild, and Alston wrote a prophetic statement about the young artist for the exhibition brochure:

> The place of Jacob Lawrence among younger painters is unique. Having thus far miraculously escaped the imprint of academic ideas and current vogues in art to which young artists are most susceptible, he has followed a course of development dictated entirely by his own inner motivations. Any evaluation of his work to date is most difficult, a comparison impossible. Working in the very limited medium of flat tempera he achieved a richness and brilliance of color harmonies both remarkable and exciting.
>
> He is particularly sensitive to the life about him; the joy, the suffering, the weakness, the strength of the people he sees every day. This for the most part forms the subject matter of his interesting composi-

tions. Still a very young painter, Lawrence symbol-
izes more than any one I know, the vitality, the seriousness and promise of a new and socially conscious
generation of Negro artists.

Almost eight decades later, Gwendolyn Knight Lawrence would
similarly reflect upon the talent of her husband of fifty-seven years
and remark, "I knew all of the artists of that time (the Harlem
Renaissance) and compared to Jacob they were all *a la mode*. Jacob
was the one who was on the cutting-edge. I might be wrong about
that, but that is what I believe."

Jacob Lawrence found in Gwendolyn Knight an intellectual
match and a fellow lover of art who, with her quiet and elegant
demeanor and striking beauty, became the most significant participant in his personal life. Gwendolyn Knight Lawrence recalled helping her friend Jake meticulously apply the written script for his
narrative when he worked on the Frederick Douglass series. She
became the first sounding board for new ideas and comments on the
art world, and she was a fellow artist in every sense of the word.

Jacob Lawrence, 1949 illustration for
Langston Hughes's poem, "Too Blue,"
when it appeared in his 1949 book of
poetry, *One Way Ticket*.
Beinecke Rare Book and Manuscript
Library, Yale University.

Together, they explored Harlem, and
Manhattan beyond, accompanying other
artists to view murals and to hear lectures, staying up hours afterwards to talk
with friends over drinks or coffee about a
major topic of the art world.

During the summer, Jacob Lawrence
worked at Camp WoChiCa (Workers
Children's Camp) in upstate New York.
There he taught art to children and
teenagers and organized art projects for
them. African American illustrator
George Ford was on the kitchen staff
that summer and he recalls a member of
the staff told him that Lawrence was "a
famous artist." He finally got up the

nerve to approach Lawrence and tell him of his love of art. Lawrence asked whom he liked and he replied "Rockwell," for the way he could render such life-like hands and anatomy. Later Lawrence would tell him not to worry about Norman Rockwell, but to follow his own vision, advice that Ford took to heart.

Lawrence's sense of community was apparent in all of his work. Whether depicting the migration of his people from the rural South to the urban North or the gripping story of abolitionist John Brown, Lawrence created a visual system that broke down these narrative epics into smaller stories, vignettes that immediately captured a viewer's attention. Consequently, viewers of all ages were able to learn from the details of his pictorial narratives in a way that literature could not immediately convey. One of Lawrence's favorite pastimes was to visit New York public schools and share these stories with the children there. These works also became popular with white viewers in part because they offered not only dynamic and ingenious design, but also provided an intimate glimpse into daily life within the black community.

It was a very methodical approach, which Lawrence would use for his projects for the rest of his life. For the narratives of his major cycles, he used simple, straightforward language that underscored his images in an understated yet direct manner. His images could easily be absorbed. As a teacher himself, Lawrence shared his experiences and his process with students for many years at the New School, Black Mountain College, the Art Students League, Skowhegan School of Painting and Sculpture, Pratt Institute, and finally, the University of Washington.

During this period Lawrence created two more series of paintings, thirty-two panels for *The Life of Frederick Douglass* and thirty-one panels on *The Life of Harriet Tubman*. In the narrative on Tubman, Lawrence produced a detailed biography, beginning with the daily struggles of a young Harriet who was struck on the head with an iron bar by an overseer, and forced to chop wood, plow fields, and haul logs. Lawrence's genius in zoning in upon the details oppression—shackled feet, a hound pulling on a leash, footprints of fugitive slaves in the snow—brought to life dramatic fragments of the harsh existence that led to Tubman's decision to devote her life to the freedom of her people. In humanizing her story without reducing her heroic stature, Lawrence brought forth Harriet Tubman as a true American icon.

In the spring of 1941 Lawrence, with the help of Gwendolyn Knight, painted his most ambitious work, the sixty-panel series, *The Migration of the Negro*. Lawrence documented an epic chapter in American history. This series addressed a universal theme in human history: the movement of a people, forced by circumstances to leave a known place for the unknown. Utilizing once again the details of human landscape—a lynching noose hanging from a tree, the smokestack of a train traveling north, a boll weevil devouring a cotton bulb—Lawrence carefully expressed the character of the South, with challenges and dangers not dissimilar to those of Harriet Tubman's era. In contrast, the movement and vibrancy of life in the North was masterfully captured by Lawrence in his compositions of

Jacob Lawrence, panel 1 from *The Migration of the Negro*, 1940-41, a sixty-panel series of images. Lawrence created several series of paintings, each of which served as a visual history of an episode in the African American experience. Often the images also contained associated text. For this image the text read: "During the World War there was a great migration North by Southern Negroes"
© 2006, The Jacob and Gwendolyn Lawrence Foundation, Seattle/Artists Rights Society (ARS), New York. Reproduced with permission of The Phillips Collection, Washington D.C.

angular diagonals of crowds moving together in one direction towards train gates and knots of people gathered in Harlem to hear street-corner orators. Life in the urban North brought its own challenges, depicted in individuals coming home from work to small apartments disconnected from the earth that had been such, part of their southern experience, or through the new image of racial violence in the form of citizens brutalized by police. Such details make Lawrence's narrative series memorable to the viewer and give them an ageless quality.

The process of breaking down an epic narrative into visual vignettes provided a comfortable point of entry for the viewer, enabling one to examine details of a scene at his or her own pace, while transforming a visual examination of American social history into an intimate and personal experience.

Like many other African American artists of the period who worked largely in the big cities in the North, Lawrence wanted to explore his southern roots. To achieve this goal, he applied for and received one of the highly competitive Rosenwald Fellowships awarded annually to young African Americans who had the potential to become future leaders in science, medicine, education, the arts, and culture. The grant enabled Lawrence to travel throughout the South and create art depicting the region, beginning with the life of John Brown. Following their marriage on July 24, 1941, Jacob and Gwendolyn Knight Lawrence traveled to New Orleans, their first trip south.

They spent the rest of the year in New Orleans living in a rooming house at 2430 Bienville Avenue while Lawrence created the twenty-two images for *The Life of John Brown*, as well as individual paintings depicting life and segregation in the South. While in New Orleans, Lawrence signed a contract with Downtown Gallery in New York and became the first African American to be represented by a major New York gallery. Included in the body of works that he created during this period is a wonderful painting of the African American town of Gee's Bend, Alabama, a small community known now for extraordinary quilters and documented during the period by

Fortune magazine photographer Arthur Rothstein.

In October 1943, Lawrence was inducted into the United States Coast Guard as a steward's mate. He went to boot camp at Curtis Bay, Maryland, and was then transferred to an officers' training station in St. Augustine, Florida. Here he confronted the full force of racial discrimination. However, his commanding officer, Captain J. S. Rosenthal, encouraged him to continue painting and was instrumental in having him assigned to the first "integrated" ship in the service, the weather patrol boat USS *Sea Cloud*. The captain of the vessel, Lieutenant Commander Carlton Skinner, was able to get for Lawrence a rating as a public relations Petty Officer, Third Class, which allowed him to devote himself to painting. During this service, Lawrence painted a series of pictures, some of which were exhibited at the Museum of Modern Art in 1961. The works are now considered lost. This Coast Guard experience led Lawrence to create his next series, *War*, in 1946. It is now regarded by many critics as perhaps his most powerful body of work.

Lawrence reached a pivotal moment in his career at the same time that avant garde arts organizations began integrating. At Black Mountain College, Lawrence was invited by Josef Albers to join the faculty during the summer of 1948. Albers rented a train to bring the couple to Black Mountain to prevent them from having to travel in segregated cars. Jacob and Gwendolyn Lawrence became part of a group of serious artists that included Walter Gropius and Beaumont and Nancy Newhall. They were immersed in the rigors of the Bauhaus style and American abstraction, while others respected Lawrence's use of abstraction in his own work. The embrace of Lawrence's talent by this group placed him in the mainstream of American art, as did his association with Edith Halpert's Downtown Gallery. That the Lawrences were a stunningly beautiful couple in a time in which there was little interaction among the races even in the arts communities made them even more significant as bridge builders between these groups.

In 1949, Lawrence voluntarily entered Hillside Hospital in Queens for treatment of depression. Edith Halpert contributed to his medical expenses and helped Gwendolyn Knight Lawrence find employment while supplying the artist with art materials. He remained there for four months, then returned for a seven-month stay, continuing to paint images of hospital life. Lawrence indicated more than once that part of the reason for his depression was his sense of isolation, having been thrust into the spotlight of the art world while leaving his mentors behind in comparative obscurity. He felt guilty that he achieved success while artists like Charles Alston and Augusta Savage never received the acclaim that he felt they were due.

During this period Lawrence demonstrated the depth of his own empathy for others by creating riveting works that reach deep into the psyche of patients—images of an external passivity moving through a world of medication. It is remarkable that the artist had the self-awareness to document a troubling period in his own life and a courage that enabled him to be proactive about an illness that was little understood during that period. Lawrence credited his wife for getting him through this period in a positive manner.

During the Civil Rights struggle, Lawrence created singular works that responded to this critical period in American history. *Ordeal of Alice*, for instance, echoes the scenes of single Negro students walking through lines of hateful white adults to pursue their education. Lawrence projected the fear and the threat of violence that surrounded these brave young spirits. In the same manner, *Praying Ministers* depicted the source of religious strength through which many leaders moved. *Two Rebels* depicted the bravery of individuals who put themselves in potentially perilous situations in their quest for racial justice.

In 1962, Lawrence worked with the American Society of African Culture (AMSAC), based in New York, to organize an exhibition of his work to be shown in Nigeria. At the invitation of the Mbari Artists and Writers Club Cultural Center, Lawrence traveled to Lagos and Ibadan, where a portion of *The Migration of the Negro*, selected by Lawrence, was exhibited. The ten-day trip was a revelation for Lawrence, and the artist returned in 1964 to Nigeria, where he remained for eight months with his wife. Although the stay was productive, the United States made it difficult for the Lawrences, as any African American traveling to Africa at the time was considered suspect of encouraging rebellion against European colonialism.

In the late 1960s, Lawrence began a series that reflected his interest in the common man. *Builders* (begun in the late sixties but not completed until the seventies) was a commentary on the ability of ordinary men to contribute to the development of a culture through their role in the formation of the institutions and structures of civilization. This series expressed his respect for the anonymous worker. It celebrated design and construction. For all of his past critiques of American culture, the several *Builders* series became Lawrence's anthem of progress. It also reflected his quiet regard and fascination for the men—and women—who built the structures that we, in turn, inhabit.

Lawrence had collected the tools of builders throughout his life. He liked tools, both large and small, because their look and feel, as he once stated, were like small sculptures. He displayed his collection on recessed shelves in his attic studio. He liked to have them around him because they gave him design ideas, they were beautiful to observe, they were satisfying to hold in one's hand, and they reminded him of man's talents as expressed through his hands.

Late in life, at the Fine Arts Center at Texas Southern University in 1991, students presented the seventy-four year old Lawrence with a pair of metal tongs. Holding them aloft, he explained to students his love of such tools. With these tools armies of workers *built,* and it is this notion of public creativity, this sense of ultimate possibility, that Lawrence regarded as uniquely American in its energy.

After setting down the major historic cycles, Lawrence always returned to the richness of the life of the common man, whether sitting on the stoop, bringing home groceries, or gathering at the local tavern. Much as Langston Hughes brought to light the voices of African Americans, so did Lawrence visually capture and define the distinctive personality as embodied in look, stance, and body language. His memory for detail was astounding, and it was this gift that distinguished the way in which he illuminated the essence and the details of life.

In 1971, Jacob and Gwendolyn Knight Lawrence moved to Seattle, settling near the University of Washington, where Lawrence had accepted a teaching position in the Fine Arts Department. In the same year, Lawrence was commissioned by Edition Olympia to create a silk screen print for the 1972 Munich Olympic Games. Lawrence created the image of five black runners with obvious references to Jesse Owens's triumphant victory in Berlin in 1936.

In Seattle, the two artists had an opportunity to spread out their work into individual studio spaces. Like artist couples everywhere, they stayed apart while working, critiquing one another's efforts only when asked. Early pictures of the couple show them as striking, sophisticated, yet simple in their public persona, and they continued to have this kind of presence throughout their years together. Lawrence was the seemingly solemn and quiet partner to Knight's evident beauty and glamour. Without children, they seemed to adopt the entire younger generation, not necessarily as hands-on mentors but as a source of wisdom and inspiration for all who met them. When one got to know the two of them well, one sensed a shared wit and an interest in and keen curiosity about the world and world events, including the art world, the role of African Americans in the United States, and the impact of globalization upon artists. Such intellectual bonds endured and created a palpable connection between them. In their presence one felt as if one were privy to a fascinating and intense fifty-year-long conversation. Their reflections on one another, the art world, and the many famous individuals that they had met over the years were often punctuated with laughter and fond recollections, combined with an enduring seriousness of memory.

They carried this conversation with them wherever they went in the world, sharing it with others. As friends and colleagues witnessed the couple age together, they sensed a true bridging of their intellects and personalities that created an eternal bond. What began as two young artists enjoying together the excitement of an incredible age of discovery and creativity evolved into a lifelong commitment of love and friendship rarely seen in the art world.

Much later in his career, in his studio in Seattle, Lawrence approached his work with the same methodical detail. This quiet technique was again a testimony to the way in which Lawrence held his own art in high regard. There was no rush, no frenzy, only calm, deliberate, and determined application of color. One color would be set down at a time on all sheets of paper, to create, as he explained, a perfect, unifying presentation of color throughout the series. Thus when all grays were applied, he moved on to blue, then to yellow, and so on until all the works had been filled in, like a puzzle. This ultimate control over the work enabled Lawrence to visually monitor the manner in which he was putting down paint while simultaneously reminding him at all times of the scope of his narrative from the first panel to the last. As a teacher, Lawrence's method of applying color remained a wonderful demonstration of how to construct a composition.

Lawrence's Seattle home studio was very much a reflection of the artist himself. The Lawrences lived in a modest, pristinely furnished bungalow in which they carefully displayed works of art dear to them. On the mantle was a portrait of Gwendolyn Lawrence as a young girl by Augusta Savage, created when Gwendolyn Knight and Jacob Lawrence were students of Savage in her Harlem Art Program. Lawrence's studio could be found in the home's finished attic. To reach the studio a visitor walked up a short flight of stairs. There, amidst honey-toned paneled walls, the artist had set up very carefully his immense drawing table and his tempera paints. Everything was perfectly orderly, and in welcoming you to the space where he created so much, he simply stated, "Here we are in my space."

Looking through the windows out across the treetops, the artist seemed to be set apart from the world. There was no music, no telephone. The only decorative elements were the collection of tools that the artist had placed on continuous ledges that wrapped around the walls of the studio at arm's height, easily accessible if the artist wished to use one of the elements for one of his compositions.

Downstairs, the first-floor sunporch was the work space of
Gwendolyn Lawrence. Both worked in quiet solitude, occasionally
checking on each other. Although the artists missed the rich energy
and culture of New York, the quiet of Seattle allowed them to work
without interruption, and the onslaught of a public who meant well
but could eat away at an artist's precious time. In many ways the
artist, like many creative individuals who began their lives or careers
in New York, never left New York City. He dressed in his later years
with the classic style of an African American male. Often sporting
his tweed hat with his pipe, Lawrence had an understated urbane
quality. He was known to enjoy a martini or nightcap with a cigarette at the end of the day. For both he and Gwen, the art of socializing involved conversation. An exchange of ideas over food or
drink was interwoven into their lives.

In his later years, Lawrence received countless awards and recognition. He was the subject of major exhibitions, including a retrospective at the Whitney Museum of Art, *Jacob Lawrence American
Painter,* followed by the retrospective, *Over the Line: The Art of Jacob
Lawrence,* which was organized during the period in which his work
was being examined in a catalogue raissone project. Lawrence continued to be an inspiration to younger artists who regarded him as a
mentor and master painter. He never stopped being aware and committed to his image of those subjects that were vital to American
history, as his series *Hiroshima* demonstrated. He was a deeply
engaged teacher and was always interested in seeing that young people were inspired to create and express themselves freely. The volume of his work and the keen vision with which he saw the world
became more crystal clear over the passing years.

Jacob Lawrence died in Seattle on June 9, 2000. He was eighty-
three. Trevor Fairbrother, curator of modern art at the Seattle Art
Museum, described Lawrence as "an artist who took on the burden
of speaking for his race as well as himself, and he did so in a manner
that was fearless, dignified, honest and beautiful."

Seven years earlier, noted African American historian Henry
Louis Gates Jr. had praised Lawrence for his ability to structure nar-

ratives through visual images: "I can't think of anyone who combines a mastery of narrative with the mastery of visual images. He brought the two traditions together."

On September 28, 2000, Lawrence's friends and admirers gathered at the Riverside Church in New York to celebrate his life. His memorial service attracted prominent African American artists and literary figures. Among the speakers was novelist Toni Morrison, who had won the Nobel Prize in literature; she discussed Lawrence's significance as an artist of the African American experience.

The ultimate importance of the work of Jacob Lawrence resides in the artist's marriage of an intellectual curiosity and a sense of cultural history with an incomparable design sensibility. Lawrence utilized visual art as a means of directly educating his people. With his own education having been abruptly interrupted during the Depression, the artist was especially aware of and sensitive to the potential of alternative sources of expression, such as the visual arts, to serve as enriching educational experiences for African Americans of all ages and backgrounds. The powerful dynamics of his painting style served to underscore the impact of the narrative content of his work upon his audience; his strong color schemes and his bold yet often finely detailed compositions were immediately engaging to audiences in pre-World War II America.

His art continues to command the attention of twenty-first century art lovers throughout the world. His aesthetic vision—a brilliance of color combined with sharply defined compositions—enables the viewer to grasp immediately the nuances of complex historic narratives. His continuous dedication throughout the twentieth century to the expression of both the small genre narrative and the epic chapters of human history, from Frederick Douglass to Hiroshima, resulted in the creation of a body of work that is essential to the study of American art.

Romare Bearden

(1911–1988)

ABDUL GOLER

*Romare Bearden was a child of the Harlem Renaissance. He was nine
years old when he arrived in Harlem. He lived with his parents a few feet
from the stage door of Lafayette Theater in a home that was a gathering
place for Harlem's political and cultural notables, including poets
Langston Hughes and Countee Cullen, singer and actor Paul Robeson,
and W.E.B. Du Bois. As a youth, Bearden entered Harlem's art scene,
spending time at Augusta Savage's Harlem studio. Following college he
easily joined the arts community through established artist Charles Alston,
his cousin and childhood companion. His art expands beyond the work of
other Renaissance artists. Absent are the African motifs favored by Douglas or the historical narrative of Lawrence. Bearden developed his own
style as he moved from cartooning and illustration to painting, and finally
to his masterful work in collage. His work situates him as a transitional
figure that moved from the Harlem Renaissance into post-Renaissance
African American art.*

Chronologically speaking, Romare Bearden was not a Harlem Renaissance artist. He was only nine years old when his family permanently settled in Harlem, just as the first stirrings of the Renaissance were emerging. Yet Bearden's work is both spiritually and thematically aligned with the movement in spite of his well-known criticisms of various aspects of it. More significantly, Bearden passed from childhood to early adulthood thoroughly immersed in the environment of the movement, and as a young artist he worked within the flourishing artistic, political, and intellectual environment that had been constructed primarily by Harlem Renaissance literary and artistic figures. These years in Harlem were interspersed with brief but repeated forays to Charlotte and Pittsburgh during his childhood. As he grew older and his desire to be an artist increased, Bearden centered himself in New York City, which he viewed as his artistic Mecca.

Fred Romare Harry Bearden was born in Charlotte, North Carolina, on September 2, 1911, to Howard Bearden and Bessye Johnson Bearden. Romare Bearden, as he was called, began his life as a member of a family with some artistic talent. His paternal great grandfather painted, his mother sketched in charcoal, and his father played the piano. During Romare's infancy, the Beardens lived with his paternal grandmother and great-grandparents, who were well established in Charlotte's black middle class. The great-grandparents had worked for a time as servants in the household of Woodrow Wilson's parents. By the time Romare was born, his great-grandfather had retired from the postal service and owned a general store and two rental houses, as well as the home where the family resided. Bearden's maternal grandparents lived in Pittsburgh, where they owned and operated a boarding house. Both of Bearden's parents attended college.

Despite the economic comforts they enjoyed living with their family in Charlotte, in 1914 Howard and Bessye Bearden and their young son left North Carolina and, like so many other African Americans, moved north. In large part the decision to migrate grew out of the racial problems they encountered in the South. Howard

Bearden was of dark complexion, while his wife and son, on the other hand, were light enough to be mistaken for white, complicating their life in the Jim Crow South. So the family headed north. For several years the Beardens were unsettled, and spent some time in Pittsburgh or back in North Carolina. Romare continued to spend time during his childhood visiting his grandparents and other relatives in North Carolina and Pittsburgh. However, by 1920 the family was firmly established in Harlem, just in time for the dawning of the Harlem Renaissance.

The Bearden family thrived in the rich cultural milieu that was Harlem in the 1920s. While Howard Bearden immersed himself in providing for his family's economic needs, Bessye Bearden became active in the community's political and artistic circles. From 1922 to 1939 she served on the New York City School Board, the first black woman to do so. From 1927 to 1928 she served as the New York-based editor for *The Chicago Defender*. In the late 1920s, Bessye Bearden managed the box office of the Lafayette Theater. In the late teens and early 20s, the Lafayette was one of the few venues for black "professional" actors and had its own company, the Lafayette Players. By the mid-1920s it catered to more popular tastes as it was also a major venue showcasing the work of talents, such as Bessie Smith, and Bill "Bo Jangles" Robinson, who performed to integrated audiences. Despite the fact that the theater rarely staged productions by black playwrights, black actors such as Paul Robeson received some of their first stage time there. The theater also screened films. In the spring of 1921, black filmmaker Oscar Micheaux premiered his film, *The Gunsaulus Mystery*, at the Lafayette Theater. The film, based on an actual murder, included Bessye Bearden as a member of its cast, along with the blues legend Ethel Waters.

Given Bessye's political and artistic activities, it is not surprising that the Bearden home became a gathering place for Harlem's intellectual and creative community, especially after the Bearden family moved to 154 West 131st Street, in the heart of Harlem's entertainment district. Their home was across the street from the backstage entrance to the Lafayette Theater, and around the corner from Connie's Inn and other nightspots like the Rhythm Club and Muzzie Anderson's. Growing up as a child, the Bearden household was a social nexus for prominent politicians, artists, composers, and musicians. Visitors included poets Langston Hughes and Countee Cullen, writer/journalist George Schuyler, singer, actor, and political activist Paul Robeson, and race leaders W.E.B. Du Bois and Mary McLeod Bethune. Experimental cross-cultural fermentation was typical of the period, and as a youngster Bearden was surrounded by people who encouraged him to enter the arts by the examples they provided in their own lives and careers. Bearden was directly influenced by legendary musicians such as Fats Waller and Duke Ellington, a Bearden family cousin. He also was influenced by the black spiritual music tradition through exposure to the work of such composers as W. C. Handy and brothers James Rosamond and James Weldon Johnson, creators of the "Negro National Anthem"—"Lift Every Voice and Sing" (1900).

The effect of this cultural environment on Bearden can be seen in his artistic creations later in his life. For example, James P. Johnson, a classically trained pianist and prolific composer who was a teacher of Fats Waller, created what many considered to be the first recorded jazz piano solo, *Carolina Shout,* in 1921. A half century later Bearden produced a collage that shared its name with Johnson's jazz piece. Both compositions incorporated the interplay of the holy and the profane, reflections of urban life and the memory of the rural south, and the influences of the classical traditions of the West and funky roots of the black Atlantic.

Romare Bearden grew up surrounded by the sounds, the personalities, and the creativity of the Harlem Renaissance, and this culturally rich environment had an impact on the young man. His first direct exposure to the world of the visual arts came when, as a teenager, he joined a group of young men who frequented Augusta Savage's Studio of Arts and Crafts on West 143rd Street in 1925 and 1926. In a 1979 interview for the *Amsterdam News,* Bearden recalled that Savage allowed the young men to use her studio as a workshop and gathering place, and she served as an artistic role model. "She was open, free, resisted the usual conventions of the time, and lived for her art." Bearden cited this experience as his artistic awakening.

During this period Bearden also met the artist Aaron Douglas, who was a frequent visitor at his parents' home. In the late 1920s Douglas was the most acclaimed black artist associated with the Harlem Renaissance, noted for his illustrations in *The Crisis* and *Opportunity*, his illustrations and cover work for the books of Harlem Renaissance writers, and for the African motifs he incorporated into his illustrations and paintings. Douglas became well known in the mid-1920s for stunning, kaleidoscopic work that depicted aspects of Negro history. In the early 1930s, Douglas had his first one-man gallery show, created striking murals at the 135th Street YMCA in 1933, and produced the mural cycle, *Aspects of Negro Life*, at the 135th Street branch of the New York Public Library. Bearden surely viewed Douglas's creations; the murals in particular provided stunning visual lessons in what could be learned from combining the geometric forms of African sculpture and stylized negroid features with a modernist sensibility.

Bearden's interest in art was also nourished by his cousin, Charles Alston. As a child "Spinky," as he was called, was very much a part of the Bearden household. By the early 1930s, Alston had achieved some success in Harlem art circles and was in a position to provide support in helping Bearden connect to the Harlem artistic scene. Bearden credited Alston with teaching him about painting.

Bearden had many anecdotal tales of Harlem from this period. He recalled the creation of the dance the "Lindy Hop" in a Harlem club as a kind of spontaneous tribute to Charles Lindbergh's successful completion of the world's first transatlantic flight in May 1927. Likewise, the death of the entertainer Florence Mills in November 1927 had a lasting impact. He remembered the streets of Harlem thronged with fans who had gathered to give their final respects to the much-loved comedienne of humble origins, star of the musical revue *Blackbirds*, who had gotten her first break in Noble Sissle and Eubie Blake's all-black production *Shuffle Along* in 1921. The crowds threw roses into the air as the horse-drawn hearse made its way to the church. After the ceremony blackbirds were released. The event was one of the most attended in the history of Harlem, and Bearden's recollection of it, montage-like and cinematic in its layering of imagery, imparts a lasting mental impression.

After graduating from high school in 1929, Bearden enrolled in Lincoln University, an African American private college southwest of Philadelphia. A year later he transferred to Boston University, and then in 1932 he transferred to New York University. As Bearden progressed through these three universities, his academic focus shifted. At Lincoln, Bearden took a traditional academic program with courses in mathematics, science, philosophy, and classical languages—possibly as preparatory classes for medical school, honoring his mother's wish that he pursue the study of medicine. At Boston University, Bearden enrolled in the Art Department of the School of Education, where he took such courses as painting, design and color, cast drawing, perspective, drawing of ornament, freehand drawing, and art history. He also submitted cartoons for the student publication, *The Beanpot,* and played on the varsity baseball team.

Following a meeting in 1931 with the noted black cartoonist and illustrator E. Simms Campbell, Bearden transferred to New York University in 1932. He continued to major in art education and enrolled in a number of art courses including figure drawing, water color painting, and linoleum block printing; he also took several art-related courses like mechanical drawing, lettering, appreciation of art, literature, and a number education courses, including teaching of art, and observation of teaching in high schools. Bearden received his bachelor of science degree from NYU in education in 1935. While at NYU, Bearden was a very active member of the student publication, not only contributing numerous cartoons to *The Medley* but also frequently serving on its managing and artistic boards from December 1934 through May 1936.

During his years at NYU, Bearden achieved his first successes as an artist, expanded his art education beyond the courses he took at the university, entered the Harlem arts scene, and made contacts with downtown artists. While enrolled at New York University, Bearden took on side projects producing cartoons and illustrations for several prominent black publications. He created the March 1932 cover for the National Urban League's journal, *Opportunity*, and sold cartoons to *The Crisis* beginning in 1934. He continued as a freelance cartoonist providing material to *The Crisis* for approximately two years. These initial successes intensified his interest in cartooning and led to further work, including a series of cartoons in *The Crisis* from April 1934 to January 1936. He also served a stint as the editorial page cartoonist for the Baltimore *Afro-American* from September 1935 through May 1937.

Romare Bearden in army uniform, circa 1942.
Beinecke Rare Book and Manuscript Library, Yale University.

Bearden considered cartooning to be serious artistic work, and expressed this view in a well-researched paper he wrote on the history and development of cartoons while a student at NYU. More significant for Bearden's development as an artist, his cousin Charles Alston and black cartoonist Elmer Simms Campbell convinced him to enroll in German artist George Grosz's art classes at the downtown Art Students League. Bearden officially enrolled in Grosz's class in August 1933 and continued to study with Grosz in an unofficial capacity for about two years. In a 1972 interview with Jim Hatch and Camille Billops, Bearden recalled, "I couldn't wait to get to class. George Grosz showed me other people who drew—[Hans] Bellmer, [Albrecht] Durer . . . [he was a] very good teacher for me." Grosz introduced him to such great masters of European drawing as Honoré Daumier, Francisco de Goya y Lucientes, Kathe Kollwitz, Jean-Louis Forain, and Jean August-Dominique Ingres—artists known for often embodying stinging social commentary in their work.

Grosz himself is a particularly important figure in the development of the Dada movement in Germany during the Weimar Republic. He, along with John Hartfield and Hannah Hoch, are attributed with creating Dada collage—an art form that involved the manipulation of photographic images into a montage form, often for propaganda. Grosz's tutelage influenced Bearden's work in two ways. First, the German artist's own work as an excellent draftsman helped the budding young artist develop his skills as an illustrator; more important, Grosz likely introduced Bearden to the power and potential of collage work, a form that dominated much of Bearden's later output. In particular, Grosz's 1919 watercolor on paper, *Untitled* (Panorama), with its sharp breaks and angles, use of an underlying geometric matrix, architectural background, sharp delineation of human figures, and technique of creating overlapping planes and doors leading the viewer's eye further and further into the composition, seems to foretell the trajectory of Bearden's later work.

Over the course of these two years Bearden and Grosz developed a mutually admiring relationship and Bearden's drawing became less linear and more painterly in its treatment of surfaces, allowing him to better suggest mood and evoke emotion and setting.

Bearden's involvement in the Grosz courses at the Art Students League provided him the opportunity to connect with New York's downtown arts scene. The contacts he made there would continue to be important throughout his career. Also during his NYU days he became more involved with the Harlem arts scene. In the interview with Hatch and Billops, Bearden recalled the Harlem Artist Guild, and the organizational meeting he attended at the 135th Street YMCA along with about seventy other black artists. Bearden was amazed by the number of black artists practicing in Harlem—and reassured by the presence of "all those others trying to become artists—like me." Under the lead of Augusta Savage, the Guild pressured the Federal Arts Project of the WPA to hire more African American artists. In 1935, Alston became the director of the Harlem Art Workshop, which was funded by the Works Progress Administration's Federal Art Project.

Bearden graduated from NYU in 1935 with a bachelor of science degree in education. Like many young men and women during the height of the Depression, Bearden found himself looking for gainful employment. His cartooning work, while impressive, did not bring in enough money and there is no indication that he sought a teaching job. Instead he began working for the New York City Department of Social Services in the fall of 1935. Bearden's work at the department provided him with a steady income and allowed him to continue his artistic pursuits. In spite of breaks caused by his service in World War II, study in France, and health issues, Bearden remained with the department for thirty-four years, until he retired in 1969.

Graduation did not significantly impact his art or his connection to the arts community. In 1935, he became a regular participant in a group that met at Charles Alston and Henry Banner's studio at 306 West 141st Street. Bearden recalls "306" as a hangout for writers, artists, and musicians, including Augusta Savage, Robert Blackburn, Ernest Chrichlow, Jacob Lawrence, Norman Lewis, Countée Cullen, Langston Hughes, Claude McKay, Ralph Ellison, Richard Wright, Alain Locke, Katherine Dunham, Addison Bates, and Carl Van Vechten. He also continued to attend meetings of the Harlem Artists Guild, where he came in contact with Jacob Lawrence, Norman Lewis, Gwendolyn Knight, Ernest Chrichlow, and the photographers Morgan and Marvin Smith.

There was much for a young, aspiring artist to see and do both above and below 125th Street, the traditional demarcation between uptown and downtown New York—white and black Manhattan. Take, for example, Bearden's introduction to traditional African sculpture. Bearden would have been well versed in the history of African sculpture as well as its relationship to African Americans in shaping a sense of cultural identity. Such knowledge may have been first perceived by the artist in the early 1920s, when the Bearden household was first filled with discussions of such topics by visiting artists and intellectuals. Later, these issues also would have been discussed at "306," given Alain Locke's involvement there. Yet, while the influx of notable personalities in the Bearden home may have set the ground for peaking Bearden's artistic interests, his study of African sculptural form and iconography most likely took root through the collection of Charles Seiffert.

"Professor" Charles Christopher Seiffert was a collector of African art and had an extensive collection of related books in his home that was utilized by many in the Harlem community in the 1930s. Bearden was among the artists who acknowledged a debt of gratitude to Seiffert's collection, and he recalled viewing the Museum of Modern Art's exhibition *African Negro Art* in a group led by Seiffert in 1935.

While the excitement and fervor of the early Harlem Renaissance years had faded somewhat, Harlem in the mid to late 1930s was still a vibrant place for black artists, writers, and musicians. The Depression years did take a toll on creative folk. Thankfully, though, through the Works Progress Administration and the efforts of such Harlem-based organizations as the Harlem Artist's Guild, black painters, writers, educators, and others were able to find some funding for their work. And in spite of the Depression, Harlem continued to swing, its clubs alive with the sounds of jazz and the flailing of dancers' limbs, seemingly in defiance of the hard times. Harlem's streets were convivial too, Bearden remembered: "You could walk down Seventh Avenue. . .and see James Weldon Johnson, Langston Hughes or Countee Cullen. They were very accessible. We had a community."

During this period Bearden formed enduring friendships with writers, artists, and musicians. In 1936, writer Ralph Ellison relocated to Harlem after three years of study at Tuskegee Institute. Bearden and Ellison met through mutual acquaintances sometime after the latter's arrival in Harlem. The two men had much in common. They shared an interest in music as well as a love of literature, especially the work of T. S. Eliot, the poems of Federico Garcia Lorca, and the novels of Hemingway—writers with whom, Ellison admitted in his naiveté, he had not expected Bearden, a painter, to be familiar. Ellison had opportunities to visit and watch Bearden work in his studio at 125th Street, where the artist explained his working method and what he hoped to achieve through his painting. Ellison felt that "Romie's approach to art and his line of development seemed closer to my own. . .Thus when it seemed impossible that I would get anywhere with my writing, I could talk with him, take heart from his progress, and feel encouraged. Better, I could observe and discuss his search for more effective techniques with which to give artistic form to his conceptions of our general experience. Each of us was concerned with the relationship between artistic technique and individual vision, and we were especially concerned with the relationship between our racial identity, our identity as Americans, and our mission as writer and artist."

Toward the end of the 1930s, Bearden, with the help of fellow artist Jacob Lawrence, had found and rented a studio space at 33 West 125th Street for $8.00 a month including electricity. Jacob Lawrence had space in the same building, as did Harlem Renaissance poet and novelist Claude McKay. In his interview with Hatch and Billops, Bearden noted that McKay occupied a room in front of his studio, and that the Jamaican was "an inspiration to Jake [Lawrence] and I." McKay talked to the young artist about his experiences in Europe, where he had known George Grosz in the early 1920s. McKay was living in near poverty in his 125th Street room, and Bearden "loaned" him electrical power. Among his few possessions McKay kept two copies of *Ecce Homo* that Grosz had presented when they met in Europe.

In addition to their relationship with Grosz, Bearden and McKay shared other common issues. McKay's novels, like much of Bearden's work, celebrated black working-class culture. They both dealt with the everyday slice of life that was typical of Harlem and many other black urban areas, and did not think it necessary to hide or dismiss the seedier aspects of black urban existence. McKay was sharply criticized by Du Bois and some other black critics for focusing on the black working classes and presenting some less-than-flattering aspects of black life. Such critics feared that by exposing the life of the lower classes McKay was feeding racist stereotypes of African

Americans. Like McKay, Bearden attempted to embrace black life in its totality, warts and all. In 1934, while still a student at NYU, he expressed these views in an essay in *Opportunity*, entitled "The Negro Artist and Modern Art." He criticized other African American artists for not sufficiently portraying aspects of black life—for their dependence on so-called "positive" images and their derision of the Southern-derived black working-class culture.

As noted earlier, Bearden's first commercial success in the art world came in the early 1930s when he began selling cartoons and illustrations to black publications. His cartoons as a body of work deserve serious attention, both as an artistic statement and as social and political comment. Bearden's effectiveness as a cartoonist was based on his skills as a draftsman, which he'd honed during his studies with Grosz. Initially Bearden's cartoon work consisted of very static linear compositions; by the mid 1930s he was able to create nuanced renderings that were often less humorous and much more biting and political.

By 1935, Bearden's work at *The Crisis* and the *Afro-American* and other black newspapers demonstrated a cinematic quality that was truly moving, no doubt due to an intimate understanding of the political and social issues that faced black Americans during this period coupled with his technical skills as an illustrator. Among the issues Bearden addressed in his cartoons were: the beginning of the eventual shift of the black electorate from the Republican party to the Democratic party—a political move that his mother was very much involved in as a Democratic party organizer in Harlem; the debates over anti-lynching legislation; Mussolini's invasion of Ethiopia in 1935; the 1931 Scottsboro incident and the ensuing trials; the symbolism of the boxer Joe Louis's defeat of the German boxer Maxx Schmeling on June 22, 1938; and the Methodist Episcopal Church's 1939 decision not to denounce segregation in its religious body at its annual conference. Bearden portrayed these historical events not merely as a satirical illustrator with sharp insight and a wicked tongue, but as an artist whose work, at its best, passionately emoted a depth of feeling that conveyed loss and the tragic results of human folly.

As stated earlier, Bearden's decision to pursue cartooning was greatly influenced by the example of E. Simms Campbell. Campbell was the first black cartoonist to become a staff member of a major mainstream publication, working for such magazines as *Esquire, Saturday Evening Post,* and the *New Yorker.* In 1937, Bearden published six drawings for the National Urban League reprint of *They Crashed the Color Line,* which included a tribute to E. Simms Campbell illustrated by Bearden's black-and-white block drawing of an artist working at his easel. Bearden credited Campbell along with Charles Alston, Carl Holty, and William Baziotes with helping him along in his process of "self-realization."

In the late 1930s, Bearden began to shift from cartoons and illustrations to paintings. His first paintings, created between 1937 and 1940, seem to be his artistic answer to the call he himself generated for more committed portrayals of black life in "The Negro Artist and Modern Art." He exhibited six of his paintings as part of a group show in Harlem in 1939. A year later he had his first solo show at the 306 West 141st Street studio that Harlem activist Addison Bates had taken over. That show was reviewed in the New York *Amsterdam News* as "distinctive." The reviewer observed that Bearden was "among the few of the young Negro artists who have been interested in showing the transition of the colored worker from the agricultural to the urban industrialized community. Not only that, but he completely has absorbed the environment of such a change in the life of these people." Bearden also had two paintings in a 1940 exhibition, *Exhibition of the Art of the American Negro,* at the Tanner Arts Gallery in Chicago, and he participated in two downtown New York shows in 1941.

Bearden's early paintings were fairly large in scale, and in style reflected the social realism of Jacob Lawrence and the Mexican muralists, especially Diego Rivera and José Clemente Orozco, both of whom had exhibits and projects in the northeast U.S. in the 1930s. Two other Mexican artists, Siqueiros and Tamayo, also were part of the late 1930s New York art scene that included Bearden, and both influenced the African American artist's work at this point in his career. In terms of subject matter Bearden's early paintings feature black working-class public and private or family life; they also incorporate religious themes and symbols. In terms of style they reflected both the traditions of abstract art, especially cubism, and representational art with bold depictions of clearly delineated characters. Color use was also bold.

Just as Bearden was beginning to gain recognition outside of Harlem, his enlistment in the army in 1942 diverted his interests and removed him from the New York artistic scene for three years. A year later, his mother's sudden death was a major blow. These developments temporarily stopped his production of paintings. Nevertheless Bearden's reputation continued to grow during the war years. A notable achievement occurred when Caresse Crosby, an internationally prominent promoter of the arts, organized Bearden's first one-man show outside Harlem with the 1943 exhibit *Ten Hierographic Paintings by Sgt. Romare Bearden* at her avant-garde Washington, D.C. gallery. Crosby had heard about Bearden's work through the artist William H. Johnson, who took her to Bearden's studio while he was serving in the army. Following his discharge from service and return to New York in 1945, Crosby introduced Bearden to the modernist gallery owner Samuel Kootz. Subsequently, Bearden became part of the downtown New York art scene as a member in the artists' stable of the Kootz Gallery.

In 1946, Bearden published an essay, "The Negro Artist's Dilemma," in *Critique: A Review of Contemporary Art*, which modified the approach to African American art that he had voiced in his 1934 *Opportunity* essay. In the earlier essay he had demanded that black artists should depict all aspects of the African American experience, especially that involving working-class and rural southern blacks, even if the resulting images offended some African American critics and political leaders. The 1934 essay was in the tradition of Langston Hughes's 1926 essay "The Negro Artist and the Racial Mountain." Twelve years later Bearden was well connected to the downtown art world. His 1946 essay backed away from a racially defined art. Instead he insisted that "the Negro artist must come to think of himself not primarily as a Negro artist, but as an artist." He also called for black artists to free themselves and their works from the confines of "all-Negro art exhibits," which he felt consigned black art to a separate but unequal status. Bearden argued that the quality of the art, not the skin color of the artist, was the primary concern, a point of view also voiced by poet and novelist Claude McKay.

The effect of this ideological shift on Bearden's art is worth noting. Between 1945 and 1947, Bearden had three solo exhibitions at the Samuel Kootz Gallery. The subject of the paintings in these shows reflected Bearden's new explorations into the Western literary cannon. His first show at Kootz, *The Passion of the Christ*, marks a brief diversion for Bearden—it is devoid of depictions of black "folk." The 1946 and 1947 Kootz exhibitions were inspired by European culture. The first was a series of paintings and watercolors inspired by Federico Garcia Lorca's poem about death in the bull ring, "Lament for Ignacio Sanchez Mejias"; the second consisted of eighteen drawings and watercolors based on François Rabelais's early sixteenth-century comic novels, *Pantagruel* and *Gargantua*. While Bearden's new work did not depict African American people or readily identifiable "black" subject matter, Bearden continued to show earlier work in group exhibitions—presenting himself on two fronts so to speak, one as a socially committed artist and the other as the universal artist concerned with archetype. As a member of the Kootz stable the exploration of African American subject matter may not have even been a direction he could further follow. Market forces may have made such interests unwise.

It is important to note that Bearden did not abandon African American themes and topics. Throughout his career these subjects dominated his body of work, although his personal and professional contacts covered both Harlem and downtown, and the subject matter of his art was not exclusively African American. Rather, as his career progressed, he felt free to explore a variety of themes, both racial and non-racial, and although he in no sense turned his back on his African American heritage, like novelist Claude McKay, he sought success as an artist—only an artist.

In many respects, the Harlem Renaissance phase of Bearden's career ended about 1949. His relationship with the Kootz gallery ended as the gallery changed its artistic direction and dropped Bearden and several other artists. In 1950, financed by his veteran's benefits, Bearden traveled to France for the first of several extended trips to study art. Also in the 1950s, he temporarily shifted the focus of his artistic interests from painting to song writing and his permanent residence from Harlem to downtown. For a time in the 1950s Bearden lived in Harlem with his father, but in 1956 he moved with his wife to an apartment in downtown Manhattan at 357 Canal Street, where he remained for the rest of his life. Although Bearden would state that he did not paint at all during this period, from about 1949 to 1961, he actually produced a number of works, including one or two early works in collage. In addition, his works continued to be exhibited, although he had no solo shows between 1955 and 1960. His work was interrupted when he suffered an emotional breakdown in 1956.

In the early 1960s, Bearden shifted from art based on painting to the extensive use of collage as his primary art form. Beginning in the 1960s, he became the master of the collage, producing a large body of work in this medium. He continued to produce collages for the rest of his career. In 1963, he became involved with Spiral, a group of African American artists involved in the civil rights struggle. Bearden proposed a group collage as part of the 1963 March on Washington activities. When his colleagues showed no interest in the project, Bearden went ahead on his own and produced a set of more than twenty collages, then photographically enlarged them for an acclaimed exhibition in 1964.

After the 1960s, Bearden returned to painting, although he continued to produce a significant number of collages. He also now devoted himself full time to art, retiring from his job with the Department of Social Services in 1969. His other work during this time included watercolors and monotypes, a hybrid process that combines painting and drawing with printmaking. He also experimented with works that combined collage and painting. Bearden remained very productive through the 1970s and into the 1980s, producing many of his most significant works. He also mentored younger artists and continued to write about art. In 1969, with abstract artist Carl Holty, he co-authored A *Painter's Mind: A Study of the Relations of Structure and Space in Painting*. In 1993, his co-author, Harry Henderson, finally published A *History of African American Artists: From 1792 to the Present*, a book the two had finished in the late 1970s.

In 1988 Romare Bearden died after a brief hospitalization. Since his death the recognition of his importance to American and African American art has continued to expand, resulting in major retrospective exhibitions. The most significant of these was *The Art of Romare Bearden*, which opened at the National Gallery of Art in 2003 before traveling to other major museums.

Romare Bearden was one of the most celebrated and successful of all African American artists. His life and career began in the Harlem Renaissance and spread across most of the twentieth century. His ability and willingness to experiment and adopt new styles, and to absorb influences from wherever they might originate, provided the basis for the diversity of his work and contributed to his success at marketing his work to diverse elements of the public and the art world.

As a personal note, when I was in college at the University of Michigan in the 1980s, it was common to find images of Bearden's work reproduced on posters in college dorms and off-campus apartments. At the Detroit Institute of Art, an institution I visited frequently as a child, *the* major work by a "black" artist on display was Bearden's mural *Quilting Time*, second only to Henry Ossawa Tanner's *Banjo Lesson*. Not only had Bearden become the poster child (literally speaking) of "black art" by the last quarter of the twentieth century, with the publication of his writings on the theory and history of African American art; he was also considered one of its deans. By the end of the century Bearden's reputation as an artist largely had become confined to the world of black artistic achievement, and the dynamism of his ideas as embodied in his work was relegated to the black art sector. Some have said that this is something Bearden would have deplored, but much of the process that led Bearden and his work in this direction took place while he was alive, and if he did not give tacit approval he at least had first-hand knowledge.

With all said and done, what has been the lasting impact of Bearden's art? Keith Morrison, in his article, "The Global Village of African American Art," quoted Bearden's friend Ralph Ellison on this question. Ellison states that "all of the paintings of Jacob Lawrence, Romare Bearden, and Norman Lewis don't add up to the power of one musical note by Charlie Parker." This statement highlights the difficulty visual artists have in their efforts to capture the attention of black audiences. However, we must not forget that both Bearden and Parker were part of the avant-garde of their time. Just as other musicians were the first to be attracted to Parker's style of playing, artists, art historians, and critics, not the masses, were the first to be attracted to Bearden's style of painting. In both cases, in the beginning it was the ideas in the work being presented that were of paramount importance.

The fact that these ideas no longer seem to be the most important element in the appreciation of either of the artists' work is probably a natural outcome. We have come to settle on the surface of things, the ornamentation, which Bearden time and time again admitted wanting to have highlighted as an element of his work because it emphasized his skill as an artist. All artists want this. So what of the message?

In his 1958 essay, "The Charlie Christian Story," Ellison described the method by which such artists work as "spring[ing] from a contest in which each artist challenges all the rest; each solo flight, or improvisation represents (like the successive canvases of a painter) a definition of his identity: as an individual, as a member of the collectivity and as a link in the chain of tradition. Thus, because jazz finds its very life in an endless improvisation upon traditional materials, *the jazzman must lose his identity even as he finds it.*"

So, what does this tell us about Bearden? First, we know he was not merely a protest or political artist. His art, and his writing about art, even as they embodied a political or social message, were always eloquently wrought because he realized that his message was tanta-mount to his method. The two could not be easily separated. The launching of the National Gallery of Art's retrospective of his work in 2003 has widened the lens through which we regard Bearden's complete body of work by highlighting his erudite interests and sensibilities and the processes he utilized in creating his art. Hopefully this exhibit and the publicity attached to it will stimulate more in-depth scholarly exhibitions and spawn new ways of thinking about Bearden. Bearden the artist was not just fomented in the cauldron of ideas that characterized the Harlem Renaissance; he was also in many ways a Renaissance man.

Josephine Baker

(1906–1975)

ASLI TEKINAY

Josephine Baker was the first international sex symbol of the twentieth century. Baker escaped the poverty of her childhood by joining a vaudeville troupe at the age of thirteen. Four years later she reached "Broadway," first as a member of the chorus line of one of the touring companies of Shuffle Along *and then as a cast member in* Chocolate Dandies. *Baker captivated audiences through her stage presence and her seemingly nonhuman dance style patterned on the movements of African animals, but she quickly passed through the Harlem Renaissance. In 1925 she was in Paris as a dancer in "la Revue Negre." The scantily clad Baker quickly gained fame throughout Europe as a much-beloved entertainer and celebrity. Occasional forays back to Harlem in the late 1920s were less successful. The cool reception she received from American critics along with her intolerance of American racism reinforced her decision to remain in Paris, where she became an icon, notorious for her strolls down the Champs-Élysées with her pet leopard on a leash.*

E veryone has a life story. Josephine Baker was one of those people blessed with more than one. She played many roles in her private life and starred in them all: as Cinderella, as the most famous American expatriate in France, as the first modern sex symbol, as a human rights activist, and as a mother of twelve adopted children. By the time she died in 1975, she had become an international legend.

Josephine Baker was born in a poor, black slum in East St. Louis on June 3, 1906, to Carrie McDonald and Eddie Carson. Of mixed ethnic background, her mother descended from Apalachee Indians and black slaves in South Carolina. Together with her mother and her sister Elvara, Carrie McDonald migrated from South Carolina to St. Louis two years before Josephine was born. They had joined the mass migration of blacks from the rural South to the industrialized northern cities during the first two decades of the twentieth century. Carrie McDonald buried her dream to be a music hall dancer and ended up doing laundry. Josephine's father Eddie, a vaudeville drummer who loved dancing, left Carrie and his daughter within a year after her birth. Soon, Josephine's mother became attached to Arthur Martin and had three more children with him. The family lived in utter poverty, often freezing cold and surrounded by bugs and rats.

Josephine Baker. This photo captures Baker's youth and beauty early in her career.
Beinecke Rare Book and Manuscript Library, Yale University.

When Baker turned eight, she was hired out by her mother to be a maid for a white woman, Mrs. Keiser. She was forced to sleep in the coal cellar with a pet dog and get up at five every morning to do all kinds of house chores—cleaning, doing the laundry, and carrying coal—before she went to school at eight. She was slapped around and beaten by her employer. Keiser burned Baker's hands with boiling water so badly that she had to be hospitalized. After this traumatic incident, Baker's mother rented her to another white woman, Mrs. Mason, who treated her with more kindness. Baker worked for Mason briefly and then was sent back home. However, she was not welcome in the shack where her mother, step-father, and step-siblings lived. This time she was sent to live with her grandmother and aunt Elvara. A skinny and meager-looking girl, Baker was in fact agile and used to hard domestic labor. In 1917, when she was eleven, she witnessed the cruel East St. Louis race riot, one of the most violent and brutal riots in the history of the United States. Black neighborhoods were ravaged, and thirty-nine blacks as well as nine whites died. Baker's memory of it was so powerful that, throughout her life, she returned to it over and over again. She often had nightmares related to the fires, beatings, and lynchings she had seen as a little girl.

Baker left St. Louis when she was thirteen. Her Cinderella story was gradually approaching the ball scene. There was no Prince Charming in this version, but the elemental passage from rags to riches and bondage to freedom certainly did occur. Baker, ambitious and optimistic, desired to be the queen of the dance, to wear glamorous clothes and be admired by all who watched her. She learned to dance on the streets and back alleys of St. Louis. She went to the zoo, observed kangaroos, camels, and giraffes, and imitated their steps. Most likely she did not know that animal movements were the very basis of the black vernacular dance tradition. However, by the time she left St. Louis, she had mastered a rich repertoire of moves. She was ready to dance professionally. Baker joined the troupe called the Dixie Steppers, working as the dresser of the troupe's star, Clara Smith.

Baker traveled around the South with the Dixie Steppers. She also married for the first time when she was thirteen, to a steelworker, Willie Wells. The couple parted after a few months when Josephine cut Wells's head open with a beer bottle. She married for the second time in Philadelphia when she was fifteen to Willy Baker, taking his last name. This second husband worked as a porter, and their marriage lasted longer than the first one. The year was 1921 and the fifteen-year-old, newly wed Josephine, promoted to the role of a comic chorus girl, was playing with the Dixie Steppers in Philadelphia. Her dream, however, was Broadway. At that time, a musical comedy written by Eubie Blake and Noble Sissle, *Shuffle Along*, had begun to enchant Broadway audiences. The enormous success of the show led to the formation of a second *Shuffle Along* company. Baker left her husband and her job with the Dixie Steppers in Philadelphia, went to New York, and was hired for the cast of the show.

The audience came to see the funny chorus girl who clowned, crossed her eyes, and moved every part of her body in a different way. She began to attract public and critical attention and soon started to build a reputation of her own and become a box office draw.

After *Shuffle Along* closed, Josephine played in *The Chocolate Dandies*, a show also written by Sissle and Blake. She was seen by white audiences as the real colored thing. Clowning, mugging and improvising, she came across as different from everyone else. Her special style as an entertainer was slowly evolving.

Josephine Baker mesmerized white audiences. However, this fact should certainly be seen as part of the general aura of the times. Baker was by no means an isolated phenomenon. Many artists of the Harlem Renaissance used primitive, sensual images and music to celebrate African American culture. Some artists genuinely believed that African American art had to be authentic and reflect the African roots of black people in America. Others wanted to cater to the demands of white audiences and guarantee a box office success. These differing views led to one of the basic intellectual controversies of the Harlem Renaissance. According to one of the leading figures of the Harlem Renaissance, W.E.B. Du Bois, the black artist did not have the liberty to express himself freely because, unlike his white colleagues, he was seen as a spokesman of his culture. It became his responsibility to create a proper cultural identity for blacks via proper art, which in this context meant white American art. W.E.B. Du Bois's criticism of Claude McKay's novel, *Home to Harlem*, for example, was angry and totally negative. McKay's vision of the black intellectual as a social misfit, and his aesthetic retreat into African primitivism, ran counter to the wishes of Du Bois and like-minded critics who wanted to see in black art a picture of middle-class respectability. This same concern caused Alain Locke and Charles Johnson, editors of *Opportunity* magazine, to report, "we did not enthuse" after watching *Shuffle Along* with Josephine Baker. In historian David Levering Lewis's words, "musical comedies, whatever the Afro-American contribution, were decidedly not the coming art form for the *Opportunity* muses."

Unlike the conservative critics, Langston Hughes, arguably the greatest poet of the Harlem Renaissance, wrote poems that exalted the blues singers and jazz dancers. In his famous essay, "The Negro Artist and the Racial Mountain," he advocated the need for authentic cultural expression of the black artist. He announced that the young artists of the Harlem Renaissance were determined to "express [their] individual dark-skinned selves without fear or shame." Hughes did not care about the response of either white or African American critics: "We know we are beautiful, and ugly, too." He proclaimed, "we will build our temples for tomorrow, strong as we know how, and we will stand on top of the mountain, free within ourselves."

The interest in authenticity was inseparable from the interest in primitivism and spontaneity. Baker's dance and her mannerisms embodied all these qualities. However, despite the huge success of *Shuffle Along, Chocolate Dandies,* and the floorshow at the Plantation Club in Harlem, she found herself in an excruciating dilemma, one that confronted all black artists of this period. If she were to aspire to be an excellent dancer in terms of style and technique and transcend race, she would cease to be of any interest to white audiences. Yet, as her biographer Phyllis Rose noted, if she "supplied the fast dancing and Negroid humor," she would be "reinforcing dumb stereotypes and killing her own artistic growth." Rather than embracing one alternative or another, Baker chose to escape this dilemma by leaving America for France.

In 1925, Baker embarked for Paris to dance at the Theatre des Champs-Élysées as a variety dancer in *La Revue Negre.* She would receive a respectable weekly salary of $250. Then, at the peak of the jazz era in Paris, the sensational *La Revue Negre* exploded on the stage. Its talented young star, then only nineteen, captivated the audience. She made her first entrance clowning. In *Jazz Cleopatra*, Phyllis Rose described the act vividly:

> Like a strange creature from a distant world, she walked or rather waddled in, her knees bent and spread apart. Her stomach was sucked in, her body contorted. She looked more like an animal than a human being, a weird cross between a kangaroo, a bicyclist, and a machine gun …
>
> She screwed up her face, crossed her eyes, puffed out her cheeks, and made noises in a high-pitched voice. Then she did the split. She splayed her arms and legs as if they were dislocated. She shook and shimmied constantly, moving like a snake. Instead of her moving to the music, the music seemed to come from her body. Finally, she left the stage on all fours, legs stiff, rear end in the air, higher than her head, looking as awkward as a young giraffe.

Josephine Baker, "Sirene des Tropiques." When Baker arrived in Paris she first attracted audiences as an exotic and erotic presence in the reviews for which Paris was notorious. Beinecke Rare Book and Manuscript Library, Yale University.

The last scene of the revue was set in a Harlem nightclub. After several acts of singing and tap dancing, Josephine and her partner performed an "authentic" black dance invented by Jacques Charles, a director of music-hall spectacles. The dance was called "danse sauvage" (savage dance). Josephine, bare-breasted, wore a bikini with feathers on it and a collar of feathers hanging around her neck like a necklace. Beads hung around her partner's ankles and his neck, as well as feathers around his hips. Their wild dance, fast, improvisational, and combining various moves of the belly dance, bordered on obscenity in the eyes of the Parisian audience. Some people fell in love with Baker and the show while others, disgusted, left the theater. *La Revue Negre* quickly became a notorious but immensely popular hit, and created a star who would become the first modern sex symbol of the twentieth century.

Josephine Baker, "Banana Dance," c. 1926. The "Banana Dance" with its unique and scanty costume made Baker famous. Her ability to combine near nudity with humor and an original dance style became her trademark. Beinecke Rare Book and Manuscript Library, Yale University.

Inspired by the huge popularity of the Revue Negre, French poster artist Paul Colin created *Le Tumulte Noir*, which was described as "a gorgeously colored portfolio of pictures affectionately mocking the infatuation of Parisians with all things black—the Charleston, jazz, Josephine in her grass skirt." Colin combined music, dance, and the great energy of the jazz era to create his dynamic images. African sculpture, cubism, and Art Deco modernism inspired the lithographs in *Le Tumulte Noir*. Two images in the portfolio immortalized Josephine: one captures her exotic beauty wearing a miniskirt of palm leaves; the other shows her in her banana skirt.

Josephine traveled to Berlin, Germany, with *La Revue Negre* and stayed there for almost two months. She transfixed postwar Berliners with her wild sexiness and erotic appeal. During the Golden Twenties, Josephine Baker became one of the magic names, like Greta Garbo and Marlene Dietrich. In *Naked at the Feast: A Biography of Josephine Baker,* Lynn Haney described Bakers's Berlin performance:

> In Berlin Josephine displayed a joyous pagan appetite for life, a hunger to grab at new experiences

with both hands. Her way of dancing, a frenzied fertility rite set to the syncopated rhythm of jazz
reflected much of her inner state, a craving for
action without reflection, a deep need to sate her
physical senses in a desperate effort to keep at bay
the hobgoblins lurking in the dark corners of her
psyche, the fears and loneliness that had stalked her
since childhood.

After Berlin, *La Revue Negre* headed to Moscow, but Baker had
already accepted a star billing at the Folies-Bergere. While this was
a smart decision, it resulted in a breach-of-contact lawsuit charging
she had abandoned the revue before its run had ended.

The Folies-Bergere, which had opened in 1869, was the first and
the greatest music hall in Paris. By the mid 1920s, its reputation had
been established worldwide as a luxury palace, a citadel of entertainment. Baker chose a perfect time to be a Folies star. Music hall entertainment was at its peak in Paris between the two world wars. In Lynn
Haney's words, "the postwar boom afforded lavish spending on public
entertainment. [Paris witnessed] the reign of nudes and sumptuous
decors, the ascendancy of electricians, of engineers and intricate stage
machinery, of the *maitre du ballet* and of equating stars with royalty."

Josephine Baker, as the dark star of *La Folie du Jour* in the Folies-
Bergere, stunned the Parisians. Josephine was Fatou, the native girl,
descending from the high dome of the theater in a golden, egg-
shaped cage. She was naked except for gold bracelets on her upper
arm and a girdle of rhinestone-studded rubber bananas, attached to
a g-string around her hips. As she danced the Charleston, the
bananas shook violently around her hips. Many critics thought that
the dancing Josephine was like an African sculpture come to life.
Her posture in the "banana dance," just as in "danse sauvage," was
similar to that of an African statuette. In both cases, the knees are
bent and the derriere is protruding. In fact, with the emphasis she
put on the posterior in her dance, Josephine changed the direction
of the masculine erotic gaze and popularized a new area for desire.

This was not entirely her own doing. In the African tradition, women dance with the rear end and with their feet flatly planted on the ground. Josephine was bringing African tradition to Paris by way of New York. Her exceptional aura consisted of a blend of youth, vigor, and unusual flexibility. She danced as if she were double-jointed and moved in ways seemingly impossible for the human body. Baker at the Folies-Bergere would cast a spell over Paris. Embodying the unrestrained joy of the jazz age, she became the Ebony Venus. Watching her as Fatou, e. e. cummings, the great American poet, said that she reminded him of "a creature neither infrahuman nor superhuman, but somehow both; a mysteriously unkillable Something, equally nonprimitive and uncivilized, or beyond time in the sense that emotion is beyond arithmetic."

Baker's great success as an exotic dancer created an extraordinary star status, the first of its kind in the twentieth century. Baker began to be equated with luxury, eroticism, primitivism, and passion. Her success was commercialized. Banana-clad Josephine dolls, bathing suits, and skin-care and beauty products named after her were only part of the Baker industry. At this time, Baker, not yet aware that her dark color was a major component of her success, was trying to bleach her skin with lemons.

In the 1920s, the Parisian cultural scene was ready for everything that came from Africa. Jazz and blues were heard all over the city. African sculpture and art had a major impact on the cubist movement and art deco. Painters like Matisse and Picasso were collecting tribal objects like masks and figures from Africa. Picasso's enthusiasm for African art went hand in hand with his association of blackness with female sexuality. So, Josephine Baker's black body was partially an ideological artifact in the 1920s, and the limitless enthusiasm shown to her was not only for her art but also for her race. Finding more acceptance as a black performer in Paris than she had in the United States, Baker would become a French citizen and stay in Paris until the end of her life. She was the favorite of artists and leftist intellectuals such as Picasso, Pirandello, e.e. cummings, Jean Cocteau, Le Corbusier, and Ernest Hemingway.

Baker was certainly not alone as an African American expatriate in France. France, because of its cosmopolitan and international character, was a racially more tolerant place than the United States, and many African American artists lived in Paris between the two world wars. Sculptors like August Savage and Nancy Elizabeth Prophet, painters like Palmer Hayden, Hale Woodruff, Archibald J. Motley Jr., and Albert Alexander Smith all found in Paris some kind of a magnetic attraction. Away from a limiting and oppressive homeland, they found a haven in this tolerant foreign city. They all fell in love with their newfound freedom of identity and artistic voice. The African American artists of the Harlem Renaissance, who became self-exiles in France, fit better with the French mentality than with the American. France adored the exoticism of African American art–jazz music, paintings, sculptures–and respected the talent of the artists. The most important writers and poets of the Harlem Renaissance could not resist the lure of Paris, either. Langston Hughes, Claude McKay, and Countee Cullen made frequent visits to this magical city. Baker's success in Paris fit into this tradition perfectly.

The year 1926 was an important one for Josephine. Twenty years old, she opened her own nightclub, Chez Josephine, in Pigalle, and met Pepito Abatino, who was to become her lover, husband, and manager for nine years. At Chez Josephine, known for its outrageous prices, Baker danced, clowned, and teased her clients. She had become "La Baker" to the Parisians. A luminous presence, she was all over Paris. *Vanity Fair* magazine reported, "As irresistible as the Queen of Sheba, Josephine Baker is the current rage of the Parisian stage. Indeed, she is all but the dictator of Paris." She was a chic, affluent, exquisitely dressed woman with eccentric idiosyncrasies. She loved all creatures and kept them as pets: white rats, rabbits, chickens, cats, dogs, pigs. Her energy seemed to be endless; she performed at the Folies-Bergere and Chez Josephine, and attended meetings and parties all over Paris.

Mostly through her husband's influence, she began a process of education to transform herself into a European. A new Josephine Baker was in the making. She wanted to train her voice, discipline her dancing, and learn French.

She left France in 1928 for a year-long tour of Europe. During this tour, out of Baker's conversations with Pepito mostly about the nature and injustice of race discrimination, a novel was born: *Mon Sang Dans Tes Veins* (*My Blood in Your Veins*). The novel, written with the collaboration of the writer Felix de la Camara, allows the reader to see Josephine's inner psyche in the 1920s. Based on a story Baker heard when she was a young girl, the novel tells of a black girl who saves the white man she loves by giving him a transfusion of her blood. Upon learning this, the man's white fiancée abandons him since he has become a "white negro." The topic of a black woman sacrificing for a white man must have obsessed Baker because that theme became the plot of all the movies she was to make later in her life.

TRACK 23

In 1926 Josephine Baker, already a star in Paris for her nightclub act, began her singing career. One of her first recording successes was "Bye Bye Blackbird".

Upon returning to Paris, Baker was hired by Casino de Paris, the most respectable music hall in Paris in the 1930s. The producer of the show *Paris Qui Remue* (*Swinging Paris*), Henri Varna, gave Baker a pet leopard, named Chiquita, as a present. Paris loved Baker and Chiquita. People cheered whenever the elegant star paraded Chiquita down Champs-Élysées. Baker and her leopard became one of the most photographed couples in 1931, the year of the Colonial Exposition in Paris.

The show at Casino de Paris was one of the cornerstones in Josephine's life because her singing career started with this show. The song, "J'ai deux amours/Mon pays et Paris" (I have two loves/My country and Paris), became so associated with Josephine that she sang it at every concert and show until her death. The song was written by Vincent Scotto and Varna himself. Biographer Stephen Papich suggested that "Varna had based it on countless stories Josephine had told him about America, which he had never visited and with which he was fascinated." It was a reminder to the audience of her status as a star expatriate in Paris and her love of her adopted city.

Baker made two major films in the 1930s. One was *Zou-Zou* (1934), a light romantic comedy with Jean Gabin. Directed by Marc Allegret and with music by Spencer Williams, this film used a great deal of autobiographical material from Baker's own life. The young heroine in the film, just like Josephine Baker, yearns for a successful career on the stage. She becomes a star but is lonely because she has no one with whom to share her life. The other film was *Princess Tam-Tam* (1935), produced by Arya Nissotti, a Tunisian casino owner. Shot in Tunisia, it was the tale of an Arab urchin who became a social butterfly in the hands of a French nobleman. Of these two films, *Zou-Zou* appealed to Baker and to audiences much more than did *Princess Tam-Tam*. Baker also played the starring role in Offenbach's operetta *La Creole* in 1934.

By the mid-1930s, Josephine had conquered Paris as dancer, singer, and actress. It was time for her, after fourteen years, to return to the United States and to bewitch Broadway audiences just as she had done in Paris. In 1936, she went to New York to perform in the Ziegfeld Follies, the American counterpart of the revues in Paris. In the Winter Garden Theater, Josephine's voice could hardly be heard. The reviews she received were devastating. In fact, of the entire cast, she alone received totally negative comments. The *New York Times* wrote that "Miss Baker refined her art until there is nothing left of it." Baker needed a scapegoat for her failure and that was Pepito, who could not endure Josephine's attacks and left her alone in New York. He died in Paris a few months later. It would be very hard for Baker to find another man who loved, supported, and cared for her as much as Pepito had.

Upon the invitation of her old boss from the Folies-Bergere, Paul Derval, Baker returned to Paris to star in the Folies-Bergere revue in 1937 at the age of thirty-one. She also opened a new Chez Josephine, which attracted tourists who came to Paris for the Colonial Exposition. In the meantime, she fell in love with a multimillionaire sugar broker, Jean Lion, and married him. The couple separated within a year.

In 1939, Hitler attacked Poland and plunged Europe into war. With the war, a new phase started in Baker's life. Her humanitarianism replaced her self-indulgent behavior. When Germany occupied Belgium, she became a Red Cross nurse, watching over refugees. When Germany occupied France, she worked for the French resistance as an underground courier. She performed with Maurice Chevalier for the French Troops posted along the German frontier. While touring in North Africa, she fell ill and remained in a Casablanca clinic for more than a year. She was very weak, but she defeated the near-fatal peritonitis.

Josephine visited and performed at the American army camps in North Africa. Jim Crow laws had permeated into the army and racism was very much alive. During her performances, Josephine insisted that blacks be seated with the same equality as whites. She also visited the Middle East as a sub lieutenant in the women's auxiliary of the Free French forces. Between 1943 and 1944, she performed in Jerusalem, Corsica, Sardinia, and Italy. After the liberation of Paris on August 25, 1944, she returned to France in her military uniform. She would occasionally wear this uniform in her concerts and shows until she died.

Baker was awarded the Croix de Guerre and the Legion d'Honneur by General Charles de Gaulle and the Rossette of the Resistance, for her contributions to the French cause in the war. The war caused her to develop a social consciousness and faith in God. She married her fourth husband, Jo Bouillon, a French jazz bandleader. In 1950, she began to adopt orphaned babies of all races and religions. She would take care of them at her 300-acre estate, Les Milandes, which included a grand medieval chateau. It was her dream to create a brotherhood among children of different backgrounds. She called them her "rainbow tribe."

Baker made visits to the United States in the 1950s and 1960s. She fiercely challenged the "separate but equal" ideology in her home country. She refused to perform to segregated audiences. She

Noble Sissle and Eubie Blake with Josephine Baker, 1951. Three icons of twentieth century African American entertainment.
The Maryland Historical Society, Baltimore, Maryland.

Josephine Baker with her twelve adopted children in Monte Carlo. Baker became famous for her selfless political and humanitarian service—in the French resistance during World War I, and with her rainbow children after the war.
Beinecke Rare Book and Manuscript Library, Yale University.

voiced her anti-American sentiments on several occasions. Believing that race relations constituted the most visible scar on American democracy, she took part in the civil rights march in Washington, D.C., in August 1963 at the age of fifty-seven.

Baker continued to perform in Paris until she died in 1975 at the age of sixty-nine. It seemed to many that she was finished in 1969, when she was evicted with her adopted children from her chateau because of financial debts. However, Princess Grace Kelly offered her a villa in Monaco and Josephine was back on her feet once again. Having overcome poverty, traumas, and humiliation, Josephine died of a stroke in 1975. She was working again under a new contract doing a series of concerts in Paris. She had just completed fourteen great performances when she died suddenly in her sleep. She departed this life a great star, a war hero, a civil rights activist, and a mother of twelve adopted children.

PART FIVE

The Renaissance Men of the Harlem Renaissance

INTRODUCTION

The Harlem Renaissance occurred during a vibrant era of social, political, economic, and demographic change. The Renaissance itself, as well as the concept of the "New Negro," were multifaceted movements that addressed many separate ideas, disciplines, and activities. The Harlem Renaissance, for example, involved literature, art, music, drama, musical theater, and film. It was deeply influenced by race, politics, political and racial theories, criticism, economics, the black migration, literary criticism, and the whole economic structure for marketing and distributing the work of writers, musicians, and artists. The New Negro encompassed both political and cultural concerns that ranged from racial pride to a militant demand for equal rights, to a nationalistic or pan-African separatism.

Out of this cauldron of ideas, movements, and social change came several Harlem Renaissance figures who defy simple categorization. What these people have in common is that they were creative artists in one or more fields and also were involved formally or informally in the racial politics of the period, usually in connection with the struggle for racial justice. A number of persons fit this description. Both Langston Hughes and Claude McKay, for example, identified themselves as writers with a political cause, and both associated themselves, at least for part of their careers, with the political left and with Soviet communism. Singer Marian Anderson made a powerful statement against racial segregation with her famous Easter Sunday concert from the steps of the Lincoln Memorial in Washington, D.C., in 1939. Singer, actress, and performer Josephine Baker resisted fascism by working with the French underground during World War II.

Other persons known primarily for their role as political or civil rights leaders also dabbled, sometimes quite successfully, in the arts—usually literature. Walter White, for example, is best known for his work with the NAACP, first as an undercover agent investigating racial violence in the South, then as an officer and ultimately the executive secretary of that organization. In 1924, he published a novel, *The Fire in the Flint,* with Alfred Knopf. Two years later he published *Flight,* his second novel; then, in 1929, he published a study of lynching, *Rope and Faggot,* that was based largely on his personal investigations. In addition to his three books, White was closely connected to Harlem's literary and cultural scene. He and his wife were famous for the gatherings in their home, which always included literary figures.

Jessie Fauset, White's colleague at the NAACP during the early 1920s, also published her first novel, *There Is Confusion,* in 1924, and then published three more in the late 1920s and early 1930s, after she had left the NAACP. Her job there had been more involved with cultural issues than civil rights. She served as

Du Bois's assistant, working on *The Crisis* and functioning as its literary editor. Her home was known as a place where penniless and would-be writers could always get a meal and conversation.

The three figures that will be discussed in the following chapters are exemplars of the political-cultural Renaissance man. The first, W.E.B. Du Bois, was acknowledged as the premier African American scholar and intellectual of the twentieth century. As a scholar and university professor, he was an accomplished historian and sociologist whose books had a great impact on our understanding of race in American history. His civil rights work is also well known. As an early advocate of a more militant and uncompromising approach to racial problems, he was a founder of the Niagara Movement and the NAACP and served as the only African American on the latter organization's original Board of Directors and the editor of its journal, *The Crisis*. Less well known are his literary achievements, which include poetry, two novels, and a musical production.

Paul Robeson as Othello, London, 1930. Robeson combined music, theater, film, and politics in his long and successful career.
Beinecke Rare Book and Manuscript Library, Yale University.

James Weldon Johnson is no less a renaissance man than Du Bois. After a career in Florida as a teacher, lawyer, and school principal who wrote poetry on the side, he came to New York and joined with his brother, Rosamond Johnson, and Bob Cole to become one of the turn of the century's most successful songwriting teams. He then entered the foreign service, worked as a journalist, and became the first African American executive secretary of the NAACP. Along the way he published a book of poetry and a novel, *The Autobiography of an Ex-Coloured Man*—all of this before 1920. During the Renaissance he remained head of the NAACP, promoted black literature and the arts, and published poetry, anthologies, and a history of Harlem.

The third featured Renaissance man is Paul Robeson. Robeson was an internationally famous actor, singer, and film star. He also had a deep commitment to racial and social justice. Unlike Johnson or Du Bois, he had no formal position with a political or civil rights organization. Rather, he molded his professional career to reflect his political beliefs. He became an ardent advocate of Soviet communism and spent much of his career as an expatriate. Ultimately, he sacrificed his career to his political beliefs.

The three chapters that follow underscore how politics, civil rights, and the arts were interwoven during the Harlem Renaissance.

W.E.B. Du Bois

(1868–1963)

KEVIN GAINES

Acknowledged as the most significant African American intellectual of the first half of the twentieth century, it is no surprise that W.E.B. Du Bois played a significant role in the Harlem Renaissance. He was, after all, the editor of the influential journal The Crisis, *and a published poet and novelist, and consequently was well situated to guide the emerging literary movement. What is surprising is that most of the young writers turned their back on Du Bois's efforts at leadership, considering him too stodgy and too mired in an outdated Victorian morality to appreciate or understand "modern" art and literature. Du Bois in turn became more of a critic than a promoter of the Harlem Renaissance.*

W.E.B. Du Bois, for whom the Harlem Renaissance was a brief interlude within a long career as the pre-eminent African American intellectual, author, editor, and activist of the twentieth century, was born in 1868 in Great Barrington, a small western Massachusetts town in the Berkshire Mountains. With a handful of blacks among a population of about 4,000, Great Barrington offered little in the way of opportunity for its African American residents, who were confined to personal service jobs. Du Bois's childhood there was less idyllic than he would later portray. The union of Du Bois's parents was short-lived. His father, Alfred Du Bois, a free man of color and a Union Army veteran born in Haiti, abandoned the family for good when the child was two. Soon after her husband's departure, Du Bois's mother, Mary Silvina Burghardt Du Bois, was disabled by a stroke. Mary Du Bois was a devoted, if strict parent who, like her son, reveled in his academic prowess. Thrown into poverty by his father's desertion and his mother's illness, Du Bois and his mother were supported by relatives. Determined to escape his meager surroundings, Du Bois recalled taking a vengeful pleasure in excelling over his white schoolmates academically. An aloof demeanor that many throughout his life would perceive as arrogance probably had its origins in disturbing memories of a broken family, deprivation, and social ostracism.

At a time when barely one percent of all Americans attended college, Du Bois attended Fisk University in Nashville from 1885 to 1888, cultivating his gifts as writer, scholar, and orator. He also deepened his understanding of the plight of African Americans in the South. During the summers, Du Bois taught in rural Tennessee, where he routinely saw the freedpeople's hunger for literacy denied by the brute realities of peonage and poverty.

After graduating from Fisk, Du Bois attended Harvard University with scholarship support, majoring in history and philosophy. He received his bachelor's degree in 1890 and pursued post-graduate studies there. He spent two years studying at the University of Berlin in Germany, before returning to Harvard to complete his Ph.D. His doctoral thesis, *The Suppression of the African Slave Trade in America*, was published in 1896 as the first volume in Harvard's *Historical Series*. While in Germany, Du Bois celebrated his twenty-fifth birthday in solitude. On that occasion he boldly imagined his future and dedicated himself to the advancement of his people, albeit in the fashion of a late victorian gentleman. "These are my plans: to make a name in [social] science, to make a name in literature and thus to raise my race. Or perhaps to raise a visible empire in Africa thro' England, France or Germany." The youthful Du Bois had embraced the "great man" theory of history of the nineteenth century. Although he himself would ultimately reject that theory, it is undeniable that Du Bois exerted a profound influence on African American and African freedom movements over the course of the twentieth century.

Du Bois's political and social thought evolved considerably over the course of a public career spanning more than seven decades. The bourgeois product of Fisk, Harvard, and doctoral training in Germany was radicalized by glacial progress in race relations and the ineluctable force of modern ideas, movements, and revolutions.

Du Bois would reflect on events in his young life, the nation, and the world in *The Souls of Black Folk*, his 1903 masterpiece. In that collection of essays—a panoramic survey linked by Du Bois's theme of the plight of African Americans living behind a "veil" of segregation and exclusion—Du Bois vividly recounted, from his summers in rural Tennessee, the unrequited strivings of black sharecroppers. In that volume, Du Bois wrote movingly of the death of his firstborn son, who died suddenly at the age of two while Du Bois and his wife, Nina Gomer Du Bois, resided in Atlanta. That tragedy cast a pall on the young couple, who remained bound in an unhappy union for over fifty years until Nina's death.

The romantic anti-materialism of *Souls*, in which he declared his opposition to the industrial education program of Booker T. Washington, yielded to the growing influence of Marxism from the 1920s onward. And in his early contention that the problem of the twentieth century was the problem of the color line, Du Bois signaled his future affiliation with global struggles against imperialism. Before his embrace of leftist ideas, however, the activism of his "Talented Tenth" theory of black leadership was rooted in bourgeois assumptions. It was the educated class among black Americans, actually amounting to about a hundredth, that would lead the race out of the wilderness of southern tyranny.

Du Bois's insistence on higher education as the path to black advancement was a direct, if genteel, challenge to Booker T. Washington's well-financed program of industrial education, which promised to mold the southern black masses into a tractable labor force. Washington was a former slave, tireless orator, and founder of the Tuskegee Institute in Alabama. He rode his compromise with southern Jim Crow laws and his partnership with the nation's captains of industry to considerable fame and power during the early years of the twentieth century. Washington deployed that power against those who might dare to challenge his leadership. Du Bois had done so, weathering a stream of attacks, and by 1905 had organized fellow members of the Talented Tenth into the Niagara Movement. The prospects of agitators for equal rights were improved by the tragedy of the 1906 Atlanta race riot, which targeted members of that city's proud, striving, African American middle-class and demonstrated the folly of Washington's exhortations that blacks eschew protest and apply themselves to acquiring wealth and property.

The Niagara movement was a precursor of the National Association for the Advancement of Colored People (NAACP), which Du Bois co-founded in 1910 with white liberals, radicals, and progressive reformers. The Talented Tenth could only watch in frustration as President Woodrow Wilson, who had received Du Bois's endorsement, presided over the establishment of racial segregation in federal buildings and gave a hearty thumbs up to D. W. Griffith's film, *Birth of a Nation*. That film's vicious propaganda depicted the Ku Klux Klan heroically riding to the rescue of southern whites oppressed by corrupt and degenerate black politicians during Reconstruction. Du Bois fought back through *The Crisis*, building an avid following with its impassioned denunciations of anti-black atrocities and inspirational accounts and images of black achievement and dignity.

As a commentator on global affairs, Du Bois's Victorian inclinations were trumped by an alertness to modern ideas and processes. In 1915, Du Bois provided a prescient and prophetic analysis suggesting that the European colonial conquest and exploitation of Africa was a major cause of World War I. He made it clear that colonialism would cause future wars if "European civilization" permitted greed to triumph over principles of justice and democracy. His

TRACK 24

In 1910, W.E.B. Du Bois co-founded the NAACP. In this interview excerpt, he comments on how he made his role fit his desires, and the beginnings of *The Crisis*.

analytical *tour de force*, "The African Roots of the War," anticipated Lenin's *Imperialism: The Highest Stage of Capitalism* by two years. In it, he recast imperialism as a system that defused class antagonisms between European labor and capital, as "the white workingman has been asked to share the spoil of exploiting 'chinks and niggers.'"

As the U.S. entered World War I, Du Bois appeared torn between his elitist expectations of racial leadership and the radical implications of his critique of imperialism. In *The Crisis*, Du Bois interrupted his tirades against racial outrages with an editorial urging African Americans, rampant violations of their rights notwithstanding, to "close ranks" and join the U.S. war effort during World War I. For that statement Du Bois was roundly condemned by black radicals and socialists. To such critics the modernizing events and trends of the postwar global situation seemed to be leaving Du Bois behind.

With the national epidemic of murderous violence against blacks spreading to several major cities during the "Red Summer" of 1919, Du Bois regained his voice as the fearless defender of the race, largely through his indispensable work in *The Crisis*. The myriad and often lethal attacks on black humanity fueled a peak in the membership of the NAACP and the circulation of its magazine. Du Bois's late-Victorian mores may have been passé for some, but he continued to set the tone for the political mood of black Americans. African Americans of all walks of life devoured the masterful, denunciatory essays and sketches in *Darkwater: Voices From Within the Veil* (1920), which distilled the militant fury of New Negroes, north and south. Modern almost in spite of himself, Du Bois's essay "The Damnation of Woman" advanced an incipient feminism in his defense of African American womanhood. And in that volume's "The Souls of White Folk," Du Bois flayed the modern "phantasy" of "personal whiteness," that warped perception that regarded blacks with amused contempt and pity, creating the hostile and dangerous world that blacks glimpsed from their side of the veil.

TRACK 25

Du Bois recalls how during World War I, despite prevalent racism, he was able to convince the Army to promote African-Americans to the officer ranks.

By the Harlem Renaissance of the 1920s, given the new receptivity of publishers to African American subject matter and writers, Du Bois had more than made a name in social science and letters. Besides the acclaimed *Souls*, his classic study of urban conditions among African Americans in *The Philadelphia Negro* (1899) tested its author's conviction that empirical social science research could eliminate racial prejudice. But scholarship was no match for such atavisms as lynching and the folkways of racial subordination, routinely upheld by white leadership. Such barbarism had diverted Du Bois from the path of scholarship to the forefront of the struggle for equal rights. While the younger, bohemian set of writers, artists, intellectuals, and cultural radicals associated with the New Negro renaissance in and around Harlem had been weaned on Du Bois's eloquent broadsides in defense of aggrieved African Americans, many of them dismissed Du Bois as retrograde in his late-Victorian mores and aesthetics. Yet there was more common ground between Du Bois and the younger generation than these young writers were perhaps prepared to admit. Du Bois had been committed to the discovery and nurturing of African American literary talent in the pages of *The Crisis*. And *Souls* had made him a beacon in the African American quest for equality and an autonomous identity. Langston Hughes acknowledged as much by dedicating his figuration of ancestral African wisdom, the poem "The Negro Speaks of Rivers," to Du Bois.

However much of Du Bois's attention was fragmented by the latest lynching outrage, the challenge from Marcus Garvey's rival mass movement, or pressure to boost the circulation of *The Crisis*, he could not remain on the sidelines. Du Bois also contended with such rival cultural arbiters as Alain Locke and Charles Johnson, who scoured black communities for fresh artistic, literary, and theatrical talent. But Du Bois's investment in the vogue of New Negro writing soured as modernist white readers remained fixated on Jazz Age stereotypes of racial primitivism. And he was chagrined as other African American intellectuals settled for a high-minded program of literary and cultural achievement as a substitute for mass agitation, even as lynchings, anti-black riots, and a resurgent Klan raged unabated well into the 1920s.

By 1926, Du Bois had rejected the vogue of writing by and about "the Negro," asserting in "Criteria of Negro Art" that "all art is propaganda and ever must be, despite the wailing of the purists." However old-fashioned Du Bois seemed to be in viewing "propaganda" as the main criterion for aesthetic value, he was uncannily prescient about the dilemma of the black artist of the future. With the arrival of the black artist and writer whose achievement compels the recognition of white America, Du Bois remarked, "some one touches the race on the shoulder and says, 'He did that because he was an American, not because he was a Negro...He is just human'..." As David Levering Lewis has written, Du Bois had powerfully articulated the question of group identity for African Americans. Du Bois's proposition was two-fold: he insisted that the black writer and artist possessed a distinct perception of America; and furthermore, that that perception was the basis for universal literary expression.

TRACK 26

In 1896, the University of Pennsylvania employed Du Bois to conduct a research project in Philadelphia, but refused to offer him a faculty position or let him teach. Du Bois used the opportunity to produce the groundbreaking study *The Philadelphia Negro*, which became his second book.

In an apparent struggle for the hearts and minds—and organizational resources—of U.S. blacks, Du Bois was drawn into a nasty public feud with Marcus Garvey, leader of a mass movement that encouraged economic cooperation between African Americans, West Indian blacks, and Africans. Both Garvey and Du Bois imagined Pan-Africanism as a bourgeois, pro-capitalist venture, a secular version of the civilizing mission led by men of African descent. Garvey's attempted joint venture with the Liberian government was thwarted by U.S. imperialism. For his part, Du Bois advised the Firestone Company to provide a humane alternative to British, French, and Portuguese colonialism by entrusting enlightened American whites, African Americans, and Liberians with the task of supervising African labor. Years later, Du Bois's Pan-Africanism would more closely reflect the radicalism of an African-led anti-colonial movement.

Du Bois exerted a profound impact on younger, educated blacks during the 1920s and after. Invited to speak at his alma mater Fisk University at his daughter's graduation, the students laid eyes on the familiar stern-faced, bronze-colored man with the prominent forehead, familiar from photographs, but perhaps shorter, at five feet, six inches, than they had imagined. The indignant speech was accented by the downward curl of his mouth under the Kaiser Wilhelm mustache. Most were shocked, then gratified, to hear Du Bois excoriating the school's president and administration for their humiliating paternalism, which included singing Negro spirituals on demand for visiting white benefactors. The speech touched off a student rebellion at that and other prominent black colleges that revived the spirit of New Negro radicalism. However much Du Bois regarded black literary modernism as a harmful diversion, he defended black college students' entitlement to the modernist standards of thought and behavior enjoyed by their white counterparts.

Another area in which Du Bois eventually transcended the ideological limitations of his training was his involvement with the Pan-African movement. At Pan-African congresses in Paris and London in the early 1920s, Du Bois expressed a preference for what he viewed as the more enlightened French imperialism over that of

England. He applied the Talented Tenth theory to the colonial situation, endorsing the European consensus that most Africans were ill prepared for self-government.

His novel, *Dark Princess* (1928), meant to underscore his literary criteria of Negro elevation, was further evidence of the importance of a nascent anti-imperialism in Du Bois's political imagination. But its prophetic account of African American solidarity with a global anti-colonial movement, specifically the nationalist movement in India, trafficked in eugenicist gender politics. The novel suggested the birth of an international Talented Tenth through a dynastic union of an Afro-American male and South Asian princess, yielding a brown messiah of the world's dark and downtrodden.

The onset of the Depression and the prominence of left-wing politics prompted among black leadership a re-examination of its assumptions and strategies. Three years before the stock market crash the ripple effect of the Bolshevik revolution led Du Bois to impulsively add the Soviet Union to his 1926 European travels. Du Bois praised that nation's commitment to making workers "the center of modern power and culture." His biographer, David Levering Lewis, writes that "[t]he teleology of global class revolution now began to vie powerfully with the concept of the superordinate power of race in Du Bois's thinking. If race was the problem of the twentieth century, after this first encounter with the Soviet Union he also began to regard class as a dilemma of comparable magnitude."

Upon his return, Du Bois tested anti-capitalist analyses and revisionist expositions of Marxian theory in the pages of *The Crisis*. American racism ensured that the destiny of the Talented Tenth—the black middle class—was linked to that of the black working class. The racism of white workers kept the African American and white proletariats, for the time being, separate and unequal.

As the African American intelligentsia explored new strategies for advancement, Du Bois, while drawn to Marxian theories of economic conflict, ran afoul of both the NAACP and black leftists alike with his independent course. For black Americans, Franklin Roosevelt's New Deal was actually a case of more of the same,

PROF. W. E. B. DUBOIS,
Sociologist and Writer, Atlanta, Ga.

Professor W.E.B. Du Bois, Atlanta University, circa 1900. Du Bois began his long and amazing career as a university professor.
Photographs and Prints Division, Schomburg Center for Research in Black Culture, The New York Public Library, Astor, Lenox and Tilden Foundations.

defined by tokenism and discriminatory relief programs. The rigidity of the color line compelled African Americans to consolidate their resources behind the veil. "The next step," Du Bois wrote in 1934, "involves the organization of intelligent and earnest people of Negro descent for their preservation and advancement in America, in the West Indies and in Africa; and no sentimental distaste for racial or national unity can be allowed to hold them back from a step which sheer necessity demands." A former Du Bois protégé, Walter White, had earned his stripes as an undercover investigator of lynchings in the deep South. Now the executive secretary of the association, White strongly objected to Du Bois's separatist views, which were being used by southern federal bureaucrats to justify segregated New Deal programs.

Undaunted, Du Bois published "Segregation" in the January 1934 issue of *The Crisis*. There was a crucial distinction between segregation as discriminatory policy and the positive aspects and cultural and material benefits of imposed racial solidarity. The argument that African Americans pursue the distant goal of integration through an immediate agenda of economic cooperation sent shockwaves throughout the black intelligentsia. The idea was debated (and mostly respectfully disputed) for weeks afterward in the black press. Demands for integration over a quarter century had brought negligible results, and Du Bois had wearied of the incessant power struggles with White and others to maintain his intellectual and editorial independence.

Du Bois's departure from the association enabled his return to the tranquility of teaching and research at Atlanta University. The ensuing years brought the magnum opus, *Black Reconstruction* (1935), Du Bois's black Marxian synthesis, which anticipated recent scholarship on the social invention of white identities in America with its formulation of a compensatory psychological wage of white-ness that induced "southern white laborers...to prefer poverty to equality with the Negro..."

The work was influential as well for subsequent scholars of the Reconstruction and post-emancipation. *Black Reconstruction* revised Marxian themes of consciousness and revolutionary agency. Like C. L. R. James's pioneering study of the Haitian revolution, *Black Jacobins* (1938), which chronicled the victorious slave uprising, led by Toussaint L'Ouverture, that overthrew the French Caribbean colony of San Domingue, Du Bois's work placed peoples of African descent at the center of world historical processes of Western modernity and revolutionary change. Du Bois's account of the actions of former slaves and black political leadership under Recon-struction state governments portrayed them as self-determining avatars of social democracy in the American South. But it took years for these works and their authors to receive the recognition they merited.

The decidedly mixed reception of *Black Reconstruction* speaks volumes about the genteel racism of intellectual life in those times. In those days it was an arguable proposition, and thus a political statement, to insist, as Du Bois did in his study, on the humanity of the freedpeople against prevailing accusations of black politicians' corruption and incompetence. To refute "the propaganda of history," Du Bois quoted the speeches of black legislators at length.

While praised in some quarters of the northern press, the work and its author met with what David Lewis described as the "code of snide denigration prevailing in upper-middle-brow publications such as the *New Yorker*," which noted that the author held the "odd view, in distinction to most previous writers, that the Negro is a human being." *Time* magazine regarded the book "a wonderland," distorting or concealing the "familiar scenes and landmarks" of Reconstruction, and its author an "ax-grinder." With the anti-black

slanders of generations of U.S. historians constituting the gold standard in Reconstruction historiography, Du Bois argued that African
Americans were at the vanguard of a gallant, and tragically defeated,
social movement of authentic American democracy. The failure of
Black Reconstruction, and the triumph of white supremacy in the
United States, lent momentum to the brutal suppression and
exploitation of the majority of the world's colored peoples under
imperialism and colonialism.

At the turn of the century, a gruesome lynching shocked Du Bois
to the realization that scholarship was no match for the violent
eruptions of the white American racial subconscious. Agitation was
the only appropriate response to the systemic madness of racism.
Now, having clashed with the NAACP's leadership, scholarship
regained its appeal for Du Bois.

But the obstacles to independent scholarly inquiry were forbid-
ding, even for Du Bois. Since 1909, he had dreamed of an "Encyclopedia Africana," a definitive reference work on Africa and its
Diaspora. In the early 1930s, as Du Bois labored at his history of
Reconstruction, major foundation support became available for such
a project. What was planned as the "Encyclopedia of the Negro"
would emphasize U.S. racial conflicts. But the pre-eminent African
American scholar was, for the project's sponsors, tarnished by his
substantial record of activism. Conspicuously excluded from a pre-
liminary planning conference called by the Phelps-Stokes Fund, Du
Bois belatedly joined the interracial board of directors after Walter
White shamed the fund into including him. Du Bois soon gained
editorial directorship of the project, outmaneuvering his paternalist
sponsors. But Phelps-Stokes's fundraising was hampered by the lack
of enthusiasm among philanthropists for new knowledge about race
generated by African American scholars.

Du Bois sought to allay concerns about his objectivity, knowing
that, as Lewis writes, "the objectivity bar was never set higher than
when the scholarship to be vetted concerned the study of the American Negro." For Du Bois, the chance to supervise an interracial
team of the finest social scientists appeared to be a dream about to

come true. However, the iced champagne remained untouched by Du Bois and his assistant Rayford Logan, as the anticipated call from Phelps-Stokes confirming the project's final approval never came.

Later, Du Bois would learn that independently of Phelps-Stokes, the Carnegie fund had embarked on a major study of the Negro in America. Soon afterward, the Swedish economist Gunnar Myrdal received the surprising news that Carnegie had commissioned him to embark on "a comprehensive study of the Negro in the United States." The Carnegie-Myrdal study, funded at $300,000, employed leading black and white academic social scientists, torpedoing Du Bois's project.

A chagrined Du Bois was gracious, if reserved, in offering Myrdal (whose status as a foreign scholar resolved the objectivity issue) an appraisal of his research plan. Myrdal's *An American Dilemma* (1944) delivered to its Carnegie sponsors "a new master theorem of race relations that was interpretively progressive but not socially destabilizing." Du Bois welcomed the Myrdal study as an opening against the racial parochialism of American society. In doing so, Du Bois, like other black reviewers (with the exception of Ralph Ellison, whose critique went unpublished at the time), looked past Myrdal's downplaying of African American resistance and his assertion of the primacy of psychological rather than economic factors in explaining the subordination of African Americans.

The racial liberalism fostered by the Second World War helped Du Bois gain recognition from such previously hostile quarters as the American Historical Association. Such appreciation, and the auspicious political climate, were to prove fleeting. Du Bois updated his involvement in anti-colonial activism, presiding over a session at the historic Manchester Pan-African Congress in 1945. Having rejoined the NAACP as a member of a delegation participating in the drafting of the United Nations charter, Du Bois denounced the indifference to the colonized world shown by the architects of the global Pax Americana. Again, Du Bois clashed with Walter White, who regarded the doctor's blunt criticisms of Truman's domestic and global Cold War policies a dangerous liability. Ousted a second time from the association and abandoned by a black intelligentsia cowed by Cold War repression, Du Bois allied himself with the radical left. For his involvement with a short-lived peace organization calling for reconciliation with the Soviet Union, Du Bois and its other officers were prosecuted in 1951 by the Justice Department for failing to register as agents of a foreign country. The doyen of the African American intelligentsia was handcuffed at age eighty-three, a clear object lesson for potential black dissenters. As the Talented Tenth ran for cover, Du Bois found crucial material and moral support from the left. He and his co-defendants were acquitted. While the case against them was threadbare, it did serve notice to prominent African Americans that dissent would be hazardous for their freedom and livelihood.

Du Bois's staunch support for the Soviet Union, despite disclosures of Stalin's atrocities, was certainly motivated by his outrage at his prosecution and the deprivation of his passport by the State Department for some eight years. But even if the government had not targeted him, Du Bois could not have found common cause with an anti-communism that was essentially synonymous with white supremacy. According to Lewis, Du Bois "adjusted the Russian casualty tables in light of the Atlantic slave trade, the scramble for Africa, the needless First World War, Nazi death camps, and the color-coded poverty and wage slavery waging within and beyond North America." Du Bois's anti-American diatribes were as self-serving as they were justified.

But the pronounced radicalism of Du Bois's later years was not simply a matter of a pro-Soviet alliance with the enemy of his enemy. To claim so is to emphasize Du Bois's vengeful Stalinist outbursts at the expense of his (and Paul Robeson's) primary commitment to anti-racist struggle in the U.S. and anti-colonial liberation abroad. For Du Bois, the exponents of Cold War anti-communism were indistinguishable from the apologists for white supremacy and colonialism. It is critical to remember that Du Bois ran afoul of the government not simply because of his Stalinism but also because of his forthright advocacy of the socialist emancipation of the colo-

nized world, and his insistence on an economic as well as a civil
rights revolution in the U.S. All too willing to forget its alliances
with a broad-based anti-colonial movement, the civil rights establishment and the black intelligentsia caved in to the inquisition
against Du Bois. Du Bois's pro-Soviet statements constituted a
frontal assault on America's entrenched racist hypocrisy rather than
a total endorsement of the Soviet system. He and singer-actor Paul
Robeson believed, justifiably, that African aspirations for freedom
and social justice would be an immediate casualty of the Cold War.

Ironically, given his insistence that Americans of African
descent assert their distinctive historical and cultural heritage in
their demand for inclusion and full citizenship, Du Bois rejected
America at the dawn of the civil rights movement. He and his second wife, the author Shirley Graham Du Bois, moved to Ghana in
1961, choosing self-imposed exile there as a final gesture of defiance
against those United States officials who had tried to silence and
isolate him. Du Bois had moved to that West African nation at the
invitation of its president, Kwame Nkrumah, to serve as director of
the Ghana-sponsored Encyclopedia Africana project. When Du
Bois celebrated his ninety-fifth birthday, Conor Cruise O'Brien, the
vice chancellor of the University of Ghana, conferred on Du Bois an
honorary degree. On that occasion, Du Bois spoke of such long-
departed rivals as Washington and Garvey in conciliatory terms.
That birthday was his last. Frail but lucid, and unable to complete
the Encyclopedia project, Du Bois died on August 27, 1963, the day
before the landmark March on Washington, at which NAACP
executive director Roy Wilkins, an old nemesis, paid tribute to him.
In his last formal speech in 1968, shortly before his assassination,
Martin Luther King, who surely must have identified with Du Bois's
plight during the 1950s anti-communist witch hunts, praised him for
his refusal to yield to the Cold War onslaught.

Although Du Bois had renounced the New Negro renaissance,
his voluminous contributions to American political life over his
long public career did more than wage a gallant struggle against a
maddeningly persistent and adaptable racism. Like his essay,

"Criteria of Negro Art," that body of work hearkened back to his manifesto in *The Souls of Black Folk*, challenging black Americans to embrace the struggle for full-fledged American citizenship while maintaining a distinctive "Negro" cultural identity. With this far-sighted turn-of-the-century formulation, Du Bois set the terms for subsequent debates among African American intellectuals on the relation of the black writer and artist to the American nation. Undoubtedly, future generations of scholars and activists will ponder and mine his trenchant reflections on the problems of race in American life and global affairs.

James Weldon Johnson

(1871–1938)

ANNE E. CARROLL

No single person was more important to the Harlem Renaissance than James Weldon Johnson. His literary and musical accomplishments earned him the respect of African American writers and artists, while his leadership position in the NAACP brought him contacts and influence among liberal whites. His work as a cultural and literary critic, and his anthologies of African American poetry and spirituals, placed him in a position to promote African American literature and culture, while his close friendship with the publisher Alfred Knopf and with novelist and editor Carl Van Vechten enabled him to assist individual writers in getting their work published. Unlike Du Bois, Johnson was an enthusiastic supporter of the Renaissance and was convinced that the appearance in shop windows of books by African Americans would prove to be a powerful tool in the struggle against American racism.

James Weldon Johnson at NAACP desk, circa 1920. Among his many careers, Johnson played a major role in bringing black leadership to the NAACP. He also was multifaceted—an educator, a successful songwriter, a poet and novelist, a diplomat, and a promoter of the arts, as well as serving as the first black executive secretary of the NAACP. Beinecke Rare Book and Manuscript Library, Yale University.

At the time of his death in 1938 at the age of sixty-seven, James Weldon Johnson was in the midst of growing success in yet another career. Having served as the first black high school principal and the first black lawyer in Florida, a songwriter whose career took him to New York City and then to Europe, a newspaper publisher and columnist, a diplomat for the United States government, a novelist, a poet, an editor, and a civil rights advocate, fundraiser, lobbyist, and officer for the National Association for the Advancement of Colored People (NAACP), Johnson was now a college professor establishing the brand-new field of African American literary studies.

The range of Johnson's activities and his success in so many different fields often go unrealized by scholars today who remember him primarily as the author of the novel, *The Autobiography of an Ex-Colored Man*. But even during the decade of the Harlem Renaissance, his contribution was significant and wide ranging. Always impeccably dressed, this cosmopolitan man was kind-hearted, gentle, and courteous, and he used his many friendships to secure opportunities and resources for younger writers and artists—so much so that the historian David Levering Lewis, in his seminal study of the Harlem Renaissance, *When Harlem Was in Vogue*, named Johnson one of "The Six," a "handful of Harlem notables," whose advocacy and support willed the movement into being. Johnson also worked tirelessly on his own writing and editing projects, producing groundbreaking anthologies in which he collected and preserved African American poetry and songs. He also published, in the leading black and white magazines of the period, essays in which he articulated the most important cultural, political, and social issues facing African Americans in the 1920s. And, particularly in his own autobiography, he provided a life story that served as an example of what might be achieved by a relentless, restless, ambitious individual who set his sights high and was always looking for the next way to make a contribution.

As a child, Johnson enjoyed a comfortable family life. His father, James Johnson, was born to a free family in Virginia. He married James's mother, Helen Dillet, in Nassau, her hometown in the Bahamas. Their first child, a daughter, died in infancy. By the time James was born in 1871, his parents had moved to Jacksonville, Florida, where the elder James was a headwaiter at a luxury hotel. The Johnsons' second son, J. Rosamond, was born in 1873. Although segregation and racism were present in Jacksonville, the Johnsons were solidly middle class and James was insulated, for the most part, from discrimination.

His ambitions and his quest for education, however, conflicted with the Jim Crow practices of the South. Through the eighth grade, Johnson attended the Stanton School, a large public school where his mother taught and where he received a rigorous education. But there was no public school in Jacksonville that offered any high school classes for African Americans. The Johnsons had high ambitions for their sons, and they sent James to Atlanta University, where he would complete both preparatory school and college. James spent summers teaching in rural Georgia, working at the Chicago World's Fair, and touring with the Atlanta University Quartet, singing and telling stories to raise money for the school. By the time he graduated from the university in 1894, Johnson had published four poems and two prose pieces in the *Atlanta University Bulletin*, had heard Frederick Douglass speak, and had begun a friendship with the young black poet Paul Laurence Dunbar. He also had conceived of his own goal of serving as "a leader and helper to my race," although it was not clear in which fields he would make that contribution.

His first job was promising: in 1894, at the age of twenty-three, he returned to Jacksonville and became the principal at Stanton, one of the most prominent schools in the state for African American students. Johnson furthered its significance when he added ninth- and tenth-grade courses to its curriculum, making it the first public high school for African Americans in Florida. He continued his work as principal until 1902, but he simultaneously pursued other careers. In 1895, he founded and began editing *The Daily American*, the first daily newspaper in the nation specifically aimed at African American readers. It circulated in Florida and southern Georgia. Johnson wrote many editorials, which ranged widely in their focus. Some offered advice to African Americans about improving their conduct and behaving with dignity; others were more political, presenting arguments, for example, against segregation in education. Johnson found the newspaper work exciting, but it was not financially successful and he had to stop publishing the paper in early 1896, only eight months after he had launched it.

Later that year Johnson embarked on the study of law, working in his spare time with a young white lawyer. After eighteen months, Johnson became the first African American to seek admission to the Florida bar. He was examined by a judge and three prominent city attorneys, one of whom left the room rather than being part of the committee that would swear in a black man. In 1898, Johnson began legal work with a friend, Douglass Wetmore, but found the paperwork of their law practice boring. He also was unfulfilled by his work at Stanton: the segregation in education, and the fact that there still were no other public high schools for African Americans in the area, meant that there was no possibility for career advancement for him in that field.

In the meantime, Rosamond was enjoying a successful musical career, touring with a vaudeville show and working as a music teacher. In 1898 he convinced James to begin writing song lyrics. Together they composed a libretto and a comic opera and then began to write songs for the musical comedy stage. In the summer of 1899, they traveled to New York to try to market their work. Though they were unable to get their comic opera produced, they met a number of black musical performers and struck up a friendship with Bob Cole, a writer and performer. In September, James returned to Florida and his post at Stanton, but he returned to New York in the summers of 1900, 1901, and 1902. By 1902, it was clear that racial conditions in Jacksonville were deteriorating: segregation was being expanded into streetcars, and when a fire destroyed the Stanton School building, it was replaced by an inferior building that demonstrated the city's lack of support for education of African Americans. In contrast, Cole and the Johnson Brothers were becoming one of the most successful songwriting teams of the period. In 1902, then, at the age of thirty-one, James resigned from his position at Stanton and moved to New York City.

Johnson loved the cosmopolitan nature of New York. Always well dressed, he became even more suave and polished. He attempted to bring more sophistication to music for black performers, too. Given the conventions of popular music at the time, Cole and the Johnson Brothers wrote and performed "coon songs" for vaudeville shows and musicals, but the trio worked to bring "a higher degree [of] artistry to Negro songs," as James remembered in his 1933 autobiography. They managed to make their songs more genteel than many others and to gently push beyond common stereotypes of African Americans. Their work was very successful: dialect songs like "The Congo Love Song" and "Under the Bamboo Tree" received critical and popular acclaim when they were performed onstage, and the trio sold hundreds of thousands of copies of the sheet music. Cole and Rosamond also became a successful vaudeville duo; in 1905, they were offered a six-week booking at London's Palace Theater, and James accompanied them as their road manager. Their show was widely advertised, with postcards and posters everywhere, and audiences loved it. The three also visited Paris, Brussels, Antwerp, and Amsterdam, and James found the trip hugely enjoyable, particularly as it was mostly free of the racism of the United States.

However, James's role with Cole and the Johnson Brothers soon came to an end. Bob and Rosamond decided to create their own musical comedy and take it on tour. While James was an excellent lyricist, Cole wanted him to serve as their business manager, which James found uninspiring and which would leave him little time to pursue his own interests. So, in 1905, he decided to switch careers again.

This time, it was literature and politics that he decided to pursue. First, Johnson began to explore the more socially committed possibilities of creative writing. He already had written a number of more serious songs, including "Lift Every Voice and Sing," an assertion of the achievements and persistence of African Americans that Johnson penned in 1900 for a celebration of Abraham Lincoln's birthday. It still is often sung and is widely known as the "Negro National Anthem." In 1902, to fill his time while Cole and Rosamond were on the road, James began taking English classes at Columbia University, most notably with Brander Matthews, one of the period's most well-known critics of literature and drama. Johnson also started writing *The Autobiography of an Ex-Colored Man*, but it was only after he left New York City—thanks to his interest in politics— that he found the time to finish it.

Johnson had become involved in politics by 1904, as a member and then an officer in the local Colored Republican Club. One of the club's goals was to convince African Americans to vote for Theodore Roosevelt. Cole and the Johnson Brothers wrote two songs for the 1904 presidential campaign, "You're All Right, Teddy" and "The Old Flag Never Touched the Ground," which drew them the compliments of the candidate. Through the club, Johnson also met Charles W. Anderson, New York's most powerful black politician and a close associate of Booker T. Washington. In 1906, Anderson, working through Washington, arranged a job for Johnson with the United States Consular Service in Puerto Cabello, Venezuela, where he certified shipping invoices and monitored trade. In 1908, he was promoted to a similar but more demanding position in Corinto, Nicaragua. Johnson's work as a consulate in this busy port city grew to include supporting the U.S.-backed rebellion against the government of dictator General José Santos Zelaya in 1910; however, Zelaya's successor, Juan Estrada, stayed in power only until 1911, when he was ousted by Adolfo Diaz. In 1912, Johnson hosted the

U.S. Marines as they attempted to suppress a rebellion against Diaz. He was able to keep the city relatively calm, and he hoped his success at routine consular duties and as a diplomat would earn him a promotion. However, when Woodrow Wilson was elected president of the United States in 1912 and began resegregating the federal government, Johnson's prospects for more prolonged service dimmed, and he resigned from the Consular Service in 1913.

While he was in Central America, Johnson had courted and married Grace Nail, whom he had met in 1902 in New York City. She was fifteen years his junior, and Johnson had first gotten to know her father, a tavern-keeper who made a fortune in real estate. Johnson visited the Nails when he traveled to New York while on leave from Venezuela and Nicaragua; he and Grace became engaged in 1909 and married in 1910, when Johnson was thirty-eight years old.

Johnson's work as a consulate also had given him free time to devote to his writing. He continued to write poetry, including such well-known verses as "O Black and Unknown Bards," a tribute to the early singers and developers of the spirituals that first appeared in *Century Magazine* in 1908. He also finished *The Autobiography of an Ex-Colored Man*, a novel about a light-skinned protagonist who eventually decides to pass as white, marries a white woman, and has two children with her. The book was published anonymously in 1912 by Sherman, French, and Company, a small publishing house in Boston. As Johnson remembered in his autobiography, most reviewers accepted it as a true account, and many African American readers speculated on who the main character might be, comparing his experiences to those of men they knew who were likewise passing as white. Johnson even recalled meeting a man who claimed to have written the book, but he kept relatively quiet about his own authorship until it was republished in 1927 under his name—now changed from James William Johnson to the more literary-sounding James Weldon Johnson.

Parts of the book offer an almost sociological description of African Americans in various cities. Johnson carefully described what he called the "desperate class," the servant class, and the more

well-to-do working class. But most significant is what *The Autobiography* reveals about its narrator; as his first-person account of his
experiences, it offers, through his example, extensive insights into
how a young African American might imagine his place in the
world and the kind of work he might do. The book also draws attention to the effect of racism on African Americans' understanding of
their identity: the protagonist's surprised discovery that he is "a
Negro" propels him through a painful process of self-doubt and
analysis, in which he can imagine nothing positive about being
black. Slowly he realizes, with the help of books like Frederick Douglass's autobiography, *Narrative of the Life of an American Slave,* that
he might become a credit to his race. He develops and articulates an
important appreciation for black folk culture, especially performance practices, storytelling traditions, and music. When he becomes
a ragtime composer and a piano player, he determines that, by working with the spirituals and blending them with classical music, he
will be able to bring them to a wider audience and earn glory for
African Americans. However, the Ex-Colored Man also develops
the kind of double-consciousness defined by W.E.B. Du Bois in *The
Souls of Black Folk* in 1903. When Johnson's narrator witnesses the
brutal lynching of a black man, he is overwhelmed by "the shame
that [he] belonged to a race that could be so dealt with." His awareness of how he could be perceived and treated by white Americans
drives him to "raise a moustache" and let "the world take [him] for
what it would": in other words, he refuses to identify himself as black
and therefore allows others to assume that he is white.

The book did not sell particularly well in 1912, and only a handful of reviews were published. By the time the Harlem Renaissance
was gathering steam in the 1920s, though, Johnson had become an
important figure in the movement; his status thus lent significance
to the book. Furthermore, its themes were of interest to participants,
especially its exploration of black identity, its positive evaluation of
black culture, its treatment of passing, and its assertion of the relationship between art and social change, seen both in its narrator's
attitude toward ragtime and his long tributes to black preachers and

singers. Recent literary critics have also heralded Johnson's blending of fiction and autobiography, the complexity of his unreliable narrator, and his use of irony and ambiguity.

Between the initial and second publications of *The Autobiography*, Johnson's career took a number of important turns. When he returned from Central America to the United States in 1914, he first looked for work in Jacksonville; unsuccessful, he and Grace moved to New York City, where he took over the editorial page of the *New York Age*. He continued to write for this influential African American weekly newspaper for nearly a decade, resigning only in 1923. Johnson's "Views and Reviews" columns were not as conservative as one might expect, given the newspaper's connections to Booker T. Washington: Johnson used his pieces to protest showings of D. W. Griffith's racist movie, *The Birth of a Nation*, in 1915; to critique President Wilson's policies; to protest lynching; and to demand recognition of African Americans' artistic and social contributions to America. He continued to write and publish poetry, including "Fifty Years," a tribute to the fiftieth anniversary of the Emancipation Proclamation, which first appeared in the *New York Times* in 1913 and became the title work of a collection of poems published in 1917. He also wrote, in 1920, an essay for *The Nation* and *The Crisis* in which he exposed the unjust activities of the United States military in Haiti, thus ironically opposing the same kind of military occupation he had supported in Nicaragua.

In this time period Johnson also began to work with the NAACP. After Washington died in 1915, NAACP leaders made a concerted effort to heal the breach between the Du Bois and Washington factions in the African American community. Johnson had met Du Bois in 1904 at Atlanta University, and Du Bois clearly liked and admired Johnson. Johnson did not join the NAACP until 1915, but its leaders quickly identified him as someone who could help unify African Americans behind the organization. Toward this end, in 1916 Du Bois and Joel Spingarn, the chairman of the NAACP board, recruited Johnson to become a field secretary, a position in which he recruited members and started chapters around the country. In 1920, he became the organization's first black secretary, its ranking administrative officer. He served in that position until 1930. His legal training was particularly useful to the NAACP's efforts to fight discrimination against African Americans through court cases and lobbying efforts, and Johnson played an important role in the organization's unsuccessful efforts to get a federal anti-lynching bill passed into law.

Johnson agreed to work with the NAACP on the condition that he could continue his literary activities. He kept writing for the *New York Age*, and he used his column to publish reviews of books, poetry, and performances. It was in this role as cultural critic that he made his next major contribution. In 1922, while the Harlem Renaissance was just getting under way, Johnson published *The Book of American Negro Poetry*. The anthology is important both for the fact that it brought together the work of thirty-one African American poets,

The Silent Parade, July, 28, 1917, was organized as a response to lynching and racial violence such as that of the recent East St. Louis race riot. "Four hundred thousand dollars' worth of property was destroyed, nearly six thousand Negroes driven from their homes, hundreds of them killed; some burned in the houses set afire over their heads," explained James Weldon Johnson in his autobiography, *Along This Way*. In a meeting of the National Association for the Advancement of Colored People to discuss plans to register a protest, Johnson suggested a silent parade. In the front row are James Weldon Johnson [far right], and W.E.B. Du Bois (second from right).
Photographs and Prints Division, Schomburg Center for Research in Black Culture, The New York Public Library Astor, Lenox and Tilden Foundations.

Children in the Silent Parade. James Weldon Johnson wrote: "The streets of New York witnessed many strange sights but, I judge, never one more impressive. The parade moved in silence and was watched in silence." Photographs and Prints Division, Schomburg Center for Research in Black Culture, The New York Public Library Astor, Lenox and Tilden Foundations.

most of them still relatively unknown at the time, and for the essay Johnson wrote as its foreword, which articulated several issues that would continue to resound throughout the Harlem Renaissance. First, Johnson insisted that literature might serve the purpose of undermining racism, both by presenting positive images of African Americans and by demonstrating the achievements of African Americans in the arts. This argument, of course, would be much more explicitly made in the following years by Du Bois and others; Du Bois, for example, called for art to work as propaganda for the race in his essay, "Criteria of Negro Art," in 1926. But the argument also would be famously rebuked by younger artists like Langston Hughes and Wallace Thurman, who insisted that the artist needed freedom to create as he or she saw fit. Johnson's statement, then, was an important early volley in this debate.

The second major argument in Johnson's foreword is his assess-ment of the possibilities of dialect in poetry by African Americans.

Insisting that dialect poetry could evoke only pathos and humor, Johnson asserted that dialect was incapable of communicating the complexities and subtleties of African Americans' experiences and character. In other words, poetry written in dialect could not achieve the kind of reassessment of African Americans that was necessary, given the racist context of the time. By 1931, when he published a second edition of the book, the work of writers like Hughes, Zora Neale Hurston, and Sterling Brown had convinced Johnson to revise his argument; he acknowledged that these younger writers had successfully broken out of the conventions of traditional dialect and been able to capture in their work "the common, racy, living, authentic speech of the Negro in certain phases of real life," as he wrote in his foreword to that edition. In any case, though, Johnson's praise for black poets and the interest he stirred with the first edition has been seen as a major force in launching the Harlem Renaissance.

Johnson also published two collections of spirituals in the 1920s. *The Book of American Negro Spirituals* (1925) and *The Second Book of American Negro Spirituals* (1926) each included sixty-one songs, arranged by Rosamond Johnson and songwriter Lawrence Brown. As was the case in his collection of poetry, Johnson's forewords to these books asserted the merits of the collected material. Opening the first volume with his poem, "O Black and Unknown Bards," Johnson went on to offer a fifty-page assertion of the distinctive qualities of the spirituals, emphasizing their technical merits and insisting on their importance as African American contributions to American culture. At the time of the publication of these books, performances of the spirituals were quite popular, but Johnson and others believed that contemporary singers could not recreate the contexts and nuances of the songs as they originally would have been composed and performed. Thus, they felt the spirituals were a form of musical and artistic expression that was in danger of being lost; Johnson's collections, then, could serve the archival role of preserving vanishing materials while also raising awareness of the importance and the beauty of this music.

In many ways, Johnson's 1927 book, *God's Trombones*, serves the same purposes for the work of African American preachers. It includes seven sermons typically preached by African American preachers and one opening prayer, all written as poetry by Johnson. He wrote the first, "The Creation," in 1918, inspired by the performance of a preacher he heard at a meeting; he created the rest of the poems and published the book during the following decade to demonstrate the oratorical skills of black clergymen and to increase the respect granted to them. Again, language was crucial to Johnson: as he explained in his foreword, he tried to capture the preachers' distinctive speech patterns, combining traditional dialect with biblical phrasing and standard English. Moreover, Johnson used the formal aspects of his poetry to suggest the rhythms of the preachers' delivery, using varied line lengths and punctuation to suggest the speed and intensity with which they spoke these lines. He acknowledged that the written transcriptions could only hint at the emotional impact of hearing these sermons performed, and he demonstrated their evocativeness when he movingly recited the poems at social gatherings. Johnson's respect for the preachers' power is all the more impressive given that he himself was an agnostic.

Significantly, *God's Trombones* also includes lettering by C.B. Falls and illustrations by Aaron Douglas, by 1927 one of the most well-known African American visual artists of the Harlem Renaissance. Thus, the book fuses written and visual texts to create a moving demonstration of African Americans' accomplishments in numerous media. Bringing recognition to such work and raising awareness of its wide-ranging dimensions were among Johnson's ongoing interests, ones that he pursued in a number of essays published during the Harlem Renaissance. Particularly significant is "Race Prejudice and the Negro Artist," in which Johnson surveyed the work being done by black writers, dramatists, actors, musicians, singers, painters, and sculptors, concluding that all were helping to revise outdated conceptions of African Americans and thus to undermine racism. Johnson also addressed the conflict inherent in writing for both black and white audiences in "The Dilemma of the Negro Author," in which he applied Du Bois's concept of double consciousness to the situation of African American artists as they imagined their readers.

Johnson's essays show that he was not afraid to disagree with other black intellectuals. In "The Negro Artist and the White Publisher," for example, he countered the common complaint of the time that white publishers were too limiting in the portrayals of African Americans they would accept; he insisted that they were open to a range of texts, an argument that he supported with a list of publications from recent years. Johnson was especially successful in delivering these messages to a broad audience, since he was one of the African American writers of the period who was able to place his work not only in predominantly black magazines like *The Crisis* and *Opportunity* but also in predominantly white magazines like *Harper's* and *American Mercury*.

TRACK 27

James Weldon Johnson reads his poem "The Creation" from *God's Trombones*. Johnson's reading captured the power in the language of a black preacher to create drama in the familiar story.

Johnson's publications during the Harlem Renaissance also included a historical essay on Harlem, which he contributed to the *Survey Graphic* issue on the New Negro in March 1925; he revised and expanded the essay for the anthology, *The New Negro*, later that year. In these pieces, he traced the development of Harlem from its first settlement by the Dutch in the 1600s through its emergence as a cultural and social hub of black America in the 1920s. Johnson expanded this focus on both the history and the contemporary significance of Harlem in his 1930 book, *Black Manhattan*. The book is wide ranging: Johnson discussed political activity in Harlem, developments in schools and churches, the rise of black leaders, the accomplishments of African American soldiers in the Civil War and World War I, and cultural and creative work by African Americans. He devoted extensive attention to developments in theater and the performing arts; the interest he had shown in the role of the stage in revising ideas about African Americans when he was writing music at the turn of the century clearly remained with him.

By the late 1920s, Johnson, now in his fifties, had become recognized, David Levering Lewis argues, "as Afro-America's senior statesman." In 1925, his achievements as an "author, diplomat, and public servant" were recognized by a Spingarn medal given by the NAACP. In 1927, he won a $400 prize from the Harmon Foundation for God's Trombones, and in 1928, he was granted honorary doctorates in literature from Howard University and Talladega College. He played key roles in directing the charitable gifts of a number of organizations toward projects that benefited African Americans. One of the most significant was the establishment of annual fellowships from the Julius Rosenwald Fund to black writers and artists. In 1929 Johnson received the first fellowship, which allowed him to take a one-year sabbatical from his duties leading the NAACP. Instead of returning to the organization, he resigned in December 1930 to become a professor of creative writing at Fisk University, a historically black college in Nashville, Tennessee. The NAACP honored his resignation with a dinner in early 1931 that was attended by more than three hundred guests.

At Fisk, Johnson had time to continue his creative writing. In 1930, he had a small book of poetry privately published. St. Peter Relates an Incident is generally considered of lesser artistic merit than God's Trombones, but its political importance is significant. As Johnson explained in his foreword, his long title poem was inspired by a recent event: the U.S. government had sent a number of gold-star mothers to visit their sons' graves in France, but it had sent the African American women on a second-class ship. The poem satirizes the event through St. Peter's retelling of the events of the Resurrection Day, when the Unknown Soldier is found to be black. Johnson added a number of additional poems to the collection and republished it with a larger press in 1935.

At the same time, Johnson was working on his autobiography, Along This Way, which he published at age sixty-two in 1933 to high acclaim from black and white reviewers alike. In it, Johnson posited himself as a representative black man; he thus described his achievements in a manner that might draw attention to the potential of African Americans. Johnson ended the book with his typical insistence on the need to provide positive images of African Americans but also with a more political argument, emphasizing the need to improve the treatment of African Americans and warning about the potential consequences of a failure to do so.

Johnson continued in that vein in *Negro Americans, What Now?*, a brief book he published in 1934. In it, he assessed the various methods of fighting discrimination, concluding that integration was necessary despite the frustrations of dealing with white resistance to it; he also emphasized that unity among African Americans was essential to racial progress. Furthermore, he insisted on the need for education for both black and white Americans, particularly in terms of experiences that would demonstrate to white Americans the errors of some of their perceptions of African Americans.

Johnson taught at Fisk only in the winter and spring terms; in the summer and fall, he lectured around the country. In 1934, he began teaching each fall as a visiting professor at New York University, becoming the first African American to teach black literature at a predominantly white university. He planned to do the same at other universities on behalf of NYU; had he lived to do so, he would have begun a program of black studies in the 1930s.

However, Johnson's ongoing work was tragically cut short when he was killed in a car accident in June 1938, shortly after his sixty-seventh birthday. He and Grace were on their way to their summer home in Great Barrington, Massachusetts. In a terrible rainstorm, Grace drove across an unguarded railroad crossing and into the path of an oncoming train. James died soon afterward, and Grace spent weeks in the hospital. Johnson's funeral was held in New York City on June 30, and it drew more than two thousand mourners. His significance was also marked by the eulogies published by both the black and white presses, including many collected in a special section of the September 1938 issue of *The Crisis*.

Some of Johnson's contemporaries concluded that he was too optimistic, too idealistic about the potential of overcoming racism, or too accommodating to whites. Kelly Miller, for example, argued that Johnson's popularity was a result of his conciliatory nature. Du Bois, despite his deep respect for Johnson, felt that he sometimes was unrealistically optimistic about social and economic conditions that faced African Americans. But perhaps his optimism and his tendency to focus on the positive—even as he fought for African Americans' rights—demonstrated that his diplomatic skills carried into other parts of his life. It seems significant, for example, that he was able to work with both Washington and Du Bois. The range of his activities matches the range of his friends: they included everyone from sports figures like Jack Johnson to President Roosevelt, writers from H. L. Mencken to Paul Laurence Dunbar, critics and commentators from Brander Matthews to Carl Van Vechten. In connecting such disparate figures, and in using his friendships and relationships to open up opportunities for other African

The James Weldon Johnson songwriting team. Beinecke Rare Book and Manuscript Library, Yale University.

American writers and artists, Johnson had a crucial impact on the development of black literature and culture during his lifetime. Van Vechten acknowledged as much when he created the James Weldon Johnson collection at the Beinecke Library at Yale University; this repository of primary materials from the 1900s has become an important archive of Johnson's papers, as well as those belonging to other major figures of his era.

In their eulogies, those who knew Johnson paid tribute to the complexity of his life. Calling him a "many-faceted genius," a man whose greatness knew no bounds, they praised him as a man of action, but also one of poise and self-restraint; as an "ambassador of understanding" between black and white Americans, but also as a "champion of justice" and a "valiant fighter" for African Americans' rights; and as an artist and activist who made many "lasting contributions to the cultural life of the nation." Today, with growing attention to the complexity and range of Johnson's career, aided by new editions of his collected writings and new books of critical essays on his work, his extensive legacy may finally begin to get the attention it deserves.

Paul Robeson

(1898–1976)

Paul Finkelman

A college football All American with a Phi Beta Kappa key, a Columbia University law student who played professional football on the weekends, a powerfully handsome actor, singer, and movie star—this was Paul Robeson, larger than life, a true Harlem Renaissance superstar. During the 1920s, the Harlem-based Robeson excelled on the stage, on the concert tour, and in the recording studio. Key roles such as that of Joe in the London production of Showboat, where he sang a memorable "Ole Man River," made him an international star. He also was active in the Harlem social scene that brought together poets, writers, and artists. By the late 1920s Robeson became increasingly political. Frustration with American racism prompted him to move to London in the late 1920s; in the 1930s it led him to the Soviet Union and communism. The multitalented Robeson continued to achieve success after success on stage and in film, and his career flourished throughout the 1930s in both Europe and the United States. In the post-war period his politics became a liability and eventually shut down his career.

In 1995 Paul Robeson was elected to the College Football Hall of Fame. The "member biography" for Robeson begins with the typical and predictable account of his career as a star athlete at Rutgers University. It notes that the six-foot three-inch, two hundred and ten-pound end was selected as an "All-American" in 1917 and 1918. In the four years that "Robey," as he was known in his playing days, was on the team, Rutgers won twenty-two games while losing only six and tying three. In addition to starring on the gridiron, Robeson lettered in track, baseball, and basketball, accumulating twelve varsity letters in four years. Indeed, he was the first black to play on any of those teams at Rutgers. At that time, pro football was in its infancy. Nevertheless, the Hall of Fame biography notes that Robeson had a brief professional career with Hammond (1920), Akron (1921), and Milwaukee (1922), in the nascent American Professional Football League.

Paul Robeson.
Beinecke Rare Book and Manuscript Library, Yale University.

The Hall of Fame biography then takes a strange twist for a college athlete, highlighting his subsequent career as an actor, singer, recording artist, and film star, illustrating the impressive range of Robeson's career. Indeed, few remember his feats on the gridiron, although at the time they made him famous in black and white households alike. Rather, he is remembered as an actor, a singer, and a political activist. He revived the "Negro spiritual," giving that genre of music a new credibility among serious lovers of music.

When Robeson arrived at Rutgers University he was only the third black student in the history of the school, and the first to play sports. Not the typical "jock," he came to college after winning a statewide contest for an academic scholarship. While at Rutgers he won prizes for his oratory, was chosen to give one of the commencement addresses, and graduated with a Phi Beta Kappa key. The All-American college athlete went on to play professional football, then became a lawyer, singer, actor, and political activist.

His father, Rev. William Drew Robeson, was born a slave. He escaped to the North in 1860, served in the U.S. Army during the Civil War, graduated from Lincoln College in Pennsylvania, and was then ordained as a Presbyterian minister. His mother, Maria Louisa Bustill Robeson, a schoolteacher, came from an elite black family in Philadelphia. The Bustills had been free for a number of generations, and were of mixed ancestry, with blacks, Indians, and whites in their family tree. Mary Bustill Robeson died in a fire when Paul was six years old. The light-skinned Bustills never warmed to their very dark-skinned, southern-born son-in-law (despite his many accomplishments), and after his mother died Paul had few contacts with her family until after the death of his father.

In 1907, when Robeson was nine, his father moved the family to Somerville, New Jersey. Paul was one of four blacks at Somerville High, where he became a top student, winning prizes for public speaking and debate. He sang and participated in school plays, and despite the racism of rural New Jersey, his teachers, especially his music teacher, worked to nurture his obvious talents. He was also a star of the school's football team. Robeson was first in his graduating class, but the racism of the principal led the school to change its graduation program to prevent him from giving the valedictory address. As a senior Robeson scored high enough on a statewide exam to win a scholarship to Rutgers University. This exam was usually taken in two parts, the first part in the eleventh grade, and the second part in the twelfth grade. However, no one had told Robeson about the exam when he was a junior, perhaps because none of the teachers in his school expected Robeson, or any other black, to aspire or be accepted to a "white" college like Rutgers. Thus, when he sat for the exam as a senior he had to complete the entire exam in the same period that all the other seniors took just the second half of the exam. Nevertheless, he scored high enough to win a scholarship.

When he entered Rutgers in 1915 he was the only black on the campus. Throughout his years at Rutgers he faced discrimination and sometimes outright rejection because of his race. However, he usually responded by simply trying harder. Initially, the football coach made it clear he did not want a black player, but when Robeson almost knocked out another player while running over him in practice, that changed—Robey's athletic ability, his fearless determination, and his size made it impossible for the coach to reject him. Robeson was soon a star of the football team and in 1917 was named to Walter Camp's list of "college all-stars." After the 1918 football season he was again named to the All-American team. Ultimately, he earned twelve varsity letters, sometimes playing two sports in one season. One year he earned letters in both track and field and baseball, and on some occasions baseball games had to be held up while Robeson left to throw the hammer, shot-put, or javelin.

When not on the gridiron, the basketball court, or the track, Robeson sang and did some acting at Rutgers, but racial barriers prevented him from joining the college glee club. In addition to his athletic and musical success, Robeson was an outstanding student, although not at the top of his class. He won oratorical awards, was elected to Phi Beta Kappa, and unlike at his high school, was asked to address the senior class when he graduated in 1919. His commencement speech focused on racial progress and the hope that in the wake of World War I, African Americans would soon have equal rights and opportunities in the United States. The *New York Times* praised the speech, as did papers in New Jersey. His deep, sonorous voice was impressive, as was his physical presence. He towered over most men of his generation, even on the football field. Tall, handsome, athletic, poised beyond his years, and musically gifted, Robison was able to overcome a great deal of racism simply because he was so attractive and charismatic. His deep, powerful bass voice matched his overwhelming physical presence.

Robeson's athletic and academic success made him something of a minor celebrity within the national black community. He was an ebony athletic hero in a predominately white sport. Moreover, in an age when college was mostly for the children of the wealthy, college football was still something of a gentleman's game. Robeson, with his

All-American honors, his Phi Beta Kappa key, his actor's poise, and his movie-star good looks, was the living embodiment of the black "Talented Tenth" just as the Harlem Renaissance emerged in arts and culture and the NAACP began its crusade for racial equality.

After graduating from Rutgers, Robeson moved to Harlem, but enrolled at NYU Law School downtown. He hated NYU in part because of the long commute downtown, but mostly because he felt it lacked intellectual rigor. In the middle of this first semester he spoke with the dean of Columbia Law School, Harlan Fiske Stone (a future Chief Justice of the United States Supreme Court). Stone, a rare racial egalitarian in the Ivy League, agreed to waive the school's rules and allow him to transfer there after his first semester at NYU.

Living in Harlem at the birth of the Harlem Renaissance, Robeson was surrounded by singers, actors, writers, and other intellectual and cultural figures. His first roommate was a young actor, Clarence Muse, and thus from the beginning of his post-college years Robeson was connected to the arts. Initially he earned money through a variety of jobs—as a redcap porter at Grand Central Station, a singer, and as a part-time coach for both Rutgers and the all-black Lincoln University football teams. His summer jobs included singing, and in 1920 he missed a final exam because he was too busy rehearsing for a play. This would ultimately delay his graduation, which should have taken place in spring 1922.

While active in local theater and musical life, Robeson missed an opportunity that might have launched his career more quickly. In the spring of 1920, Eugene O'Neill offered Robeson the lead in his new play, *Emperor Jones*. That role, Brutus Jones, presented an unflattering portrait of a black man who gambled, drank, womanized, committed murder, and ultimately went insane. That O'Neill offered this role the unproven actor suggests both how impressive the young Robeson was and also how well known he had become because of his successes in college. However, Robeson believed the role belittled blacks and thus rejected it. Ironically, later in life this would become a major role for Robeson on the stage and in film.

That year he did do some singing and acting, and played some professional football in Hammond, Indiana.

In August 1921, Paul married Eslanda "Essie" Cardozo Goode, whose grandfather, Francis Lewis Cardozo, was a leading black politician during Reconstruction, serving as secretary of state and state treasurer in South Carolina. After Reconstruction, Cardozo moved to Washington, D.C., where his family helped create an upper-class black elite in the nation's capital. Essie grew up in this atmosphere, graduated from the University of Illinois, and, as a chemist, was the first black staff member at New York Presbyterian Hospital. That fall of 1921, the recently married Robeson returned to Columbia Law School, but also accepted an offer to play professional football for the Akron Pros on the weekends. Football, as well as the long train trips to Akron, would prove exhausting, as Robeson usually played the entire game, on both defense and offense.

Paul and Eslanda Robeson in *Borderline*, 1930.
Beinecke Rare Book and Manuscript Library, Yale University.

Instead of making up his exams so that he could graduate from law school, Robeson accepted the lead in the play, *Taboo*, in the spring of 1922. As "Jim," Robeson was both a free black minstrel in the antebellum South and a voodoo king in Africa. The plot was almost incoherent, with even theater critics unable to follow it. Not surprisingly, the play was a flop, but critics praised Robeson's voice and acting. In July he went to England, where he performed the same role but with the play retitled *Voodoo*. The production once again failed but Robeson received high marks for his singing.

At the end of the summer he returned to New York and to Essie, with no job prospects and still no law degree. Black Harlem greeted him with great affection, as though his acting career in Great Britain had been a triumph, when in fact it had not. But adulation did not lead to a job, and law school did not interest him; nor would it feed him.

The out-of-work singer thus returned to sports, moving to Wisconsin to play football for the Milwaukee Badgers. Once again the work was exhausting, but it did enable him to make up a missing course at Marquette Law School. Despite the high pay, after his year with the Badgers he never again seriously contemplated an athletic career. He returned home at the end of the season and in February 1923 he received his law degree from Columbia. Unlike his years at Rutgers, his record at Columbia was hardly impressive. Moreover, having completed his degree, he had little interest in practicing law. He lethargically looked for a law job, and may have worked at a firm for a short while. He registered for the New York bar, but in March 1924 he failed to take the exam.

By this time Robeson had moved away from law and sports and concentrated his efforts on the theater. In 1924 he accepted Eugene O'Neill's offer of the lead in *All God's Chillun Got Wings*, his controversial new play about interracial marriage. The script required that Robeson kiss his white female co-star. Previous performances had used a white male lead in black face. But O'Neill and the Greenwich Village-based Provincetown Players were prepared to challenge social convention by putting a real African American, Robeson, in the lead. The play dovetailed with the rise of the "new" Ku Klux Klan and came in the aftermath of bloody race riots in East St. Louis, Chicago, Tulsa, and elsewhere. The kissing scene led to a huge controversy, with demands by some newspapers that the play be banned. The Ku Klux Klan threatened to bomb the Provincetown Theater and kill Eugene O'Neill's son.

The threats of the Klan and the complaints of some newspapers led to increased support for the play, Robeson, and O'Neill. The financial backers of the play raised their support while black and white civil rights leaders in Harlem and elsewhere spoke out in defense of the play. Among the vocal supporters of Robeson and O'Neill were the national officers of the NAACP, James Weldon

Johnson (himself an accomplished novelist and literary figure), and the distinguished black scholar/activist, W.E.B. Du Bois. In the midst of this controversy the white female lead, Mary Blair, became ill, and the production was postponed. To fill in the gap, the Provincetown Players revived *The Emperor Jones,* and this time Robeson agreed to play the lead role. His performance was a tour de force for which he received rave reviews. This play was probably the turning point of his career, although at the time he may not have realized it. From the moment he played Emperor Jones, Robeson was a star. He would play the Emperor throughout his career, making the role his own. Moreover, the reviews guaranteed that Robeson would have other roles in other performances.

"Emperor Jones" by Aaron Douglas, from his *Emperor Jones* illustrations. Provided by an anonymous donor.

The triumph of *Emperor Jones* was followed by *All God's Chillun Got Wings,* which finally opened without any bombings, violence, or rave reviews. Robeson did well, and the play was a financial success, in part because the controversy brought people to the theater. The critics thought the play was weak, but were kind to Robeson, whose stage presence mesmerized audiences. Throughout the summer of 1924, Robeson had steady work—no small accomplishment for a young black actor with no formal training and little experience. Most importantly, his success as the Emperor Jones and his calm response to the controversy of *All God's Chillun* made him a significant up-and-coming figure in Harlem and the national black community. His growing fame also brought him new social contacts in Harlem and with the whites who patronized the Renaissance. Yet despite his fame and critical success, Robeson earned under $2,000 in 1924 from his theater work.

By the end of the year he was hired by Oscar Micheaux, the greatest black movie producer of the period, to appear in the film

Body and Soul. Scholars today refer to this and similar films as "race films" because they were produced by black filmmakers for black audiences. At the time almost no whites saw these films, which were shown in theaters that catered almost entirely to black audiences. For his role in *Body and Soul,* Robeson earned the handsome sum of $100 a week while the film was in production and a small percentage of the film's profits. The role gave moviegoers a glimpse of Robeson's sensuality and highlighted his sex appeal. Like most race films of the period, it was of limited commercial or artistic success. In later years scholars focused on the movie as an important example of race films, as well as an important documentation of the young Robeson.

In the spring of 1925, Robeson teamed up with Lawrence Brown, an accomplished singer and pianist, but even more skilled as a composer and arranger of music, especially traditional black music, including spirituals. In April 1925, with Brown accompanying him (and occasionally singing with him), Robeson gave his first vocal concert, using the Provincetown Theater in Greenwich Village as his concert hall. Walter White, the assistant general secretary of the NAACP, was a key player in arranging for the concert. Soon Paul and Essie Robeson were regular guests at parties where White brought together talented blacks and white intellectuals, critics, impresarios, and philanthropists. Robeson already had a following among some of New York's key critics, including Heywood Hale Broun of the *New York Tribune.* The Robesons attended social gatherings in Harlem but also in the homes of whites in the more elite sections of the city.

Walter White also introduced Robeson to Carl Van Vechten, who, in addition to being a novelist and major promoter of black literature, was also the music critic at the *New York Times.* Like Broun, Van Vechten immediately recognized Robeson's enormous talent and his great potential for stardom. The two critics, along with White and others, helped launch Robeson's career. For example, Broun praised Robeson and Brown in his column on the day before the concert, urging his readers to attend, which many of them did.

Robeson's first public concert with Brown, in April 1925, was a spectacular success and was followed by ecstatic reviews. It was held in Greenwich Village, in the theater owned by the Provincetown Players. The audience was racially mixed, although most were white. It was also almost certainly the first concert of the period made up entirely of slave songs, spirituals, black folk songs, and contemporary music by black composers performed before a mostly white or mixed audience. Robeson and Brown began with "Go Down Moses," nearly bringing the audience to its feet. Later half the audience would be in tears as he sang "Sometimes I Feel Like a Motherless Child." Brown and Robeson had to give eight encores before a nearly delirious audience would let them leave.

The concert was a breakthrough in three ways. First, it established Robeson as a major musical talent. On the heels of his triumph as Emperor Jones, he was now a major force as a singer as well as an actor. Second, the concert allowed Robeson to educate white audiences about the sophistication of black folk music and slave music. Never again would the "Negro spiritual" be seen as a quaint

Portrait of Paul Robeson, by Winold Reiss, 1925. This portrait appeared in the New Negro issue of *Survey Graphic,* March 1925.
Manuscripts, Archives and Rare Books Division, Schomburg Center for Research in Black Culture, The New York Public Library, Astor, Lenox and Tilden Foundations.

song offered up by an exotic race. Robeson's powerful renditions of songs about slavery, oppression, and freedom would change the way many Americans, black and white, thought about African American music. Finally, the concert launched Robeson's musical career as a black performer who could appeal to both black and white audiences.

Just as *Emperor Jones* led to his first movie role, this concert launched his recording career. A month after the concert he had signed a contract with Victor Records (later RCA Victor), a major white label. In 1925, working under the contract for less than half a year, Robeson and Brown would earn more than $1,000 from Victor recordings. Robeson also acquired a white booking agent, which meant he could perform throughout the nation before white audiences in bigger theaters and for more money. Ironically, while his white agent could book him into theaters that catered to white audiences, there was a political and psychic cost for Robeson: these theaters might let him perform but would not allow members of his race to purchase tickets. If blacks *were* allowed to come to these theaters, they might be forced into segregated seating.

By this time, Robeson was fully integrated into the social and intellectual world of the Harlem Renaissance. He partied with white literary and musical figures such as O'Neill, Van Vechten, George S. Kaufman, Rudolph Valentino, Margaret Leech, Dorothy Parker, F. Scott Fitzgerald, Noel Coward, Theodore Dreiser, Alfred A. Knopf, Cole Porter, Tallulah Bankhead, and George Gershwin, and with such black figures as Langston Hughes, James Weldon Johnson, Roland Hayes, Claude McKay, and Walter White. Robeson had achieved stardom and was surrounded by Harlem's and New York's brightest stars and star makers in art, music, poetry, literature, and the theater.

In the summer of 1925, Robeson performed *Emperor Jones* in London and sang on British radio. He and Essie stayed in Europe until December, moving on to Paris for a few weeks before returning to the United States. He was now a star with a national and international reputation.

In early 1926, Robeson and Brown began their first American concert tour. Reviews of the tour were stellar but audiences were small and the financial rewards minimal. America was not quite ready for a black vocal star, no matter how good he was. After his failed concert tour, Robeson tried to regain his momentum with the lead in the play *Black Boy*, but it closed in three weeks after terrible reviews. Even Robeson's talent could not overcome a poorly conceived play. After this failure, Essie organized another tour. As with the earlier tour, it began with a hugely successful concert in New

York City. But once outside of New York, bookings were poor, audiences small, and the tour was an emotional and financial failure.

In the fall he headed for Europe for yet another concert tour. Essie, eight months pregnant with their first child, remained in New York. Robeson had not wanted children this early in his marriage—perhaps he did not want them at all. But Essie had other plans. Her pregnancy may have been an attempt to cement their marriage, which was coming apart as Robeson's celebrity and his travels made Essie increasingly insecure. She was clearly aware of his enormous sex appeal to black and white women, and whether he had already begun to stray from his marriage vows (as he would openly do later), Essie surely was worried that he might. With his marriage in trouble, his career going nowhere, and a child on the way, Robeson headed to Paris.

In Paris he was warmly received by audiences of black expatriats, intellectuals, and celebrities, such as James Joyce and Mrs. Cole Porter, and sophisticated locals. He received thunderous ovations while Essie, back in New York, gave birth to their son, Paul Jr., on November 2. He returned to New York in December, with his finances in a little better shape and his reputation enormously enhanced.

In early 1928, Robeson signed a contract to perform in a "Negro Revue" organized by the white socialite Caroline Dudley Reagan. The revue was to open in September. In March, Robeson accepted the role of Crown, the rival of Porgy in the musical by the same name (later known as *Porgy and Bess*). He earned $500 a week and again won rave reviews. The producers enhanced the role with more songs, to capitalize on Robeson's voice. This play might have been another career-making move for him, playing a powerful role in an important play. He was in New York, and while he did not have the title role, he was stealing the show. But a better opportunity soon appeared: the role of Joe in a London production of the Jerome Kern-Oscar Hammerstein musical, *Show Boat*.

In April, Robeson returned to England to begin rehearsals for *Show Boat*. His rendition of "Ole Man River" was the key to the play's success and brought him new fame and fortune. Again, though he did not have the lead role, he was the instant star of the play. Indeed, most British critics disliked the play but loved Robeson. The play, because of Robeson, was enormously successful, running for more than a year and earning more than one-and-a-half million dollars. When not performing in the play, Robeson and Brown were giving matinee recitals in a packed concert hall. Robeson was a hero, making more money than he ever had made, and he was in constant demand. Even the King and Queen came to the theater to see him perform.

Away from the segregation and racism in the United States, Robeson flourished. At home he had always avoided a direct confrontation with segregation and discrimination. At Rutgers he had to overcome a coach reluctant to allow a black on his team; in New York he had silently ignored slights caused by race. He knew well that he could not eat with his white friends at most restaurants, but he refused to push the issue. He avoided fights and political confrontations, but at the same time, saw his prospects and his career harmed by bigotry. He also felt the slights and insults that assailed a black who ventured into the world of white America, even if he arrived there by invitation. Like so many other talented black men and women, he flourished in the midst of the Harlem Renaissance, but found that he could achieve even more in Europe. Robeson was enormously popular in England. Fans almost mobbed him, asking for his autograph or just trying to touch him. The demands for his time were so great that the theater manager hired a personal assistant, Joseph Andres, to help his star fend off fans and steer him through crowds and other places. Andrews, a native of the British West Indies, would remain with Robeson for more than thirty years.

In September, Robeson refused to return to the United States to fulfill a contract he had signed to perform in the "Negro Revue." With his success in England he did not need the job in the United States. Nor did he want to return to his homeland, which held no charm for him. Robeson's self-imposed exile was similar to that of other black artists and intellectuals, such as Josephine Baker, who brought the

Harlem Renaissance to Europe because they could not tolerate the racism of the United States. Earlier that year, in July, every prominent American in London had been invited to the Embassy for an Independence Day celebration, except the most prominent of all Americans in Britain, Paul Robeson. This was the sort of racism he would have to expect if he returned to America, and he was not willing to face it. His refusal to fulfill the contract jeopardized his ability to work in the United States, and the Actors Equity Association threatened him with suspension if he did not return. The Equity Association also hinted that his failure to return might harm other black actors. This led Walter White to intervene, but even he could not convince Robeson to return to America to fulfill his contract.

Robeson's decision illustrated the dilemma of talented blacks. If he stayed in England, he risked harming the chances of other black actors and singers succeeding in the white-dominated world of entertainment. Actors Equity might retaliate against other blacks, as might impresarios. But America could not offer Robeson equality or even true equity. He would be paid less in America than abroad and would have to face the constant insults and slights of being black in America. The King of England came to see him perform in London, but the American ambassador would not invite him to a Fourth of July party. Robeson's choice was in part personal—he had a better deal in England—but the decision to remain in England was also political. His value in Europe could in fact be a form of leverage against racism at home. The message Robeson sent was clear: if the United States would not treat its talented blacks as they deserved, then they had other options.

The Robesons remained in England until 1933. They lived in luxury, with white servants in their house, while they socialized with the elite of England and famous visitors from the United States and elsewhere. Robeson performed in England and on the Continent. In 1930, he played *Othello* with some success, opposite the British actress Peggy Ashcroft. Unlike his roles in the United States opposite white women, only a few people in England were bothered by the race issue, although both Robeson and Ashcroft received some hate mail after he kissed her on stage. But, unlike in the United States, there were no serious threats and the shows went on without incident. While in London, Robeson faced some prejudice and slights, but where race relations were concerned it was a different world from the United States.

The reviews of *Othello* were mixed, with some Shakespearean scholars praising his interpretation of the Moor but other critics arguing that his portrayal was based purely on emotion. In fact, for all his success as a singer and actor, Robeson had had almost no formal training in either. Talent and emotion could carry him in most roles, especially where his physical presence and singing voice could wow the audience. It worked for a time with *Othello*, as the play grossed $20,000 a week, but critical analyses of the lead's weaknesses led to diminished audiences and the play closed early.

Robeson returned to the concert stage in England and on the Continent. In 1931 he was listed in the British *Who's Who*, a significant accomplishment for the young foreigner. Robeson experimented with other forms of music—more classical material in German and French—but in the end he came back to his strength: African American music, recent compositions coming out of the Harlem Renaissance, and show tunes that reflected black life in America. In the spring of 1933 he once again performed *All God's Chillun Got Wings*, but this time, in England, there would be no threats of violence or mobs, and the play would be a great success. Throughout his years in England his concerts were often spectacular successes, including a 1929 near sell-out of the cavernous Royal Albert Hall, which had seating for 10,000.

While his career flourished, Robeson's marriage nearly collapsed. Complicating his marriage was a poorly conceived biography Essie wrote, *Paul Robeson, Negro*, which appeared in 1930. Critics had little good to say about the book, which turned into an emotional attack on her husband by a very unhappy wife. The book ends with Essie declaring her husband afflicted with "Laziness with a capital L," and declaring that his success was due to "his usual good luck" and his "instinct." She also accused him of being dishonest and a coward. Reviewers called it "trite" and "mediocre." Langston Hughes said it was "naively intimate" and said "as much about Mrs. Robeson" as it did about her husband. In the wake of this book, Essie found some love letters from his *Othello* co-star, Peggy Ashcroft. This confirmed Essie's fears of his philandering, and in 1930 they separated. Their marriage would remain in limbo for the next two years before Essie filed for divorce. Paul and Essie would ultimately reconcile, but they would never be deeply happy.

Meanwhile, Robeson briefly returned to the United States for a concert tour. He still had no love for his native land, but the financial opportunity offered by the tour was too great to resist. He sold out Carnegie Hall, and the audience was not satisfied until he had given at least seven encores. He sang his traditional repertoire, but also added songs in German and English folk music, although gradually the German lieder disappeared because the audience wanted more of his traditional songs. The tour was an overwhelming success. Essie was no longer there to watch over him (they were still separated, she in England) and he thrived on his independence and his overflow crowds.

Some blacks criticized his heavy use of spirituals, which the black intelligentsia thought did not improve race relations, but rather stereotyped blacks. Middle-class blacks and those who spoke for them wanted a black artist who would sing traditional opera and other music, and in effect prove that blacks were "equal" to whites. These critical comments illustrated the divisions within the African American community: traditionalists, middle-class blacks, sought to create a world where they would be equal and respected by rejecting black culture. However, some artists, such as Robeson, saw a "new pride in their race" from the songs of slavery and oppression, as he mentioned in a speech in April 1931.

The hostility of some black critics, combined with the pervasive racism in the United States, was more than Robeson was willing to bear. By May he had returned "home" to London, where he told reporters he found that "every man is a potential friend and people are unprejudiced and fair."

London thrilled at the return of its idol. Robeson starred in O'Neil's *The Hairy Ape*, which explored the nature and oppression of the lower and working classes of the industrialized world. The play made London's upper-class audiences deeply uncomfortable. Critics focused much of their praise on Robeson's voice and his acting, while attacking the play itself. Whether the play would have been a success cannot be known because Robeson caught a severe cold, and temporarily lost his voice, and the play closed.

But the critics also were thrilled because for the first half of the play Robeson appeared naked from the waist up, shoveling coal into the boilers of a steam ship. Londoners had not tired of his fabulous physique and great looks. One London theater critic declared: "That Mr. Robeson should be stripped to the waist is my first demand of any play in which he appears."

While obviously high praise, such comments also illustrate how Robeson and other African Americans in Europe were seen as exotic. For Londoners the black American body was a text, a spectacle, perhaps the very personification of forbidden carnal pleasure. This sort of praise was positive in the sense that white Londoners adored Robeson, but the adoration was in part a kind of racism because it reduced Robeson to an exotic creature—a great black body—and ignored his talent.

In January 1932, Robeson, lured by the likelihood of strong ticket sales, once more returned to America for a tour that took him to Canada as well as the Midwest and Northeast. He then began a run of *Show Boat* in New York. Still separated from Essie, rumors tied him to various English women, including Lady Edwina Mountbatten, the wife of Lord Louis "Dickie" Mountbatten, a cousin of the King. In June 1932, Essie, still in London, announced she would divorce Robeson. Her husband had "one affair too many," as their son would later put it. In response to the divorce filing, Paul made it clear he was in love with a white English woman from high society. He also indicated he was ready to move permanently to England if he could not live with his white wife-to-be in the United States.

These scandals had no effect on his career. He played to packed houses. His alma mater, Rutgers, awarded him an honorary degree at the same commencement at which the school awarded an honorary degree to the president of Princeton. The poor black kid from Somerville sat on stage with the president of the elite white school that he could never have attended. Clearly, Robeson had "made it" in America, as much as any black man could. But he knew that no black man could be completely free in America, and since he planned to marry an English woman, he knew he might have to accept permanent exile. In September, Robeson left *Show Boat* (which his contract allowed him to do) and traveled to France to meet the women he hoped to marry, the love of his life, Olivia Jackson, the stunningly beautiful daughter of a wealthy Englishman who had helped administer the colonial government in India. Olivia, however, refused his proposal. Her family could not accept a black son-in-law, and she was not willing to be disowned from her family and its wealth.

Robeson, devastated, became deeply depressed. In October, he gave a series of concerts in London and Manchester. His views of England had now been altered. He was, after all, not "good enough" to marry into the very class in England that had been lionizing him and socializing with him for nearly five years. He was college educated, with a Phi Beta Kappa key. He was a lawyer and had received an honorary degree alongside the president of Princeton University. He was perhaps the most famous black man in England or America. Yet even in England he was still too black to be truly accepted by elite society. In the wake of his failed romance he and Essie began to reconcile.

In February 1933, Robeson signed a contract to return to the United States to perform in a film version of *The Emperor Jones*. Before leaving London, Robeson did one more stint playing the lead in *All Gods Chillun Got Wings*. Here he played a black man denied the opportunity to wed the white woman he loved. In the wake of Olivia Jackson's rejection of him, art was now imitating Robeson's life. This, perhaps his best stage performance ever, was a fitting end to this phase of his life in England.

In May 1933, Mr. and Mrs. Paul Robeson returned to New York. The lucrative contract for the film version of *The Emperor Jones*, in addition to various expenses and first-class travel back to the United States, would pay Robeson $15,000 for six weeks' work and $2,000 a week after that. In the depths of the Great Depression, Robeson was about to make significant money. Despite his prosperity, Robeson was once again discouraged by the racism and discrimination he faced in New York. In England he might not be able to marry into the upper class, but for the most part he could live where he wished, stay in any hotel, eat in any restaurant.

Thus his return to the United States led to overwhelming frustration and anger. He was once invited to a Park Avenue home for a black-tie party, only to be told by the doorman at the building that he would have to use the freight elevator. Robeson was on the verge of striking the doorman when his movie producer arrived to defuse the situation. However, nothing could defuse Robeson's daily outrage. Meanwhile, black middle-class leaders condemned Robeson for playing the part of Emperor Jones—gambler, womanizer, thug, and murderer. Brutus Jones was not the role model that the black-middle class desired.

The film opened in segregated theaters around the nation on September 19, 1933. Some critics lauded Robeson, while others carped, perhaps unable to accept Robeson's powerful portrayal of Jones. Black critics attacked the film, the story, and O'Neill. In the *Amsterdam News* Joel Rogers denounced the whole production and attacked Robeson for agreeing to be in the film, which he argued did nothing for the image of blacks in America. Many blacks were uncomfortable with a script that had Robeson say the word "nigger" fourteen times. Middle-class blacks did not understand how Robeson's use of the word altered its meaning, just as his stunning portrayal of Emperor Jones undermined black stereotypes.

Robeson was not around to witness the controversy. He returned to London as soon as the film was finished. He could no longer tolerate the racism of American whites or the patronizing, petty debates of black cultural leaders who could not appreciate the complexity of the film, the power of his portrayal, and the ways in which Brutus Jones, despite all his flaws, challenged white America.

In England, Robeson was again lionized. He sang on the radio and in concerts. He studied foreign languages—Russian, Yiddish, Gaelic, even Chinese—to better sing the songs of other nations, other oppressed peoples. He started to sing in Russian, Polish, Hebrew, Yiddish, and Finnish. He added Scottish and Irish songs, in the original languages, to his repertoire. He toured the British Isles for most of 1934, astounding audiences and selling out concert halls.

Robeson also immersed himself in African culture and history, and met with black students from Africa, the Caribbean, and the United States. He added poetry to his concerts, and discussed the history of English abolitionists in Manchester and other textile cities. He accepted the lead role in *Sanders of the River,* a movie set in Africa that required hiring about 250 blacks to play Africans. His fame and box-office draw could now help unemployed blacks from all over the world find at least some work in Britain. One of the extras was a Kenyan named Johnstone Kenyatta, who was studying in London at the time. Twenty-five years later, as Jomo Kenyatta, he would lead the independence movement in his home country. Ironically, *Sanders* would be attacked by colonials living in Britain because the movie glorified British imperialism. After *Sanders,* which appeared in 1935, Robeson went on to star in four other movies set in Africa: *My Song Goes Forth* (1937), *Song of Freedom* (1937), *King Solomon's Mines* (1937), and *Jericho* (1937).

At the end of 1934, after completing work on *Sanders,* Robeson visited the Soviet Union, where he met the great Russian director Sergei Eisenstein, who wanted Robeson to star in a movie about Toussaint L'Ouverture, the leader of revolutionary Haiti who helped overthrow slavery and the French. To reach Russia he had to pass through Hitler's Germany. Once a center of avant-garde culture, he feared for his life when confronted by Nazi guards and the overwhelming sense of hatred in the nation. He left Germany, a country that clearly had worse race relations than even the United States. When he arrived in the Soviet Union he was initially wary of the openness of the society and apparent lack of racism. But at the same time, after Nazi Germany and even England, it must have seemed like an oasis of racial tolerance. He knew he was a celebrity and could not be certain if his treatment was just a show. Nevertheless, he found even less racism in the Soviet Union than he had in England. He was shocked, and pleased, when young children mobbed him with affection and joy. He met other American blacks who'd had similar experiences. People stared at him because they had never seen a black and because he was a giant of a man, but they were stares of wonderment and affection, not hatred. Here was a place, he thought, where racism really did not exist. He was also impressed by the strong Yiddish theater and the apparent lack of anti-Semitism in a nation infamous for its pogroms and intolerance. By this time Robeson could speak Yiddish reasonably well, and felt great kinship with the actors at Moscow's Jewish Theatre.

Robeson, enamored by the lack of racism in the USSR, returned in 1936 for a concert tour. The Soviet Union denounced racism and provided enormous public support of the arts. Moreover, Soviet officials wooed Robeson at every turn. He later said that during his first trips to the Soviet Union he, for the first time in his life, could walk with dignity and without fear of racism, prejudice, or some kind of slap in the face. In 1936, the Robesons decided to send their son, Paul Jr., to the Soviet Union for schooling. It was the only place they believed he could grow up without facing racial prejudice and discrimination. England was surely an improvement over America, but neither could match the equality offered in Russia.

As the Harlem Renaissance was coming to an end, Robeson, who had long before abandoned Harlem and the United States, gradually drifted into the Communist Party. He journeyed to Spain to support the anti-fascists, and in doing so he became increasingly political. He returned to the United States at the outbreak of World War II, just after finishing his last British film, *Proud Valley* (1939), written and directed by Herbert Marshall, a member of the Communist Party Robeson had met in Russia.

During World War II, Robeson used his music to inspire patriotism, performing the "Ballad for Americans" on the radio and then in public concerts across the nation. In 1943 he began to perform *Othello* in the United States and Canada, but refused to perform in any city or state where segregation was practiced. In 1945, he received the Spingarn Medal from the NAACP, the highest award of that organization and probably the most coveted civil rights award in the nation. In the winter of 1945–46, he gave a spectacularly successful concert tour across that part of the nation that did not discriminate against blacks. By this time, however, he was becoming increasingly political, denouncing segregation and lynching, while supporting the Communist Party. In the party he found dedicated anti-racists and proponents of world peace. At the same time, he ignored the excesses of Stalinism, including the "disappearance" of some of his Russian friends when their work no longer pleased Stalin. Robeson said nothing when his friend Eisenstein was forced to recant and denounce himself because he was also out of favor with Stalin. Robeson ignored this public humiliation of his friend and fellow artists, just as he ignored the execution and imprisonment of many of his other Russian friends.

TRACK 28

In 1925 Paul Robeson introduced black folk songs and spirituals to concert audiences as valuable expressions of the African American creative genius. "No More Auction Block" serves a powerful reminder of the suffering that blacks have overcome as well as their strength and determination. He imbued his reading of the song with the memory of his father, who had been a slave.

By 1947, Robeson was considered a Communist, and for many "un-American." He supported the Progressive Party candidate Henry Wallace in 1948. Wallace was emphatically not a Communist, but the Communist Party in the United States supported him. As the Cold War deepened, Robeson became increasingly tied to Communism and increasingly alienated from the nation and the potential audiences. By 1950, he was considered a subversive; his passport was seized and he could neither travel abroad nor get bookings at home. He had earned over $200,000 in 1944 but grossed under $20,000 a decade later. Finally, in 1958, at age sixty, he regained his passport and immediately went to England. He remained out of the country until 1963, traveling in Eastern Europe, where he was still lionized. By the time he returned to the United States, his career was over. Although only sixty-five years old, his spirit was broken and he avoided public appearances. He spent the rest of his life all but forgotten, living with a sister in Philadelphia.

Robeson's contributions to American culture are complicated. He was almost certainly the greatest black singer of his age. His voice and stage presence were enormously powerful. His legacy includes the many color lines he broke, onstage and in film, with his great talent. Most importantly, he almost singlehandedly resurrected the Negro spiritual, slave songs, and African American folk music, bringing it to all Americans. As a performer he was a force in the Harlem Renaissance, although most of his successes occurred after the Renaissance and away from Harlem.

At the same time, he also personified the tragedy of a racism that could torment and undermine even a man of unprecedented talent. His support for communism was a reflection of his distaste for American racism and Western imperialism in Africa and in what would today be called the Third World. At the same time, his unwavering support of Stalin and Stalinism undermines his reputation as a bright, well-educated, humane artist. Despite his failure to see, or admit, to the horrors of the regime he defended, Robeson remains a towering figure in American culture. The old black-and-white films still show the power of his presence, and recordings of his voice still thrill listeners.

PART SIX

The New Negro: Politics and Criticism in the Harlem Renaissance

INTRODUCTION

The post-World War I years were a period of intense political debate and struggle for African Americans as they strived for the most effective away to address the prejudice, discrimination, and racial violence that characterized American life. This effort was influenced by a wide range of options and ideas that emerged both from African American experience in the United States and new anti-colonial and socialist-communist ideologies that characterized the political climate of the post-war era. From the perspective of the Harlem Renaissance, these political deliberations raised two major issues. The first was the identification and assessment of the political options that faced African Americans. The second was the role, the responsibility, and the relationship of the arts to this political struggle. As noted in the previous section, politics and the arts were intertwined.

As the twentieth century opened, the fundamental political reality confronting African Americans was the withering away of political and social rights achieved following emancipation. Simply put, the problems were the imposition of Jim Crow segregation throughout the South and in many parts of the North, and the systematic denial of the right of African Americans to vote in all of the states of the former Confederacy. These conditions added to the economic subjugation of blacks and left them defenseless in the face of intensifying racial violence—especially lynching and race riots. It also deprived blacks of the traditional means of addressing such problems through the courts and political action.

In the early twentieth century, the response of African Americans to these conditions generally followed one of two strategies, each identified with a specific personality. One approach, associated with Booker T. Washington, tended to stress development within the African American community through building up black educational, social, and economic institutions, and focusing on gaining wealth before pursuing equal rights. The second, associated with W.E.B. Du Bois, insisted on confronting segregation and discrimination and demanding immediate equal rights.

In the post-war period, the debate became more complicated. The death of Booker T. Washington in 1915 and the rise of the NAACP left Du Bois ascendant, at least temporarily. At the same time, forces unleashed by the war—anti-colonialism and Pan-Africanism on the one hand and Marxist-Leninist socialism on the other—altered the political debate. Furthermore, the growing impact of the black migration, and the turmoil and violence of Red Summer in 1919, seemed to destabilize the old order and portend even greater change. Harlem, the New Negro, and the emerging Harlem Renaissance sometimes seemed to be at the center of this expected revolutionary change.

The three figures discussed in the chapters that follow participated in the politics of this period, and each sought to define the new

order. Garvey and Randolph approached
the problem from a mostly traditional
political perspective. Garvey began as a
disciple of Booker T. Washington and
came to the United States primarily to
raise funds to replicate Tuskegee Institute
in his native Jamaica. In the tumultuous
war and post-war period, his ideas rapidly
evolved and he founded the first black
mass political movement in the United
States. His message combined the development of black-owned businesses, the
linking of all the peoples of the African
Diaspora into an international force to
protect black rights, and the redemption
of Africa from European colonialism.

Title page, *The New Negro: An Inter-
pretation,* edited by Alain Locke; book
decoration by Winold Reiss. 1925.
Photographs and Prints Division,
Schomburg Center for Research in
Black Culture, The New York Public
Library Astor, Lenox and Tilden Foun-
dations.

Alain Locke, a Harvard-educated
Ph.D. and professor of philosophy at the
all-black Howard University in Washington, D.C., eschewed traditional politics and approached the racial problem through culture.
As a philosopher and critic, Locke emerged as an intellectual leader
of the Harlem Renaissance and sought to define the aesthetic of the
movement. Though based in Washington, he was a frequent visitor
to New York and played a pivotal role in the origins and development of the Harlem Renaissance.

A. Phillip Randolph took an alternate political route. Shortly
after arriving in Harlem from his native Florida, he embraced
socialism and became active in street-corner and university-based
radical politics. He believed that racism was the inevitable byprod-
uct of capitalism, and that socialism was the only remedy. In the
early 1920s, his views began to evolve. Rejecting Bolshevism and
Soviet-dominated communism, he drifted towards the center,
became the head of the largest African American labor union, and
led the struggle to end discrimination in the workplace and in
organized labor.

There were other players in the political arena of the Harlem Renaissance—Du Bois, of course, and James Weldon Johnson being just two examples—but Garvey, Randolph, and Locke serve excellent examples of the connection between politics and art during this period.

Marcus Garvey

(1887–1940)

CLAUDRENA N. HAROLD

The milestones in Marcus Garvey's brief but meteoric career in the United States attest to both the grandness of vision and the depth of his failure. In March 1916, Garvey arrived in the United States for the purpose of fundraising for his programs in Jamaica. Within a year he had decided to relocate permanently to the U.S. and established the headquarters of his Universal Negro Improvement Association in Harlem. Over the next three or four years his success was phenomenal. He articulated a coherent program of black pride, Pan-Africanism, and economic self-sufficiency, and he established visible components of this—the weekly Negro World, and the stunningly ambitious Black Star Line. The African American working class responded enthusiastically. By 1920, when the UNIA held its first international assembly, Garvey could boast of one million members—the largest African American mass organization in U.S. history. Garvey's fall was just as rapid. Arrested in 1922, sentenced to federal prison in 1925, and deported in 1927, Garvey and the UNIA, for all practical purposes, had ended their spectacular run.

Three years after Marcus Garvey's deportation from the United States in 1927, James Weldon Johnson, in his magisterial study, *Black Manhattan*, reflected on the charismatic leader's brief tenure in the United States. Garvey, Johnson opined, "stirred the imagination of the Negro masses as no Negro ever had. He raised more money in a few years than any other Negro organization had ever dreamed of. He had great power and great possibilities within his grasp." Moved by Garvey's clarion call for race pride, Pan-African unity, and economic uplift, thousands of African Americans and West Indians invested heavily in his economic ventures, stood behind him during his numerous legal struggles, and labored earnestly to transform his Pan-African dreams into reality.

A controversial figure, Garvey had an almost visceral appeal among thousands of black working women and men in New York City, but his impassioned rhetoric provoked anger, apprehension, and even trepidation among various members of the civil rights establishment. "Garvey," Johnson recalled in *Black Manhattan*, "made several vital blunders, which, with any intelligent advice, he might have avoided." To the detriment of not only his movement but black racial unity, the UNIA leader "proceeded upon the assumption of a triple race scheme in the United States; whereas the facts are that the whites in the United States, unlike the whites of the West Indies, make no distinction between people of color and blacks, nor do the Negroes." Terribly frustrated by what he viewed as Garvey's inability to grasp fully the uniqueness of America's racial situation, Johnson scolded the UNIA leader not only for his focus on color distinctions and divisions within the African American community but also for his colonization efforts in Liberia. "Thoughtful colored Americans," Johnson hissed, "knew that, under existing political conditions in Africa, that plan could ultimately meet with nothing but failure." Repelled by the UNIA's political program, Johnson portrayed Garvey as a "tragic figure" who had been blessed with the opportunity to build a truly unique and transformative movement, but "clutched greedily at the glitter and let the substance slip from his fingers."

Such a view was definitely not shared by the thousands of black women and men in New York who rallied behind the Pan-African agenda of the UNIA. Few leaders, if any, had a more indelible impact on the masses of ordinary black women and men during the 1920s than Marcus Garvey. A proud, ambitious man whose formal education ended at the age of thirteen, Garvey significantly influenced the ways in which thousands of women and men conceptualized race and class, evaluated the strengths and weaknesses of international political formations, and staked their hopes in the American democratic project. Audley Moore, the celebrated Harlem activist whose organizational affiliations included the UNIA, the Communist Party, and the Revolutionary Action Movement, noted in 1977, "Marcus Garvey raised in me a certain knowledge of belonging to people all over the world, the African people, and he gave me pride...It was Garvey who brought consciousness to me."

Living in Harlem between 1916 and 1925, Garvey transformed the lives of countless other black New Yorkers through both his writings and speeches. A gifted orator, Garvey drew hundreds and sometimes thousands to the UNIA's weekly meetings in Liberty Hall. Spectacularly attired in militaristic uniforms with gold trimmings and sashes, Garvey captured the imagination of domestic workers, pullman porters, draymen, and factory workers with his nationalist vision of a new future for Africa and its children.

Forever presenting himself as a servant of the people, Garvey constantly reminded his followers of his dedication to the black liberation struggle. "Some people die for their wives," Garvey thundered to a packed audience at Liberty Hall in 1922, "some people die for their money; some die for their property, and some people die for a national ideal. Among the many things that I would die for is the national ideal—a free and independent Africa."

"I am not going to trouble anybody," he continued, "I am not going to disturb anybody; I am not going to rob anybody; I am not going to get in anybody's way, but everybody will get out of my way on the way to Africa." Seemingly undeterred by the global forces aligned against him and his movement, Garvey was quite confident about the UNIA's potential for success: "We are traveling towards a destination that we claim to be ours and we are going to win out and we are going to get it if it takes a year or a hundred years or a thousand years; we are bound to get the complete freedom of Africa. I trust you who make up the rank and file of the Universal Negro Improvement Association are prepared and ready at any time to find a man when the hour strikes for your deliverance."

Even though Garvey was based in Harlem for much of the 1920s, his Pan-African vision struck a responsive chord in the hearts and minds of black women and men in various parts of the United States. Timing played a significant role in his massive popularity. Terribly frustrated with the permanency of white supremacy at the end of World War I, a growing number of black women pledged their support to new and existing civil rights organizations, increased their involvement in revolutionary politics, and even defended themselves against white physical aggression. Fully cognizant of the rising militancy in black America during the post-World War I period, Marcus Garvey labored to build a mass-based movement for racial redemption and economic advancement.

Garvey encouraged his followers to direct their attention toward the creation of an autonomous nation state in Africa. Neither voter registration campaigns nor lobbying for the passage of anti-lynching bills would secure American blacks their citizenship rights. Trying to prove one's humanity through the mastery of the arts was equally futile. "The white man," Garvey explained, "will only respect your rights constitutionally as a citizen of this country, when you have some government behind you. When you can compel a nation to respect your rights because of your connection with some government that is sufficiently strong to support you, then and only then will you be respected."

Familiarity with the marginalized status of blacks in various parts of the globe contributed significantly to Garvey's embrace of Pan-African nationalism. A St. Ann's Bay, Jamaica, native born to Sarah Richards and Malchus Mosiah Garvey Sr. on August 17, 1887, Garvey had traveled extensively before his arrival in the United States in 1916. Not particularly satisfied with the economic opportunities in his hometown, in 1906 Garvey moved to the capital city of Kingston, where he worked as a printer for the Government Printing Office. Four years later at age twenty-three, Garvey decided to follow the scores of Jamaican workers who searched for better economic opportunities in Central America. Garvey landed a job as a timekeeper on a United Fruit Company plantation in Costa Rica.

Shortly thereafter, Garvey traveled to England, where his Pan-African perspective deepened significantly. Once in London, the Jamaican befriended the noted Pan-Africanist Duse Mohamed Ali, published an article in Ali's *African Times and Orient Review*, and socialized with West Indian and West African students in the metropolis. Garvey's sojourn in England, historian Tony Martin notes, "was of great importance to his career. The workings of British democracy made a lasting impression on him, and like later generations of visitors from the colonized world to the metropolis, he noted the contrast to the autocracy which the very same colonizers maintained in their tropical dependencies." Living in London proved to be an excellent political experience for the West Indian, but poverty forced Garvey to return to his native land after three years abroad.

Less than a week after his return to Jamaica, Garvey, with the assistance of his future wife, Amy Ashwood, organized the Universal Negro Improvement Association (UNIA) and African Commercial League (ACL) on August 1, 1914. Ten years younger than Garvey, Ashwood had been born in Port Antonio, Jamaica, but had spent her childhood in Panama and Columbia. Even though her parents objected to her relationship with Garvey, Amy was committed to her beau and their Pan-African dreams. Very serious about the liberation of their people, Ashwood and Garvey labored to build the UNIA into a formidable organization. A testament to its founders' lofty ambitions, the UNIA's stated goals were:

> To establish a universal confraternity among the race.
> To promote the spirit of race pride and love.
> To reclaim the fallen of the race.

> To administer to and assist the needy.
> To establish commissaries or agencies in the princi-
> pal countries of the world for the protection of all
> Negroes, irrespective of nationality.
> To promote a conscientious Christian worship
> among the native tribes of Africa.
> To establish universities, colleges, and secondary
> schools for the further education of the boys and girls
> of the race

Shortly after the organization's formation, Ashwood and Garvey launched a fundraising campaign to build an industrial school along the lines of Booker T. Washington's Tuskegee Institute. Soon, Garvey hoped to "erect several colleges, (educational and industrial) at different centers in the island for the purpose of supplying free secondary and industrial education to our boys and girls." Support for Garvey's proposed plan was minimal. Frustrated by local blacks' disinterest in his plans, Garvey asked Booker T. Washington, the principal of Tuskegee Institute, to supply the newly formed organization with a small donation. In a letter dated September 17, 1914, Washington denied the West Indian's request for financial assistance, but invited the young man to "come to Tuskegee and see for yourself what we are striving to do for the colored young men and women of the South."

Sensing greater potential for success in the United States, Garvey wrote back to Washington and accepted his invitation. Unfortunately, Washington died in November 1915, before Garvey's trip. Instead, Garvey traveled to New York City, arriving on March 23, 1916.

To familiarize black Harlemites with his organization's goals, on May 9, Garvey held his first public lecture at St. Mark's Church Hall. No exact record of the speech is available, but according to Wilfred A. Domingo, Garvey's first address was a complete failure:

> Shaking like an aspen leaf and with a tremor in
> his voice he started to deliver his oration. He hadn't
> gone very far when the audience began to vent its

disgust by whistling and hooting. You can easily imagine the sorry figure and the pitiable spectacle the poor discomfited orator presented. He looked around in affright and pulling a manuscript from his pocket began to read. The more he read the greater was the din created by the audience ... From all sides of the small hall came shouts of 'Sit down,' 'Shut up,' 'Away with him,' interspersed with catcalls and ear-splitting whistles."

Such a dismal performance would have led most to question their fitness for leadership, but as was the case throughout his life, the supremely confident Garvey put this horrific experience behind him. Undeterred by his unsuccessful performance at St. Mark's, Garvey embarked on a year-long speaking tour which included thirty-eight states. Traveling across the country provided Garvey with the opportunity to gain a better understanding of the position of the Negro in America. "I have seen Negro banks in Washington and Chicago," he wrote in an article in *Champion*, "stores, cafes, restaurants, theaters and real estate agencies that fill my heart with joy to realize that at one center of Negrodom, at least, the people of the race have sufficient pride to do things for themselves." An impressed Garvey praised black Americans for their achievements in the economic and cultural arenas. "Let not the American Negro be misled," he explained, "he occupies the best position among all Negroes up to the present time." Thoroughly impressed by the women and men who welcomed him into their churches, social clubs, and private homes during his lecture tour, Garvey returned to New York in May 1917.

Staying busy after his return, Garvey found himself devoting more attention to racial discrimination in the United States. Saddened by the news of whites' brutal murder of thirty-nine blacks during the race riots in East St. Louis in July, Garvey registered his disgust at "the savagery of a people who claim to be the dispensers of democracy . . . I do not know what special meaning the people who slaughtered the Negroes of East St. Louis have for democracy of which they are the custodians, but I do know that it has no literal meaning for me as used and applied by these same lawless people." Of course, Marcus Garvey was hardly alone in his criticism of the race riots and the federal government's unwillingness to protect its black citizens. More vocal and militant denunciations of American race relations emerged from New York activists like A. Philip Randolph, Chandler Owen, and Hubert Harrison.

Few individuals impressed Garvey more than Harrison. A month after his return from his lecture tour, Garvey had spoken at the inaugural meeting of Harrison's Liberty League. A brilliant orator whose writings and speeches on race, socialism, Pan-Africanism, and free thought influenced many black radicals, Harrison had served as a leading organizer and theoretician in the Socialist Party of New York from 1911 to 1914. According to his biographer, Harrison was the "most class conscious of the race radicals and the most race conscious of the class radicals." Frustrated by the political tactics of the civil rights establishment, Harrison organized the Liberty League on

TRACK 29

In this 1921 speech, Garvey discusses the efforts of his political opponents to undermine his organization. He defends the UNIA, emphasizing its goals and objectives as well as its loyalty are to the U.S. government.

June 12, 1917. The League not only agitated for the passage of a federal anti-lynching bill and the enforcement of the Fourteenth and Fifteenth Amendments, but also promoted self-defense as a viable method in the struggle for black equality. Garvey supported Harrison's endeavors, but he never abandoned his own organization.

Quite confident in his abilities, Garvey started to hold weekly meetings in Lafayette Hall, which, according to the Harlem-based *Home News*, drew hundreds of people. To capitalize on his growing popularity, Garvey incorporated the New York chapter of the UNIA and ACL on June 20, 1918. Vibrant UNIA locals eventually developed in Philadelphia, Boston, Washington, D.C., Cleveland, Chicago, Los Angeles, New Orleans, Norfolk, and Miami. A testament to the widespread popularity of the UNIA, the organization even had a large following in the Jim Crow South. Firmly anchored in the South by early 1921, the Universal Negro Improvement Association's base of supporters included domestic workers and longshoremen in the port cities of the Gulf Coast, disgruntled share-croppers in the cotton regions of the Black Belt, tobacco hands in eastern Virginia, and Bahamian immigrants in South Florida.

No small factor in the growth and popularity of the UNIA among Southern blacks was the organization's official organ, the *Negro World*. A superbly edited weekly sold at poolrooms, dance halls, convenience stores, and beauty shops across the country, the *Negro World* introduced thousands of black women and men to the UNIA, provided detailed information on the association's various programs, and cultivated a diasporic sensibility among its readership. "It is impossible to say," M. Harrold of Blackton, Arkansas, explained in 1925, "how much we learn from the *Negro World*. There are so many things that we would never know or understand if we did not see it there."

Fully cognizant of the critical role of the *Negro World* in the growth of the UNIA, many whites sought to prevent the paper's cir-culation in the South. Convinced that the continued distribution of the black nationalist weekly would "cause riots, revolutions, rebel-lions and finally chaos," one Bureau of Investigation agent in Nashville, Tennessee, urged the Postmaster General, Albert Burele-son, to ban the sale and distribution of the *Negro World*. Officials at the Bureau of Investigation and Post Office departments discussed the possibility of banning the weekly, but they proved unable to stop the circulation of the *Negro World*. Nor were they able to stop the outpouring of support for Garvey's Pan-African initiatives.

A strong desire to raise the necessary funds to establish a Jamaican industrial school along the lines of Tuskegee Institute brought Garvey to the United States, but after gaining a strong fol-lowing in New York City and building support across the country, he shifted his political emphasis from industrial education to the creation of a shipping line and the formation of a strong Negro nationality in Africa. After World War I, Garvey increasingly

The Black Star Line office was the headquarters of Garvey's most ambitious project, the creation of a black-owned and black-operated steamship line that would carry trade among the peoples of the African diaspora and transport blacks back to their African homeland.

Photographs and Prints Division, Schomburg Center for Research in Black Culture, The New York Public Library Astor, Lenox and Tilden Foundations.

asserted that any program of racial uplift had to concern itself with the material improvement of the black masses as well as the removal of white colonialists from the African continent. Worried over the potential impact of postwar demobilization on black workers, Garvey preached a message of economic preparedness to black audiences across the country. "We have to prepare against the hard times of the future," he repeatedly informed his followers, "and the best way we can do that is by strengthening our present economic position." The underlying philosophy behind the UNIA's economic agenda was relatively simple: the improvement of blacks' economic position was dependent on a strategy that emphasized economic integration and cooperation among African-descended peoples on the continent and in the diaspora.

To improve the commercial links between blacks in the West Indies, the Americas, and West Africa, Garvey organized the Black Star Line Steamship Corporation (BSL) in the summer of 1919. An undercapitalized shipping venture, the Black Star Line became the cornerstone of the UNIA's efforts to create an integrated community of workers, producers, and consumers with the collective power to improve blacks' economic position globally. "We want an exceptionally good passenger service," Garvey explained to potential shareholders, "so that in the event of any economic setback in this Western Hemisphere, we will be able through our own ships of the Black Star Line, to transport our people in the United States of America, the West Indies, and anywhere else to new industrial fields and thereby enable them to make a satisfactory livelihood." Only blacks could buy stock in the Black Star Line and shareholders could not purchase more than two hundred dollars worth of stock. To generate funds for the UNIA's new enterprise, Garvey sold shares in the Black Star Line at five dollars apiece. Of course, it was not easy for working-class blacks to amass the necessary funds to acquire stock in the line, especially after many industries slashed wages during the economic recession, but many Garveyites viewed racial enterprise as the best way to improve their material condition.

Thanks largely to the generous contributions of blacks in New York City, Philadelphia, Newport News, Virginia, and Colon, Panama, the BSL purchased its first ship, the SS *Yarmouth*, on November 5, 1919. A relatively small, thirty-two year old vessel of only 1,452 gross tons, the *Yarmouth* was hardly worth its purchase price of $165,000. Notwithstanding the *Yarmouth's* numerous mechanical problems during its two trips to the West Indies, UNIA officials soon purchased two additional ships in the spring of 1920. An excursion boat of approximately 450 tons, the SS *Shadyside* was purchased by the UNIA for use on promotional trips and summer excursions along the Hudson River. Less than one month after the *Shadyside* began its excursion trips along the Hudson, BSL officials announced the acquisition of another vessel, the SS *Kanawha*, on May 9. A 375-ton yacht whose defective boilers did not prevent the United States Shipping Board from approving its sale to the BSL, the *Kanawha* suspended operations after only one trip to the Caribbean. None of the BSL's trips to the West Indies proved profitable, but as Michelle Stephens points

Marcus Garvey on his wedding day, 1919. Garvey married his first wife, Amy Ashwood Garvey, in December, 1919; The marriage lasted less than three years. The couple divorced shortly before Garvey married his second wife, Amy Jacques Garvey, in 1922.
Photographs and Prints Division, Schomburg Center for Research in Black Culture, The New York Public Library, Astor, Lenox and Tilden Foundations.

out in her recent study, *Black Empire*, the *Yarmouth* and the *Kanawha* played an important role in "mobilizing the black world's sense of itself as a global racial community."

UNIA Parade, 1924. UNIA parades became a regular feature in Harlem during the early 1920s. They attracted thousands of marchers and spectators emboldened by the concept of "the New Negro."
Photographs and Prints Division, Schomburg Center for Research in Black Culture, The New York Public Library Astor, Lenox and Tilden Foundations.

Simultaneously with his effort to build a viable shipping enterprise, Garvey worked to establish a political and commercial relationship with the West African country of Liberia. Negotiations between the UNIA and the Liberian government officially commenced in May 1920, when Elie Garcia, auditor general of the UNIA, arrived in Monrovia, Liberia. Very interested in attracting foreign investment, Liberia's secretary of state, Edwin Barclay, assured Garcia of the government's intention to "afford the association every facility legally possible in effectuating in Liberia, industry, agriculture, and business projects." Moved by Barclay's encouraging words, Garvey launched the Liberian Construction Loan in the fall of 1920. "The purpose of this loan," Garvey explained in an editorial in the *Negro World*, "is to start construction work in Liberia, where colleges, universities, industrial plants, and railroad tracks will be erected; where men will be sent to make roads, and where artisans and craftsmen will be sent to develop industries." An industrially developed Liberia, Garvey insisted, would "offer great opportunities to all men and women who desire to start off independently to build fortunes for themselves and their families."

No doubt, the association's entrepreneurial pursuits and colonization endeavors pulled many into the movement, but blacks also derived much uplift from the association's social activities. Weekly meetings at the UNIA's Liberty Hall in Harlem attracted thousands of women and men who greatly enjoyed the impassioned lectures, poetry, drama, and live music provided by movement participants.

The movement's appeal and importance extended beyond its cultural value. Working-class blacks, denied participation in the mainstream political culture, valued highly the opportunity to participate in the Universal African Legion, the Black Cross Nurses, and the Juvenile Department. Occupying leadership positions within the movement was a source of pride for many laboring people in Harlem. "A Negro might be a porter during the day, taking his orders from white men," E. Franklin Frazier perceptively noted in his analysis of the Garvey movement's mass appeal in an August 1926 article in *The Nation*, "but he was an officer in the black army when it assembled at night in Liberty Hall." Satisfying black workers' thirst for "self-magnification," the UNIA, with its numerous offices, "made the Negro an important person in his immediate environment." True, UNIA supporters appreciated public recognition, but their embrace of the UNIA must also be placed within the broader context of their growing frustration with the traditional black leadership class. Frustrated with the direction of many of the leading racial advocacy groups in black America, many workers searched for institutional spaces where their concerns could be articulated, their voices heard, their ideas taken seriously, and their leadership skills developed in order to ensure a better future for themselves and their children. To thousands of women and men in New York and other locales across the country, the UNIA constituted such a welcoming space.

Not everyone, however, approved of the UNIA. Troubled by the Garvey movement's growing popularity, the Justice Department's Bureau of Investigation launched an extensive investigation and surveillance of the organization in 1919. J. Edgar Hoover oversaw much of the surveillance activity. Between 1919 and 1923, Hoover relied on the services of several black informants—Dr. Arthur Craig, James Wormley Jones, William A. Bailey, Herbert S. Boulin, and James Edward Amos—to uncover criminal activity within the leadership ranks of the UNIA. Needless to say, the Bureau focused specifically on Garvey. In a letter to Hoover's assistant, George Ruch, Chief Frank Burke wrote: "As Marcus Garvey is an alien, it is particularly desirous of establishing sufficient evidence against him to warrant the institution of deportation proceedings. Any avocation by him of opposition to law and order would be grounds upon which to have a request for deportation. Therefore, kindly have the informant give particular attention to this phase of the question."

TRACK 30

Marcus Garvey outlines the international perspective of the United Negro Improvement Association, and its objectives and beliefs, in this excerpt from a recorded 1921 UNIA membership appeal.

Two years after the Bureau launched its investigation of the UNIA, Garvey, along with three other Black Star Line officials, was arrested for fraudulent use of mails. Federal officials accused the UNIA leader of advertising and selling stock in a non-existent ship purported to be used for the Black Star Line's Liberian route. Speaking before an enthusiastic crowd at the Liberty Hall in New York, Garvey denied involvement in any attempt to swindle his followers: "Let me say to you that, as far as I am concerned, I have no cause to rob anybody," he assured his supporters. "I have no cause to defraud anybody; for the simple reason, thank God, or whosoever gave it to me, I was endowed with strength and ability always to do something for myself, for I can handle a pick or a shovel, or handle a pen, or handle a wheelbarrow. I always feel in such form as to be able to earn a livelihood anywhere, even in a desert." Fervent UNIA supporters pledged their loyalty to Garvey, but several African American leaders applauded the UNIA leader's arrest. Writing off the BSL as a fraudulent scheme designed solely to rob money from misguided blacks, W.E.B. Du Bois of the NAACP, Cyril Briggs of the

African Blood Brotherhood, and Chandler Owen and A. Philip Randolph of *Messenger Magazine* had already advised blacks to cease their purchase of BSL stock.

There was some truth in critical comments leveled at Garvey's organization. The BSL had been a valiant attempt at economic integration and cooperation between African descended peoples, but the line and its officers lacked the financial capital, nautical experience, political connections, and business contacts necessary to survive, let alone turn a profit, during the postwar recession. The line's vessels, the *Yarmouth*, *Kanawha*, and *Shadyside*, were constantly plagued with mechanical problems and financial difficulties. Over the period between 1918 and 1922, UNIA supporters across the globe contributed close to one million dollars towards the BSL, but more money was needed to succeed in the shipping industry. Nearly two months after Garvey's arrest on mail fraud charges, the April 1, 1922, edition of the *Negro World* announced the suspension of the Black Star Line.

The UNIA faced more problems in the coming months. Nearly two months after the BSL's demise, Garvey found himself under attack for his controversial meeting on July 22, 1922, with the Ku Klux Klan Acting Imperial Wizard, Edward Young Clarke. Impressed by a Garvey speech on the benefits of Jim Crow segregation, Clarke informed the president of the Atlanta UNIA of his desire to talk with the black nationalist. Quite concerned about KKK physical and verbal assaults on UNIA followers in the South, Garvey agreed to meet with the avowed white supremacist. Reporters were kept out of the meeting, but according to Garvey, the two had the opportunity to explain the true intent of their organizations, their mutual hostility towards many integrationist groups, and their belief in the emigration of blacks to Africa as the most effective solution to America's racial dilemma. Garvey's summit with Clarke infuriated his detractors. Understandably troubled by Garvey's actions, A. Philip Randolph and Chander Owen of the *Messenger* publicly voiced their disapproval at Garvey's decision to meet with the white supremacist in their July 1922 issue: "We urge all ministers, editors and lecturers who have the interests of the race at heart to gird up their courage, put on new force, and proceed with might and main to drive the menace of Garveyism out of this country."

Ironically, Randolph had been critical of the federal government's deportation of labor radicals during World War I, but he openly called for the expulsion of the UNIA's president-general. Spending more time criticizing Garvey than building their own movement, Randolph and Owen rallied other black leaders around the slogan "Garvey Must Go." An eclectic group of activists lectured at various churches on the disruptive influence of the Garvey movement, its dangerous separatist politics, and its inability to solve the problem of racial oppression.

Frustrated by numerous delays in the start of Garvey's trial, A. Philip Randolph, Chandler Owen, Robert Abbott (editor of the *Chicago Defender*), John Nail and Harry Pace of the New York Urban League, Julia Coleman (president of a cosmetic company), and William Pickens and Robert Bagnall of the NAACP even urged the attorney general to "speedily push the government's case against Marcus Garvey for using the mails to defense."

Garvey's long-awaited trial started in May 1923. Though he lacked legal experience, he decided to represent himself in court. Garvey denied any involvement in fraudulent activities and attributed the BSL's problems to his associates' incompetence and dishonesty. Unsuccessful in his efforts to convince the jury of his innocence, on June 21 Garvey was found guilty of mail fraud and sentenced to five years in prison. Garvey and his lawyers immediately petitioned for an appeal. Believing U.S. Assistant Attorney Maxwell Mattuck's claim that Garvey had ammunition stored at the Liberty Hall in New York, the federal courts denied the leader's request for bail for three months. Finally, on September 10, 1923, the UNIA Parent Body secured his release on $25,000 bail pending his appeal.

Immediately after his release, Garvey revitalized the organization's African plans. In late December 1923, he dispatched Robert

Lincoln Poston, Henrietta Vinton Davis, and J. Milton Van Lowe to Monrovia, Liberia, where they negotiated with the ex-Liberian president Edwin Barclay and other governmental officials over the possible acquisition of five hundred square miles near the Cavilla River in Maryland County. Understanding that the success of the organization's Liberian plans depended on its ability to provide affordable transportation to prospective colonists, Garvey organized the Black Cross Navigation and Trading Company (BCNTC) in March 1924. Laying out the BCNTC's prospectus in the pages of the *Negro World*, Garvey urged his followers to rally behind the organization's latest venture into the shipping industry. "There are hundreds of shiploads of cargo waiting for us in Africa, in the West Indies, [and in] South and Central America to convey back to the United States of America. Millions can be made for the race in the conveying of raw materials from one part of the world to the other, and the return to them of our finished products."

The BCNTC's first ship, Garvey announced, would carry "the first organized group of colonists to Liberia," but other ships would also be purchased to develop "a trade relationship between Negroes of Africa, the United States of America, the West Indies, and South and Central America." All across the nation, Garveyites enthused over the opportunity to start anew in Liberia. Carlise D. Arsenburg of New Orleans, in a letter to the *Negro World*, welcomed the opportunity to leave the United States: "I am greatly enthused over the movement with its great cause and success. I had been taught about Africa since I was fourteen years old by my mother, and I had always lived in hopes that the time would come that her words would come to pass. Surely that time has come. It is now." Only through emigration, many blacks increasingly believed, could African Americans achieve full emancipation. Until blacks established a strong Negro nationality in Africa, in their view, full emancipation would remain an elusive dream. "The Negro needs a flag and a country of his own," Sara Maclin of Memphis, Tennessee, reasoned. "He can never expect to get any protection or recognition without a government of his own to back up his demands."

Five months after Garvey revealed his plans for the newly organized line to the UNIA's rank and file, BCNTC officials purchased the *General Goethels,* rechristened as the *Booker T. Washington,* for $100,000. Still committed to the idea of racial enterprise as an effective method of economic uplift, Garveyites contributed thousands of dollars towards the line, but their hopes of achieving economic independence would not be realized. Unable to attract much business, the *Booker T. Washington* was taken out of service in the summer of 1925 and sold at a fraction of its original cost in March 1926.

Even worse, Garvey and his representatives in New York had been unable to strike a deal with the Liberian government. Worried about the potential strength of a UNIA colony, Liberia's State Department in the summer of 1924 banned the entrance of anyone associated with the UNIA. A team of UNIA technicians and representatives arrived in Liberia on June 14 with plans to prepare the projected UNIA settlement, but the group was seized, detained, and then deported. Garvey vowed to take the necessary steps to improve the Liberia situation, still hopeful that a deal could be reached between the two parties. However, his plans to mend the UNIA's fractured relationship with the black republic in early 1925 were complicated when he lost his appeal for a new trial. In February, he commenced serving his five-year sentence at the federal penitentiary in Atlanta, Georgia.

Unwilling to give up on his African agenda, Garvey, in an act of extreme desperation, formed an alliance with the Anglo-Saxon Clubs of America (ASCOA), a Virginia-based, white supremacist group that lobbied for the passage of legislation authorizing the federal government to finance the removal of blacks to Liberia. The ASCOA was led by well-known white supremacists John Powell and Ernest Sevier Cox. Certain that the success of their lobbying efforts for repatriation depended on their ability to gain black support for their cause, Cox and Powell were eager to form an alliance with Marcus Garvey and his followers. Even though Garvey routinely criticized blacks in the NAACP and the Communist Party for their close relationship with the white left, he enthusiastically cooperated with

Cox and his cohorts. In a letter to Cox written in 1925, Garvey admitted that the "The White American Society, Anglo Saxon-Clubs, and [the] Ku-Klux-Klan have my full sympathy in fighting for a pure white race even as we are fighting for a pure Negro race." Writing from his prison cell in Atlanta, Garvey advised his followers to extend to the Anglo-Saxon Clubs of America "the courtesy and fellowship that is logical to the program of the Universal Negro Improvement Association." To those within the UNIA who may have harbored doubts about the organization's alliance with the ASCOC, he wrote: "I feel and believe that we, the two organizations, should work together for the purpose of bringing about the ideal sought—the purification of the races, their autonomous separation and the unbridled freedom of self-development and self-expression."

Garvey encouraged his followers to remain steadfast in their commitment to the UNIA, but this was not an easy task. Leading UNIA Parent Body officials fought over who would replace Garvey as president-general, the central office's relationship to UNIA branches outside New York, and the general direction of the movement. Infuriated by Garvey's reluctance to relinquish more of his authority within the organization, George A. Weston convinced hundreds to break away from the New York UNIA. Still, Garvey had the support of thousands of blacks in Harlem and elsewhere. Identifying with the legal struggles of their leader, Garveyites flooded the *Negro World* with letters of support, held celebrations in Garvey's honor, and petitioned leading politicians for the black nationalist's release. Undoubtedly, those working towards the release of the imprisoned leader enthused over President Calvin Coolidge's decision to commute Garvey's sentence in November 1927. Turning down Garvey's request for a brief respite in New York City, the Immigration Office immediately dispatched the black nationalist to New Orleans for deportation to Jamaica.

Not surprisingly, given Garvey's popularity in the Crescent City, hundreds of black citizens showed their respect for the charismatic leader. Anyone strolling down the docks at Algiers Point on December 2, 1927, could not have missed the large crowd of

African Americans gathered at the foot of the S.S. *Saramacca*. One thousand blacks had trekked to the immigration station at Algiers Point in east New Orleans on the rainy Friday morning to bid farewell to Marcus Garvey, scheduled for deportation to his native land at 12:30 p.m. Around 11:30 a.m., immigration officials permitted Garvey, already aboard the S.S. *Saramacca,* to address the hundreds of black folk huddled along the dock.

A brilliant orator who could move a crowd to fever pitch in a matter of seconds, Garvey expressed his appreciation for those who had provided financial and moral support during his eleven-year stay in the United States, restated his adherence to the ideology of black nationalism, and assuaged the fears of those concerned about the negative impact his deportation might have on the future of the Universal Negro Improvement Association. "Nothing that has happened has daunted my courage," Garvey assured the crowd. "I want you to be impressed that wherever I may go I shall direct the affairs of the Universal Negro Improvement Association."

Garvey not only continued to supervise the affairs of the UNIA's central office, but also followed closely the major political and cultural developments in black New York. Given his firm belief in the political potential of culture, Garvey was vocal about the outpouring of literature on black art, culture, and life during the late 1920s. Interestingly enough, several of the writers associated with the Harlem Renaissance had published in the *Negro World*. Claude McKay started writing for the UNIA in 1919 and Zora Neale Hurston published several poems and short stories in the *Negro World*. Eric Walrond served as the literary editor of the newspaper during the early 20s and frequently contributed to the book review section. Garvey encouraged blacks to develop their artistic talents, but he was not afraid to criticize them for their representations of black life. Garvey was not at all comfortable with the writings of the New Negro artists . "Our race, within recent years," Garvey hissed in his review of Claude McKay's *Home to Harlem*, "has developed a new group of writers who have been prostituting their intelligence, under the direction of the white man, to bring out and show up the worse traits of our people." Aggrieved not only by these writers' subject matter but also by their reliance on white patronage, Garvey encouraged his followers to "boycott such Negro authors whom we may fairly designate as 'literary prostitutes.'"

Far from the center of his declining movement, Garvey continued to voice his views on black art and other issues of importance, but by the end of the 20s, Garvey's influence had diminished considerably. Spending the last five years of his life in London, Garvey never achieved the popularity he experienced during the 1920s. Neither did the UNIA. As the economy foundered, Garveyites could no longer contribute to their divisions' various programs. Many questioned the wisdom of the organization's political agenda. Not only was the UNIA's self-help strategy unpersuasive during the economic depression, but the association's apolitical stance hindered its ability to recruit blacks who searched for activist organizations during the radical 30s. Eclipsed in popularity by the Brotherhood of Sleeping Car Porters, the Congress of Industrial Unions, and the American Communist Party, the UNIA struggled to attract members throughout that decade.

Nearly thirteen years after his departure from the United States, Marcus Garvey died in Europe in June 1940 after suffering a massive stroke.

To a large extent, Garveyism as a political movement failed to achieve most, if not all, of its objectives. Working women and men labored earnestly to turn Marcus Garvey's Pan-African vision into a reality, but time and time again they experienced disappointments and setbacks. To label the Garvey movement a complete failure, however, would be erroneous, especially if we consider the UNIA's accomplishments in the cultural arena, the space in which ordinary black people imagined a new world, put forth positive images of black identity, and challenged pejorative representations of blackness. Moreover, Garvey inspired many black people to become activists for social change.

Nearly fifty years after Garvey's death, James B. Nimmo, an ardent Garveyite from Miami, reflected on the UNIA leader's profound influence on his political development. Over the course of his adult life, Nimmo embraced black nationalism, trade unionism, and then revolutionary socialism. In his testimony before the U.S. House Un-American Activities Committee on November 29-December 1, 1954, Nimmo described himself as a committed activist who worked extensively with the Congress of Industrial Organizations and the Communist Party during the 1940s and 1950s. He stated that he had acquired many of his political and organizing skills as head of the UNIA's paramilitary group, the Universal African Legions (UAL), during the post-World War I years. "I despised and hated the treatment of the Black man," Nimmo recounted, "and was determined to fight for the hopes and aspirations of Black people. I was impressed and strongly motivated by the Garvey movement."

Staunch critics of the UNIA dismissed Garvey as a tragically flawed demagogue who led the black masses down the road of racial chauvinism, but his followers remembered the flamboyant black-nationalist as a courageous leader who constantly reminded the race of its potential for greatness. Defiantly pro-black, Garvey's words and actions inspired African American activists as diverse as Malcolm X and Louis Farrakhan of the Nation of Islam, Max Stanford of the Revolutionary Action Movement, and Audley Moore of the Republic of New Africa. Very much a celebrated figure in contemporary black nationalist circles, Garvey's deeds have received praise in the rhymes of such noted rap artists as KRS-ONE, Mos Def, Talib Kweli, and Dead Prez, and he remains important to the "conscious reggae" artists that have been emanating from Jamaica for decades. More than sixty-five years have passed since Garvey's death, but many blacks in the United States and other parts of the African Diaspora are still moved by his Pan-African vision of racial redemption and uplift.

Alain Locke

(1885–1954)

Martha Jane Nadell

Alain Locke envisioned himself as the master of ceremonies of the Harlem Renaissance. He was present in that capacity from the beginning (at least of the literary phase of the movement) at the 1924 Civic Club dinner, and he attempted to define its aesthetic parameters in the two works he edited—the Harlem issue of Survey Graphic *and the anthology that followed,* The New Negro. *Locke, with his Harvard Ph.D. in philosophy and his status as the first African American Rhodes Scholar, had the intellectual credentials for this role. He also had the position and the contacts—he wrote extensively on black literature, including an annual review of literature for* Opportunity *in the 1930s, and he effectively connected writers and artists with sources of financial support. He also had an aesthetic vision that he hoped would define and guide the movement. All he lacked was the cooperation of the writers and artists. While many benefited from and appreciated Locke's guidance, others resisted. In spite of these difficulties, Locke was one of the two or three intellectual leaders of the movement.*

Alain Locke, 1926.
Beinecke Rare Book and Manuscript
Library, Yale University.

In 1926, the critic Leon Whipple announced a momentous event in American arts and letters: the second printing of the seminal anthology *The New Negro: An Interpretation*. Whipple described the volume as "comprehensive, full of passion and faith, brimming with fact and new viewpoints, and starkly clear in its revelation that there is a 'new Negro,' keenly and naturally at times bitterly aware of himself and his place in our civilization." Initially published in 1925 by the well-known publishing house Albert and Charles Boni, the anthology gathered a variety of interpretations and accounts of the state of African American culture and the "New Negro." It also brought together the work of some of the most important African American writers and artists of the 1920s: Gwendolyn Bennett, Countee Cullen, Aaron Douglas, Rudolph Fisher, Langston Hughes, Zora Neale Hurston, Claude McKay, Jean Toomer, and others. These were the Harlem Renaissance's major figures, and the collection was, as Arnold Rampersad writes, "its definitive text, its Bible."

The editor of this seminal text was Alain Locke, one of the most highly educated African Americans in the country. Locke came to *The New Negro* after acting as the master of ceremonies at the March 1924 Civic Club dinner and guest editing the Harlem number of *Survey Graphic*, a monthly magazine devoted to social issues. His work on this complex anthology placed him at the center of the Harlem Renaissance.

The Civic Club dinner had drawn members of New York's white literary establishment, older African American leaders, and young, relatively unknown African American writers. Officially, they gathered to celebrate the publication of *There Is Confusion*, the first novel of *The Crisis* magazine's literary editor, Jessie Fauset. Yet the organizer, *Opportunity* magazine editor Charles S. Johnson, had other motives for bringing together over one hundred prominent publishers, writers, and others. He conceived of the dinner, he wrote in a letter, as a "coming out party" that marked "a "growing self-consciousness" in a "newer school of writers," a group of young writers who would come to be identified with the New Negro and the Harlem Renaissance.

Locke, a slight and dapper man, took center stage at the event. Johnson had invited the Harvard- and Oxford-educated professor to be the Master of Ceremonies for the fete, something that would solidify his position as the "virtual dean of the movement." Indeed, Locke's importance at the dinner anticipated his centrality to the Harlem Renaissance as a whole. He would "interpret the new currents manifest in the literature of this younger school," as an *Opportunity* article reported he did at the dinner. He would publish articles, write reviews and introductions, and edit anthologies, articulating a particular conception of the Harlem Renaissance. And, perhaps

Portrait of Alain Locke by Winold Reiss, 1925.
Manuscripts, Archives and Rare Books Division, Schomburg Center for Research in Black Culture, The New York Public Library, Astor, Lenox and Tilden Foundations.

more importantly, he would also act as the master of ceremonies for the Harlem Renaissance as a whole, navigating the complex worlds of publishers and patrons and linking young African American writers and artists of his choice with those worlds.

Locke's ascension to this dual role in the Harlem Renaissance followed a remarkable education and career in academia. He was part of what W.E.B. Du Bois called "the Talented Tenth," the "leaders of thought and missionaries of culture among their people." He had undergraduate and graduate degrees from Harvard and was the first African American Rhodes Scholar to study at Oxford. By 1924, at the age of thirty-nine, he had already started his teaching career at

Howard University and had begun to mentor a number of young, male, African American writers.

The only child of a highly educated, middle-class family, Locke was born on September 13, 1885, in Philadelphia. His grandfather, Ishmael Locke, taught at the Institute for Colored Youth, a high school founded by Quakers to train African American teachers excluded from the Philadelphia school system. Locke's father, Pliny, worked in education and government throughout his short life (he died in 1892 at the age of forty-two). Like his father, he was also a teacher at the Institute and was the first African American clerk to serve at the Freedmen's Bureau in Washington, D. C. Locke's mother, Mary Locke, nee Hawkins, graduated from the institute and taught in both Pennsylvania and New Jersey. She had a profound influence on her son; she instilled in him and her students, scholar Jeffrey Stewart writes, "the values of piety, thrift, respectability, and personal culture." Locke imbibed her lessons, embracing the idea of respectability and culture, and remained strongly attached to her throughout her life and even afterwards. He even lived with his mother until her death in 1922; he sat with her embalmed body in their parlor during her wake.

Locke graduated from Philadelphia's Central High School in 1902 at the age of sixteen. Later that year, he began to study at the Philadelphia School of Pedagogy, a college that prepared students to teach after two years. After attending these predominately white schools, Locke entered Harvard in 1904, where he was a popular and successful student. He studied a wide range of subjects, including the English literary tradition, composition, Greek, and philosophy and graduated *magna cum laude* in 1907.

Locke's academic experiences at Harvard would prove important for his thoughts on race and on the Harlem Renaissance. He worked with a number of literary scholars. They included George Pierce Baker, who insisted on the importance of native material for dramatic composition; the conservative Irving Babbitt, who called for the study of the classics; and Barrett Wendell, who stressed the importance of the European past and argued for the connections between literature and social environment. Baker's influence would surface in Locke's attention to drama, especially in the 1927 anthology, *Plays of Negro Life*, which Locke edited with fellow Harvard graduate and Howard professor Montgomery Gregory. Babbitt's and Wendell's thought emerged in Locke's "ancestralism"—though Locke was interested in a different past, an African one—and the links he saw between artistic production and demographic and social change. Locke was also part of a general student interest in aestheticism and European literature and culture, interests that would drive his yearly summer sojourns to Paris, Berlin, and other European locales.

Locke's exposure to a number of strains of philosophy was especially important; he later recalled, "Under the spell of Royce, James, Palmer, and Santayana, I gave up Puritan provincialism for critical-mindedness and cosmopolitanism." Locke either studied or was aware of the conflicting schools of philosophy at Harvard, what he described as "the genteel tradition of Palmer, Royce, and Munsterberg...the disillusion of Santayana and the radical protest of James." Ultimately, Locke would turn toward a form of "cultural pluralism," the idea that difference in "color, faith, sex, occupation, possessions, or what have you," as Horace Kallen, the philosopher who originated the term put it, was valuable and necessary to national and group identity in the United States. As Locke described himself later, "Finally a cultural cosmopolitan, but perforce an advocate of cultural racialism as a defensive counter-move for the American Negro."

Shortly after Locke received his BA from Harvard, he traveled to England, where he began studies at Oxford. As an undergraduate, Locke had not felt or, perhaps, did not accept, the sting of racial discrimination, probably because he was one of a number of young African Americans studying in Cambridge. Locke, however, had a difficult time at Oxford, both academically and personally, because of his experience of racial prejudice, something that would inform his future work. Many of his fellow Americans disapproved of the Rhodes committee's decision to award the scholarship to an African

American. In fact, in 1907, at the behest of Southern Rhodes scholars, the American club did not invite Locke to its annual Thanksgiving dinner.

Other, more liberal American students and some European students, however, socialized with Locke at Oxford, because they were both outraged by his treatment at the hands of the Southerners and intrigued by his racial identity. He became, for them, a "curiosity," "a Chinese puzzle," as Locke wrote to his mother. As Locke became more familiar with the Commonwealth students, he grew aware of British colonial practices and anti-American attitudes, something he found problematic. He even went as far as to defend the American Rhodes scholars, despite his difficulty with many of them. Oxford, then, was where Locke realized that he had to wrestle with race and nationality, two ideas that would emerge in his Harlem Renaissance writing.

At Oxford, Locke embraced the dandyism and aestheticism that characterized England during the Edwardian period. Partly in response to the racial discrimination he experienced, he threw himself into that social world. There were some days that he had to change his clothing five times as he went from one engagement to another. A mere five feet tall (he weighed only ninety-nine pounds at Oxford), he had his formal wear as well as his cap and gown made for him. He also spent a great deal of time away from Oxford, in London and elsewhere in Europe. According to Jeffrey Stewart, he cultivated the "wit, dress and snobbish tastes that later identified him as the 'perfect gentleman.'" He would continue his formal, effete habit of dress throughout his life. Historian Steven Watson describes Locke as he walked around Harlem in later decades: he carried "a tightly wound umbrella as his stick (and in later years as a form of protection), delivering erudite pronouncements in high-pitched rapid-fire sentences."

Locke left Oxford without receiving a degree. He found the study of Greek too taxing, after what was probably insufficient preparation at Harvard. And he spent a great deal of time away from Oxford as he attempted both to avoid the racism of the Southern Rhodes scholars and to enjoy his European sojourn. He briefly attended the University of Berlin before returning to the United States. In 1912, he accepted an appointment at Howard University's Teacher's College, where he would later become a professor and chairman of the philosophy department. In 1916, as he turned thirty, Locke took a leave in order to attend Harvard again, where he wrote a dissertation entitled, "The Problem of Classification in the Theory of Value," which argued for the connections between social and historical environment and the development of values.

After receiving his Ph.D. in philosophy in 1918, Locke, then thirty-three, returned to Howard, where he was an active member of the faculty, advocating the study not only of the classics and European languages and literature but also of African American history. He advised *The Stylus*, a literary magazine for students he had founded in 1916 and which published Zora Neale Hurston's first short story in 1921. Locke, however, was not immune to playing favorites and preferred his young, male students. In fact, he told his female students that they would, in all likelihood, receive Cs in his class.

In 1924, Locke took a sabbatical from Howard, and a year later he was fired due to a conflict with the administration. He traveled widely during that time, even visiting Cairo with the French Oriental Archaeological Society, a trip during which he saw the opening of Tutankhamen's tomb. Yet it was in Harlem where Locke made his mark and began his career as, he later wrote, "more of a philosophical mid-wife to a generation of younger Negro poets, writers, and artists than a professional philosopher."

The Civic Club dinner that year placed Locke firmly on his path. Among the guests was Paul Kellogg, the editor of *The Survey*, a weekly magazine of social work, and *Survey Graphic*, a monthly magazine geared toward an educated, general audience. Kellogg was so impressed with the gathering that he planned a special issue of *Survey Graphic*, which would be devoted to social and cultural changes in Harlem. Kellogg invited Locke to be the guest editor, thereby providing a forum for Locke's interpretations of the movement.

In March 1925, *Survey Graphic* published its New Negro number. The magazine contained diverse material, ranging from sociological analyses of Harlem to literary works by young African American writers. Charles S. Johnson discussed black workers in New York City, while James Weldon Johnson speculated about the development of Harlem into an African American community and center. Winthrop Lane discussed the "grim side of Harlem," poverty, quack medicine, rent gouging, and the ubiquity of "the numbers"—Harlem's version of the lottery. Elise Johnson McDougald contributed an article entitled "The Double Task" about African American women, and Kelly Miller wrote about "race prejudice." Albert Barnes wrote about African American literary artistry, and J. A. Rogers discussed jazz. Countee Cullen, Angelina Grimke, Langston Hughes, Claude McKay, and Jean Toomer contributed a range of poetry, while Rudolph Fisher's short story, "The South Lingers On," meditated on Southern migrants' experiences of the city. The magazine included a range of visual material: photographs of Harlem and portraits of "Harlem Types" by Winold Reiss, which acted as evidence or accompaniments for many of the claims of the authors.

As the guest editor of the magazine, Locke contributed introductions to the material and articles about the state of Harlem and the Harlem Renaissance. Continuing the role he had begun as master of ceremonies at the Civic Club dinner, he articulated a particular interpretation of the era in this magazine, one that he would enlarge and modify in the months and years to come.

Locke was concerned with the changes in Harlem, the social, spiritual, and psychological nature of its population, and the consequent emergence of a literary and artistic movement. In his first essay in the magazine, "Harlem," Locke explored the relationship between the demographic shifts in early twentieth-century African America and the development of a new group consciousness. The Great Migration, the mass movement of African Americans from the rural South to the urban North, and the movement of other people of African descent to New York City, was making Harlem a new "race capital":

Here in Manhattan is not merely the largest Negro community in the world, but the first concentration in history of so many diverse elements of Negro life. It has attracted the African, the West Indian, the Negro American; has brought together the Negro in the North and the Negro of the South; the man from the city and the man from the town and village; the peasant, the student, the business man, the professional man, artist, poet, musician, adventurer and worker, preacher and criminal, exploiter and social outcast.

With the growth of this diversity, Harlem had become a "crucible," a "laboratory for great race-welding" in which "group expression and self-determination" were taking hold.

Although Locke was highly educated, one of the "Talented Tenth," he saw the importance of the "migrant masses" in this changing racial self-consciousness. They were in a "deliberate flight not only from countryside to city, but from medieval America to modern." They pressed on the elite African American, the "poet, student, artist, thinker," forcing him to concentrate on the "racial side of his experience and [to] heighten his race-consciousness." Out of this interaction came the New Negro, the subject of Locke's next piece in *Survey Graphic*.

In "Enter the New Negro," Locke connected the demographic change he described in "Harlem" to a new racial consciousness, evident in the literary and artistic scene celebrated at the Civic Club dinner. Something new was afoot, Locke argued, "something beyond the watch and guard of statistics," something for which "The Sociologist, The Philanthropist, the Race-leader" could not account. Locke was describing the development of the New Negro, a figure he cast in opposition to an imaginary, mythic Old Negro. That figure was the product of the stereotypes of African American identity that dominated nineteenth and early twentieth-century American culture. Indeed, both white and black America contributed to the ideas circulating around this Old Negro, "more of a formula than a human being—a something to be argued about, condemned or defended, to be 'kept down,' or 'in his place,' or 'helped up,' to be worried with or worried over, harassed or patronized, a social bogey or a social burden."

The New Negro, in contrast, was emerging from the African American community itself, which was, Locke argued, experiencing "renewed self-respect and self-dependence" and "a spiritual Coming of Age." African Americans, in short, were changing their senses of themselves and of their communities. And this was occurring across the African American population:

> The migrant masses, shifting from countryside to city, hurdle several generations of experience at a leap, but more important, the same thing happens spiritually in the life-attitudes and self-expressions of the Young Negro, in his poetry, his art, his education, with the additional advantage, of course, of the poise and greater certainty of knowing what it is all about. From this comes the promise and warrant of a new leadership.

With these changes and the new leadership emerging in arts and letters, it was time, Locke argued, to "scrap the fictions, garret the bogeys and settle down for a realistic facing of facts." And it would be in the poetry, drama, fiction, and art of young African American artists, as well as in Locke's own work, where this new era would take place.

In many respects, Locke's writing and editing throughout the Harlem Renaissance was an answer to this charge to "settle down for a realistic facing of facts." In the remainder of *Survey Graphic* and in his other publications, he would attempt to account for the New Negro and the significance of the movement that produced him.

In "Enter the New Negro," Locke wrote about the importance of interracial relations—describing the past and current intertwining of the African American and non-African American populations as at once "too close" and "too light"—and called for connections among the "enlightened minorities of both race groups." The New Negro, "on the right side of the country's professed ideals," was "an augury of a new democracy in American culture." Through him, "a new American attitude" and a shift in race relations would take hold. Locke also maintained that the New Negro would act as the "advance-guard of the African peoples in their contact with Twentieth Century civilization." Harlem would be home to the "Negro's 'Zionism,'" akin to other international centers.

Within all of his talk of democracy and internationalism, one could perceive Locke's belief in the importance of culture as an alternative and viable political strategy for African Americans. Arts and letters would educate white and black alike, thereby transforming race relations and American democracy. And in Harlem, Locke wrote in a later essay, "the arts movement in this case happens to coincide with a social one—a period of new stirring in the Negro mind and the dawning of new social objectives," movements that were not "a reformer's duty or a prophet's mission" but investments in an "ethics of beauty itself."

Locke was especially interested in codifying an African American aesthetic. In "Youth Speaks," a later essay in *Survey Graphic*, he discussed the new trends in literature and art emerging from the young African American writers of the era. Organically connected to the African American population, they were, he declared, not writing "for the Negro—they speak as Negroes." Race, for them, was "but an idiom of expression" one that "affords a deepening rather than a narrowing of social vision." They were no longer bound by earlier art forms—"the minstrel tradition" and "dialect"—and were able to "seek and find art's intrinsic values and satisfaction." Toomer, he wrote, "gives a folk-lilt and ecstasy to the prose of American modernists," while Hughes "put Biblical fever into free verse," and "Cullen blends the simple with the sophisticated." These writers are linked because "they are thoroughly modern" and in "stepping alignment with contemporary artistic thought, mood and style."

Locke was not above manipulating the literary works he chose for *Survey Graphic* so that they conformed to his standards. At Locke's behest, the Jamaican expatriate Claude McKay submitted a number of poems for *Survey Graphic*. Locke refused one poem, "Mulatto," claiming that it was too "strong." He also changed the title of another poem, "The White House," to "White Houses," thereby diminishing the power of its angry stance. Neither poem fit in with Locke's pluralistic New Negro aesthetic; they were too combative. McKay did not take kindly to Locke's actions and accused him of being "a dyed-in-the-wool pussy-footing professor."

The New Negro number of *Survey Graphic* sold over 40,000 copies in two printings, prompting Albert and Charles Boni to publish *The New Negro: An Interpretation* in 1925. Again edited by Locke, the anthology was a collection of fiction, poetry, drama, critical essays, art, and studies of African American life. It included new essays about Howard, Tuskegee, and Hampton, as well as a piece about Durham. Locke added a range of poetry, fiction, drama, and commentary about jazz. He eliminated much of the material about the negative aspects of Harlem, evidence of his elitism, according to some critics. Yet, Locke was responsive to the exigencies of publishing, as he had been when he edited *Survey Graphic*. He wanted to expand the focus and hence the readership for his volume.

Consider his choice of illustrations. *Survey Graphic* contained two types of drawing by the German artist Winold Reiss: formally experimental images entitled *Interpretations of Jazz*, and type sketches, realistic, almost photographic portraits of unnamed Harlem residents, as well as Harlem celebrities Paul Robeson and Roland Hayes. In *The New Negro*, Locke dropped Reiss's abstract work and most of the unidentified portraits and included images of his favorite New Negroes (Jean Toomer, Countee Cullen, and himself) and other African American leaders (W.E.B. Du Bois, Mary McLeod Bethune). Changes such as these, George Hutchinson argues, made *The New Negro* more appealing to colleges and middle-class African Americans.

Locke also included several images by the African American

artist Aaron Douglas for the 1925 volume and even more for the second printing in 1927. Douglas's work was experimental and abstract; with its black-and-white, geometric design, it evoked not only the nineteenth-century tradition of silhouettes but also African masks and contemporary cubism, which mined African art for its challenge to older, representational forms. This was a key part of Locke's visual aesthetic. The "ancestral arts," as he called African sculpture, produced a "ferment in modern art" and provided "the lesson of a classic background, the lesson of discipline, of style, of technical control pushed to the limits of technical mastery." And this should be, he argued, the inspiration of African American artists.

Locke also wrote a number of essays for magazines that articulated his sense of the importance of African American arts and letters. In "Beauty Instead of Ashes," published in *The Nation* in 1928, Locke defined and defended the young school of African American writers from their critics. In "Art or Propaganda?" published in the short-lived magazine *Harlem*, Locke asked if art should "preach and exhort or sing" and concluded that it should "function as a tap root of vigorous, flourishing living." Locke also wrote reviews of the work of young African American writers and edited the anthology *Four Negro Poets*, which included Cullen,

Winold Reiss, "African Phantasy," *The New Negro*, 1925. The striking African style of this illustration reflects Locke's interest in African art and African heritage as an essential component of African American culture and art. Manuscripts, Archives and Rare Books Division, Schomburg Center for Research in Black Culture, The New York Public Library, Astor, Lenox and Tilden Foundations.

Hughes, Toomer, and McKay, despite the fact that the young poet did not give Locke permission to publish his work.

Locke was also extraordinarily active in navigating the complex social world, which included publishers and patrons that emerged from the meeting of America's cultural establishment and the young

New Negroes that Locke fancied. He enthusiastically took to the role of Master of Ceremonies of the movement as a whole. He helped carefully chosen younger writers and artists acquire the means to work on and publish their work. Hughes described Locke, along with Fauset and Charles S. Johnson, as "the three people who midwifed the so-called New Negro literature into being. Kind and critical—but not too critical for the young—they nursed us along until our books were born. Countee Cullen, Zora Neale Hurston, Arna Bontemps, Rudolph Fisher, Wallace Thurman, Jean Toomer, Nella Larsen, all of us came along about the same time." And Wallace Thurman, in his roman-a-clef, *Infants of the Spring*, satirically described his stand-in, Dr. Parkes, and his engagement with younger New Negroes:

> He was a mother hen clucking at her chicks. Small, dapper, with sensitive features, graying hair, a dominating head, and restless hands and feet, he smiled benevolently at his brood. Then, in his best continental manner, which he had acquired during four years at European Universities, he began to speak.
>
> "You are," he perorated, "the outstanding personalities in a new generation. On you depends the future of your race. You are not, as were your predecessors, concerned with donning armor, and clashing swords with the enemy in the public square. You are finding both an escape and a weapon in beauty, which beauty when created by you will cause the American white man to re-estimate the Negro's value to his civilization, cause him to realize that the American black man is too valuable, too potential of utilitarian accomplishment, to be kept downtrodden and segregated."

Yet Locke's activities were not without complex motives. Consider his relationships with Langston Hughes and Zora Neale

Hurston. Countee Cullen, who had been enamored with Hughes, sent Locke Hughes's address in 1923, the year before the Civic Club dinner. Probably frustrated with Hughes' willful blindness to his overtures, Cullen passed Hughes on to Locke with a note that read, "You will like him; I love him." Locke quickly wrote to Hughes, "Countee already means so much to me, but he generously insists on deeding over a certain part of me to you."

The thirty-seven year old professor and the twenty-one year old poet cum sailor began an active correspondence. Locke wrote to Hughes not only of the younger man's poetry but also of his own "early infatuation with the Greek ideals of life," subtly suggesting his sexual interest in Hughes. These were seductive moves to which Hughes, according to his biographer Arnold Rampersad, did not respond. Rather, he played with the elder philosopher, asking at one point if Locke was married and writing, at another point, "And how delightful it would be to come surprisingly upon one another in some old world street! Delightful and too romantic!"

Hughes dissuaded Locke from a meeting in 1923, but during the summer of 1924, the thirty-nine year old Locke knocked on the door to Hughes's Paris apartment, and the two soon began to spend a significant amount of time together. Locke was so smitten—and perhaps calculating—that he raised the possibility of securing Hughes admission to Howard and offered him lodging in his house, a prospect that was not unattractive to the determined Hughes. After Hughes left for Italy, Locke wrote to him "to tell you how I love you" and to ask that he join him in Venice. The two soon met and spent their time viewing the artistic treasures of the city but never consummating their relationship. After Hughes's passport was stolen, the frustrated Locke left him in Genoa. Later, Hughes chose Lincoln over Howard, avoiding the pressure Locke exerted on him. Locke's interest in Hughes, then, was just as much personal as it was artistic.

In 1927, the forty-one-year-old Locke met the wealthy and elderly Charlotte Osgood Mason, who would become one of the most influential white patrons of the Harlem Renaissance. Mason had introduced herself to Locke after he delivered a lecture on

African art. He soon began to spend time with her, enjoying tea at her Park Avenue home as he cultivated what would become a lucrative and emotional relationship that was reminiscent of the one that he had had with his deceased mother. Mason was attracted to what she saw as the inherent spirituality of "primitive" peoples, native American, African, and other non-Western groups. She imagined that African Americans, especially those who were economically disadvantaged, had a special connection to the cosmos, one that they should cultivate. In his autobiography, *The Big Sea*, Hughes described her:

> Concerning Negroes, she felt that they were America's great link with the primitive, and that they had something very precious to give to the Western World. She felt that there was mystery and mysticism and spontaneous harmony in their souls, but that many of them had let the white world pollute and contaminate that mystery and harmony, and make of it something cheap and ugly, commercial and, as she said, "white." She felt that we had a deep well of the spirit within us and that we should keep it pure and deep.

As Locke guided Mason through the Harlem literary and artistic scene, he became even more influential. He helped her decide how to spend her funds, becoming, essentially, a broker for the patron and the artists, writers, and projects she would support. Shortly after their meeting, Locke and Mason began to work, ultimately unsuccessfully, on the Harlem Museum of African Art, where Mason imagined "the mystical vision of a great bridge reaching from Harlem to the heart of Africa, across which the negro world, that our white United States had done everything to annihilate, should see the flaming pathway...and recover the treasure their people had in the beginning of the African life on the earth."

Mason, however, wanted to develop a more personal relationship with the "primitives" in whom she was interested. She asked Locke to introduce her to the young African American writers Locke was mentoring so that she could promote their spirituality through her understanding of their art. She wrote, "I believed I could find leaders among themselves to react and publish far and wide the truth about their art impulse that daily lived in all their common acts."

Locke introduced Langston Hughes to Mason during the intermission of a concert in Carnegie Hall in February, 1927, and arranged a meeting between the elderly woman and the young poet two months later. Mason was taken with Hughes. She saw in him a strong Native American ancestry—and hence a deep, earthly spirituality—and began to see herself as so central to his life and art that she insisted he call her "Godmother," something that other writers and artists for whom she was a patron did as well. Mason supported Hughes financially, eventually providing him a monthly stipend and luxuries, such as expensive food, elegant stationery, and travel in her chauffeur-driven car, so that he could devote his time to his writing.

Mason also supported a number of other writers and artists who she asked to sit on footstools at her feet, including Douglas, Hurston, and the Mexican artist Miguel Covarrubias, who published the 1927 collection of caricatures *Negro Drawings*. In fact, in her efforts to develop their native and primitive spirituality in contrast to the vulgar consumerism of white society, Mason spent almost $75,000 on her protégés, all the while promoting their dependence on her. Hughes later described her efforts to control her protégés:

TRACK 31

Throughout his career Alain Locke had sought the roots of African American culture in the race's African and Southern heritage. In 1940, he stressed the importance of "Negro Spirituals" in these introductory remarks for the Library of Congress concert commemorating the 75th anniversary of the end of slavery.

> Great wealth had been given to a woman who
> meant to be kind the means to power, and a technique

of power, of so mighty a strength that I do not believe she herself knew what that force might become. She possessed the power to control people's lives–pick them up and put them down when and where she wished.

Hughes advised Hurston about negotiating the demands of their common patron and Godmother's relationship with Locke, for it was between Mason and the two writers that Locke maneuvered. At Godmother's expense, in the spring of 1930, the two young writers were ensconced in Westfield, New Jersey, supposedly hard at work on the folk opera *Mule Bone* they had planned after traveling together in the South.

Hurston was wary of Locke; she wrote, "The trouble with Locke is that he is intellectually dishonest. He is too eager to be with the winner." To a certain degree, Hurston was correct. Locke reported to Mason about the shenanigans going on in New Jersey. The pair were having too much fun and not working, in his mind, enough on their play. After hearing this, Mason became cold and distant to her protégés and, despite Hughes' efforts, ultimately broke with the young man.

Hughes recalled that part of the problem was Mason's insistence on his playing the part of the primitive:

> She wanted me to be primitive and know and feel the intuitions of the primitive. But, unfortunately, I did not feel the rhythms of the primitive surging through me, and so I could not love and write as though I did. I was only an America–Negro—who had loved the surface of Africa and the rhythms of Africa—but I was not Africa.

Locke, however, continued to cultivate Mason at the expense of his relationship with Hughes. Even though he nominated Hughes for a Harmon Foundation Award for Distinguished Achievement Among Negroes, he wrote to Mason that it would "swell the false egotism that at present denies its own best insight." And when Hughes complained to him that Hurston copyrighted their joint work without giving him credit, Locke was not sympathetic. Hughes wrote, "That week I received the award, I wired Alain Locke, who knew the circumstances of our having written the play and had, I believe, seen a first draft. I asked him kindly to talk to Miss Hurston for me. Alain Locke wired back, YOU HAVE HARMON AWARD SO WHAT MORE DO YOU WANT. Exactly ten cooling words."

Hughes was not Locke's only target. Between 1929 and 1931, he wrote to Mason that Hurston was "disloyal," that Wallace Thurman was a "traitor" for publishing *Harlem* and that James Weldon Johnson was "profiteering" from the publication of his anthology of African American poetry.

This period marked the end not only of Hughes's relationship with Mason but also of Locke's position. He no longer had New Negroes to cultivate. He wrote to Mason in 1931, "I hear almost no news from New York; a younger crowd of 'Newer negroes' are dancing in the candle flame. The older ones are nursing their singed wings."

Locke, however, did not give up his interest in African American arts and letters. In the decades to follow, he would write annual retrospective reviews of books by and about African Americans for *Opportunity* and *Phylon*. He returned to the New Negro a number of years later, planning a volume entitled, *The New Negro: Fifteen Years Later* or *The Newer Negro: 1939*, a collection that included not only Hughes and Huston but also Richard Wright.

In the years following the Harlem Renaissance, Locke returned to Howard, where he taught until his retirement in 1953. Among his projects was his effort to establish an African studies program, which ultimately was implemented in 1954, the year of *Brown v. Topeka Board of Education* and a year after he retired from the university. He continued to write, publishing a number of essays and books about art and music, and was in high demand as a lecturer in universities and colleges across the country. He was active in adult education and was named the first African American president of the American Association for Adult Education. No longer was he at the center of a movement; instead, he maintained his preeminence as a scholar of African America.

Locke died in New York City on June 9, 1954, at the age of sixty-eight. A year earlier, following his retirement from Howard University, he had moved to the city and acquired a home at 12 Grove Street in Greenwich Village. His health had deteriorated throughout the year, and his death from heart disease followed a six-week illness. Following his funeral service in Brooklyn, his body was cremated. No immediate relatives survived him.

While the Harlem Renaissance, and hence Locke's centrality to it, were short lived, Locke's importance to the movement remains uncontested. He articulated and disseminated the idea of the New Negro. He shepherded young artists and writers, though he was not above manipulation and favoritism. And, above all, he insisted on the centrality of African American arts and letters for American culture and democracy.

A. Philip Randolph

(1889–1979)

WILLIAM H. HARRIS

A. Philip Randolph achieved his success during the Harlem Renaissance as the first major African American labor leader. Initially attracted to New York by his dream of becoming an actor, he quickly shifted his interest to politics, especially radical politics. By the time the United States entered World War I, Randolph was a player in the socialist left of Harlem cafe politics. His journal, The Messenger, proclaimed itself "The Only Radical Negro Magazine in America." By 1926 the magazine had moved to the political center (writer Wallace Thurman described it as endorsing the policy of whoever paid best), while Randolph had left socialism behind and become the head of the largest black labor union, the Brotherhood of Sleeping Car Porters. He led the union in a successful struggle against the Pullman Company and against the discriminatory policies of the American Federation of Labor. For two decades beginning the 1930s, Randolph was the most effective civil rights leader in the country.

Hughes's thoughts on the Harlem Renaissance help us to understand that the "New Negro Movement," an idea that allows inclusion of ideas and persons beyond the arts, is perhaps a more accurate term for the period, especially if one is accustomed to thinking of the Renaissance in narrow terms reminiscent of the European Renaissance in art and literature during the fifteenth and sixteenth centuries.

A. Philip Randolph was a major personality of the twentieth century who gained true prominence during the New Negro period and directly helped define "the New Negro"—though not through art. (However, we should not overlook the fact that Randolph and Chandler Owen, his cofounder and coeditor of *Messenger* magazine, published numerous poets and essayists of the Harlem Renaissance.)

Asa Philip Randolph was born on April 15, 1889, in Crescent City, Florida, from which his parents moved to Jacksonville, a larger town, shortly after his birth. Randolph grew up in a home that nurtured learning and intellectual activities. He was the second of two sons. His father was a tailor who also served as a minister in the African Methodist Episcopal Church (AME). In addition to preaching he worked in odd service jobs to support his family. Randolph grew up in a home with books and in which ideas were discussed. He was aware of and conversant with the ideas of the radical AME Bishop Henry McNeil Turner and Booker T. Washington of Tuskegee Institute, and the emerging views of W.E.B. Du Bois. Further, Randolph knew firsthand the work of James Weldon Johnson, who had grown up in Jacksonville and attended and graduated from Atlanta University. After graduation Johnson returned home, where he served as principal of the elementary school for blacks while he studied law and prepared for admission to the bar. Randolph took great pride in this older man from his hometown who went on to become an American ambassador and, eventually, a major poet and author of prose, and a leader of the National Association for the Advancement of Colored People (NAACP) in New York City.

The Randolph brothers graduated from high school at Cookman Institute, a private high school for African Americans in the

absence of a public high school in their North Florida city. Financially unable to attend college, they worked as laborers around town.
James Randolph eventually became a Pullman porter, and Philip a
messenger for the local telegraph company. Randolph chafed under
those restraints and determined to improve his lot. In 1911, at age
twenty-two, he took the fateful step to do just that when he
requested and received permission from his parents to work for the
summer in New York City, with the promise that he would return to
Jacksonville in the fall. He left knowing that despite his promise, he
had left for good.

A strikingly tall and handsome man with a deep, melodious baritone
voice, Randolph arrived in New York City in the vanguard of the
trickle of African Americans who, in increasingly larger numbers,
migrated from the rural South to the urban North; a trickle that
would become a flood known as the Great Migration. In addition to
bringing their creativity and skills, the newcomers also brought with
them numerous needs to which older, established residents
attempted to respond. As early as 1909, Du Bois had led a group that
founded the NAACP to improve the overall condition of African
Americans. On a more practical basis, followers of Booker T. Washington, who had been left out of the NAACP group, in 1911
founded the National League on Urban Conditions Among
Negroes, which became the National Urban League (NUL). This
latter group intended to ease the transition from rural southern to
urban Northern living by helping blacks find jobs, housing, health
care, and access to social services.

Randolph, charismatic but socially shy, flourished in this big sea
of new ideas and new people. During the years 1911 to 1914, as a
bachelor, he devoured the cultural and intellectual opportunities
that New York offered, easily moving from address to address and
from job to job as he pursued his interests in economics and his
desire to become a Shakespearean actor. During this period he
acquired an Edwardian English accent of broad a's, speaking often of
the "grand struggle between the maasses and the claasses." He stud-

ied at City College of New York and the Rand School of Economics, and actually lectured on black history at the latter institution. During his time at those institutions, Randolph became enthralled by the teachings of Lester Frank Ward, the father of scientific sociology, and by the thoughts and ideas of Karl Marx. Marx's work led Randolph to determine that the remedy for the plight of black people lay in the teachings of socialism. Randolph also developed a friendship with the Socialist leader Morris Hillquit and with Eugene V. Debs, the longtime labor leader. From them he learned the activist side of politics and came to believe that the only way in which blacks, the vast majority of whom were workers, could advance in American society was to organize and jointly present their interests to the captains of industry, and, strangely, to the court of American public opinion.

In 1914, Randolph met two people who would profoundly affect the rest of his life. In the spring he met Lucille Green, a thirty-one-year-old widow who shared his birthday and was six years his senior. A graduate of Howard University, Green was trained as a schoolteacher, but she had given up that job and become a successful businesswoman, running a fashionable beauty salon marketing the beauty and hair dressing processes that had been developed by Madame C. J. Walker. Green and Randolph were married during the summer of 1914 and that same year they met Chandler Owen. Owen was slightly older than Randolph, and the two men shared an interest in economics and politics. They became lifelong friends and spent many evenings in the Randolphs' apartment discussing the great issues of the day and plotting ways to improve the status of the black masses. They were drawn to the political activities of the time and both were members of the "faculty" of Street Corner University, who lectured from soapboxes at the corner of Lenox Avenue and 135th Street and other "campuses."

Randolph was fortunate and truly grateful that Lucille Randolph paid most of their expenses from her salon's income and later from her earnings as the first African American social worker in New York City. Her support provided him with an opportunity to concentrate freely upon his activist mission without making "compromises" in order to earn a living. The Randolphs and Owen became Socialists, and in 1917 all three ran for elective office; all lost. Always the organizer, Randolph also used this time to form the Independent Political Council, a vehicle to bring together black students from Columbia University, City College, and New York University for political activity. He succeeded in getting them to attend political conversations but failed to get them active.

The year 1917 was pivotal in the life and work of A. Philip Randolph. Early that year the Head Waiters and Side Waiters Society of Greater New York invited Randolph and Owen to publish a magazine on its behalf in exchange for office space for the Independent Political Council. The two agreed and for eight months put out *Hotel Messenger*. The magazine was short lived, however, because of its editorial honesty and its editors' incessant urging to organize and help the downtrodden. During their time with the waiters' association, side waiters complained to Randolph and Owen about their mistreatment by the head waiters. The two men editorialized against these practices in *Hotel Messenger*, and the head waiters—who paid the editors—fired them and kicked them out into the street.

Thus began the public career of the pair that would courageously take on any entity that they perceived dangerous to the interests of black working-class people. In November 1917, within days after being dismissed by the head waiters, Randolph and Owen dropped *Hotel* from the title and launched an independent magazine, the *Messenger*, whose masthead proclaimed it "The Only Radical Negro Magazine In America." Though independent, much of the early financial support for the magazine came from the Socialists, mainly through the editors' management of the Harlem arm of the Hillquit mayoralty campaign.

The *Messenger* debuted at an interesting time for a radical magazine, especially a black one. On April 6, 1917, Congress approved President Woodrow Wilson's request for a declaration of war against Germany and ushered in a high fervor of patriotic Americanism and a fierce animosity against any person or group perceived to be anti-American. Congress also passed the Espionage and Sedition Acts, which contained broad language on a wide range of activities that could lead to fines or imprisonment for American citizens deemed to be involved in hindering the war effort. Left-leaning labor leaders and organizations were high on the list—as were Randolph and Owen because of their writings in the *Messenger* and their speeches in opposition to the war.

The *Messenger's* anti-war stand was based on its editors' personal opposition to war and their belief that African Americans, mistreated in America, had nothing to fight for in World War I. Their response to W.E.B. Du Bois's editorial in *The Crisis*, "Close Ranks," in which he exhorted blacks to "forget our own special grievances and close our ranks shoulder to shoulder with our own white citizens ... that are fighting for democracy" makes the point.

In an editorial titled "New Leadership for the Negro," the *Messenger* wrote derisively of Du Bois's piece as the "'Close Ranks' editorial in *The Crisis* which will rank in shame and reeking disgrace with the 'Atlanta Compromise' speech of Booker T. Washington." The editors declared that blacks had gained nothing by fighting in the war. It said "he has been the most loyal, but in turn, as is his deserts, he is most lynched, most Jim-Crowed, most segregated, most discriminated against, most disfranchised."

The *Messenger* editors' opposition did not stop with editorials and stories in the magazine. They also spoke brazenly and often against the war on street corners and in churches, when they could find one open to them, to any African American and to radical whites who would gather to hear them. They even took their crusade to Washington, where they castigated President Wilson. While speaking in Cleveland, the authorities arrested Randolph and Owen and detained them briefly until a judge, because of their youthful appearance, released them and sent them home. Rather than go east to New York, the two headed west to Chicago to continue their anti-war tour. The government did not take such activities lightly and marshaled its efforts to silence the *Messenger's* activists, as it did other opponents of the war effort. Owen was drafted into the army, a fate

Randolph escaped because of his marital status, but he always maintained that he would not have served even if he had been drafted.

During and after the war, the *Messenger* continued its criticisms of the conditions of black life and gave no quarter to either blacks or whites whom it considered obstacles to making improvements. In one piece Randolph takes a generally unsympathetic view of "ignorant" blacks, but he saves his greatest criticism for what he considered the misguided leadership of the older, educated group, in which he included W.E.B. Du Bois and James Weldon Johnson. Randolph criticizes both Republican and Democratic African Americans. "Negroes of national prominence," he claimed, "had turned Democratic" in order "to make Republicans repentant." Further, he accused the "old school" black political leaders of "playing the game of politics" mainly "to get next to campaign slush funds and land a rubber stamp job." In the end he concludes that the only hope for blacks lay in the Socialist Party.

While criticizing black leaders, Randolph also attacked the conditions of black life. Now thoroughly a Socialist, he claimed that the American capitalist system was the cause of all of the adverse conditions under which blacks lived. It was, for example, the root cause of lynching, he concluded. But neither Randolph nor the *Messenger* would stop there. When major race riots broke out during 1919, the *Messenger* was in the forefront of those who demanded that blacks arm themselves and fight back. In an essay on "The New Negro," Randolph listed self-defense, "violent if necessary," among the responses of the New Negro. It is important to note that he did not just say one should defend oneself alone, but also organize to do so. He called on African Americans to "form little voluntary companies which may quickly be assembled" to respond to mob violence. The magazine published a lead editorial following the Chicago Riot titled "If We Must Die" in which it included the text of Claude McKay's poem of that title and exulted in the fact that blacks had inflicted considerable damage upon white attackers in both Chicago and Washington. The piece concluded that in the future blacks would follow McKay's admonition:

> Like men we'll face the murderous, cowardly pack,
> Pressed to the wall, dying, but fighting back.

Further, the *Messenger* also took the position that the New Negro would demand social equality, including challenging the national taboo against interracial sexual relations and interracial marriage.

Government officials on both the federal and state levels were deeply concerned about the positions that Randolph and the *Messenger* had taken, especially those demanding social equality. Under the leadership of Attorney General A. Mitchell Palmer, assisted by J. Edgar Hoover at the Justice Department and Post Master General Albert S. Burleson, federal agencies considered ways to silence the magazine. Palmer considered Randolph "the most dangerous Negro in America," and major federal and state investigations of radical publications, black and white, concluded that the *Messenger* was "by far the ablest and most dangerous Negro publication" in the nation. Randolph and Owen relished this distinction, but their efforts were hindered when Burleson considered some of their issues seditious and unfit for the mails. Indeed, Burleson delayed the September 1919 issue, that included the "If We Must Die" editorial, for weeks and, perhaps more important, he denied the magazine a second-class mailing privilege from 1918 to 1921, a costly action.

In addition to its radical political and social action activities, the *Messenger* and its editors were directly involved in the artistic endeavors of the Harlem Renaissance. Though not as dedicated to the arts as were some other organs, the *Messenger* was an important magazine for the publication of literature from new authors, as well as criticism. Indeed, the major artists of the time published in its pages. Further, through the work of Theodore Lewis, a post office employee by day and a regular at theaters by night, the *Messenger* had the best theater critiques of the period. The emphasis on the arts came without the deep interest of Randolph, who was particularly opposed to much of the music that developed in Harlem and other black communities. Unlike Langston Hughes, who embraced the blues, using the term to title such poems as "The Weary Blues,"

Randolph abhorred the blues. In an editorial in the *Messenger* Randolph described the blues as "loud, boisterous, cheap, tawdry, unmusical." He noted that blacks liked the blues while European immigrants turned to opera and he lamented that "a race that hums opera will stay ahead of a race that simply likes the 'blues.'" Such ideas as this perhaps contributed to Langston Hughes's conclusion that in time the *Messenger* became "God Knows What," a magazine that "reflected the policy of whoever paid best at the time."

By 1920–21, Randolph and Owen began an ideological shift indicated by the *Messenger's* editorial stance. In February 1920, the *Messenger* ended its run as "The Only Radical Negro Magazine in America" and became a "Journal of Scientific Radicalism." The editors claimed that the change was due to the fact other radical black organs had come into existence because of the *Messenger's* leadership. Yet the movement toward the center represented both Randolph's bid to become an accepted member of black leadership and Owen's intellectual disenchantment with socialism, especially after he moved from New York to Chicago in 1923.

In 1920, Randolph and Owen led in founding the Friends of Negro Freedom (FNF), an organization of all-black leadership that was designed to take positions that neither the NUL or the NAACP could take because of what Randolph called the white control under which they worked. The FNF founders considered the new organization necessary because neither of the older organizations paid any attention to the problems of working-class blacks except as they would be affected by improvements in race relations. The call for a meeting to organize the Friends, which appeared in the May 1920 issue of the *Messenger*, was signed by many of the outstanding leaders of the day, including some prominent members of the NAACP. The *Messenger* was the official organ of the new movement, and its leaders undertook the major task of creating a national organization. This task fell mainly upon Owen, who had already begun to tire of the regular work with the *Messenger*. He seemed to relish the idea of traveling about the country lecturing about the FNF and stirring up interest in the needs of working-class blacks, especially within organized labor.

The FNF was short lived, lasting only about three years. It spent most of its energy establishing forums in New York and other cities where members of the branches talked about "the Negro question" and other topics. The role the FNF played in the "Garvey Must Go Movement" brought its greatest notoriety.

In 1914, Marcus Garvey founded the Universal Negro Improvement Association (UNIA); in 1917 he established a UNIA branch in New York City. Garvey's group had a sizable following and established several businesses: grocery stores, a newspaper, and a steamship company, the Black Star Line—the latter intended to carry on trade and to transport African Americans to Africa in order to carry out the "Back to Africa" scheme of Garvey's ideology. The UNIA's businesses, especially the Black Star Line, suffered from mismanagement and underwent a major public failure. Leading blacks began to call for Garvey's removal from the country, especially after news developed that Garvey had met with the lead Kleagle of the Ku Klux Klan in New Orleans and had, in effect, endorsed the Klan's position on relationships between the races.

The *Messenger* was ambivalent in its attitude about Garvey, at first reluctant to oppose him, but later unrelenting in its attack. Randolph, in an editorial, particularly took offense when Roscoe Conkling Simmons criticized Garvey in the *Chicago Defender* and wrote that "if Garvey doesn't like this country, let him go back to Jamaica, where he came from." Randolph was deeply resentful of Simmons's position, especially his effort to pit native-born African Americans against the West Indians, a position he considered divisive. He pointed out that "we have heard too much talk of anti-West Indian intolerance. We take no stock in this argument." But the *Messenger's* position on Garvey was about to change, loudly and radically.

Just three months after its defense of Garvey's right to speak, the *Messenger* ran a banner headline editorial: "Marcus Garvey! The Black Imperial Wizard Becomes Messenger Boy of the White Ku Klux Kleagle." The article, which Randolph wrote, rehearsed a long series of reasons why black people should oppose Garvey. He ridiculed Garvey's "row-boatless steamship line and his voteless election to the presidency of a nonexistent nation." In the next month's issue, the editor described Garvey as a "half-wit, low grade moron, whose insufferable assumption is only exceeded by his abysmal ignorance ..." In case anyone remained unclear, the *Messenger* announced in the July editorial that "here's notice that the MESSENGER is firing the opening gun in a campaign to drive Marcus Garvey and Garveyism in all its sinister viciousness from American soil."

The *Messenger* crowd joined with other well-placed blacks in opposition to Garvey, an opposition that ended only with Garvey's conviction in federal court on charges of mail fraud in connection with selling bonds for the Black Star Line, his imprisonment in federal prison in Atlanta, and his eventual deportation to Jamaica.

Randolph continued his move toward the center that had begun in 1920. When the NAACP led a delegation to the White House in 1924 to lobby President Calvin Coolidge to pardon black soldiers who had been convicted in courts martial for their part in a riot in Houston, Texas, in 1917, Randolph went along as a respected member of the delegation. The larger public recognition of his standing as an important leader of African Americans came in 1926, when leaders in Philadelphia invited Randolph to address the opening session of the Philadelphia Sesquicentennial of the Declaration of Independence.

Randolph's effort to take on different activities coincided with a decline in fortunes of the *Messenger*. The magazine had never made much money, but by 1925 Owen was living in Chicago and Randolph was turning to foundations and other philanthropists for funds "to ease the financial position" of the magazine. He found some help for his publication in 1925, when he became associated with efforts to organize the sleeping car porters into a union.

Randolph had long been interested in organized labor as a method to improve the status of black workers. He had made several small efforts to organize workers on some of the many jobs he had held in New York, and he was a constant critic of the stance of white organized labor toward organizing blacks. He pointed out in the *Messenger* that the American Federation of Labor (AFL) could hardly help to solve the problems of black workers as long as it was led by reactionaries like Samuel Gompers, "the Chief Strike Breaker" in the United States. But as on other matters, Randolph was ambivalent about organized labor. Though he vilified Gompers and other AFL leaders, he proudly pointed to the fact that the federation had granted "federal" union status to a small union of elevator operators that he and Owen had organized for a short time.

Randolph possessed charismatic qualities that would serve him well as he tried to become a labor leader. A leading scholar defines charismatic leadership as "certain qualities of an individual personality by which the leader is set apart as endowed with supernatural, super human, or at least specifically exceptional powers and qualities." Such leaders usually originate under conditions of stress, show an absence of regard for formal rules of routine administration, reject rational economic conduct, and usually prevail for short or intermittent periods. Moreover, charismatic leaders have the ability to issue statements clearly at variance with the facts and have their words taken as truth, and they demonstrate at all times an air of personal incorruptibility.

Randolph was handsome, almost exquisite in bearing, and a master of rhetoric and oratory. His speeches had a hypnotic effect upon audiences. He carried himself with an air that exuded such confidence that opponents found it almost impossible to deny the wisdom of his arguments and his supporters were loyal almost to his every word. So powerful was Randolph as a speaker that his associates in the porters union advised local unions to take up a collection before he spoke because "The Chief" was "sure to break up any meeting" and send the participants screaming into the streets, too excited to contribute to the cause. Yet despite his ability to stimulate people, Randolph possessed few routine organizational skills. He moved in the public realm, stirring up questions about black unionism and generating propaganda and ideas to publicize his views and the goals of his union.

Though he had functioned as the lead editor for the *Messenger* since 1917, Randolph first became a nationally recognized personality in 1925 when disgruntled porters of the Pullman Palace Car

Company decided to organize a union and invited Randolph to join their effort. Randolph agreed to conversations with these men and, in August 1925, the group organized the Brotherhood of Sleeping Car Porters (BSCP) with A. Philip Randolph as its general organizer and the *Messenger* as its official organ. Despite his charismatic qualities, Randolph was poorly thought of in some black circles. He carried himself with such pride and dignity that some people considered him haughty and aloof. The Oxford English accent he affected, full of "maasses and claasses," did not help matters. In the view of one critic, Randolph's problem was a "bootleg superiority complex." Moreover, some black spokesmen distrusted him, though there was little in his past upon which to build such suspicion. Soon after the union's organizational drive got underway one newspaper wrote that Randolph had failed in everything he tried to do and added that the "path of failure is said to be bedecked with shady deeds." Randolph, the claim went, was using the porters only to enhance sales of the *Messenger*—Randolph liked the "reds" and intended to take the porters' money and run off to Russia.

Whatever the criticisms, Randolph moved quickly to create a national organization of sleeping car porters, and to personify that union. Writing that "public opinion is the most powerful weapon in America," he was convinced that a favorable image, especially among influential whites, was as important to the union as were the porters themselves. He spent much time and effort trying to line up support for the BSCP among established black leaders and organizations—the very people he had spent years vilifying in the *Messenger*—and soliciting aid and money from liberal whites. These activities were representative of how Randolph would function in coming years. He was to serve as a high moral force who would articulate the porters' aspirations and demands, and he would become a symbol of their struggle. The chore of bringing in members fell to his lieutenants. Within months he put together a network of agents across the country: Milton P. Webster in Chicago, Morris "Dad" Moore at Oakland, Benny Smith at Detroit and Pittsburgh, and E. J. Bradley in St. Louis. Except in rare cases, those men remained in their positions throughout the long struggle for recognition and demonstrated strong personal loyalty to Randolph and his ideas. Likewise, Randolph secured money and endorsements from black and white groups and assembled a battery of white legal and economic experts to work for the union, many of whom served without compensation.

To achieve its specific goals, the Brotherhood needed to impress upon a large number of men the revolutionary idea that they could improve their standards of living through collective bargaining and ease their fears of Pullman reprisals. By 1925, with approximately twelve thousand porters, Pullman was the largest single employer of blacks in the United States. This gained Pullman widespread support among African American spokesmen.

However, at this time there was general hostility between blacks and organized labor. In most of his speeches, Randolph emphasized that the problems of black people in the United States were essentially economic and that the remedy lay in organized labor, and he believe that if the BSCP succeeded the lesson would be driven home, and the general economic and political awareness and status of black Americans would improve. If the union failed, his lifelong goal of finding a way to improve conditions for the masses would fail with it. Randolph also recognized that his personal fortunes had become intertwined with the BSCP. If the union failed, so would he. Though he talked big, he moved with caution, sacrificing immediate gains for long-range success.

Randolph hungered for publicity and respectability for his union, and he believed that the only way the BSCP would succeed would be to maintain public discussions of the porters' grievances at a high level. Utilizing the craft he had honed through the long years of editing the magazine, Randolph filled the *Messenger* and favorable newspapers with derogatory comments about Pullman's labor policies and punctuated his speeches and writings with attacks against his opposition, black and white. He was particularly caustic towards porters who would not immediately join the union, referring to them as "Uncle Toms." Black opponents of the union were "conscienceless, crooked and corrupt...mad dervishes" who used their "murderous fingers of graft and corruption" in efforts to destroy the union. The strategy did not contribute much to recruitment but it did gain press exposure for the union and marked Randolph as fearless and wholly committed to his cause. If much of the press opposed Randolph and his activities, his style made it impossible for newspapers to ignore him. Indeed, their opposition only added to Randolph's reputation. Because his organization was weak and without tradition, Randolph had to operate on a hit-or-miss basis, formulating policy as he went along, projecting himself as a man of initiative, creativity, and daring.

The BSCP made little tangible progress during the first three years. The disparity between Randolph's brave words and cautious behavior caused problems for the union. Some of his staunchest supporters took issue with his nonassertive policy, and the rank and file left the union in droves. By summer 1928, conflicting views and a series of union failures led to a crisis in the brotherhood and threatened Randolph's career as a labor leader. The union suffered four major defeats between August 1926 and June 1928. It failed to achieve a meeting with Pullman to discuss porters' grievances; it failed to raise porters' pay through having the Interstate Commerce Commission outlaw tipping, an intriguing and unique effort; it failed in its threat to strike against Pullman; and the *Messenger* ceased publication. During the same period the Brotherhood lost the support of the Pittsburgh *Courier*, a leading black weekly and until then the BSCP's staunchest supporter. Placing full blame for the union's failure on Randolph, the *Courier*'s influential publisher Robert Vann personally demanded that Randolph serve the porters' cause by resigning.

The most difficult and publicly humiliating of these failures was the strike fiasco of 1928. In the end, the strike threat was only part of Randolph's policy of operating from a position of weakness, using his skills and contacts to bring influential individuals and organizations to support his cause. Characteristically, his announcement of an imminent strike was for public consumption. He only wanted to raise enough noise about a strike against Pullman to cause the federal government to intervene on the BSCP's behalf under provisions of the Watson-Parker Railway Labor Act of 1926. But on this occasion Randolph found himself caught between the need to appear militant and firm in the eyes of Pullman and the mediation board and at the same time allay the fears of porters about what they could expect from a strike.

His actions during the spring of 1928—such as making a public statement to the porters that a "strike vote does not necessarily mean that the porters will strike"—convinced both the Pullman Company and the federal mediators that the whole episode was little more than a gesture. Many porters also came to question his intent. The mediation board, recognizing the contradiction, called Randolph's bluff and refused to recommend emergency measures. The mediation board informed James Weldon Johnson, who as executive secretary of the NAACP had intervened on behalf of the BSCP, via telegram that there would be no disruption of service, and thus no emergency, "if every Pullman Car stood idle." After the mediation board's decision, the BSCP did not carry through on its threat and instead "postponed" the strike, despite endorsement of the strike by a majority of the porters. Randolph's activities in 1928 amounted to a bluff that failed.

After 1928, the BSCP lost organizational rigidity as various organizers transformed their formal roles and became a social group, a "unity of persons rather than technicians." Since close associations during shared failures had forged strong bonds among them, they were able to reach their new organizational relationship with a minimum of friction. Erosion of BSCP membership continued, and as the nation moved into the Great Depression the brotherhood became little more than a cell. Of the 4,632 members in the union in 1928, only 658 remained in 1933. The BSCP could hardly consider itself a national organization. But its leaders were convinced that if they kept the doors open, the union would triumph in the end.

The period between the crisis of 1928 and the coming of the New Deal in 1933 marked a hiatus in Randolph's style, as the needs of the union demanded that he take control of routine functions. The

BSCP changed its tactics and sought to attain its goal of recognition through the federal courts rather than through the press and propaganda. Randolph continued to devote full attention to the BSCP, but he utilized different methods than before, toning down his rhetoric and working through the American Federation of Labor (AFL).

Indeed, the BSCP's need in 1928, if it ever hoped to succeed, was to achieve legitimacy. Since there was no possibility at that point of gaining recognition from the Pullman Company, Randolph and his colleagues turned again to the AFL and applied for a charter. The AFL did not accept the BSCP's application for an international charter in 1928, but in 1929 the executive council of the federation chartered thirteen BSCP locals as federal unions, each independently affiliated with the AFL. Though fully aware of the Jim Crow nature of the charters they received, brotherhood leaders believed that receipt of the charters marked the union with a certain legitimacy and responsibility. But more important for the relationship between black workers and the general organized labor movement, the charters granted Randolph and his BSCP colleagues access to the floor of AFL meetings, from which they could challenge the racist attitudes and activities of member unions and fight for the rights of black workers.

From the strike fiasco to the coming of the New Deal, the brotherhood remained largely a paper organization, struggling simply to survive as its leader awaited an opportunity to reassert his rare abilities. Randolph's failure to perform a miracle in 1928 had dampened his followers' faith in his charismatic qualities and he had to await a victory before he could function as a symbolic figure again. The New Deal, with its liberalized labor laws and the emphasis the new administration placed on organized labor, opened new fields for Randolph and provided renewed opportunity for him to operate with the initiative and daring that had characterized his leadership of the BSCP in the days before 1928.

The Amended Railway Labor Act of 1934 assured for the first time federal support of the BSCP's claim to the right to represent porters. Under protection of that legislation, Randolph convinced an overwhelming majority of the porters, many of whom were not members of the BSCP, to endorse the brotherhood as their bargaining agent in disputes with Pullman. After it won a bitter campaign with the Pullman Porters and Maids Protective Association—a company front union—for endorsement from the porters, the BSCP gained recognition from Pullman as the legitimate representative of the porters and maids in 1935. The victory identified Randolph again as a major figure among black spokesmen and leaders.

The BSCP's success in gaining recognition from Pullman was but one factor contributing to Randolph's standing among black leaders. Long concerned about the impact of the AFL's discriminatory policies on the economic status of black workers, Randolph made numerous appeals to AFL leaders to alter the federation's policies. After his success with Pullman, Randolph capitalized upon his increased stature among both labor leaders and blacks and demanded improved opportunity for blacks within the federation. At the 1934 convention, with support from a few powerful industrial unions and a mass street demonstration that Randolph had convinced Walter White and the NAACP to organize, Randolph forced the AFL to establish a committee to study discrimination in federation affiliates and report its findings to the convention the following year.

The hearings in 1935 of the Committee of Five on Negro Discrimination in the AFL brought enormous prestige to Randolph as he used every effort to make the sessions an event of importance to all blacks. He brought before the committee testimony from the NAACP and the National Urban League, other black spokesmen, and some African American workers. When AFL leaders received the report in advance of the 1935 convention and tried to downplay its findings of widespread racial discrimination and its recommendations for remedy, Randolph enhanced his standing even more by the straightforward manner in which he carried to the floor of the convention the fight to save the report and make the federation responsive to the needs of black workers.

The original committee report had called for the expulsion of racist unions, but the executive council had set those recommendations aside and submitted a report of its own. Randolph excoriated the council's report as a "dignified, diplomatic camouflage." George M. Harrison, author of the executive council's draft, heatedly defended his position and maintained that organized labor had done more for the advancement of blacks than had any other institution in America. The convention supported Harrison's view and ended by angering a large segment of the African American population. Walter White wrote to John L. Lewis of the United Mine Workers that the AFL had "destroyed the last vestige of confidence" that blacks had in that organization.

But White's comments were perhaps a bit hasty. Though Randolph had made himself obnoxious to white delegates, the 1935 convention of the AFL granted the Brotherhood of Sleeping Car Porters an international charter, marking it as the first black union to achieve that status. Although Randolph had written in *Messenger* magazine in 1919 that "the dissolution of the American Federation of Labor would inure to the benefit of the labor movement in this country . . . because it holds that there can be a partnership between labor and capital" and that the "American Federation of Labor is the most wicked machine for the propagation of race prejudice in this country," he accepted the charter. He did so because, as he told John L. Lewis, "My fight, the fight to organize Negro workers, is in the AFL. I must stay here and carry on that fight."

In 1935, at the end of the New Negro Movement, A. Philip Randolph was far from done. Randolph would live forty years longer and would be involved in many ventures at the center of American life. Randolph had gained great prestige in both black and white circles as a result of his success with the Brotherhood of Sleeping Car Porters and used that prestige to become the leading civil rights leader and spokesman in the country. In 1937, he founded the National Negro Congress (NNC), a civil rights umbrella organization of which he was president until the Communists took it over in 1940. Randolph was at his eloquent best in his resignation speech from the NNC, using it to warn blacks that they must finance and lead their own organizations.

Randolph moved on quickly, continuing his efforts to improve the quality of life for African Americans and to tie together the relationship between economics and civil rights. In late 1940 and early 1941, Randolph began talking increasingly about what many others had come to recognize: white workers were coming out of the Depression while blacks remained on unemployment and relief rolls. Randolph organized the March on Washington Movement to demand that President Franklin D. Roosevelt issue an executive order ending discrimination in employment and segregation in the military. During the spring of 1941, the idea of the march gained considerable motion as clergymen and newspapers came to support Randolph's movement. Roosevelt, who clearly did not want to see thousands of blacks marching in protest on the National Mall, dispatched high-placed whites and friends who had supported Randolph in the past—including the president's wife, Eleanor, and New York City Mayor Fiorello LaGuardia—to talk Randolph into calling off the march. Randolph's response was that nothing short of an executive order ending discrimination and military segregation could stop the march.

In the end, the president issued Executive Order 8802, which outlawed discrimination in employment on federal contracts and established the Fair Employment Practice Committee (FEPC) to oversee implementation of that decision. But the executive order did not mention segregation in the military, the second aspect of Randolph's demand. FEPC was at best a symbolic victory, and Randolph received stiff criticism for accepting the compromise. Nonetheless, he had caused the federal government to admit racial discrimination and promise to outlaw it, and his continued arguments with both the Roosevelt and Truman Administrations eventually led to the latter president's executive order that ended segregation in the military in July 1948.

Despite these successes, Randolph was not finished in his effort to improve the economic and civil rights status of African Americans and to fuse the two issues in Americans' minds. And he worked against considerable odds, especially within organized labor. Under the shadow of McCarthyism in the 1950s, organized labor engaged in red-baiting to purge left-leaning unions and union leaders, some of which had been most supportive of blacks. And when the AFL merged with the Congress of Industrial Organizations (CIO), a group of industrial unions that had split from the AFL in 1935, leadership of the new group went to the former AFL instead of the more militant CIO. This new AFL/CIO even began siding with unions in court cases that challenged unions on charges of racial discrimination.

Randolph also used his influence and status to help other civil rights leaders. In Montgomery, Alabama, in 1955–56, he assisted in a yearlong boycott of that city's buses to demand that they be desegregated. That effort, known as the Montgomery Bus Boycott, launched the public careers of Rosa Parks and Martin Luther King Jr. Parks's decision to remain in her seat when ordered by the bus driver to yield it to a white male passenger launched the boycott; King became head of the hastily organized Montgomery Improvement Association (MIA) to lead it. King, well educated, highly articulate, and a charismatic personality, went on to found the Southern Christian Leadership Conference and to earn a Nobel Peace Prize for his civil rights activities. During the dark days of the Montgomery Bus Boycott, the Brotherhood of Sleeping Car Porters provided much needed money and personnel in support. Edgar D. Nixon, a Randolph lieutenant and BSCP vice president, actually paid the initial bond to get Parks out of jail. After a year of boycotting and a Supreme Court decision upholding the MIA's activities, the city gave in and the buses were desegregated. This was the first major civil rights victory in the Deep South.

Randolph, who was elected to the executive council of the AFL/CIO, used his position to continue to press for support of black

TRACK 32

In the 1930s and 1940s, A. Phillip Randolph had evolved from a labor leader to the most significant spokesperson for civil rights. His message, as presented in this speech, was racial equality and the need to secure for all Americans their legal and Constitutional rights.

workers' rights. Randolph was so doggedly determined in his advocacy that George Meany, president of the AFL/CIO in 1959, wondered aloud "who the hell appointed you the guardian of all the [Negro members] in America?" Though intended to intimidate Randolph, the "who the hell" remark only energized him and raised his standing among African Americans as their fearless guardian. Meany even had the executive council censure Randolph, but the BSCP president was undaunted. In 1960, he led in founding the Negro American Labor Council (NALC), intended to "secure membership of Negro workers in the unions and employment and promotions on the jobs as well as participation in the executive, administrative and staff areas of unions." Further, despite opposition from some leaders, in 1963 Randolph forced the AFL/CIO to create a Special Task Force on Civil Rights, a group that even included George Meany.

These two events, the creation of the NALC and the special committee on civil rights, proved timely for Randolph. Dating back to 1941, Randolph still believed in the importance of mass demonstrations and dreamed of a major march on Washington. For several years he had been talking with his friend, Bayard Rustin, and other civil rights leaders about such a march. Now, with the support of organized labor, or at least its acquiescence, he called for a March on Washington for Jobs and Freedom for August 28, 1963. Though Dr. Martin Luther King Jr., president of the Southern Christian Leadership Conference, stole the day with his "I Have a Dream" speech, it was Randolph's march. He told the assembled masses, and millions on television, that the march represented "the advance guard of a massive moral revolution for jobs and freedom."

His words were prophetic. Within two years the nation experienced a virtual revolution in racial policies as Congress passed the Civil Rights Act of 1964 and the Voting Rights Act of 1965. Much remained to be done, but the United States was clearly a different nation after this legislation. During his long life, A. Philip Randolph played a major role in bringing about this remarkable transformation of the nation. When Randolph died in his beloved Harlem in 1979, in his ninetieth year, his vision of a just society and his demand that "the sanctity of private property take second place to the sanctity of human personality" were as clear and firm as they had been in 1917 when he launched *Messenger* magazine and began his public career.

SELECTED READINGS

The number of books on the Harlem Renaissance and the writers, musicians, and artists associated with the movement is quite large and grows every year. In addition, numerous articles, both scholarly and popular, add substantially to this body of literature. The material listed below is meant to provide a starting point for the reader who wishes to look deeper into the Renaissance. We have made no attempt to include everything. Instead, we have listed books that will provide more intensive reading on this subject.

In addition to books, we have included suggestions of recorded music that will provide an introduction to the work of the musical artists featured in this book. We have also included a short list of web sites that feature material on the Harlem Renaissance. There are literally thousands of these sites that a web search will uncover. We have selected a handful that are of high quality, and are connected with institutions that will likely keep these sites on-line.

GENERAL REFERENCE

West, Aberjhani and Sandra L. eds. *Encyclopedia of the Harlem Renaissance*. New York: Checkmark Books, 2003.

Wintz, Cary D. and Paul Finkelman, eds. *Encyclopedia of the Harlem Renaissance*. 2 Volumes. New York: Routledge, 2005.

THE HARLEM RENAISSANCE: OVERVIEW

Anderson, Paul Allen. *Deep River: Music and Memory in Harlem Renaissance Thought*. Durham: Duke University Press, 2001.

Bontemps, Arna, ed. *The Harlem Renaissance Remembered: Essays*. New York: Dodd, Mead, 1972.

Carroll, Anne Elizabeth. *Word, Image, and the New Negro: Representation and Identity in the Harlem Renaissance*. Bloomington: Indiana University Press, 2005.

Fabre, Genevieve and Michel Feith, eds. *Temples for Tomorrow: Looking Back at the Harlem Renaissance*. Bloomington: Indiana University Press, 2001.

Floyd. Samuel A., Jr., ed. *Black Music in the Harlem Renaissance: A Collection of Essays*. Knoxville: University of Tennessee Press, 1993.

Hayard Gallery. *Rhapsodies in Black: Art of the Harlem Renaissance*. Berkeley: University of California Press, 1997.

Helbling, Mark. *The Harlem Renaissance: The One and the Many*. Westport, CT: Greenwood Press, 1999.

Huggins, Nathan Irvin. *Harlem Renaissance*. New York: Oxford University Press, 1971.

Huggins, Nathan Irvin, ed. *Voices from the Harlem Renaissance*. New York: Oxford University Press, 1976.

Hutchinson, George. *The Harlem Renaissance in Black and White*. Cambridge, MA: Belknap Press of Harvard University Press, 1995.

Krasner, David. *A Beautiful Pageant: African American Theatre, Drama, and Performance in the Harlem Renaissance, 1910-1927*. New York: Palgrave Macmillan, 2002.

Lewis, David Levering. *When Harlem Was In Vogue*. New York: Oxford University Press, 1981, 1989.

Lewis, David Levering, ed. *The Portable Harlem Renaissance Reader*. New York: Viking, 1994.

Nadell, Martha Jane. *Enter the New Negroes: Images of Race in American Culture*. Cambridge, MA: Harvard University Press, 2004.

Porter, James A. *Modern Negro Art*. Washington, D.C.: Howard University Press, 1992.

Schwarz, A.B. Christa. *Gay Voices of the Harlem Renaissance*. Bloomington: Indiana University Press, 2003.

Scruggs, Charles. *The Sage in Harlem: H. L. Mencken and the Black Writers of the 1920s*. Baltimore: Johns Hopkins University Press, 1984.

Singh, Amritjit. *The Novels of the Harlem Renaissance: Twelve Black Writers, 1923-1933*. University Park: Pennsylvania State University Press, 1976.

Spencer, Jon Michael. *The New Negroes and Their Music: The Success of the Harlem Renaissance*. Knoxville: University of Tennessee Press, 1997.

Wall, Cheryl A. *Women of the Harlem Renaissance*. Bloomington, IN: Indiana University Press, 1995.

Wintz, Cary D. *Black Culture and the Harlem Renaissance*. College Station: Texas A&M University Press, 1997.

HARLEM

Anderson, Jervis. *This Was Harlem: A Cultural Portrait, 1900-1950*. New York: Farrar, Straus, Giroux, 1981.

Boyd, Herb, ed. *The Harlem Reader: A Celebration of New York's Most Famous Neighborhood, From the Renaissance Years to the 21st Century*. New York: Three Rivers Press, 2003.

Clarke, John Henrik. *Harlem: A Community in Transition*. New York: Citadel Press, 1964

Clarke, John Henrik. *Harlem, U.S.A.*, rev. ed. New York: Collier Books, 1971.

Greenberg, Cheryl Lynn. *Or Does It Explode?: Black Harlem in the Great Depression*. New York: Oxford University Press, 1997.

Johnson, James Weldon. *Black Manhattan*. New York: Alfred A. Knopf, 1930.

Osofsky, Gilbert. *Harlem: The Making of a Ghetto: Negro New York, 1890-1930*. New York: Harper & Row, 1966.

Schoener, Allon, ed. *Harlem on My Mind: Cultural Capital of Black America, 1900-1968*. New York: New Press, 1995.

Willis, Deborah and Jane Lusaka, eds. *Visual Journal: Harlem and D.C. in the Thirties and Forties*. Washington, D.C.: Smithsonian Institution Press, 1996.

ARMSTRONG, LOUIS

Armstrong, Louis. *Satchmo: My Life In New Orleans*. New York : Da Capo Press, 1986.

Armstrong, Louis. *Swing That Music*. With an introduction by Rudy Vallee and a new foreword by Dan Morgenstern. New York: De Capo Press, 1993.

Armstrong, Louis. *Louis Armstrong, In His Own Words: Selected Writings*, ed. Thomas Brothers. New York: Oxford University Press, 1999.

Bergreen, Laurence. *Louis Armstrong: An Extravagant Life*. New York: Broadway Books, 1997.

Collier, James Lincoln. *Louis Armstrong, an American Genius*. New York: Oxford University Press, 1983.

Jones, Max and John Chilton. *Louis: The Louis Armstrong Story, 1900-1971*. New York: Da Capo Press, 1988.

Storb, Ilse. *Louis Armstrong: The Definitive Biography*. Translated by Bertram Thompson. New York: Peter Lang, 1999.

BAKER, JOSEPHINE

Baker, Jean-Claude and Chris, Chase. *Josephine: The Hungry Heart*. New York: Random House, 1993.

Baker, Josephine and Jo Bouillon. *Josephine*. Translated from the French by Mariana Fitzpatrick. New York: Harper & Row, 1977.

Bennetta Jules-Rosette and Simon Njami. *Josephine Baker in Art and Life: The Icon and the Image*. Urbana: University of Illinois Press, 2006.

Haney, Lynn. *Naked at the Feast: A Biography of Josephine Baker*. New York: Dodd, Mead & Company, 1981.

Papich, Stephen. *Remembering Josephine*. Indianapolis: The Bobbs-Merrill Company Inc., 1976.

Rose, Phyllis. *Jazz Cleopatra: Josephine Baker in Her Time*. New York: Doubleday, 1989.

BEARDEN, ROMARE

Fine, Ruth, with contributions by Mary Lee Corlett, Nnamdi Elleh, Jacqueline Francis, Abdul Goler, and Sarah Kennel. *The Art of Romare Bearden*. New York: Harry N. Abrams, Inc., 2003.

Schwartzman, Myron. *Romare Bearden: His Life and Art*. New York: Abrams, 1990.

BLAKE, EUBIE

Carter, Lawrence T. *Eubie Blake: Keys of Memory*. Detroit: Balamp Publishing Company, 1979.

Kimball, Robert and William Bolcom. *Reminiscing with Sissle and Blake*. New York: Viking Press, 1973.

Rose, Al. *Eubie Blake*. New York: Schirmer Books, 1979.

CULLEN, COUNTEE

Du Bois, W. E. B. *The Souls of Black Folk*. 1903. New York: Barnes and Noble Classics, 2003.

Early, Gerald, ed. *My Soul's High Song: The Collected Writings of Countee Cullen*. New York: Anchor Books, 1991.

Ferguson, Blanche E. *Countee Cullen and the Negro Renaissance*. New York: Dodd, Mead, 1966.

Perry, Margaret. *A Bio-Bibliography of Countee P. Cullen, 1903-1946*. Westport, CT: Greenwood Publishing Company, 1971.

Shucard, Alan R. *Countee Cullen*. Boston: Twayne Publishers, 1984.

DOUGLAS, AARON

Kirschke, Amy Helene. *Aaron Douglas: Art, Race and the Harlem Renaissance*. Oxford, Mississippi: University Press of Mississippi, 1995.

Works Cited:

Douglas, Aaron. "Autobiography," unpublished manuscript, Aaron Douglas Papers, Fisk University Special Collections, Nashville, TN.

Interview of Aaron Douglas by Ann Allen Shockley. November 19, 1975. Black Oral Histories, Fisk University Special Collections, Nashville, TN.

Du Bois, W.E.B.

Huggins, Nathan, ed. *Du Bois, W.E.B. Writings*. New York: The Library of America, 1986.

Lewis, David Levering. *W.E.B. Du Bois: Biography of a Race, 1868-1919*. New York: Henry Holt and Company, 1993.

Lewis, David Levering. *W.E.B. Du Bois: The Fight for Equality and the American Century, 1919-1963*. New York: Henry Holt and Company, 2000.

Marable, Manning. *W.E.B. Du Bois: Black Radical Democrat*. Boston: Twayne Publishers, 1986

Moore, Jacqueline M. *Booker T. Washington, W.E.B. Du Bois, and the Struggle for Racial Uplift*. Wilmington, DE: Scholarly Resources, Inc., 2003.

Rampersad, Arnold. *The Art and Imagination of W.E.B. Du Bois*. Cambridge, MA: Harvard University Press, 1976.

Rudwick, Elliott M. *W.E.B. Du Bois: Propagandist of the Negro Protest*. New York: Atheneum, 1969.

Wolters, Raymond. *Du Bois and His Rivals*. Columbia: University of Missouri Press, 2002.

Ellington, Duke

Ellington, Edward Kennedy. *Music Is My Mistress*. Cambridge, MA: Da Capo Press, 1976.

Ellington, Mercer with Stanley Dance. *Duke Ellington in Person: An Intimate Memoir*. Cambridge, MA: Da Capo Press, 1979.

Ellison, Ralph. *Living with Music: Ralph Ellison's Jazz Writings*. New York: The Modern Library, 2002.

Hasse, John Edward. *Beyond Category: The Life and Genius of Duke Ellington*. Cambridge, MA: Da Capo Press, 1995.

Tucker, Mark. *Ellington: The Early Years*. Urbana: University of Illinois Press. 1991.

Tucker, Mark. *The Duke Ellington Reader*. New York: Oxford University Press, 1993.

GARVEY, MARCUS

Kornweibel, Theodore Jr. *Seeing Red: Federal Campaigns against Black Militancy, 1919-1925*. Bloomington: Indiana University Press, 1998.

Martin, Tony. *Race First: The Ideological and Organizational Struggles of Marcus Garvey and the Universal Negro Improvement Association*. Dover, MA: The Majority Press, 1976.

Martin, Tony. *Literary Garveyism: Garvey, Black Arts, and the Harlem Renaissance*. Dover MA: The Majority Press, 1983.

Stein, Judith. *The World of Marcus Garvey: Race and Class in Modern Society*. Baton Rouge: Louisianan State University Press, 1986.

Stephens, Michelle Ann. *Black Empire: The Masculine Global Imaginary of Caribbean Intellectuals in the United States, 1914-1962*. Durham: Duke University Press, 2005.

Sundiata, Ibrahim. *Brothers and Strangers: Black Zion, Black Slavery, 1914-1940*. Durham: Duke University, 2003.

Works cited:

Hill, Robert A., ed. *The Marcus Garvey and Universal Negro Improvement Association Papers*. 9 Volumes. Los Angeles: University of California Press, 1983-2006.

Perry, Jeffrey B., ed. *A Hubert Harrison Reader*. Middletown: Wesleyan University Press, 2001.

Sherman, Richard B. "The Last Stand: The Fight for Racial Integrity in Virginia in the 1920s." *Journal of Southern History* 56, no. 1 (February1988):70.

HUGHES, LANGSTON

Berry, Faith. *Before and Beyond Harlem: A Biography of Langston Hughes*. New York : Random House, 1995.

Hughes, Langston. *The Big Sea: An Autobiography*. New York: Knopf, 1945.

Rampersad. Arnold. *The Life of Langston Hughes*. Volume I: *1902-1942: I, Too, Sing America*, and Volume II: *1941-1967: I Dream a World*. New York: Oxford University Press, 1986, 1988.

Rampersad, Arnold, ed. *The Collected Poems of Langston Hughes*. New York: Alfred A. Knopf, 1995.

Tracy, Steven C. *Langston Hughes and the Blues*. Urbana: University of Illinois Press, 2001.

HURSTON, ZORA NEALE

Boyd, Valerie. *Wrapped in Rainbows: The Life of Zora Neale Hurston*. New York: Scribner, 2003.

Hurston, Zora Neale. *Dust Tracks on a Road*. With a new foreword by Maya Angelou. New York: Harper Perennial, 1991.

Hemenway, Robert. *Zora Neale Hurston: A Literary Biography*. Urbana, Illinois: University of Illinois Press, 1978.

Meisenhelder, Susan. *Hitting a Straight Lick with a Crooked Stick: Race and Gender in the Works of Zora Neale Hurston*. Tuscaloosa, AL: University of Alabama Press, 1999.

Walker, Alice. *In Search of Our Mother's Gardens: Womanist Prose*. New York: Harcourt Brace Jovanovich, 1983.

Wall, Cheryl A, ed. *Zora Neale Hurston: Folklore, Memoirs and Other Writings*. New York: Library of America, 1995.

Wall, Cheryl A, ed. *Zora Neale Hurston: Novels and Stories*. New York: Library of America, 1995.

Works Cited:

Cliff, Michelle. "Within the Veil," *The Norton Anthology of African American Literature*. Eds. Henry Louis Gates, Jr. and Nellie Y. McKay. 2nd ed. New York: W. W. Norton, 2004. 2505-08.

Schuyler, George. "Views and Reviews." Rev. of *Their Eyes Were Watching God*, by Zora Neale Hurston. *Pittsburgh Courier* 25 Dec. 1937: 12.

Wright, Richard. "Between Laughter and Tears." Rev. of *Their Eyes Were Watching God*, by Zora Neale Hurston. *New Masses* 5 Oct. 1937: 22, 25.

Johnson, James Weldon

Andrews, William J., ed. *James Weldon Johnson: Writings*. New York: Library of America, 2004.

Fleming, Robert E. *James Weldon Johnson*. Boston: Twayne Publishers, 1987.

Johnson, James Weldon. *Along This Way: The Autobiography of James Weldon Johnson*. New York: Da Capo Press, 2000.

Johnson, James Weldon. *Black Manhattan*. New York: Da Capo Press, 1991.

Levy, Eugene. *James Weldon Johnson: Black Leader, Black Voice*. Chicago: University of Chicago Press, 1973.

Price, Kenneth M. and Lawrence J. Oliver, eds. *Critical Essays on James Weldon Johnson*. New York: G. K. Hall—Prentice Hall, 1997.

Wilson, Sondra K., ed. *The Selected Writings of James Weldon Johnson*. New York: Oxford University Press, 1995.

Larsen, Nella

Davis, Thadious M. *Nella Larsen, Novelist of the Harlem Renaissance: A Woman's Life Unveiled*. Baton Rouge: Louisiana State University Press, 1994.

Hutchinson, George. *In Search of Nella Larsen: A Biography of the Color Line*. Cambridge, MA: Belknap Press of Harvard University Press, 2006.

McLendon, Jacquelyn Y. *The Politics of Color in the Fiction of Jessie Fauset and Nella Larsen*. Charlottesville: University of Virginia Press, 1995.

Miller, Erica. *The Other Reconstruction: Where Violence and Womanhood Meet in the Writings of Ida B. Wells-Barnett, Angelina Weld Grimke, and Nella Larsen*. New York: Garland Publishing, Inc., 2000.

LAWRENCE, JACOB

Brown, Milton W. *Jacob Lawrence*. (Exhibition Catalog). New York: Whitney Museum of American Art, 1974

Nesbett, Peter T. and Michelle Du Bois, eds. *Over the Line: The Art and Life of Jacob Lawrence*. University of Washington Press, Seattle and London in association with Jacob and Gwendolyn Lawrence Foundation, Seattle and New York, 2000.

Wheat, Ellen Harkins. *Jacob Lawrence: American Painter*. (Exhibition Catalog). Seattle and London: University of Washington Press in association with the Seattle Art Museum, 1986.

LOCKE, ALAIN

Harris, Leonard, ed. *The Critical Pragmatism of Alain Locke: A Reader on Value Theory, Aesthetics, Community, Culture, Race, and Education*. Lanham, MD: Rowman & Littlefield, 1999.

Harris, Leonard, ed. *The Philosophy of Alain Locke: Harlem Renaissance and Beyond*. Philadelphia: Temple University Press, 1989.

Linnemann, Russell J, ed. *Alain Locke: Reflections on a Modern Renaissance Man*. Baton Rouge: Louisiana State University Press, 1982.

Locke, Alain, ed. *The New Negro: An Interpretation*. (Book decoration and portraits by Winold Reiss). New York: Albert and Charles Boni, 1925.

Posnock, Ross. *Color & Culture: Black Writers and the Making of the Modern Intellectual*. Cambridge, MA: Harvard University Press, 1998.

Stewart, Jeffrey C. *The Critical Temper of Alain Locke: A Selection of His Essays on Art and Culture*. New York: Garland Publishers, 1983.

McKAY, CLAUDE

Cooper, Wayne F. *Claude McKay: Rebel Sojourner in the Harlem Renaissance: A Biography*. Baton Rouge: Louisiana State University Press, 1987.

McKay, Claude. *Complete Poems*. Ed by William J. Maxwell. Urbana: University of Illinois Press, 2004.

McKay, Claude. *A Long Way from Home*. New York: L. Furman, Inc., 1937.

McKay, Claude. *Harlem: Negro Metropolis*. New York: E.P. Dutton & Company, Inc. 1940.

Tillery, Tyrone. *Claude McKay: A Black Poet's Struggle for Identity*. Amherst: University of Massachusetts Press, 1992.

RANDOLPH, A. PHILLIP

Anderson, Jervis. *A. Philip Randolph; A Biographical Portrait*. New York, Harcourt Brace Jovanovich, 1974.

Davis, Daniel S. *Mr. Black Labor; The Story of A. Philip Randolph, Father of the Civil Rights Movement*. Introduction by Bayard Rustin. New York, E. P. Dutton, 1972.

Harris, William H. *Keeping the Faith: A. Philip Randolph, Milton P. Webster, and the Brotherhood of Sleeping Car Porters, 1925-37*. Urbana, Illinois: University of Illinois Press, 1977.

Pfeffer, Paula F. *A. Philip Randolph, Pioneer of the Civil Rights Movement*. Baton Rouge: Louisiana State University Press, 1990.

Taylor, Cynthia. *A. Philip Randolph: The Religious Journey of an African American Labor Leader*. New York: New York University Press, 2006.

Work cited:

Harris, William H. (ed) *Records of the Brotherhood of Sleeping Car Porters: Series A, Holdings of the Chicago Historical Society and the Newberry Library, 1925–1969, Part 1: Records of the BSCP, 1925–1969*. Chicago: Chicago Historical Society, 1994.

ROBESON, PAUL

Boyle, Sheila Tully and Andrew Bunie, *Paul Robeson: The Years of Promise and Achievement*. Amherst: University of Massachusetts Press, 2001.

Brown, Lloyd L. *The Young Paul Robeson: On My Journey Now.* Boulder, CO: Westview Press, 1997.

Duberman, Martin B. *Paul Robeson.* New York: Alfred A. Knopf, 1988.

Foner, Philip S., ed. *Paul Robeson Speaks.* Secaucus, NJ: Citadel Press, 1982.

Graham, Shirley. *Paul Robeson, Citizen of the World.* New York: J. Messner, Inc., 1946.

Robeson, Eslanda Goode. *Paul Robeson, Negro.* New York: Harper & Brothers, 1930.

Robeson, Paul. *Here I Stand.* Boston: Beacon Press, 1958.

Robeson, Paul, Jr. *The Undiscovered Paul Robeson: An Artist's Journey, 1898-1939.* New York: John Wiley & Sons, Inc., 2001.

Seton, Marie. *Paul Robeson.* London: D. Dobson, 1958.

SMITH, BESSIE

Albertson, Chris. *Bessie.* New Haven: Yale University Press, 2003.

Brooks, Edward. *The Bessie Smith Companion: A Critical and Detailed Appreciation of the Recordings.* New York: Da Capo Press, 1982.

Davis, Angela Y. *Blues Legacies and Black Feminism: Gertrude "Ma" Rainey, Bessie Smith, and Billie Holiday.* New York: Pantheon Books, 1998.

Feinstein, Elaine. *Bessie Smith.* New York: Viking, 1985.

WATERS, ETHEL

Harris, Sheldon. *Blues Who's Who.* New Rochelle, NY: Arlington House, 1979.

Jasen, David A., and Gene Jones. *Spreadin' Rhythm Around: Black Popular Songwriters, 1880-1930.* New York: Schirmer Books, 1998.

McCorkle, Susannah. "The Mother of Us All," *American Heritage* (February-March 1994).

Pleasants, Henry. *The Great American Popular Singers.* New York: Simon and Schuster, 1974.

Stearns, Marshall and Jean. *Jazz Dance*. New York: Schirmer Books, 1979.

Waters, Ethel. *To Me It's Wonderful*. New York: Harper & Row, 1972.

Waters, Ethel, with Charles Samuels. *His Eye Is on the Sparrow*. Garden City, NY: Doubleday & Co., 1951.

WRIGHT, RICHARD

Bone, Robert. *Richard Wright*. Minneapolis: University of Minnesota Press, 1969.

Fabre, Michel. *The Unfinished Quest of Richard Wright*. Jackson: University Press of Mississippi, 1985.

Gilroy, Paul. *The Black Atlantic: Modernity and Double Consciousness*. Cambridge: Harvard University Press, 1993.

Kinnamon, Keneth and Michel Fabre, ed. *Conversations with Richard Wright*. Jackson: University of Mississippi Press, 1993.

Macksey, Richard and Frank E. Moorer, eds. *Richard Wright: A Collection of Critical Essays*. New York: Prentice Hall, 1984. See the "Introduction" by Macksey and Moorer.

Rowley, Hazel. *Richard Wright: The Life and Times*. New York: Henry Holt, 2001.

Walker, Margaret. *Richard Wright: Demonic Genius*. New York: Amistad Press, 1988.

Wright, Richard. *Black Power*. 1954. Introduction by Amritjit Singh. rpt. New York: Harper Collins, 1995.

Wright, Richard. *The Color Curtain*. 1956. Foreword by Gunnar Myrdal. Afterword by Amritjit Singh. rpt. Jackson: University Press of Mississippi, 1994.

Works Cited:

Howe, Irving. *A World More Attractive*. New York: Horizon, 1963.

Hughes, Langston. "The Negro Artist and the Racial Mountain," in *African American Literary Theory: A Reader*, ed. Winston Napier. New York: New York University Press, 2000.

Thurman, Wallace. *Collected Writings of Wallace Thurman: A Harlem*

Renaissance Reader, ed. Amritjit Singh and Daniel M. Scott. New Brunswick: Rutgers University Press, 2003.

Wright, Richard. "Blueprint for Negro Writing," in *Richard Wright Reader*, ed. Ellen Wright and Michel Fabre. New York: Harper and Row, 1978.

MUSIC

Louis Armstrong, *The Essential Louis Armstrong* (Columbia, 2004).

Josephine Baker, *Gold Collection* (Dejavu Retro, 2001).

Eubie Blake, *The Eighty-Six Years of Eubie Blake* (Columbia, 1969).

Eubie Blake, *Memories of You* (Shout Factory, 2003).

Duke Ellington, *The Essential Duke Ellington* (Sony, 2005).

Paul Robeson, *Ol' Man River: His 25 Greatest* (Asv Living Era, 1998).

Bessie Smith, *Bessie Smith: The Complete Recordings, Vol. 1* (Sony, 1991).

Ethel Waters, *The Incomparable Ethel Waters* (Sony, 2003).

Ethel Waters, *Am I Blue: 1921-1947* (Jazz Legends, 2004).

WEB SITES

The Art of the Harlem Renaissance. Web site for the exhibit "Rhapsodies in Black: The Art of the Harlem Renaissance." Institute of International Visual Arts.
http://www.iniva.org/harlem/index2.html

Chicago Renaissance: Images and Documents from the Vivian C. Harsh Research Collection. Chicago Public Library.
http://www.iniva.org/harlem/index2.html

A Guide to Harlem Renaissance Materials. The Library of Congress. http://www.loc.gov/rr/program/bib/harlem/harlem.html

Harlem, 1900-1940: An African American Community. The Schomburg Center for Research in Black Culture. The New York Public Library.
http://www.si.umich.edu/CHICO/Harlem/index.html

Harlem: Mecca of the New Negro. The complete contents of the March 1925, Harlem issue of *Survey Graphic*. The University of Virginia. http://etext.lib.virginia.edu/harlem/

Langston Hughes National Poetry Project. University of Kansas. http://www.kuce.org/hughes/index.html

Shuffle Along—The Eubie Blake Collection. Maryland Historical Society. http://www.mdhs.org/eubieblake/

AUDIO CREDITS AND PERMISSIONS

In all cases, we have attempted to provide archival audio in its original form. Some audio segments have been edited for time and content. While we have attempted to achieve the best possible quality on the archival audio, some audio quality is the result of source limitations.

All efforts have been made by the editors to contact the copyright holders for the material used in this book. The editors regret any omissions that have occurred and will correct any such errors in future editions of this book.

Louis Armstrong: "I'm Not Rough" performed by Louis Armstrong and His Hot Five, from the recording entitled *Jazz, Vol. 2: The Blues*, Folkways 02802. © 1950

Josephine Baker: "Bye Bye Blackbird" from the recording Josephine Baker: Déjà Vu Retro Gold Collection 2001. Courtesy of Recording Arts. "Bye Bye Blackbird," by Dixon/Henderson, courtesy of Olde Clover Leaf Music (ASCAP) Administered by Bug, and Ray Henderson Music Co, Inc. (ASCAP)

Eubie Blake: Interview and medley of songs from *Shuffle Along* courtesy of Terry Waldo.

Eubie Blake: "Troublesome Ivories" from the album *Eubie Blake introducing Jim Hession* (EBM-6), published by Eubie Blake Music, Brooklyn, New York, (1974). "You Ought to Know" from the album *Sissle & Blake: Early Rare Recordings, vol. 2* (EBM-7), published by Eubie Blake Music, Brooklyn, New York, (1976). Used by permission of the Maryland Historical Society and the Estate of Eubie Blake.

Sterling Brown: "Ma Rainey" (text) from Collected Poems of Sterling Brown, published by Harper & Row (1980). Used by permission of HarperCollins. "Ma Rainey" (audio), from the recording entitled *Anthology of Negro Poets*, Folkways 09791, provided courtesy of Smithsonian Folkways Recordings. © 1954. Used by Permission.

Countee Cullen: "Incident" and "Heritage" from *My Soul's High Song: Collected Writings of Countee Cullen* edited by Gerald Early. Used by permission of The Amistad Research Center at Tulane University and the Estate of Countee Cullen.

Countee Cullen: "Heritage" (audio), from the recording entitled *Anthology of Negro Poets*, Folkways 09791, provided courtesy of Smithsonian Folkways Recordings. © 1954. Used by Permission.

W.E.B. Du Bois: "Early College Years, Fisk U," "N.A.A.C.P.," "The Crisis," "World War I Pan-African Conference," and "Atlanta U." From the recording entitled *W.E.B. Du Bois: A Recorded Autobiography, Interview with Moses Asch*, Folkways 05511, provided courtesy of Smithsonian Folkways Recordings. © 1961. Used by Permission.

Duke Ellington: "The Creeper" performed by Duke Ellington and His Kentucky Club Orchestra from the recording entitled *Jazz Volume 7: New York (1922-1934)*, Folkways 02807 © 1953.

James Reese Europe: "Too Much Mustard" from the recording entitled *A History of Jazz: The New York Scene*, Folkways 00RF3. © 1961

Marcus Garvey: Recordings courtesy of The Marcus Garvey and UNIA Papers Project, UCLA.

Langston Hughes: "The Weary Blues," "Mother to Son," and "Dream Variation" (text) from *The Collected Poems of Langston Hughes* by Langston Hughes, copyright © 1994 by The Estate of Langston Hughes. Used by permission of Alfred A. Knopf, a division of Random House, Inc.

Langston Hughes: "The Weary Blues," "Mother to Son," and "Dream Variation" (audio) from the recording entitled *The Dream Keeper and Other Poems of Langston Hughes*, Folkways 07774, provided courtesy of Smithsonian Folkways Recordings. © 1955. Used by Permission.

Zora Neale Hurston: Recordings of "Mama Don't Want No Peas No Rice," "Halimuhfack," "Mr. Brown," and "Uncle Bud," from the *Florida Folklife from the WPA Collections*. Used with the permission of the Estate of Zora Neale Hurston.

Charlie Johnson's Paradise Orchestra: "Boy in the Boat" from the recording entitled *A History of Jazz: The New York Scene*, Folkways 00RF3. © 1961

James Weldon Johnson: (text) "The Creation," from GOD'S TROMBONES by James Weldon Johnson, copyright 1927 The Viking Press, Inc. renewed © 1955 by Grace Nail Johnson. Used by permission of Viking Penguin, a division of Penguin Group (USA) Inc.

James Weldon Johnson: (audio) "The Creation," from GOD'S TROMBONES by James Weldon Johnson, from *Voices of Black America*, courtesy of Naxos Audiobooks.

Alain Locke: "The Negro Spiritual" from the "Emancipation Celebration, 1940, at the Library of Congress Collection," American Folklife Center, Library of Congress. *FREEDOM: The Golden Gate Quartet and Josh White at the Library of Congress*. Copyright 2003. Bridge Records, Inc.

Claude McKay: "If We Must Die" and "The Tropics in New York" (text) originally published in HARLEM SHADOWS, republished in SELECTED POEMS OF CLAUDE MCKAY. Courtesy of the

PHOTO CREDITS

Manuscripts, Archives and Rare Books Division, Schomburg Center for Research in Black Culture, The New York Public Library, Astor, Lenox and Tilden Foundations: 370, 413, 423.

Photographs and Prints Division, Schomburg Center for Research in Black Culture, The New York Public Library. Regina Andrews photo collection: 41.

The Picture Collection of The New York Public Library: 30

Picture Collection, The Branch Libraries, The New York Public Library, Astor, Lenox, and Tilden Foundations: 30, 31

General Research and Reference Division, Schomburg Center for Research in Black Culture, The New York Public Library: 35, 37, 46, 74, 75, 104.

Milstein Division of United States History, Local History & Genealogy, Schomburg Center for Research in Black Culture, The New York Public Library, Astor, Lenox and Tilden Foundations: 42

The Maryland Historical Society, Baltimore, Maryland: 155, 156, 158, 159, 160, 161, 162, 250, 322.

Institute of Jazz Studies: 186, 194, 212, 218, 219, 236

Fisk University: 258; photo by George Adams.

Anonymous donor: 264, 265, 269, 368.

The Jacob and Gwendolyn Lawrence Foundation, Seattle/Artists Rights Society (ARS), New York [reproduced with permission of The Phillips Collection, Washington, DC]: 280.

INDEX

C

Colin, Paul, 315
collaboration, 220, 226–27, 254, 265
collage, 289, 292, 296, 304
Collected Writings (Thurman), 140
College Football Hall of Fame, 362
College Inn (Chicago), 271
Collier, Constance, 177
Collins, Johnny, 200–201, 202, 203
colonialism, 386
 Du Bois, W. E. B., 331, 334–35, 338,
  339–41
 Garvey, Marcus, 387, 390, 393
 Hughes, Langston, 59
 McKay, Claude, 103, 104, 107
 Robeson, Paul, 380
 Wright, Richard, 132, 135, 144, 145, 146
Color (Cullen), 71, 72
Color Curtain, The (Wright), 135
color discrimination, 18. *See also* discrimination;
 race and racism
Colored Republican Club, 348
Colored Waif's Home, 185, 188–89, 201
Color Struck (Hurston), 120, 125
Columbia (country), 393
Columbia Broadcasting System (CBS), 226
Columbia Records, 10, 164, 174, 175, 222,
 244–45
Columbia University, 29
 Douglas, Aaron, 272
 Hughes, Langston, 57, 58
 Hurston, Zora Neale, 121
 Johnson, James Weldon, 348
 Lawrence, Jacob, 274, 276
 Randolph, A. Philip, 435
 Robeson, Paul, 361, 365, 366, 367
"Coming Revolution, The" (Thurman), 141–42
Comintern, 110
Committee of Five on Negro Discrimination, 448
communism
 Du Bois, W. E. B.,324, 340–41
 Hughes, Langston, 67
 McKay, Claude, 99, 109, 110–11,
  113, 114
 Randolph, A. Philip, 387
 Robeson, Paul, 326, 361, 381,
  382, 383
 Thurman, Wallace, 141–42
 Wright, Richard, 132, 133, 134,
  141, 142
 See also Marxism
Communist Party
 Garvey, Marcus, 391, 406
 McKay, Claude, 110, 114
 National Negro Congress and, 449
 Nimmo, James B., 410
 Robeson, Paul, 381, 382
 UNIA and, 409
 Wright, Richard, 132, 133, 141
"Concert of Sacred Music" (concert), 231–32
Condon, Eddie, 169
Congo, 207, 268

"Congo Love Song, The" (song), 347
Congress of Industrial Organizations (CIO),
 410, 451
Congress of Industrial Unions, 409
Connie's Inn, 37
 Armstrong, Louis, 185, 199, 200,
  201, 203
 Bearden, Romare, 292
 Ellington, Duke, 218
 Smith, Bessie, 180
Conscience of the Court, The" (Hurston), 125
Constabulary Ballads (McKay), 103
controlled improvisation, 226–27
Cook, Will Marion, 9, 214
Coolidge, Calvin, 407, 441
Copper Sun (Cullen), 75
Costa Rica, 393
Cotton Club, 20, 35–36, 43–44
 Armstrong, Louis, 199, 200
 Ellington, Duke, 212, 224–26,
  227–28, 231
 Waters, Ethel, 247
"Cotton Club Stomp" (song), 226
"Court Order Can't Make Races Mix"
 (Hurston's letter to *Orlando Sentinel*), 118–19
Covarrubias, Miguel, 427–28
Coward, Noel, 371
Cox, Ernest Sevier, 406–7
Cox, Ida, 169
Craig, Arthur, 402
Crane, Hart, 12
Cravath Hall, 268
Cravath Library, 271
"Crazy Blues" (song), 173
"Crazy for This Democracy" (Hurston), 121
Creamer, Henry, 160
"Creation, The" (Johnson), 355, 356
"Creeper, The" (song), 220
Creole Jazz Band, 193, 194
"Creole Love Call" (song), 226
"Creole Rhapsody" (song), 230
Crisis, The (magazine), 12, 19, 21
 Bearden, Romare, 293, 295, 300
 Cullen, Countee, 72
 Douglas, Aaron, 254, 261, 263,
  265–66
 Du Bois, W. E. B., 325, 326, 330,
  331, 332, 333, 335, 336
 Fauset, Jessie, 325
 Hughes, Langston, 58, 59–60
 Hurston, Zora Neale, 125
 Johnson, James Weldon, 351, 356,
  358
 Larsen, Nella, 94
 Locke, Alain, 413
 McKay, Claude, 106, 108
 Randolph, A. Philip, 436
 Wright, Richard, 138, 144
"Criteria of Negro Art" (Du Bois), 136, 333,
 342, 353
critical writing, 7

Y-Z